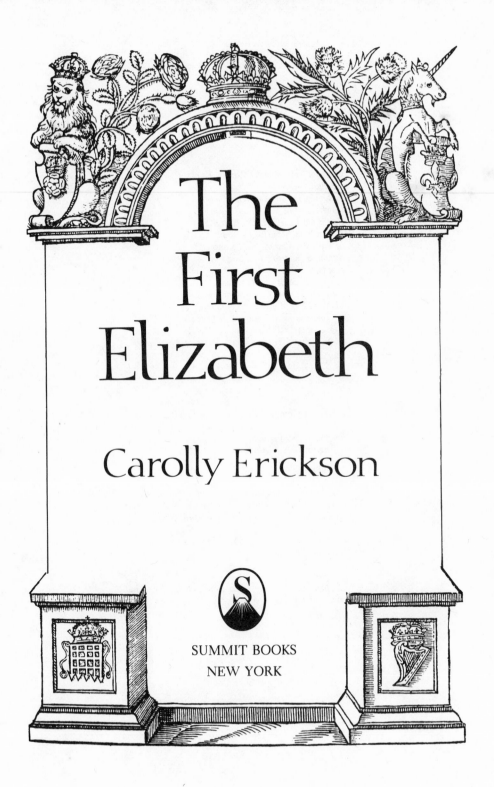

The First Elizabeth

Carolly Erickson

SUMMIT BOOKS
NEW YORK

Published by SUMMIT BOOKS
A Simon & Schuster Division
of Gulf & Western Corporation
Simon & Schuster Building
Rockefeller Center
1230 Avenue of the Americas
New York, New York 10020
SUMMIT BOOKS and colophon
are trademarks of Simon & Schuster
Designed by Edith Fowler
Manufactured in the United States of America

Library of Congress Cataloging in Publication Data

Erickson, Carolly, date.
   The first Elizabeth.

   Bibliography: p.
   Includes index.
   1. Elizabeth I, Queen of England, 1533–1603.
2. Great Britain—History—Elizabeth, 1558–1603.
3. Great Britain—Kings and rulers—Biography.
I. Title.
DA355.E74   1983   942.05′5′0924 [B]   82-19274
ISBN 0-671-41746-0

Chapter epigraphs are taken from popular songs and
poems of the Tudor era.

Contents

PART ONE

The Improbable Child

1

The people flocked there amain
The multitude was great to see;
Their joyful harts were glad, and fain
To view her princely maiesty,
Who at length came riding by,
Within her chariot openly;
Even with a noble princely train
Of lords and ladies of great fame.

The afternoon sun was already low as the constables and marshals, their great staves ready in their hands, took up their stations along the route the royal procession would follow. They wore liveries of velvet and silk, in keeping with the pomp of the occasion, but their function would be more than ceremonial this day. The crowds that had gathered to watch the spectacle had begun to bank up behind the railings erected along one side of the route, and threatened to spill out into the path of the marchers. It was a noisy, restless crowd, sullen rather than welcoming, and the men deputed to keep order set their faces in a stern rictus and gripped their staves more tightly as the sound of hoofbeats in the distance signaled the beginning of the parade.

Anne Boleyn, wife of King Henry VIII, was to ride in ceremony on this May afternoon in 1533 through the City of London and then westward along the Strand to Westminster, where next day she would be crowned queen of England. The route of march was set by time-honored tradition: from the Tower of London the queen and her attendants would process by Gracechurch Street and Cornhill to St. Paul's, pausing frequently to enjoy the singing and pageantry prepared in Anne's honor, and then along Fleet Street to Temple Bar and so into the Strand. The houses and shops lining these streets were decorated with tapestries and silken hangings, and from their upper windows ladies and gentlewomen who had not been summoned to ride with the queen looked out expectantly, watching for the first of the riders to come into view.

As the procession snaked its way through the narrow streets tradition called for the onlookers to kneel and take off their caps when the royal litter passed, and to give a lusty cry of "God save the queen!" But few such greetings were heard. Instead there were rough snickers and laughter, or silent glares and frowns of disapproval or, when the constables and marshals were out of earshot, insults and curses.

Women jostled one another and rolled their eyes, nodding to indicate the slack lacing of the queen's white satin kirtle. They noted the elegance of her gown, cut in the French fashion and furred with ermine, but they paid more attention to her swollen belly, and to the odd bulge at her neck and the marks of scrofula that, in their eyes, disfigured her beauty and made her monstrous.

Children squinted to look hard at her hands, trying to catch a glimpse of the freak sixth finger which, they heard their parents say, was the sure mark of a witch. And men stared at her, some quizzically, some in censure, curious to see at close range the notorious woman who had caused the great scandal only to be touched despite themselves by the allure of her features and expression.

Through it all Queen Anne rode unabashed, regal, triumphant. She paid little heed to the jeers and mockery around her, and none at all to the appraising stares directed at her person. She carried her head proudly, not only to keep in place the jeweled circlet she wore but from habit, for she had a long and graceful neck and knew how to show it to advantage. She was at her best that day, her color high from excitement and her cheeks rosy in the cool spring air. The contours of her oval face had rounded noticeably in recent weeks, and now that she was in the sixth month of pregnancy her morning sickness was past and she felt as well as she ever had in her life. She sat back against the gold cushions of her litter, aware of the sensation she was creating, aware of the attractive picture she made in her satins and shining jewels, her silhouette framed by the thick black hair that fell in waves to her waist.

What if her subjects mocked her? What if they called her Concubine, Whore, the Scandal of Christendom? She had borne their taunts for years. This day, this procession was her revenge. Today all the leading nobles and gentlewomen of the kingdom—including many who were her bitter enemies—were escorting Anne to the site of her coronation. Tomorrow at the coronation itself they would attend her, kneeling reverently before her to swear fealty. Only her haughty uncle the duke of Norfolk was absent—

pardonably, as he was on a diplomatic mission in France. Norfolk's wife, however, had flatly refused to ride in the procession, though his stepmother, the aging dowager duchess, rode conspicuously beside Anne's mother in a handsome chariot; tomorrow she would have the honor of carrying Anne's train.

Yet sweet as it was, the crown was not Anne's ultimate triumph. Her child, the male heir the astrologers so confidently predicted: he was her final vindication.

He had been the real objective from the beginning, from the time seven years before when the king, Henry VIII, first began to woo her. All along the king had needed, had wanted a son to succeed him. And Anne, once she realized that her destiny was to be bound up with the king's, had been determined to bear his son—not a bastard, born in secret like Henry's son by his mistress Bessie Blount, but a legitimate scion of the Tudor line, born in a royal bed, christened true heir to the throne.

For all these years, through all the stumbling blocks and confusions of the king's infamous divorce from his formidable first wife Katherine of Aragon, Anne had held firm to her purpose. She would wait to have her son until she could be queen, until he could be prince of Wales.

Then last fall the waiting ended. The king had taken her to Calais, not as his mistress but as marquess of Pembroke, a great lady with a man's title (for she held it in her own right) and a queenly entourage. At Calais she had been provided with everything a queen could desire, new fur-trimmed silken gowns, her favorite foods—grapes and pears specially imported, porpoises and pasties of red deer—even the jewels of a queen. (These Anne's rival, Henry's wife Katherine, had at first refused to provide, saying it went against her conscience to lend her jewels to adorn a woman of ill repute, but in the end she had yielded.)

Everyone, including Katherine, had been convinced that the king would marry Anne in Calais, during his days of banqueting and jousting with the French king, far from the angry crowds that would have been certain to protest the marriage in England. But Anne's closest confidants knew otherwise. She had reportedly told one of them that even if King Henry wished it she would refuse to marry him in Calais, wanting the ceremony to take place in England, "where queens are wont to be married and crowned."[1]

But if she resisted marriage for the moment Anne had clearly calculated that, one way or another, she would very soon be queen. How long she had shared the king's bed is impossible to say. Rumor had it they had been living as man and wife for years, and beyond the large stake both had in assuring the legitimacy of any child that might be born to them, there is nothing to argue against those rumors. Now, however, in the weeks following the celebrations at Calais, the couple were certainly cohabiting, for in December of 1532 Anne became pregnant.

From then on nature ruled events. As soon as her condition was suspected Anne married Henry, in a tiny private ceremony with only her parents and her brother and two friends present. It was not the formal royal wedding Anne had set her sights on, but it was the next best thing. And open recognition of her rank was not long in coming. At Easter mass, as Henry looked nervously on, Anne made a dramatic entrance, heralded by a royal fanfare and with all of Katherine's jewels blazing on her gown of cloth of gold. Then Archbishop Cranmer presided over the final judicial resolution of the king's disputed marital status. In the last week of May the marriage to Katherine was judged invalid, and that to Anne legal and binding. The way was open for the coronation of Queen Anne, and for the birth of the prince.

The summer came on, and with it, the hunting. The king was often in the fields, his huntsmen and companions beside him, riding down the red deer from early morning until last light. King Henry loved the hunt as he loved every other vigorous, challenging sport, and he was a familiar sight in the hunting parks near the capital, a tall, red-haired figure riding a swift and splendid horse, joyously intent on his quarry.

At forty-two Henry VIII was a burly, athletic man of unusual vigor, with broad shoulders and powerful legs—legs which, though afflicted with painful chronic infections, still carried him magnificently through night after night of energetic dancing. At an age when other men were in decline he seemed to be waxing toward manly perfection; foreign visitors to his court were invariably as astounded by his handsome, vital person as they were by his lively intellect and detailed knowledge of European affairs.

Those who knew him best saw a complex man, restless with nervous energy that burst out now in hearty camaraderie, now in sharp-witted debate, often in flashes of anger. When displeased he could be chillingly royal, lowering, yet more often he disarmed all who came near him with his boyish enthusiasm, drawing them irrevocably into the circle of his mantling charm. No ruler of his time was more quick to cast aside the curtain of regality and become a high-spirited comrade, "more a good companion than a king."

He had never shown himself a better companion than in this summer of 1533, traveling through the country districts close to London and enjoying the hospitality of his favorite courtiers. "I never saw the king merrier than he is now," one of these courtiers wrote in early August, "and there is the best pastime in hunting red deer." Good cheer prevailed in the hunting parks and banquet tables of the king's favorites until midsummer and beyond, dampened only, it seemed, by a brief epidemic of the sweating sickness, that recurrent scourge of Henry's reign that invariably drove the king into a panic and sent him hurrying into seclusion with only a handful of retainers.[2]

The contagion, though not widespread, was fateful; two of his household officers succumbed quickly to choking congestion and high fever, and were carried off, and a number of other servants and courtiers were disabled for weeks. Yet alarming as the outbreak was to King Henry another issue preoccupied him. The first counterblast to Anne Boleyn's coronation had been delivered. Henry had been excommunicated. The excommunication had not yet been publicly pronounced, however; Pope Clement VII held out a fatherly hand to his erring son and offered him one last opportunity to redeem himself. If within the next few months the king would forsake his concubine and take back his true wife Katherine, he would be restored to the Roman fold. If not, the world would soon witness his final irremediable expulsion from the true church—and the damnation of his soul.

Henry went to great lengths to keep this ill news private. He installed Anne at Windsor, where she would avoid risk as the time of her delivery was approaching, and then rode off as if to the hunt but in fact to an urgent conference. Unknown to the queen he had summoned councilors and theologians to a town in the vicinity of the castle, where under his direction they were "hard at work" attempting to defend the king against this ultimate censure.

Supervising his doctors, watching out for his wife, hunting when he could, Henry can only have been annoyed by dispatches from his diplomats in Flanders, where popular rumors caricatured the truth. Henry, it was said, was the victim of "diabolic illusions," which made him dote spinelessly on his wife day and night while his people laughed at him and his gentlemen did as they pleased. As for Anne's child, it had been born dead, the rumors went, or else it was a freak.[3] The gossip stung, especially when it made Henry out to be his wife's willing slave. In truth he had got the upper hand, and only recently.

"The king," a Spanish diplomat wrote, "is courting another lady, with whom he seems to be very much in love." Who this other lady was he didn't say, but King Henry's interest in her was unmistakable. Equally unmistakable was the satisfaction of his courtiers, who encouraged and helped his suit with a vengeance in order to alienate him from Anne.[4]

Anne had, in fact, earned the opprobrium and ill-concealed hatred of many at court, from the Italian diplomat she publicly insulted to the royal comptroller Guildford, who was so affronted by her that he tried to resign his office. Her enemies were legion: household officers she had threatened to dismiss, women she suspected of arousing the king's lust, even distant relatives whom she knew to be partisans of Katherine. Her near relatives had become venomous. Her father had worked to postpone her marriage to the king, and her uncle the duke of Norfolk had been overheard to say that he feared she "would be the ruin of her family." (Norfolk had put family honor first, though, when Charles Brandon, duke of Suffolk, and his wife insulted Anne; with twenty of his men he assaulted Brandon's chief gentlemen and a bloody brawl ensued.)

Now that Anne was being humiliated by her husband all those she had offended took pleasure in her predicament, and did what they could to widen the rift between the king and queen. Anne was jealous, and told Henry so, "making use of certain words which he very much disliked." But whereas in the past her angry outbursts had stung and confused him, and sent him hurrying to her relatives for support, he now returned her anger in kind, whirling on her and telling her "that she must shut her eyes and endure as those who were better than herself had done, and that she ought to know that he could at any time lower her as much as he had raised her."

The rebuke must have struck Anne with the force of a thunderbolt. Not only had she lost as a wife what leverage she had possessed as a mistress, but there was a menacing hint of bitterness in the king's words. In a single sharp phrase he reduced her from pampered sweetheart to abused spouse —Katherine's unenviable status—and threatened to take even that from her at his whim.[5]

The quarrel bit deep, and left Anne shaken, though she concealed her fear and kept herself at an ill-tempered distance from her husband. For most of the summer there was "much coldness and grumbling" between them. Henry did not speak to Anne for days on end, until some said he had repented of his marriage and had begun to think of recalling Katherine. Thus when following custom Anne took formal leave of the court and withdrew to await the birth of her child, it was amid an atmosphere more strained than festive, and with the almost certain knowledge that her husband was playing her false.

She "took her chamber" in the time-honored ceremony at Greenwich, escorted to and from mass by the nobility and honored as she stood under her cloth of estate. Her chamberlain solemnly requested all present "in the queen's name, to pray God to send her the good hour," and then she went into the inner chamber prepared for the birth. The chamberlain drew the curtain; she was alone.

From now on no man would come near her, save King Henry, and he was not likely to be a frequent visitor. Women would take the place of her chamberlain, her ushers, her grooms, bringing her food, attending her as she bathed and dressed, watching her as she slept, waiting for signs that her "good hour" was at last come upon her. What her own thoughts may have been during these last expectant days we can only guess. Yet it seems likely that as she lay in the magnificent bed Henry had provided for his son's birth—a bed from his treasure room, hung in silks and carved in elegant scrolls—Anne thought less of the ordeal she faced than of her child's future.

She had already taken the first step in safeguarding the baby's rights, ordering fair copies of all grants recently made to her and her heirs and having them bound together for posterity. Whatever else happened, her child would inherit her title as marquess of Pembroke, with preeminence among all others of that degree. But his father's title must be assured to him, against all other claimants whoever they might be. This was paramount. In her fretful leisure these other claimants may have preyed upon Anne's musings: her obscure nephew "young Master Carey," son of the king and her sister; Henry Fitzroy, the king's acknowledged bastard and preferred heir, who bore the royal title duke of Richmond; King Henry's impetuous nephew in Scotland James V, who resembled his uncle in England with his red hair and beard "like fire shining gold."

None of these ought to prove a threat. Little Carey was too young and insignificant, King James too far away, Fitzroy unsuitable to reign despite the royal favor publicly shown him since the age of six, because of his illegitimate birth. But Katherine's daughter Mary was another matter. For one thing, she was a favorite with the people. Ballads were printed lamenting her fate, telling how her mother's ruin had left her friendless and forlorn, a princess without a throne. All the loyalty the people felt toward Katherine they felt toward her daughter as well, and Mary could count not only on their sympathy but on their allegiance, should she become the focus of a plot against the king and his heir by Anne.

Mary was a threat on other grounds. She was stubborn, she was highly intelligent, she was wedded to her cause with a force of will that gave strength to her weakened body and purpose to her shattered life. And she was important to her father. He praised her and admired her; clearly her fair blond beauty softened his heart and made him want to overlook the danger she presented. And of course, he was far too shrewd not to keep constantly in mind that, until Anne's son was born, she was still heiress of the kingdom (with Fitzroy always prepared to stand in should he be needed). As such she was irreplaceable, and would not lose her value entirely until Anne's son had reached an age to reign.

Even now Mary was at court, waiting to play her role in the drama of the prince's birth. As heir presumptive she was obliged to be present at the birth of the heir apparent, and bitter though the event would be to her she was certain to fulfill her obligation—for she obeyed her father in everything save when her conscience forbade it. The thought of Mary waiting in some remote chamber of the palace, dreading her half-brother's birth, quite possibly, Anne believed, praying for a stillbirth or a weakling who would not survive, was chilling. Yet there was no heeding it; now as always, Anne had to trust in the vigor of the infant that kicked strongly within her, and in her own formidable tenacity.

In the first week of September final touches were put to the preparations. Finery and furnishings for the royal infant were assembled—sheets and swaddling bands, a christening mantle of crimson cloth of gold, furred with ermines, a "great cradle of estate" trimmed in velvet and gold and silver gilt. All had to be made afresh for this baby, as Katherine had refused to lend Anne's child the christening robes Mary had worn seventeen years earlier, and the issue had not been pressed. King Henry's attention was elsewhere, on the jousts he was organizing to celebrate the birth, on deciding on a name for the prince (either Edward or Henry, it was said), and on the august pronouncements of the physicians and astrologers he had assembled to reassure him about the child's health and sex. There was no doubt whatever, they concurred gravely, that the baby would be a strong, long-lived male.

Then the pains began. The physicians took their places around the vast bed, their sharp instruments ready, the midwives put in position copper basins for catching the blood and rolls of linen for staunching it. Hours passed. The courtiers, only too aware of the activity in the queen's chambers, were distracted by a mildly scandalous wedding. Charles Brandon, very recently made a widower in his late forties, was marrying a very pretty, very virginal young girl of fourteen whom he had originally chosen to become his daughter-in-law. The wedding took place on the morning of September 7. That afternoon Anne's labor reached its climax.

All went as it should. Anne sweated and struggled to rid herself of her burden, and her attendants tensed themselves to see her through the last dangerous moments. The baby appeared, its flesh a living, pulsing red, its tiny body whole and unblemished. In the candlelight they bent close to check its sex, then gasped in dismay. Anne Boleyn's child was a girl.

2

It is in truth a pretty toy
For babes to play withal;
But O the honies of our youth
Are oft our age's gall!

At nightfall huge bonfires were lit in the London streets, and the bells of the city's churches rang so loudly they could almost be heard downriver at Greenwich. The queen's enemies tried to belittle the celebrating, but it was real enough. Everywhere men and women were helping themselves eagerly to the tuns of wine set out for the citizenry, and drinking healths to the baby princess; when they had drunk their fill they danced crazily and threw their caps in the air for joy, just as they had the last time England's queen had given birth to a living child.

In the palace a darker mood prevailed. Mercifully, Anne slept, so worn out by her labor she had no strength left to dread her husband's irate displeasure. Henry, at first shocked to disbelief by the news of his daughter's birth, soon became angry. He lashed out at everyone within range, first driving out the astrologers—doubtless with such threatening words that they thought themselves lucky to escape with their lives—and then swearing at the physicians and midwives until he reduced them to submissive self-reproach. Even the horse master and grooms of the stables felt the bite of his rancor when he summoned them to cancel the carefully planned jousts.

When Anne began to recover there must have been some heated scenes between husband and wife. Henry, who had abandoned his first queen because she presented him with only weak and stillborn sons and unwelcome daughters, was chagrined beyond measure to find that his second could do no better. Behind his rage was the fear that, having risked his throne, his soul and the safety of his kingdom on this child, he had been betrayed. On some level he had believed himself divinely guided to act as he had in divorcing Katherine and marrying Anne; now he must believe either that God was taunting him or that his conscience had misled him. Either view was unnerving. It was easier to blame the disaster on Anne, and to use it as an excuse for the estrangement that had already begun to divide them.

By the hearth in the nursery the tiny princess lay in her great cradle of estate, swaddled so tightly she could not move her arms or legs. With the obliviousness of the newly born she slept through her father's rages and her mother's tears, aware of nothing save the periodic hunger in her stomach and the discomfort of her overheated body.

In the first few days of her life she was easily the most talked-of child in England; as the news of her birth made its way through Europe she became the most talked-of child in Christendom. But she was not spoken of in the reverent tones due a princess of the blood royal; she was laughed at. This girl child, it was said, was the butt of an almighty joke, God's just chastisement of the king who had defied God's vicar on earth.

With the world laughing behind his back, King Henry took in hand the immediate practical concerns presented by the birth of an heir. First, the child had to have a name. Mary. She would be called Mary, taking both the place and name of Katherine of Aragon's daughter in order the more thoroughly to supplant her. Word went out that the infant princess would be known by the same name as her half-sister, and as late as the day of the christening courtiers expected to pay their respects to her as Princess Mary.

But when they took their appointed places in the friary church at Greenwich for the christening ceremony they found that the king had changed his mind, and the herald that proclaimed the princess's title saluted her as "the right high, right noble, and right excellent Princess Elizabeth, princess of England."

The christening could hardly have been more elaborate if the child had been the hoped-for prince. The chief nobles, the leading churchmen and the lord mayor and aldermen stood by as the dowager duchess of Norfolk carried the baby to the church, with Thomas Boleyn behind her bearing the long train of the purple velvet christening mantle. Hangings of cloth of gold and bright tapestries draped the interior of the chapel, and soft thick carpets covered the floor. A heavy scent of incense and perfume filled the air, disguising the strong odor of coals burning in a brazier near the font;

the brazier provided warmth for the baby while she was undressed behind a curtain, then handed to the bishop of London who immersed the back of her head and her heels in the holy water. Before her purple mantle was put on again she was anointed on back and breast with the holy oil sacred to royalty, and given her name.

Elizabeth's three godparents, the dowager duchess, the old marchioness of Dorset and Thomas Cranmer, archbishop of Canterbury, sponsored her at the font, which was raised to permit the crowds of onlookers to witness the baptism "without pressing too nigh." Then the hundreds of guardsmen standing in attendance lit their torches, and even the tiny taper enclosed in the infant's hand was lit and placed on the altar. The christening gifts were produced, and noblewomen carried them into the palace, to the queen's chamber, where Anne and Henry waited to give their formal blessing to their child.

"It is to be feared," wrote an Italian who followed events at the English court, "that the child will be weak, owing to [its] father's complexion and habits of life."[1] The speculation was justifiable, given the feebleness of Henry's earlier children and the enormously high odds against infant survival. If Elizabeth did not succumb from inherent frailty, or fall prey to disease, there were sinister forces waiting to entrap her. Ten months after her birth, when the king's breach with the pope had become complete, two friars were overheard preaching the princess's destruction. "She was christened in hot water," they told the assembled faithful, "but not hot enough."[2]

Such threats to her mortality were ignored, however, in the regulations governing the royal nursery, which envisioned an orderly and healthful environment undisturbed by any sort of menace. Under the supervision of the lady governess, a staff of yeomen and grooms were appointed to attend the infant's needs while sewers and officers of the pantry stood ready to supply her food. There were three chamber women called "rockers," a dry nurse, and a wet nurse—the latter the focus of severe scrutiny.

It was a premise of Tudor childrearing that infants were marked for life with the character of the women who nursed them. If the wet nurse was vulgar or vicious, however she might hide these faults from the parents who employed her, she would pass them on to the child entrusted to her. Did she speak a strong dialect, or slur her speech? If so, the infant would be sure to mimic her as soon as it formed words. In the case of a royal child these considerations took on added gravity, and made the choice of a nurse as important as the choice of a chaplain or tutor.

Once engaged, the woman's every move was watched, in particular her meals. "It must be seen that the nurse's meat and drink be assayed during the time that she giveth suck to the child," the regulations insisted, "and that a physician do oversee her at every meal, which shall see that she giveth the child seasonable meat and drink."

It was not enough to have a well-run nursery; the entire court must be purged of hazards to the baby's health. In 1533 the court of Henry VIII was not the lawless bedlam it had been eight years earlier, when the chaos had cried out for sweeping reform. But there were dangers to be eliminated. The most obvious was plague. A new proclamation prohibited royal servants from going to London—always the prime breeding ground of infection —and returning again to their posts. At the same time, Londoners coming to the palace had to stay outside the gates, delivering their goods and transacting their business through the iron grillwork. Vagabonds and other "followers of the court"—ragged urchins, idlers, pickpockets and prostitutes—were driven off with stern warnings not to return, and efforts were made to cleanse the large and unruly palace staff of undesirables.[3]

Despite the best intentions all did not run smoothly in Tudor nurseries. Babies either sweltered or froze in the unevenly heated rooms, and fretted in their restrictive swaddling bands. The discomforts of overheating and the close confinement combined to produce a pimply rash; drafts led to eternal coughs and dripping noses. And there were fleas, abundant and everhungry, which infested even the most exalted nurseries and left highborn babies with red and swollen fingers, ears and toes.

A month passed, two months, and the infant princess belied the prognosis of weakness. She ate, she filled out, she opened her wide blue eyes— soon to turn to brown—and began to grow a fuzz of reddish-blond hair. Her father's frowning disappointment over her sex turned to cautious faith in her survival, and to a natural resolve to exploit her usefulness. Of course, she would be of significance only until a brother was born, but in the meantime she was the sole representative of the true Tudor line, and on her behalf the cumbersome process of altering the succession was set in motion.

Unquestionable establishment of her rights was essential, for as the year 1533 drew to a close England stood in peril. Sentence of excommunication against Henry VIII had yet to be pronounced, but though it had been delayed for two months—in order that Henry "might come to a knowledge of his error"—it could not be forestalled indefinitely. With excommunication came a triple danger: an excommunicated king was automatically held to be deposed, leaving his kingdom vulnerable to invasion and civil war. The Hapsburg emperor Charles V would no doubt contrive to fill the power vacuum, and in fact the intimidating net of imperial might was growing tighter.

English travelers crossing the Channel were warned to avoid the emperor's territories. "I give you knowledge that if your king take not his queen again within thirty days," a Flemish captain threatened three English merchants who boarded his ship at Gravelines, "I would advise you nor none of your nation to pass this ways, but to keep you at home; for if you do, I will take you as good prizes." Incidents of this kind, coupled with persistent rumors that the emperor was massing fighting men in his Netherlands provinces to send to England, led many to fear that the vital cloth trade with Flanders might be cut off. And that, the imperial ambassador Chapuys noted, would be disastrous, for the king would then have to reckon with the ire of the clothworkers—"who are considerably more than half the people in England," he estimated with exaggeration.[4]

Early in December the merchants came to Henry in a body and asked pointedly whether or not their next shipments through the Channel ports would be safe. Instead of replying directly he blustered and strode angrily about, pouring out a tirade of abuse against Pope Clement and dismissing the impending censures with an imperious toss of his head. No one would dare to interfere with them, he told the merchants haughtily. As for the threatened excommunication, he "would do wonders" against the pope, whose threat was only an empty gesture. Henry's dazzling if unwarranted confidence satisfied the merchants, and in fact his luck did carry him through the crisis unscathed—for the present.[5]

To underscore his defiant stand the king went ahead with his exaltation of his newborn daughter at the expense of her half-sister Mary. A well-staffed household was prepared for Elizabeth at Hatfield, and she was escorted there "in full state," with a large retinue of lords and gentlemen. Henry used the occasion as an excuse to show his daughter to the Londoners who had responded with loyal celebrations at her birth. Though it was out of the way, the traveling party wound through the capital before turning northward, "the better to impress upon the people the idea of her being the true princess of Wales."

Meanwhile Mary, who until recently had been accustomed to a corps of a hundred and sixty servants, was reduced almost to the status of a servant herself. She was unwillingly installed in the worst suite of rooms in the turreted, red brick manor house, and ordered to serve as maid of honor to her infant sister. More humiliating still, she was denied the deference due a princess, and was forced to call the baby "Princess Elizabeth" while she herself was referred to merely as "the lady Mary." In an era when formalities were often a matter of life and death these distinctions were freighted with menace. Legally, Mary was a bastard and excluded from the succession; she lived at her father's sufferance. If he were to die, Anne Boleyn would become regent, and though Anne might hold back from ordering the execution of a princess she would not hesitate to eliminate a troublesome nobody.

Thus for the first months of her life Elizabeth was the innocent object of a grave rivalry—and of her half-sister's enduring animus. Mary Tudor was by nature a warm and loving girl with a special fondness for little children. But she would have needed the greatheartedness of a saint to overlook the deep injury Elizabeth symbolized. Tiny as she was, the baby stood between Mary and the throne. She incarnated Anne Boleyn's usurpation of Katherine of Aragon's rights and lineage; what was worse, she drew to herself what little attention the king spared for his children, leaving Mary all but fatherless.

The first encounter between the half-sisters set the tone. Mary arrived at Hatfield, where Elizabeth's household was already in operation, and Norfolk, her gruff companion on the unhappy journey, remarked pointedly that she might want to pay her respects to the princess. Mary bristled to hear the title applied to Elizabeth, and told the duke curtly that she knew of no princess in England save herself, and that the daughter of "Madame de Pembroke"—as she called Anne Boleyn—had no such distinction. Reluctantly, she would agree to call the baby "sister," just as she called the king's bastard son Henry Fitzroy "brother," but conscience forbade her any further compromise.

The duke was abusive—and he was a bruising antagonist. But Mary would not yield, and as he stopped short of striking her he left her unbowed. She sent her father the stinging message that "his daughter, the princess, begged his blessing," then when Norfolk refused to carry it she retired to her room. It was only then, with the duke out of sight and a thick oaken door between them, that she gave way to tears.[6]

Relations between the sisters became a pavane of precedence. Elizabeth was given the place of honor in the dining hall; Mary took her meals in her room rather than sit in the chair of an inferior. Anne heard of this, and ordered Mary back to the table; she obeyed, but repeated a precisely worded formula of protest before every meal. The same protest accompanied her every act that might be misinterpreted as voluntary acknowledgment of Elizabeth's higher status, until the words became almost a reflex. The struggle over primacy reached its peak when, at regular intervals, the entire household moved to a new residence so that the old one could be swept out and scoured. The princess was carried in a sumptuous velvet litter, while Mary either walked beside her or traveled in the conspicuously plain conveyance of an ordinary gentlewoman. The contrast was unbearably humiliating to Mary, who was put to shame before the country people who still held her in esteem and disregarded Anne Boleyn's daughter as an insignificant bastard. Mary begged to be allowed to ride either ahead of her half-sister's party or behind it, to avoid the comparison.

As a rule her entreaties went unheard, and more than once she was shoved forcibly into her assigned place. But at least one time she was indulged. The household was en route from a country house, possibly Eltham, to one of the palaces upriver. Told that she could ride on ahead, Mary "suddenly pushed forward," spurring her horse and leaving the rest of the party in her dust. She reached Greenwich, where the king's barge was waiting to carry the royal children the rest of the way, an hour before Elizabeth's velvet litter came into view. By the time the princess could be transferred to the barge Mary had already taken possession of the seat of honor, and she savored her preeminent position during the remainder of the trip.[7]

Dynastic politics ruled Elizabeth's earliest childhood, and distant relatives governed her nurture. A widowed cousin of her mother's, Lady Bryan, had charge of the wet nurse and other nursery staff, while another Boleyn connection, John Shelton, was steward of the household. His wife Margaret Shelton had the unpleasant task of browbeating Mary into submission. When Lady Shelton showed any tendency to leniency Anne was quick to reprimand her; in Anne's view Mary deserved to be slapped and addressed as a "cursed bastard" for her obstinacy.

The king and queen visited their child infrequently, riding separately or together to wherever the princess was staying and remaining there only a short time. They supervised Elizabeth's upbringing from a distance, through intermediaries. Someone—was it King Henry himself?—questioned the high expenses of her household in 1535 and ordered a lengthy explanation for each expenditure. Due response was made: the accounts covered the Christmas celebrations, when more table linens were used and more food consumed; more candles and coals were burned in wintertime than at other seasons; some of Elizabeth's attendants exceeded the number of personal servants allowed in the household rules laid down by the king. And so on in a lengthy list—rendered with the detached formality of a treaty negotiation.[8]

Even so delicate a matter as Elizabeth's weaning was handled at several removes. First, Lady Bryan wrote to the chief royal minister Thomas Cromwell that the princess was big enough and mature enough to leave her wet nurse and drink from a cup, and the other officers of the household concurred. Then Cromwell showed the letter to the king, who considered the issue and determined that his daughter should be weaned "with all diligence." He communicated his decision to William Paulet, then comptroller of the royal household, who put it in a letter to Cromwell. And finally Paulet wrote on the king's behalf to Lady Bryan, directing her to proceed with the weaning. Enclosed with his letter was another from Anne, perhaps giving instructions, but this letter has not survived.[9] Elizabeth was then just over two years old.

The princess was occasionally brought to court, but less for the sake of spending time with her parents than to be shown off to courtiers or visiting ambassadors. It was essential that the king's only legitimate child be seen to be healthy, particularly in an era when more infants died than survived. And if Elizabeth was healthy—"as goodly a child as hath been seen," one observer wrote of her at seven months old, in April of 1534—then she was marriageable. Just at this time King Henry proposed a match between his baby daughter and the third son of the king of France. Two French diplomats came to inspect her. She was shown to them first "in very rich apparel, in state and triumph as a princess," and then completely naked, so that they could personally refute any rumors of physical defects.[10]

During 1534 and the first six months of 1535 the proposed marriage alliance was the focus of serious negotiation. The betrothal would not take place until Elizabeth was seven years old, by which time, it was hoped, Anne and Henry would have at least one son; if they had two sons, they could spare Elizabeth to be brought up in France among her future in-laws.[11] Despite months of diplomatic discussions, in the end the negotiations came to nothing. King Francis refused to join his brother monarch in England in breaking away from the church of Rome, and he would not lend his public support to Henry's controversial second marriage. Both issues were essential to any dynastic union, from the English point of view, and so the discussions ended.

Elizabeth's babyhood witnessed the radical upheaval of the English church. The authority of the pope in England was denied, and the clergy became subject to the king in religious as well as secular matters. It was nothing short of a revolution in that the autonomy of the spirituality in England was forever broken, and the monarchy gained immensely in both wealth and power. Papal taxation was now diverted to the crown, and the clergy were heavily taxed. That close scrutiny of monastic mores and revenues began which was to lead, in 1536, to the suppression of the lesser monasteries and, a few years later, to the liquidation of the entire monastic establishment in England.

Even more important, there began in these years that crucial shift in public consciousness and in the workings of the political order which undercut the moral force of the clergy and shifted the locus of spiritual suasion toward the king. Amid a climate of religious ferment, widespread and outspoken anticlericalism and blasphemous contempt for sacred things among the people, the king and his chief minister Thomas Cromwell fashioned a new concept of sovereignty.

Henry VIII saw himself as responsible for the souls as well as the bodies of his subjects; he claimed an ultimate, imperial power that recognized no higher authority but God himself. Cromwell translated the king's vision of rulership into policy, embedding the strictly religious changes in the Reformation statutes in a broader theory of monarchical government. Parliament became the natural arena of royal legislation, and the bond formed between king and Parliament was to be fateful for England's governance in future.

But for these momentous changes to be secure and lasting the king needed a son to succeed him, and by 1535 it was becoming a worrisome possibility that the male heir Anne Boleyn hoped desperately to conceive would never be born. Her several pregnancies had ended in miscarriage, and each of her failures served only to increase the continuing tension under which she lived, making it more and more unlikely that she would give her husband a male heir. "The king despairs of other sons," the bishop of Faenza wrote prophetically in April, 1535, "so this last daughter may be mistress of England."[12]

Henry and Anne had long since ceased to be bound by either lust or affection. Henry, ever "inclined to amours," amused himself with flirtations and infatuations which drove Anne into a helpless frenzy. She was trapped, and he knew it; she dared not complain about his favorites—among them her maid of honor Jane Seymour and her cousin Margaret Shelton, daughter of that Lady Shelton who kept watch over Mary Tudor—for fear he might lose patience with her once and for all and put her aside as he had Katherine. Oddly enough, besides her continuing hopes for a son Katherine was Anne's strongest safeguard against ruin. As long as Katherine lived, Henry would hesitate to rid himself of Anne, for if he did he might be forced to return to his first wife.

Then in November of 1535 Anne took heart again, and by December she was certain she was pregnant. The holiday season came and went, and she found herself able to overlook both her husband's ceaseless gallantries and the vulgar insults of her uncle Norfolk, who at his least offensive called her "a great whore." She began to breathe more easily, and to allow her expectations to rise. She was only twenty-eight, after all, younger by three years than Queen Katherine had been when she gave birth to Mary. Perhaps this time, if she was careful, she would carry her child to term.

Unexpectedly, Katherine died on January 8, still professing to love the king who, many said, had had her poisoned. The death of her longtime rival cannot have left Anne indifferent, and her relief at the news was almost certainly mingled with apprehension. Characteristically, Henry camouflaged his own mixed feelings with frenetic activity. "God be praised," he shouted exultantly when word of Katherine's death first reached him, "now we are free from all suspicion of war!" All the machinery of celebration was set in motion, and the king outdid himself in planning banquets and tourneying to commemorate the passing of an abiding peril. He put on his gayest clothes, danced for hours with overeager abandon, and then went out to exercise in the tiltyard, forgetting his age and jousting like a young man again. This was the first good news to reach him in two years. The menace of invasion receded, the intricate arguments over the validity or invalidity of his first marriage became moot. Most important, the child Anne was carrying would be born without the stigma of bastardy.

Two fateful events interrupted the revelry. First, the king was nearly killed in a jousting accident. He fell off his mount, and as he lay pinned to the ground by his heavy jousting armor the horse fell on top of him. Two hours passed before he recovered consciousness. Then shortly afterward, on the day Katherine of Aragon was interred, Anne lost her child. In the circumstances the tragedy seemed insurmountable, especially when the midwives admitted that the tiny foetus "had the appearance of a male."[13]

For Henry the blow was very bitter, and decisive. Anne's inadequacy went beyond either blame or forgiveness; it called for a complete change of heart. All at once she was dislodged from her key position in his life, and a new rationale took shape to justify both her past disappointments and her future fate. Henry decided that all along he had been bewitched by Anne, and that now that his eyes were opened he must rid himself of her. Their daughter Princess Elizabeth would, of course, be a casualty of Anne's disgrace, but with luck a new wife—Mistress Seymour—would soon make up for the loss by presenting him with a son.

Less than three months after her miscarriage Anne was led to her execution on Tower Green. A secret royal commission had uncovered evidence sufficient to convict her of treason, and the list of her specific crimes was long and shameful. "Despising her marriage, and entertaining malice against the king," the accusation read, "and following daily her frail and carnal lust, she did falsely and traitorously procure by base conversations and kisses, touchings, gifts and other infamous incitations, divers of the king's daily and familiar servants to be her adulterers and concubines."

Anne's "incontinent living" was bad enough, especially as her brother George Boleyn, Lord Rochford, was said to be among her lovers. But there was more. Anne and her paramours had conspired to kill the king, and he had been preserved from death by the grace of God alone. The royal councilors "quaked at the danger his grace was in," Cromwell wrote piously, "and on our knees gave him laud and praise that he had preserved him so long from it."[14]

There could be no mercy for the guilty queen. Anne was sentenced to be taken to Tower Green, to the small grass-covered courtyard facing the church of St. Peter in Chains that was reserved for prisoners of the highest rank, and there "burned or beheaded so shall please the king." She was allowed the less painful death, uncommon in England, of beheading by the sword.

Several days before her execution her marriage to Henry VIII was judged to be of no force, because of her husband's prior relations with her sister. Her child Elizabeth, two years and eight months old, was no longer princess, but a bastard like her half-sister Mary. But unlike Mary, Elizabeth was the daughter of a condemned adulteress and traitor, whose headless body would be stuffed into a crude wooden box and buried, without ceremony, in St. Peter's church.

In the final months of her mother's life, two scenes may have impressed themselves on Elizabeth's memory. In both she was the focus of wide attention.

The first was on the occasion of Katherine's death. As part of his display of satisfaction King Henry dressed himself in yellow satin and sent for his little daughter. She was brought to him, no doubt arrayed in similar finery, and he carried her about for some time, holding her out to each of his courtiers, smiling at her, talking about her. The excitement of the occasion, the sight of her tall, broad-shouldered father in his bright yellow suit, the sound of his hearty voice booming out happily and repeating her name—these impressions may well have stayed in the mind of a precocious child of two and a half.

The second occasion was more poignant. Shortly before Anne was taken to the Tower, she made a last mute appeal to her husband to spare her—if not for her own sake, then for the sake of their child. A contemporary who witnessed the event described it to Elizabeth many years later. "Alas I shall never forget the sorrow I felt when I saw the sainted queen your mother, carrying you, still a little baby, in her arms," he wrote, "and entreating the most serene king your father in Greenwich Palace, from the open window of which he was looking into the courtyard where she brought you to him." The king had just received the accusations of his commissioners; though their findings were no more or less than he had ordered, he responded to the indictment with the anger appropriate to an unsuspecting husband who discovers he has been betrayed. At the moment Anne appeared outside his window he may well have been giving orders for her execution. "The faces and gestures of the speakers plainly showed the king was angry," the man went on, "though he concealed his anger wonderfully well."

Whether the king's enigmatic expression concealed anger or dark satisfaction will never be known. But he dismissed his repudiated wife and her child without a word or a look, and a few hours later the cannon thundered from the Tower to announce that Anne Boleyn, commoner and traitor, had entered by the river gate.

3

Crie not out-right for that were children's guise,
But let thy teares fall trickling downe thy face,
And weepe so long untill thy blubbered eyes,
May see (in Sunne) the depth of thy disgrace.
  Oh shake thy head, but not a word but mumme.
  The heart once dead, the tongue is stroken dumme.

Within days of Anne Boleyn's execution every evidence of her queenship was gone. Her coat of arms was removed from linens and liveries, and from the royal barge. Her servants were dispersed, many of them joining the king's engorged household. Her debts, among them bills for velvet kirtles and purple satin caps for her little daughter, were paid and buried in the comptroller's accounts. And her throne was filled by another woman.

When Elizabeth was next brought to court a pale, sweet-faced lady with a prim mouth and mild brown eyes sat at her father's side, and when this lady turned her mild eyes on the king's younger daughter there was more pity in them than respect.

For Anne's child was the only ineradicable proof of her existence, and as such she seemed to incarnate her mother's dark memory. For years Anne's enemies had called her the Great Whore; now all that was left of her was the child they called the Little Whore, a thin, fair-skinned girl with delicate features and lashes and eyebrows so light they gave her a startled look.[1] The new queen, Jane Seymour, was kind to her, but kinder to her half-sister Mary, who was given the seat of honor at her side in the dining hall while Elizabeth was placed out of sight. And there was an unmistakable difference in the way the courtiers looked at her, now frowning to themselves as they scrutinized her features, now whispering to one another, now turning their faces away as if to avoid all contact with a tainted being.

Only a month had passed between the arrest of Queen Anne and the king's marriage to Queen Jane, and during those whirling days so much had happened so quickly that no one had even begun to digest it. The court was alive with rumor and conjecture, much of it centered on the late queen's discredited child. "Here are so many tales," wrote Lord Hussey, a staunch enemy to Anne and recently Mary Tudor's chamberlain, "I cannot tell what to write."[2]

The circumstances leading to Anne's conviction lent themselves to much speculation and embroidery. She had been unfaithful to the king, but when, and how often, and with whom? Henry himself averred that Anne had slept with more than a hundred men, and in fact beyond the five convicted lovers who were executed with her several others were detained in the Tower, and the courtiers looked for "many more" to be executed before long.[3]

Anne's adultery, of course, not only imperiled Elizabeth's legitimacy but —far more important—called into question her royal lineage. For if, as many believed, someone other than the king was her father, then even the relatively debased status of royal bastard was a much higher honor than she deserved. Beyond her own base lust two things, it was alleged, had prompted Anne to faithlessness: the king's impotence (hardly broadly pub-licized, but repeatedly alluded to at the trial), and the reassurances of liberal bishops, infected with Lutheran doctrines, that it was permissible for a woman to "ask for aid in other quarters, even among her own relatives," if her husband was incapable.[4]

Armed with these inducements Anne seduced her lovers, "by sweet words, kisses, touches and otherwise," to lie with her, and so conceived not only her miscarried children but her one surviving daughter. Anne had betrayed the king, according to rumor, even before he married her. "It was proved at the trial that she had behaved in this way before the conception of the child which the king thought to be his," wrote an imperialist diplomat in Rome confidently. "It is intended to declare the child not to be the king's."[5]

Of the many candidates for Elizabeth's paternity three stood out. One was Henry Norris, the tall, handsome principal gentleman of the chamber who had long been among the king's most trusted intimates. So likely did Norris seem as Elizabeth's true father that Eustace Chapuys, the imperial ambassador, found his paternity plausible grounds for Henry's divorce from Anne. "The archbishop of Canterbury declared by sentence that the con-cubine's daughter was the bastard of Mr. Norris," he informed Charles V's minister Granvelle, "and not the king's daughter."[6]

George Boleyn was the most sensational choice—and one reinforced even more strongly by family resemblance. The charge of incest against Anne was repeated with particular relish by her continental opponents; a Portuguese contemporary noted that "after her execution the council declared that the queen's daughter was the child of her brother."[7] That both Anne and George denied the charge did nothing to brake the scandal, and George, who was widely disliked for his arrogance, was probably least mourned of the queen's alleged lovers.

The allegation that endured longest in common memory was that Mark Smeaton, musician on the virginals and organ, "deft dancer" and groom of the king's chamber, was the father of Anne's child. Smeaton, a commoner (and carpenter's son) and possibly a Fleming, was the only one of the men accused with Anne to confess, under torture, to being her lover. His confession set off imaginative speculation. By the time Charles V heard the story it was reduced to essentials: Anne, he said, had been surprised in bed with the king's organist; hence her execution. For years afterward English courtiers thought they could see in Elizabeth's maturing features the imprint of Mark Smeaton's. Mary found the likeness particularly strong, and to her dying day she asserted (to her intimates) that Elizabeth had the "face and countenance" of the hapless musician, and was neither her sister nor her father's daughter.[8]

If there was much doubt about Elizabeth's father, there was at least some doubt about her mother as well. Even before Anne's execution the imperialists had spread the tale that all along she had been unable to conceive, and that Elizabeth was the daughter of peasants, brought secretly to court while Anne was said to be in labor and represented to be her long-awaited child. There was an inescapable flaw in this argument, for surely if Anne had taken the trouble to locate a supposititious child she would have made certain it was male. Yet the story was repeated all the same, and it became more welcome than ever on Anne's death. With Henry having all but disowned her, it would have been a short step to denying Elizabeth's bond to Anne as well, and so hopelessly severing her connection to the court, much less to the throne.[9] Chapuys made much of Anne's own acknowledgment of another possible defect in Elizabeth's claim. After her last miscarriage Anne comforted her women, saying that her next child "would not be doubtful like this one, which had been conceived during the life of the [late] queen," thereby implying that Elizabeth too was "doubtful."[10]

As it turned out, of course, Henry did not disown Elizabeth (though she was declared illegitimate) and even succeeded in convincing one observer that he had a father's warm affection toward her, and loved her very much.[11] No record of his true feelings remains. Doubtless to Henry Elizabeth was many things—a fragile and pitiable little girl, the daughter of a traitress and a witch, a distasteful reminder of his greatest love and cruelest disenchantment. If he believed her to be another man's child he never said so, and the one slander he forbore to bring against Anne Boleyn was that she had not been able to conceive. But Elizabeth was primarily a political asset, all the more to be protected in that her half-brother Henry Fitzroy had recently died.

This shadowy figure, in practice heir to the throne for the last ten years and more, had reached his seventeenth year in near total obscurity, and his death was kept as veiled as his life. There was no state funeral or burial, and though the boy had been provided for in princely style his eighty-five servants, his four great warhorses, his gifts of jewels and plate from the king and even his Garter mantle were easily disposed of. Mary and Elizabeth were left as sole contenders, under the new Act of Succession, for designation as Henry VIII's successor should Queen Jane have no child.

That the king continued to acknowledge Elizabeth as his did nothing to dam the groundswell of rumors about Anne, rumors which, no doubt, reached her growing daughter throughout her childhood. Anne had not only been promiscuous—which her condemned lovers, in conventional scaffold confessions, seemed to affirm—she had been guilty of worse crimes. Some said it was Anne, not Henry, who had poisoned Queen Katherine. No less an authority than the king, weeping as he spoke, told Fitzroy shortly before his death that he and Mary "were greatly bound to God for having escaped the hands of that accursed whore, who had determined to poison them."[12] Adultery, incest, murder or attempted murder, not to mention witchcraft—to these were added the further ominous revelation of other nameless crimes, too sinful to be written or spoken, which would forever be known only to a few. The confessions of Anne's lovers, Cromwell wrote to the king's envoy Stephen Gardiner in Rome, contained disclosures "so abominable that a great part of them were never given in evidence, but clearly kept secret."[13]

All this, and behind it the added weight of public mockery and contempt —Anne the Bawd, the she-devil, the English Messalina, the "goggle-eyed whore"—tipped the scales heavily against Anne, and seemed to put her guilt beyond question. Held in the greatest contempt when she became queen, Anne was doubly to be despised for turning against the man who had raised her to his throne. Hussey spoke for many in saying that all the evil deeds ascribed to women since the time of Adam and Eve "were nothing in comparison of that which has been done and committed by Anne the queen." He could not believe that she had actually done all the scurrilous things she was accused of, yet even if only some of the charges were accurate her behavior was "so abominable and detestable" that he could hardly bring himself to set it down.[14]

It was a black legacy. But was it true? The whisperings that sounded though Elizabeth's childhood were not unanimously to Anne's discredit. Archbishop Cranmer, a humane and thoughtful man who had been a chaplain in the Boleyn household and had known Anne for years, professed to be "clean amazed" to learn of her adultery. "I had never better opinion of woman," he wrote flatly to Henry VIII, expressing with his usual candor a dangerously controversial view.[15] Cranmer's opinion was not disinterested; he spoke for the liberals in religion who had from the start been associated with Anne, and had in mind that he, Cranmer, had been the one to pronounce sentence against the king's first marriage just as he would against the second. But there were other exonerating tales. The woman who had charge of Anne during her imprisonment in the Tower sent word to Chapuys, in the greatest secrecy, that Anne had sworn her innocence "on the damnation of her soul," before and after receiving the sacrament —moments hardly conducive to deceit. And at her trial she had not only denied the accusations made against her but had "given to each a plausible answer," raising more than a few suspicions about her accusers, especially as no witnesses were brought against her.[16]

But it was King Henry's behavior that gave rise to the most serious questions. His conduct, however one looked at it, was below reproach. Leaving aside the unfathomable issue of how any man, king or no, could in cold blood send a woman he had once worshiped to her death, there was the additional scandal of his grotesque rejoicing over it, and of his hasty third marriage.

It was generally known that Henry had filled the short weeks between Anne's arrest and her execution with exuberant merrymaking, taking his barge upriver every evening to dine in the company of beautiful women, then returning after midnight, his chamber singers and other musicians filling the night with fervent song. Such celebration "sounded ill in the ears of the people," who took his gaiety to mean, not only that he was glad to be rid of a "thin, old cantankerous nag," but that there was already a new filly in his stable. As soon as he received word that Anne was dead Henry went to the house where Jane Seymour was staying, and the next day they were formally betrothed. Ten days later they were privately married, and news of the marriage spread through the court despite the king's efforts to prevent it.

There was much murmuring over this, and suspicion that Henry and Jane had arrived at an understanding long before Anne was arrested. The high-handed proceedings at her trial, the lack of witnesses, Mark Smeaton's singular, torture-induced confession reinforced the view that Anne had simply stood between Henry and his desire, and he had swept her aside. "People think he invented this device to get rid of her," wrote the regent of Flanders, sister of Charles V; what she did not add, though it must have been obvious, was that at one blow Henry had carried out a palace revolution, sweeping away not only his wife but his leading chamber gentlemen (her alleged lovers), leaving the way open for new men, prominent among them Jane's brother Edward Seymour, to surround him.[17]

The king's capering and gloating, his evident self-interest and, in one view, calculated betrayal of Anne muddled the question of her guilt almost past clarification. Her daughter, buffeted by contrary rumors and stigmatized by her mother's ill repute, was left to sort out the stories and to piece together a truth from them over time.

What that truth was cannot now be discovered, and her extreme reticence about her mother is a striking fact of Elizabeth's adult life. But at some point she must have begun to comprehend and to envision the fate that overtook the mother she only dimly remembered. There were witnesses enough to recall, at a young child's urging, how "to aggravate her grief" Anne had been forced to watch her convicted accomplices die before her, their heads severed by the sharp blade of an axe, then their bodies quartered and the bloody quarters buried without ceremony. Two days after this Anne herself had climbed the steps of the scaffold, newly built and "of such a height that all present might see it," to face the hundreds—some said thousands—of spectators that spilled out down the hill before the White Tower on the morning of her execution. To the end, these witnesses recalled, she had appeared dazed, as if in disbelief to find herself so close to death, confident, with the confidence of the condemned, that in the final moment the king would save her. Throughout her trial she had sworn that, whatever happened, she was "safe from death." Now, as she approached the block, she "looked frequently behind her," as if watching in vain for the royal messenger bearing a pardon sealed with the king's seal.[18]

No pardon arrived, and the waiting onlookers were not cheated of their spectacle. As they watched Anne stepped forward to make a brief speech. She acquitted herself with dignity; she must by then have realized that the words she spoke would be her last. She was ready, she said, to "yield herself humbly to the will of the king," and to prove it she laid aside the furred mantle of her gray gown and crushed her abundant black hair under a plain linen cap, baring her long, white neck to the executioner's sword.

All this and more Elizabeth must have heard, how the swordsman had finished his task with one stroke, how the head had been wrapped in a white cloth, how the old women who charmed herbs and cast spells crowded to the scaffold to catch drops of Anne's blood, for the blood of the condemned was especially potent.

What little Elizabeth remembered of her mother in life—a hauntingly beautiful, brooding face, a scent, a voice singing a French lullaby—must have become confused with what she imagined of her death, until the whole took on the flavor of a dark fairy tale. The years passed, and other scandals arose to lure gossip and deflect attention from Anne Boleyn's daughter, and by then she was building an armor of silence. Even so the stigma lingered, and it would be many years before Anne's ghost was laid to rest.

Not long after Anne's death Elizabeth's governess Lady Bryan wrote a long, distraught letter to Cromwell. She was newly widowed and, as she put it, "succourless, and as a redeless creature." She was totally reliant on her position as lady mistress to the royal children—a post she had held for twenty years—for her support, and now that Elizabeth's status was changing she feared to lose her own rank of baroness and the comforts that went with it. In her uncertainty and distress she felt her control over the other servants slipping. "Now it is so, my lady Elizabeth is put from that degree she was afore, and what degree she is at now, I know not but by hearsay. Therefore I know not how to order her, nor myself, nor none of hers that I have the rule of—that is, her women and grooms, beseeching you to be good lord to my lady, and all hers."[19]

Apparently the little girl had outgrown all the gowns and jeweled caps her mother had ordered for her, and no larger ones had been provided. "She hath neither gown, nor kirtle, nor petticoat, nor no manner of linen—nor forsmocks [overdresses], nor kerchiefs, nor rails [nightdresses], nor body-stitchets [corsets], nor handkerchieves, nor sleeves, nor mufflers, nor big-gens [nightcaps]." She was destitute, and poor Lady Bryan could no longer make do. Urgent enough from day to day, the need for clothing would become particularly acute next time the king ordered Elizabeth "set abroad," to be viewed in public. At such times it fell to the lady mistress to make certain Elizabeth looked and acted like a king's daughter, and proper clothes were essential to the role.

The state of Elizabeth's wardrobe reflected the general penury of the household. The steward, John Shelton, who was responsible for keeping up the supplies of beef and corn and wine and dozens of other necessary supplies, wrote to Cromwell shortly after Lady Bryan did to complain that he was running short of money and "could not continue" without more. The aid he asked for may have been a long time in coming. The king's secretary Brian Tuke had made it clear only a week earlier that he hoped Mr. Shelton would not be appealing for additional funds, as he had little or nothing to give him.[20]

Somehow, though, the beef and mutton and fowl in abundance and many kinds of fish found their way into the dining hall, heavily spiced and smothered in the rich sauces characteristic of Tudor cookery. And there, Lady Bryan explained at length to Cromwell, lay a major bone of contention between herself and Mr. Shelton. For the steward, who loudly proclaimed himself "master of the house" ("What fashion that shall be I cannot tell," the lady mistress added, "for I have not seen it before"), insisted that Elizabeth eat with the adults, where there were "divers meats, fruits and wine" to tempt her. Lady Bryan despaired of restraining her infant greed, finding Elizabeth "too young to correct greatly" and fearing that she would make herself sick.

She appealed to Cromwell to intervene and establish a more healthful (and incidentally more economical) regimen. Elizabeth should eat in her own apartments, with one plate of beef or game and "a good dish or two that is meet for her grace to eat of." Her leavings would feed all eleven of her personal servants, thinning the ranks of those to be fed in the dining hall.

There was another reason for keeping the child in her own apartments. "God knoweth," Lady Bryan wrote, "my lady hath great pain with her great teeth, and they come very slowly forth, which causeth me to suffer her grace to have her will more than I would." Evidently the lady mistress was an indulgent guardian, and her charge sometimes got out of hand. "I trust to God, once her teeth were well graft, to have her grace after another fashion than she is yet," she said hopefully, "for she is as toward a child, and as gentle of conditions, as ever I knew any in my life. Jesu preserve her grace!"

As Elizabeth struggled with her "great teeth" and Lady Bryan struggled with the steward, the household servants let their duties go and spent their afternoons poaching in the king's hunting parks. Both Hunsdon and Hatfield—the usual residences of the royal children—were full of deer, and it was some months before the park keepers uncovered the misdoings, aided by a buck's head found concealed in a wheat field, a buck and doe found in the household servants' lodging, and the talebearings of one Roger of the Bakehouse. Eventually the facts came out. Roger himself had been among the guilty, along with Ralph of the Chandlery and several of the steward's servants. In complicity with at least one of the keepers the poachers coursed the deer with dogs and, on one occasion, hunted with crossbows. The principal culprit, Ralph Shelton, also shot birds with a handgun, and "drove away all the old breeders." It is tempting to connect

38

Ralph Shelton with John Shelton the steward, but if they were related, the steward was unable to prevent his kinsman from serving a term in the Fleet prison; the lesser hunters were shut up in the stocks.[21]

All in all it was an unsettled household, and much in need of reform. In the fall of 1536 a new governess arrived at Hunsdon to take over Elizabeth's upbringing. Her tutelage, and the subsequent arrival of several other new officers, inaugurated a transformation, and set Elizabeth's be-clouded childhood on a new track.

4

My prime of youth is but a frost of cares;
My feast of joy is but a dish of pain;
My crop of corn is but a field of tares;
And all my good is but vain hope of gain;
My life is fled, and yet I saw no sun;
And now I live, and now my life is done.

When Catherine Champernowne took up her post as lady mistress to Elizabeth, she joined a moderately large household living most of the time at Hatfield in Hertfordshire. The old-fashioned red brick manor house, with its squat central tower and graceless crenellated turrets, was a shabby enough setting for a royal nursery, though its grounds were vast and inviting. The huge forested hunting park, which had given so many hours of illicit pleasure to the wayward servants, stretched away for miles, while in the nearby Innings Park domesticated animals, including hundreds of black rabbits, were raised for food. The country air was sweet and, in plague season, safer than the damp, choking atmosphere of London, full of fogs and infection. To Elizabeth Hatfield was the welcoming, homelike center of her itinerant life, and the other familiar palaces of her childhood—Hunsdon, Ashridge, the More, and lesser houses—were merely temporary quarters to be occupied for a season while Hatfield was freshened and cleaned.

Mistress Champernowne joined some thirty-two other principal servants to Elizabeth, among them Blanche and Thomas Parry, who were to have long and eventful careers in her service. The gentlemen and gentlewomen appointed to her household were drawn from the least influential, least ambitious strata of the nobility; the lady mistress herself was from an obscure Devonshire family without rank at court. Gentility, not pomp, was the keynote. Royal ceremony was to be reserved for the king's future child by Queen Jane, the child designated, well in advance of its birth, as heir to the throne.

Shortly after Elizabeth's fourth birthday that child was born. He was christened with the name Henry had once considered for the unborn Elizabeth: Edward. And his birth was celebrated with all the festive merrymaking once planned, and canceled, for the hoped-for son of Anne Boleyn. Elizabeth took part in the glorious christening, dressed in a fine gown with a long train, clutching her infant brother's heavy, jewel-studded baptismal robe. Edward Seymour, the prince's uncle, held Elizabeth in turn, though at the conclusion of the ceremony she took her sister Mary's hand for the dignified procession out of the church.

With Edward's birth Elizabeth was all but forgotten. Living among nobodies in obscure country houses—save when, for economy's sake, she was thrown together with Mary or the little prince—Elizabeth grew out of babyhood unremarked, her holiday appearances at court little more than formalities. Her father, scrupulously attentive to all his possessions, saw to it that her household costs were paid and ordered new clothes for her from time to time (in 1539 he dressed his children, his gentlemen and his fools in one sweeping requisition), but otherwise ignored her. He did keep an eye on her servants. The distasteful memory of Anne Boleyn's crimes gave cause for concern about her daughter's morals, and Henry made it known that he preferred "ancient and sad persons" for her household. When a young girl of good family applied to enter Elizabeth's service the king refused her in favor of a "gentlewoman of elder years," adding that his daughter already had too many young people around her.[1]

Given this preference of the king's it would be interesting to know how old Catherine Champernowne was when she became lady mistress in the fall of 1536. But this, like much else about her, must remain conjecture. That she was educated, personable, and of presentable appearance seems likely. She was probably reasonably well spoken—though with a hint of broad Devon in her speech—and had been trained to write with facility. Whatever her nature, she won from Elizabeth an affection and loyalty so complete and unwavering it surpassed even a parent's due.

When Elizabeth was fifteen, and her lady mistress was in the Tower in peril of her life, Elizabeth put her feelings into words which, though bookish, were sincere. "[She] hath been with me a long time, and many years, and hath taken great labor and pain in bringing me up in learning and honesty; and therefore I ought of very duty to speak for her, for Saint Gregory sayeth 'that we are more bound to them that bringeth us up well than to our parents, for our parents do that which is natural for them that bringeth us into the world, but our bringers-up are a cause to make us live well in it.' "[2]

This wordy sentiment itself owed much to Mistress Champernowne—or Kat, as Elizabeth called her—for it was she who provided all of Elizabeth's early education, including her grounding in Latin and her acquaintance with Saint Gregory and the other Church Fathers. Well into adulthood Elizabeth was to be "more bound" to this Devonshire gentlewoman than to her blood relatives, though in time Kat became a relative by marriage, taking as her husband a Boleyn cousin, John Ashley, senior gentleman attendant in Elizabeth's household.

What sort of bringing up Kat Ashley provided, though affected by her temperament and intellect, was circumscribed by the conventions of the age. Children were welcomed into the Tudor world not for themselves, but as potential adults, and in light of this everything possible was done to make them old before their time.

From infancy little girls were dressed as women, wearing uncomfortable corsets and all the layers of petticoats and underskirts that women wore over them. They toddled in voluminous long robes stiff with embroidery, and struggled with cumbersome detachable puffed sleeves that made their arms too heavy to lift. Portraits of the time show little girls barely old enough to walk, their round faces encircled by tight-fitting lace caps, their bodies encased in layers of skirts and overdresses cinched in tightly at the waist, their plump necks chafing under starched collars. Sometimes they carry gold rattles, secured by chains to their waists, but their expressions are far from playful. Often their faces express a sobriety verging on the tragic, as if their thoughts ran prematurely to the mortality that hung over them.

One writer observed with pride that the children of his day "seemed to be born wise, and have gray hairs in their youth." A similar compliment was paid to Elizabeth at age six. Thomas Wriothesley, a somewhat unimaginative man soon to become principal secretary of state and then chancellor to Henry VIII, saw her in December of 1539, and brought her Christmas greetings from the king. Elizabeth was ushered in to him, having been carefully dressed and coached by Kat Ashley on how to behave. His message delivered, Wriothesley listened for Elizabeth's response. "She gave humble thanks," wrote Cromwell afterward, "enquiring again of his majesty's welfare, and that with as great a gravity as she had been forty years old. If she be no worse educated than she now appeareth to me, she will prove of no less honor to womanhood than shall beseem her father's daughter."[3]

Slavelike obedience to parents, precocious seriousness, modesty and prim decorum: these were the hallmarks of a well-brought-up child. Fathers and mothers were treated with a pious dutifulness akin to religious reverence. God and parents alone, the child was taught, were to be supplicated on both knees; one knee sufficed for everyone else. Stubborn, willful children were commonly made to crawl to their parents on their knees, scraping them raw across the entire length of the immense Tudor galleries as penance. A father's or mother's blessing was the precious sign of parental approval. From infancy children learned to kneel morning and evening and say "Father, I beseech you your blessing for charity." The parent, holding up his joined hands, would respond with a formula of blessing: "Our Lord bless you, child," or "May God guard you and lead you to great goodness." One parents' manual of the 1530s recommended that a "stiff-hearted" child, unwilling to submit to this filial ritual, be "whipped with a rod" until he was obedient; if too old to whip he was to be subjected to general abuse, with every member of the household hurling insults at him as they would a common criminal.[4]

Failure to observe "honorable esteem" toward parents had extreme consequences. Disobedient children were thought of as unnatural beings, "cruel murderers of their parents," who would at the very least be harshly punished by God for their impiety. Sometimes a magistrate was called in to impose a father's penalty on his son or daughter. But most parents would have found this excessively nice, preferring to follow the simple maxim "Whip the devil out of them!" for all misbehavior. Whippings, thrashings, severe spankings were everywhere incident to Tudor childrearing. Beating was seen as a sort of behavioral purgative, driving out the child's inborn inclination to wantonness and vice. Even the best-behaved children were pinched and cuffed and slapped when their perfection faltered; insensitive parents teased and threatened their tortured sons and daughters almost past endurance in the vague belief that affectionate treatment bred wrongdoing.

Henry VIII fully subscribed to the prevailing view of punishment, admonishing parents "to imploy their diligence and busy care to educate and instruct their children by all means in virtue and goodness, and to restrain them from vices by convenient discipline and castigation." He seems not to have punished his children himself, but was quite merciless in instructing others to punish them for him. When Mary, stripped of her rights and title, stubbornly clung to the name of princess and would not yield precedence to Anne Boleyn or her daughter, Henry sent Norfolk to break her will. The duke shouted abuse and threatened every sort of savagery, saying at last that if she were his own daughter he would kill her, dashing her head against the wall until her skull cracked and became "soft as a boiled apple." Yet rough as Norfolk was, the king ordered him to be rougher, and was angry at him for going about his task too gently.[5]

To the little Elizabeth her father must have been a fearsome creature, toweringly tall and, by the time she was five or six, growing mountainously fat. He was no longer the nimble-footed athlete who jousted and danced with youthful abandon. He could still show agility on occasion, but he limped heavily on his painful legs and often had to rest them, and riding had become an effort. The hearty cordiality that had made the king a popular figure in his youth was not yet fully eclipsed, but darker powers of spirit were emerging in him, and the memory of friends and relatives he had sent to the block curdled his affections and stained his character. He was a stern, old-fashioned father, who believed in a father's godlike authority. "Although sons and daughters were bound to some obedience toward their mothers," he once wrote, "their chief duty was to their fathers."[6] And that duty consisted primarily in total, unhesitating obedience.

Beyond deference to parents modest, "shamefaced" behavior was a principal goal. The temptations usual to childhood—fist-fighting, spitting, breaking windows, "casting snow or balls of snow" among myriad others —were severely punished, of course, but even such innocuous habits as running with other children "in heaps like a swarm of bees," or leaning against walls, or blushing and stammering at the teasing of other children were not tolerated. In his book of instructions for young children the great humanist Erasmus prescribed in minute detail proper control of the body. Shuffling the feet or wiggling the fingers or toes, he wrote, was indecorous, as was rolling the eyes or standing about in purposeless confusion. The arms, like birds' wings, should not swing idly but find some useful task to perform, perhaps in coordination with practice in bowing "after the fashion of England," bending the right knee first and then the left. When sitting or standing, the legs should be kept together—not as in Italy, Erasmus added, where everyone seemed to stand on one leg like a stork. And in walking, the child should cultivate a grave and seemly gait, neither so fast as to be undignified nor so slow as to appear to be loitering.[7]

When speaking the child was to frame his words pithily and to the point, uttering every word "with grace." Baby talk, like all other signs of childhood, was eliminated as early as possible, and very young children were taught to memorize "godly, grave and fruitful" maxims they could not possibly understand, such as "There is one invisible God, creating himself and all creatures," and "He is of the highest good; without him nothing is good." Silence was preferable to speech in childhood, but if an adult spoke to a child the child was to answer as appositely as possible, speaking, as Erasmus put it, to clergy about God, doctors about health and painters about design. Whether adults spoke to children about childhood seems doubtful.

But the strictures imposed on speech by the childrearing manuals were one thing, real family life another. Roger Ascham, Elizabeth's tutor during her adolescence and a highly proper, if not quite priggish, schoolmaster, wrote about his visit to a gentleman's house where a young child, "somewhat past four years old," could not manage to pronounce a short grace at table. "Yet," said Ascham, "he could roundly rap out so many ugly oaths, and those of the newest fashion, as some good man of four score years old hath never heard named before." It was easy enough to see where the problem lay; the little boy spent too much time with the serving men in the kitchen and stables, and picked up every word they uttered. But "that which was most detestable of all," wrote the earnest Ascham, "his father and mother would laugh at it."[8]

Nothing revealed good or ill breeding so quickly as behavior at the dinner table, and when Elizabeth was old enough to dine with the adults she had to master yet another realm of etiquette. She had to learn to manage a spoon and knife (no forks were used), to say "I thank you" politely even to dishes she could not eat, to lay picked bones neatly on a corner of her trencher for a servant to remove, and to try to ignore the dogs that licked her greasy fingers under the table. In his own fifteenth-century childhood, Erasmus recalled, food was valued; people kissed the very bread that fell on the floor as a mark of respect. Now that respect had fallen away, and heedless parents allowed their children to stuff themselves at table until they vomited. It would have been understandable, if not excusable, if the daughter of the gargantuan eater Henry VIII had stuffed herself to excess. But Elizabeth, at least in adult life, ate lightly, and there is no evidence of her overindulgence in childhood.

Civilized eating habits called for more than proper management of food; neatness, sociability and discretion were required. To wipe one's hands on one's sleeves (or on the linen tablecloth) was unforgivable; if the sleeves were of the long and open kind that hung down in deep folds and threatened to get into the food, they should be thrown back over the shoulders, or turned up at the elbow and pinned out of the way. Caps were to be on throughout the meal, lest the hair "fall into the dishes," and the hair itself had to be kept combed to remove lice. Children had a unique problem at meals. They were taught to join in the table conversation, for to remain silent, "in stupor or ecstasy," was bad manners. Yet they could not speak until spoken to, and in households where the young were ignored this must have led to considerable tension as the meal drew to a close. Nor were they to join in any gossip that might be aired, nor reopen old quarrels, nor repeat afterward anything their elders said, especially if the elders were inebriated at the time.[9] It was an intricate initiation into the adult world, with its formalities and hypocrisies, an introduction to society in microcosm.

The moral education of girls required special instruction, and in the training of Anne Boleyn's daughter extraordinary precautions must have been taken. It was the unchallenged conviction of sixteenth-century thought that women were far inferior to men in their capacity for goodness and virtue—as well as in intelligence and sound judgment. But Elizabeth bore a double stigma. She had not only the inherent incapacity and moral weakness of a female, but the added tendency toward wantonness and sin that was her presumed inheritance from her condemned mother. To make a virtuous, modest child from such unpromising material was Kat Ashley's principal task, though there is little evidence of how she went about it. Yet always assuming that she followed convention, the watchword of little Elizabeth's instruction must have been self-control.

Self-control in avoiding "lustful movements" and other signs of sensuality; self-control in gestures, posture, and speech; self-control in keeping silent, or modestly soft-spoken, in the company of adults. Above all Kat must have sought to breed out of Elizabeth any sign of her mother's vivacious high spirits, any tendency to draw attention to herself through boisterous spontaneity or laughter. Laughter, Erasmus taught, indicated either empty-headedness or a wicked soul, or, in the extreme, utter madness. (Even smiling betokened deceit.) People whose laughter was as shrill as a neighing horse, or who showed all their teeth when they laughed, like a snarling dog, made their degeneracy plain for all to see.

Of course it was impossible for Elizabeth not to laugh at Lucretia the Tumbler, Mary's fool, or not to show pleasure when her own minstrels played. But there was proper laughter and improper laughter. Proper laughter should not distort the features, but a well-bred child ought to cover his mouth with a handkerchief whenever he laughed, just in case. There were many facial expressions to be avoided: wrinkling the nose, twisting the mouth into unbecoming shapes, furrowing the brow or working it up and down "like a hedgehog"—Erasmus' catalog of undesirable behaviors reads like a bestiary—as well as yawning, sniffling, and sneezing. Sneezing in particular was surrounded with ritual. If an adult sneezed, the child was to remove his cap and say "Christ help you," or "Christ's mercy on you." If the child had to sneeze—something he should try with all his strength to prevent—he should turn away from his companions and bless his mouth with the sign of the cross afterward, then acknowledge the blessings of others by taking off his cap.[10]

Girls, fragile creatures that they were, needed constant supervision, both by the servants and waiting women who were always in attendance on them and by a relative or lady mistress. Their days were filled with purposeful activity, leaving little time for playing with dolls or riding hobbyhorses or running with a hoop.

Needlework was their traditional pastime, and it took years of diligent labor to progress from the simple cross stitch, crewel and feather stitch of samplers to the twist, back stitch, satin stitch, and chain stitch required by intricate decorative embroidery. Little girls applied themselves to stitching the alphabet and sententious proverbs on wall hangings; by age six or seven they had progressed to fancier work and were able to decorate cushions or clothing. There were dozens of styles to master, and an accomplished needlewoman of ten or twelve could spend most of her free time hidden behind an embroidery frame, skeins of thread wound round her neck, her kirtle prickly with needles. Parents found the hours lost to needlework reassuring. One nobleman wrote that all daughters should be put to vast embroidery projects "that will ever be in the beginning and never ended." Kat Ashley seems to have held to this view, at least to an extent, for at age six Elizabeth presented her two-year-old brother Edward with a cambric shirt "of her own working," and in the following year she gave him another piece of needlework.[11]

But if Elizabeth spent a good deal of time stitching, she spent much more in the schoolroom, where under Kat's guidance she made remarkably rapid progress in learning to read and write.

She had a bright, quick intelligence and a good memory, and languages —the core of her humanist education—came easily to her. When she began to puzzle out words is not known, but most likely she read with great facility by the age of five or six, for by then she had begun her second language: Latin. In both tongues short sentences gave way to longer ones with longer words, then to the Bible and Caesar and Cicero. In time Edward's tutors allowed her to join his lessons; eventually she acquired a tutor of her own.

By then she had also begun to master the art of handwriting, with its accompanying lore of pens, paper and ink. Quill pens were made from the third or fourth feather of the wing of a goose, sharpened with a penknife, softened with spit and rubbed afterward on the underside of a piece of clothing, where the stain would be hidden. Ink too had to be mixed, the type of ink used depending on the haste of the writer and the intended permanency of the lettering. Children in Elizabeth's time wrote on paper —parchment was saved for official documents—and kept a second sheet of coarser stock at hand to blot their work and try out their pens. Some of this coarse paper used by Elizabeth as a girl has been preserved; on it she practiced again and again her brother's name.[12]

When all the materials had been made ready, writing could begin. The ink, stirred and thinned, was placed beside the right hand. Then the pen was dipped in, the excess ink shaken off, and the point touched to the practice sheet to make certain it was free of hair. Then the letters were carefully drawn, the student clenching his teeth and trying not to bend low over the page. "As much as you can," a handwriting text warned, "write with your head upright: for if one stand with his head downward, humors fall down to his forehead, and into his eyes; whereof many infirmities do arise, and weakness of sight."[13] Slowly the beginning writer traced the alphabet, a cross, the Lord's Prayer, and the invocation "In the name of the Father and of the Son and of the Holy Ghost, Amen." Later, longer passages were written, sometimes translations of Latin texts or, still later, translations from English into Italian or French.

Such was Elizabeth's early education: filial duty, submissive self-restraint, self-improving pastimes, the solid beginnings of a thorough classical education. And with it all, habits of religious devotion—morning services and evening services, Bible reading and prayer, a view of the world as God's creation blemished by human sin and redeemed by the sacrifice of God's son.

She was not raised to revere particular doctrines for themselves, but rather to believe deeply and without question the central verities of Christianity—the incarnation, death and resurrection of Christ, the miracle of blessed bread and wine consumed in worshipful remembrance, the promise of a serene afterlife. When she disobeyed, she was reminded of heaven and hell, of "the horned and hairy monster being in hell to catch bad children," and of how "the good ones go to paradise, dancing with the angels."

Such were Elizabeth's mental parameters, the fixed ideas that shaped her earliest thoughts. "For the pure clean wit of a sweet young babe," Ascham wrote, "is like the newest wax, most able to receive the best and fairest printing; and like a new bright silver dish never occupied, to receive and keep clean, any good thing that is put into it."[14] By the time she was five or six, Elizabeth's "pure clean wit" bore a strong and lasting imprint, one that would be deepened and refined, though not fundamentally altered, as she grew older.

Early in 1540, when she was six years old, Elizabeth was brought to court to be present at an unusually solemn event. Her father was to celebrate his fourth wedding, and this time his bride was to be a foreigner, the delicate blond sister of the duke of Cleves.

Jane Seymour, Edward's mother and the king's third wife, had died within days of her son's birth, and after more than two years as a widower King Henry had agreed to a political match. His bride-to-be, Anne of Cleves, came from a duchy rich in mercenary soldiers and with great strategic importance should war break out between England and the Hapsburg emperor Charles V. On the day of her public greeting at Greenwich Anne's "determined and resolute countenance" was framed by a pearl-trimmed bonnet and her thin figure was encased in an ill-cut German gown which did nothing to enhance her appearance in English eyes. Yet despite this inauspicious debut the king married her, and Elizabeth began to grow accustomed to seeing yet another woman in her mother's place at her father's side.

Queen Anne's appeal as a stepmother cannot have been great. She spoke only a few words of English, and was surrounded by ruddy-faced foreigners with such unpronounceable names as Vresvydour, Hoghsteyn and Swartzenbroch. Yet nothing in her outward behavior was objectionable enough to explain the king's decision, only a few months after the marriage, to separate from her. Elizabeth could hardly have guessed that simple physical revulsion lay behind the separation, and she must have been puzzled, to say the least, by the swiftness with which Anne was replaced by the king's fifth wife, Catherine Howard.

The new queen was not yet out of her teens, a blooming, nubile girl whose sensuality rejuvenated the king and made him besotted. His abundant gifts to his new wife—gowns, chains, jewels in an inexhaustible stream —were one measure of his affection; his constant caresses another. Catherine's Howard relatives regained entirely what favor they had lost with the disgrace of the family prodigal Anne Boleyn, and Elizabeth too was drawn closer to the circle of privilege around the queen.

Elizabeth and Catherine Howard were closely related, as Elizabeth's Howard grandmother was Catherine's aunt. Whether there was any close personal attachment between them is conjectural, but Elizabeth rode in Catherine's barge and stayed with her for a time, in the spring of 1541, at the king's riverside manor of Chelsea.[15] Evidently Queen Catherine passed on to her young stepdaughter a small share of the largesse with which King Henry showered her. An inventory of her jewels listed a small bauble, "little thing worth"—perhaps a brooch or cross—given away to Elizabeth, and also a rosary "with crosses, pillars and tassels attached."[16]

With the king's several marriages came renewed interest in Elizabeth as a potential bride. During 1538, when Henry had been engaged in the search for a wife which culminated in his marriage to Anne of Cleves, he proposed matches for himself and his children. Elizabeth was included in these grandiose schemes for multiple marriages, in which her father, brother and sister were to take brides and bridegrooms from among the relatives of Charles V. (The emperor let the English ambassador know, however, that where Elizabeth was concerned he "noted the life and death of her mother," and considered the subject closed.)

Later, while Catherine Howard was queen, the legitimacy of both of King Henry's daughters became a stumbling block in marriage negotiations with the French. "It was more honorable," the French envoys said haughtily, "for the son of France [the dauphin] to marry the poorest gentlewoman, being legitimate, than a dame of the noblest parentage, being illegitimate."[17] This being their view, Norfolk discouraged them from bargaining for Elizabeth as a bride for the duke of Orléans. "The opinion of Queen Anne, her mother, was such that it was quite decided to consider her illegitimate," he told them, "as the Act of Parliament declared." And besides, she came last among the king's children in order of succession.[18]

As the issue was being decided there came another wrenching reversal in the king's affections. After a year and a half of marriage it was discovered that Catherine Howard had not been a virgin when she married King Henry, and there were those who swore she had not been faithful to him as a wife. She was sent away, her lovers executed, many of her relatives imprisoned. Lady Rochford, wife of the executed George Boleyn and Elizabeth's aunt, was condemned as the queen's accomplice in her romantic intrigues.

Catherine Howard's swift fall reminded many of the dramatic ruin of her cousin Anne Boleyn, and led to much head-shaking over the spectacular unchastity of the Howard women. Old memories were revived, and once again Anne Boleyn's daughter came in for tacit censure.

For Elizabeth, who at eight and a half was beginning to grasp the enormity of her father's treatment of her mother, now lived through a reenactment of his vengeful authority. The queen, a terrified girl one-third her bloated husband's age, was brought to the Tower where she and Lady Rochford—the latter raving mad—awaited death. As with Anne Boleyn's execution six years earlier, the high scaffold was erected on Tower Green. The crowd assembled. The queen was led up the steps to stand before her subjects, to confess with her final words that she had broken God's commandments and offended "very dangerously" against the king, and to ask the king's pardon. And she suffered, and her headless body was taken to the Tower chapel to be buried, without ceremony, near her cousin's.

Spring came, then summer, and in September Elizabeth's ninth birthday. There was a new companion in her life, a boy of about her own age. He was Robin Dudley, the son of John Dudley, a man of rising importance at her father's court. There was a special empathy between the two children, and though Elizabeth was not a confiding child she confided in him. She told him very seriously, he recalled many years later, that she had made up her mind never to marry.

5

Think'st thou, Kate, to put me down
With a "No" or with a frown?
Since Love holds my heart in bands
I must do as Love commands.

T he destruction of his plump, young fifth wife left King Henry depressed and sometimes savagely hostile. He limped around the privy chamber on his swollen legs, ranting at his servants, cursing his subjects for their ingratitude and his councilors for their hidden plottings. He limped to the dining table, and sat down to course after course of savory delicacies, which he consumed with a methodical gluttony that kept his tailors steadily engaged in enlarging his doublets and his armorers hammering new harness to surround his enormous girth. The Herculean meals he consumed and the rivers of wine with which he washed them down blackened his temper; while the mood was on him he trusted no one, and became, to those who tiptoed into his presence, quite simply "the most dangerous and cruel man in the world."[1]

Yet after a year of this he found his equilibrium, and in July of 1543 braved ridicule by marrying for the sixth and last time. His tall, auburn-haired bride was a witty and sensitive woman with serious turn of mind. Catherine Parr had been brought to the marriage not by the king's persuasion but by a powerful conviction that it was God's will; her own will, set firmly on another course, she renounced. Her small features composed, she repeated her marriage vows in the queen's privy closet at Hampton Court, as nine-year-old Elizabeth and five-year-old Edward looked on. Mary, who at twenty-seven was only a few years younger than the new queen and had grown up with her at court, stood by as her father spoke his vows "with a joyous countenance," and put the gold wedding ring on Catherine's white finger.

Though demure and subservient in her husband's presence, Catherine was accustomed to taking command. She came from a line of dominant, enlightened women: her grandmother Elizabeth Fitzhugh had been a remarkable woman of vigorous intellect; Maud Parr, her mother, as a young widow with three children had served Katherine of Aragon as lady in waiting while looking out for her children's welfare and interests virtually unaided. Catherine Parr herself was a veteran of two dutiful, demanding marriages, neither of which can have awakened her passion. She had married her first husband, an elderly widower in declining health, at fourteen, and when he died she married Lord Latimer, a middle-aged Yorkshire gentleman who expected her to look after his London house, his magnificent border castle and his two young children. By the time he died in 1542 Catherine was no more than thirty, yet she had acquired the organizing genius of a lord chamberlain, the healing skill of a physician and the toughness and resilience of a soldier on campaign. She had the strength and skill to cope with yet another cantankerous, aging husband, and she had convinced herself that coping with him was, at least for the time being, her destiny.

Much has been made of the high-minded learning and religious devotion of Elizabeth's fourth stepmother. Her earnest study of the Christian classics and the inward-looking piety she expressed in her widely read devotional books set her apart from her contemporaries and gave her unique appeal as a woman who combined strong intellect with urgent human feeling. A member of Catherine's household left a flattering portrait of his mistress, her mind "so formed for pious studies that she considered everything of small value compared to Christ."[2] Her rare goodness, he wrote, "made every day a Sunday, a thing hitherto unheard of, especially in a royal palace." He considered himself blessed to be part of her holy establishment, "where Christ is celebrated daily," and where the queen's rich store of virtue improved and uplifted all who dwelt with her.

Yet these effusive sentiments are misleading. Catherine was indeed devout, but her capacity for passionate devotion was but one part of a general capacity for passion. She was an ardent woman, and when she married Henry VIII she was very much in love with another man.

Thomas Seymour was a handsome, energetic man with a broad brow and keen eyes. Robust and youthful at thirty-five, he was still unmarried, though consumingly eager to marry as soon as the right situation presented itself.

He was only the fourth son of a country gentleman, but his sister Jane Seymour had been queen and his nephew Edward Tudor would before long be king; his brother, Edward Seymour, far outshone him in political advancement—though not in looks or personality—yet his brotherly patronage and indulgence of Thomas' undisguised ambition was bound to be an asset in the long run. All in all, Thomas Seymour held himself worthy to marry a woman of unusually high rank and great fortune, and as Lord Latimer's widow Catherine Parr fulfilled at least the second requirement. Seymour approached her, and found her warmly responsive. "My mind was fully bent," she wrote him later, "to marry you before any man I know." But then the king intervened, and his proposal took priority.

In Henry's eyes Catherine was the perfect bride. She was a good-looking woman, an intelligent and opinionated conversationalist, an accomplished huntswoman and a good shot with a crossbow. Careful tutelage had purged her of willfulness and sensuality—though vulnerable to romance she was, as she put it, "none adulterer, nor fornicator, and so forth"—and she was old enough to show common sense should temptation present itself. She would supervise the care of his children, Henry was sure, and would serve him humbly and without resentment as he confronted old age.

It was no wonder that, after five unsatisfactory wives, his expression was joyous as he married his sixth. And no matter what malicious gossip said, it was not in perverse celebration of his wedding that he sent a priest, a chorister and a tailor to their deaths just then for heresy.[3] These were uncertain times for the church, and Henry, with his godly wife beside him, had to purge error as often as he found it, wedding season or no.

The royal couple set out almost at once on a leisurely hunting progress, riding through green fields and luxuriant meadows to the country manors of Oatlands, Guildford, Sunninghill and the More. The grasses were unusually tall, and stubborn weeds crowded the planted fields, for the summer was oppressively rainy. Henry decreed prayers to be said for sunshine; without it the crops would be ruined. But the wet weather continued, and made conditions ripe for a severe outbreak of the summer scourge, plague.

In the early weeks of the honeymoon all three of the king's children were together with their father and stepmother—until then a very rare circumstance. In August, as Henry and Catherine proceeded with their progress, Elizabeth was sent to stay with Edward, and Mary continued on with the royal party. By then the pestilence was spreading. As always it was worst in London, with tentacles of infection reaching deep into the countryside to menace market towns and villages. The king and his party took refuge in the remote hunting lodge of Woodstock, where for a month and more they isolated themselves from the surrounding region and watched the rain drench the park, ruining their sport. By mid-October, however, the sickness had run its course and, with the number of deaths subsiding, they made their way back to court, where Catherine would take up in earnest her role as mother to the heirs to the throne.

A harsh stepmother, a contemporary treatise taught, "shows herself to be an enemy, gathering up hate without cause, and wreaking it upon the weak and innocent." A good stepmother, on the other hand, "will wish to be to her husband's children that which she may often hear them call her, that is 'Mother.'" For the next five years Catherine Parr was something akin to a mother to Elizabeth and Edward, and a sisterly adviser to Mary. Her role was more that of overseer than anything else, for as always the children had their own households and followed the itinerant pattern that saw them moving in a recurring cycle from one country house to another. Sometimes the royal family did not even assemble on holidays; in fact, for a year after the wedding Elizabeth did not see either her father or her stepmother at all.[4]

Yet Queen Catherine's influence was no less powerful for being exerted at a distance. Undoubtedly she gave careful attention to Elizabeth's education, as she graduated from Kat Champernowne's rudimentary tutelage to more advanced lessons with Edward's tutors, first the learned clergyman Richard Cox and then John Cheke, regius professor of Greek at Cambridge and among the greatest scholars of his age.

Cox, Edward's first tutor, was an affectionate teacher who used the most imaginative means to make learning palatable. In 1544, when Edward was nearly seven and Elizabeth going on eleven, he built his lessons around the most interesting of contemporary events: Henry VIII's invasion of France and conquest of Boulogne. He challenged the children to "conquer the captains of ignorance" as the king was conquering the French, and presented every exercise—learning the parts of speech, conjugating Greek and Latin verbs, and so on—as a fortress to be besieged or a bulwark to be defended. He even cloaked discipline in military metaphors, referring to Edward's recalcitrance as "Captain Will" and subduing it with the "morris-pike" of a sharp slap or spank.

John Cheke succeeded Cox, and perhaps because of his own exalted abilities as a classical linguist—most of his works were translations of Greek texts into Latin—he recognized Elizabeth's precocity and, with her stepmother's acquiescence, recommended that she have her own tutor. William Grindal, a learned and patient young Cambridge scholar recently disappointed in his bid for a readership at St. John's College, was the choice. For the next three years and more, Elizabeth was to benefit from Grindal's scrupulous, attentive training, as she was steeped in the particular world view of English Protestant humanism.

Cheke, Grindal, and Roger Ascham—who though he stayed at Cambridge until 1548 was nonetheless in close touch with the others—were all from St. John's. With Cox and other Cambridge scholars they formed an intellectual bridge between the internationalist, Catholic humanism of Erasmus and Thomas More, with its distaste for fine points of doctrine and its optimistic religious tolerance, and the radical, Protestant learning that was aggressively nationalistic and that welcomed doctrinal distinctions as antidotes to heresy. Their program laid much emphasis on Greek and Latin (and, for university scholars, Hebrew as well), for without a mastery of these tongues one could not read either the works of the Church Fathers or the classics of antiquity in the original. But though the classical writers— Demosthenes, Plato, Vergil and, in particular, Cicero—were prized for their unsurpassed eloquence and depth, still their works were seen as imperfect compared to the higher eloquence, the perfect truth of the Bible. Cambridge in the 1540s, one writer has said, was in transition from a stronghold of ecclesiastical learning to a seminary for laymen; no longer clerical, it was nonetheless a training ground in Christian virtue, where gentlemen's sons were meant to form their character and sharpen their religious sensibilities for the lifelong struggle against sin. And they were to live their heroic lives within the confining bounds of the English church, devoting themselves to the untiring service of the state and the monarch.

The men who taught Elizabeth were young. Grindal was in his twenties, Cheke barely thirty, Cox an ingenuous forty-four. Yet compared to the earlier generation of humanists they were straitlaced and inflexibly devoted to purity of life. Dancing, card-playing, gambling were anathema; long hours of sermons and private meditation, combined with improving reading, fortified one, they taught, for the strife of the world. There was an occasional whiff of the medieval about these enlightened products of the Renaissance. Roger Ascham, writing to Elizabeth's cousin John Ashley, sent him a series of pictures representing the Dance of Death, in the hope that in this macabre reflection he would "discern, as in a mirror, the decay of glory, the flesh, the world, lust, and all vanities."[5]

What curriculum Grindal prescribed for Elizabeth can be guessed from the schedule Ascham designed for her later: probably the mornings were given over to Greek, with lessons in grammar and translation of simple texts giving way in time to reading the New Testament and the less demanding classical authors. Most likely she read Latin, chiefly Cicero and Livy, in the afternoons, and divided the remainder of her time between French and

Italian. Her facility in Italian Elizabeth shared with her stepmother Catherine Parr (though not with her half-sister Mary, educated in the 1520s, before Italian culture came strongly into vogue), and by at least the age of eleven Elizabeth was able to show off her mastery of the language in decorous letters addressed to the queen.

A test of Elizabeth's abilities came at about this time when John Leland, the "king's antiquary," visited John Cheke's schoolroom. Cheke presented the historian to Edward, then brought him "to the Lady Elizabeth to have a sight of her." He asked her to address Leland in Latin, "the which she did." The antiquary, favorably impressed by the learning and poise of the slim, redheaded little girl and always eager to please his patron her father, preserved the event in Latin poetry.

For her New Year's gift at the close of 1544 Elizabeth sent her stepmother something which displayed all her accomplishments to advantage. It was a handwritten book, and its cover, beautifully embroidered in blue and silver threads, with clusters of purple heart's-ease and the queen's initials intertwined, proclaimed the giver's proficiency in needlework. The penmanship was admirable in itself, while Elizabeth's translation—for she had turned a French work into fluent, if overornate, English—showed a high level of literacy in both languages. These features, welcome as they were, may have pleased Catherine Parr no more greatly than the choice of text. Elizabeth had chosen a contemporary devotional work, not dissimilar to Catherine's own writings—*The Glasse of the Synnefull Soule,* by the French princess Marguerite de Navarre. It was a cheerless, spiritually anguished little book, full of Old Testament mournfulness and self-mortification, and Elizabeth had prefaced it with a solemn, involuted dedication embroidered with classical maxims:

"Knowing that pusillanimity and idleness are most repugnant unto a reasonable creature," the dedication began, "and that (as the philosopher sayeth) even as an instrument of iron or other metal waxeth soon rusty unless it be continually occupied, even so shall the wit of a man or woman wax dull and unapt to do or understand anything perfectly unless it be always occupied upon some manner of study. Which things considered," she went on, "hath moved so small a portion as God has lent me, to prove what I could do."

Elizabeth was only too aware of the shortcomings of her efforts, she said, but she had faith in the alchemy of her learned stepmother's tolerant perusal of the book. Once Catherine read it, Elizabeth believed, "its imperfections would all be smoothed and polished by the file of her highness' excellent wit and godly learning"; "after it shall have passed through her hands, it would come forth as it were in a new form."[6]

Elizabeth made several such manuscript books at this period of her life. One of these she kept in the royal library at Whitehall until the end of her reign. It was inscribed, in French, "To the right high and right mighty and redoubtable Prince Henry, Eighth of that name, king of England, France, and Ireland, Defender of the Faith, Elizabeth, his right humble daughter, gives greeting and obedience."[7]

Though privately tutored by Grindal Elizabeth did not undertake her intellectual efforts alone. A contemporary called Catherine Parr's household "a school of virtue for learned virgins," where "it was now a common thing to see young virgins so trained in the study of good letters that they willingly set all other vain pastimes at naught for learning's sake."[8] A number of young women were educated under the queen's supervision and with her encouragement, among them her younger sister Ann Parr, the four daughters of the Cambridge scholar Anthony Cooke, and Jane Grey, great-granddaughter of Henry VII and, after the king's own children, next in line of succession to the throne. Mary Tudor, though belonging to an older generation, was also among the "learned virgins," and secured her place among them by serving as one of the translators of Erasmus' *Paraphrases on the Four Gospels,* a publishing project financed by the queen.

Like Elizabeth, Jane Grey stood out from the others. Tutored assiduously from the age of four—the tutor had carried her in his arms, teaching her to pronounce words—Jane seems to have developed preternatural ability and scholarly insight. Quickly mastering the grammatical facility needed to read the classics with her tutor, she passed on to a higher plane of appreciation, and read them on her own, for pleasure. When Roger Ascham visited her at age twelve or thirteen, he found her in her chamber, reading Plato's *Phaedo* in Greek, "and that with as much delight as some gentleman would read a merry tale in Boccaccio."

Henry VIII's reign was drawing to an end, and Elizabeth's childhood ebbed with it. She was growing tall, and acquiring the watchful self-aware-ness of a young woman, part vanity, part defensiveness. A portrait painted sometime in early adolescence catches a hint of steely vigilance in her grave, unsmiling stare—or perhaps she was merely trying to look regal. We who know what her future was to hold can read much into that tight-lipped countenance: self-control, resolute modesty, even defiance. The forced maturity in the expression is touching, for the face has not quite lost its childish contour. Still, what is telling about the portrait is how the intelli-gent power of Elizabeth's expression overwhelms all else—the elegance of her crimson kirtle and embroidered gown, her restrained adornments of pearls and jet, her sloe eyes, bright red hair and milk-white skin, clear and free of the pimply "wheals" that "disgraced the faces" of sixteenth-century adolescents, even her remarkable hands, their long, spider-thin fingers holding a velvet-bound book.

Jane Dormer, who as a child was among Elizabeth's companions, recalled her striking looks at thirteen, but noted that her "proud and disdainful" expression and manner "much blemished the handsomeness and beauty of her person." Elizabeth at thirteen and fourteen was already a figure to be reckoned with, her charisma still embryonic, her physical attraction great and her outward reserve strengthened by a singular force of mind.

In the capital the old king lay dying. Physicians and apothecaries hovered over him, forcing evil-smelling liquids down his throat, collecting and measuring every drop of his urine and cauterizing his swollen legs with hot irons. He had been ill since late summer, yet each time he took to his bed in "great danger" of death he confounded everyone by quickly getting out again to go hunting. His unwieldy body seemed unconquerable, yet the physicians continued to give one another knowing looks (they dared not speak openly of their prognoses) and foreign ambassadors, denied access to the palace, warned their governments to expect an imminent transfer of power in England. Queen Catherine and Henry's three children, staying in separate residences and not allowed to come to the dying king's bedside, fretted and waited for news; among the people it was whispered that he was already dead.

An unspoken anxiety hung over every mention of the king: would nine-year-old Prince Edward succeed him, and if so, who would govern in fact?

That Edward would succeed seemed certain, though Mary's rights and possible preeminence were not discounted. Two things weighed in her favor: she was much loved by the people, as her mother had been before her, and her powerful cousin, the Holy Roman Emperor Charles V, stood ready to defend her rights by force should his own interests make it advisable. Mary had a glaring liability, however: she belonged to that minority of the English who were still committed to the Roman faith. Despite King Henry's breach with the pope, despite his destruction of the monasteries and expropriation of monastic wealth, despite the doctrinal reversals that, with seesaw changefulness, had guided public faith for a decade and more, Mary stood firmly with those who held to the mass, the saints, and the time-honored belief.

Her Catholicism, combined with her status as heir apparent, made Mary the natural focus of any rebellion or conspiracy that might arise once the new reign began. Like it or not she was bound to come into collision with the king's ambitious councilors, who now gathered at his bedside waiting to make their bid for power.

Finally, in the early hours of January 28, 1547, Henry died. His death unleashed a maelstrom of political maneuvering, with each of the privy councilors—particularly Edward Seymour, who emerged almost immediately as leader of the new government, as Lord Protector of his nephew Edward VI, his subtle ally William Paget, John Dudley, a crafty soldier ambitious for influence, and the handsome, aggressive Thomas Seymour—intriguing to advance himself at the expense of the others.

Thomas Seymour was as flamboyant in his tactics as he was in personality. Having become a member of the privy council in Henry's final days (an appointment the king had always resolutely opposed until then), Seymour made himself very visible in the early weeks of the new reign. His tall, energetic figure was much in view at the tournaments celebrating King Edward's accession, and he was addressed now as Baron Seymour of Sudeley, having been made a peer (as well as a Garter Knight) by the young king. But these were minor honors compared to the exalted role he coveted.

He was an eligible bachelor; Edward's court was full of marriageable women, several of them in line for the throne. Cocksure and thoughtless, Thomas Seymour approached his brother and asked him to support his plan to marry Mary Tudor. According to the imperial ambassador, a quarrel broke out between them. Edward Seymour, indignant that his younger brother should presume so high, lectured him on humility and ordered him to "thank God and be satisfied" with the status he had. Besides, the Protector added, Mary would never consent.

This insult to his power over women Thomas Seymour dismissed with a smile. He would look after that problem if it arose, he said; all he wanted was his brother's blessing. But the Protector was firm, and they parted on bad terms—made worse by the intervention of Dudley, who saw in Seymour a limitless lust for power that mirrored his own, and was determined to stop him.

What Seymour did next is unclear. Apparently he did not approach Mary directly, but according to rumor he attempted to gain the assent of the royal council—without whose approval marriage to either Mary or Elizabeth was illegal—to marry Elizabeth. Failing in this attempt (and, according to the French ambassador, in his efforts to court Anne of Cleves, who had long since made herself at home in England and was a familiar presence at court), Seymour fell back on yet another alternative, and revived his long dormant suit to Catherine Parr.

Queen Catherine—for she kept her royal title, with all its prerogatives, as Henry VIII's widow—was the highest-ranking woman at court, yielding precedence only to the king's two sisters. She had long been among the wealthiest women in England, for in addition to the lands she held from her first two marriages Henry had settled on her all of Anne Boleyn's and

Catherine Howard's lands, and many others besides. Since 1543 a council of overseers had been charged with keeping the voluminous records and collecting the rents from her hundreds of estates. Now, with the king's death, her wealth was increased by £1,000 in coin and £3,000 in plate and jewels, besides all the other valuables King Henry had presented to her while he was alive. In one respect alone he might have been seen to slight her. He made no provision for Catherine's last resting place in his will, and ordered that Jane Seymour's body be interred beside his in the soaring marble tomb—as yet unfinished—that was to house his remains. But this was easily forgiven: Jane was the new king's mother, and Catherine understood that dynastic considerations took precedence. Besides, her thoughts were not on her dead husband, but on her handsome, living lover; to her inexpressible delight, Thomas Seymour had asked her to marry him.

That their wooing was secret—and politically dangerous—only added to Catherine's excitement. To avert suspicion he came to her at daybreak, frowning purposefully as he strode across the fields that surrounded her dower house at Chelsea. They dared not be seen together, and Seymour, who realized what opposition he faced from his senior colleagues on the council, was determined to marry Catherine before his intentions could be guessed. Within two or three months of the old king's death Catherine Parr married Thomas Seymour in a ceremony so clandestine its date was not recorded. The bride was as radiant, as diffident as if the marriage had been her first. Her good fortune transformed her. Normally an articulate woman, Catherine was reduced to few words. Surely, she wrote in a letter to her beloved, "God is a marvellous man."[9]

Elizabeth was living with Catherine at Chelsea during this breathless courtship. Though she was officially in mourning for her father her grief cannot have overwhelmed her. She had seen little of him in recent years, and when in his company court protocol had strictly governed her behavior. A visitor to Henry's palace had once been astonished to see Elizabeth sink deferentially to her knees before her father three times in the course of a single audience. Beyond signing the warrants that gave authorization for her household staff, her clothing, and other needs Henry paid her little or no attention. She had reached marriageable age, and in consequence his envoys did not hesitate to offer her hand—to the earl of Arran's son, to a brother of the king of Denmark, or to his son the crown prince. But it is doubtful whether she was informed of these transient bargainings, which like earlier such initiatives came to nothing in the end.

Thomas More, one of the best and wisest fathers of the Tudor age, wrote that "a man does not merit the name of father who does not weep for the tears of his children." Henry VIII was a man who wept easily, but rarely, it may be supposed, for his children's sorrows. Elizabeth, however she may have invoked his authority in later years, could hardly have felt he lived up to More's dictum.

In truth she found more to think on in the upheavals in her stepmother's life than in the passing of her father. She saw clearly the joy Catherine's marriage gave her, and welcomed Seymour into the household with excited trepidation. Probably she said little, devoting her time to diligent study and intricate needlework. But she felt an unmistakable tension in Seymour's presence, and Kat Ashley and others noticed how she smiled and blushed when she heard his name.

Everyone, perhaps even Catherine herself, had heard the rumor that Seymour had sought permission to marry Elizabeth. But only Elizabeth and Kat Ashley knew the truth, as Kat said she had it from his own mouth: Seymour had sought her, not for her royal blood and prospects, but because he truly desired her. All else aside, Elizabeth believed, she, and not her starry-eyed stepmother, had been the choice of Thomas Seymour's impetuous heart.

PART TWO

God's Virgin

6

If anyone at fifteen hath taken up and found
A pretty thing that hath her maidenhead unbound:
If any gallant have with catertray
Played the wisacre, and made all away:
*   Let him come to the crier.*
There will be laid a thousand pound to ten
That none of these will e'er be had again.

T homas Seymour, lord high admiral of England, strode boldly into Elizabeth's life just as she reached adolescence. His turbulent masculinity and forceful manner sent shock waves through the quiet household, leaving none of the women, from Catherine Parr's ladies to the young gentlewomen who attended Elizabeth, untouched by his magnetism. "Women commend a modest man, but like him not," ran the proverb, and the lord high admiral embodied many women's secret preference for immodesty and swaggering ribaldry. He was a man of action, of aggressive physicality: a flawed hero, in fact, whose very overconfidence ensured his ruin.

Seymour once sent a messenger to Kat Ashley, ordering the man to present his compliments and then ask her "whether her great buttocks were grown any less or no?"[1] He joked and teased with a Rabelaisian license, even about such dangerous issues as the succession. "I tell you this but merrily, I tell you this but merrily," he assured Elizabeth's dismayed cofferer Thomas Parry after repeating a groundless rumor about his having secret plans to marry Jane Grey.[2] He had a highly volatile sense of the absurd, and displayed it even at the expense of discretion. Yet his jests put no one at ease, for his anger was as volatile as his hilarity and his favorite oath—"By God's precious soul!"—rang out often as he talked.

In an age that valued (and fostered) circumspection the lord high admiral was uninhibited and raw, his feelings ever close to the surface and his reactions close to the bone. He was, or appeared to be, fearless, and his fearlessness made him fearsome to others. He was also completely convinced of the reliability of his own judgment—a quality which, if it led him into foolhardy undertakings, at least lent him the strength to attempt them without tormenting doubts. "If he had once conceived opinion by his own persuasions," his servant Wightman wrote, "neither lawyer nor other could turn him."[3] That his opinions lacked subtlety and his persuasions force put him at a disadvantage in the treacherous, power-hungry court of Edward VI. But he had other tactics.

Some years earlier, when Seymour had been put forward as a husband for Norfolk's only daughter Mary (who, as Henry Fitzroy's widow, was the first in a long line of royal relicts and other female relations Seymour coveted), Henry VIII remarked that Norfolk meant to "couple her with one of such lust and youth as should be able to please her well at all points." His jovial reference to the admiral's potency echoed common gossip. The admiral was, by general repute, a man of hearty sexual appetites who looked on women in frank appraisal and was more of an opportunist than a gentleman. This is not to say that, by the standards of his time, he was either lecherous or cynical about women: merely that he saw in them desirable possessions to be ranked, obtained, and used to advantage. His own attractiveness, of course, gave him an immeasurable advantage, as did the unique state of the English succession in the late 1540s: apart from the young king himself, all the claimants to the throne were women.

But the admiral would hardly have measured his political cunning by his looks or magnetism. In his own view he possessed just the sort of daring —backed by years of tough soldiering and leading men at sea—that England's parlous condition called for. It was a shaky situation at best, with a child on the throne, a wrangling council to guide him and, brooding over all, the irascible figure of Edward Seymour, Lord Protector, whose grip on the reins of power was none too firm.

The boy-king was a charming miniature—a slender, doll-like child dressed in the plumed hat and velvet doublet of a king. He wrinkled his child's brow in a frown and stalked up and down the presence chamber in stiff-legged imitation of his father, but his father's regal profanities sounded pathetic in Edward's high-pitched voice, and the son was painfully lacking in the father's robust physique. Edward looked fragile, and inspired concern. Everyone worried over him, from the councilors who had contingency plans ready in the event of his death to the citizens of the capital who expected to see his delicate, jewel-studded figure from time to time and, when they missed it, were quick to infer the worst. At age twelve the king wrote in his journal that "because there was a rumor that I was dead, I passed through London."[4]

Intellectually precocious like his half-sisters, Edward became in time so facile a linguist that he was able to converse in fluent Latin even on scientific subjects. He made considerable progress in Greek as well, and in modern languages—though the imperial ambassador, when advised that the king's Latin was better than his French, remarked that "he seemed to me to understand one just as little as the other."[5] Certainly his linguistic accomplishments exceeded those of his councilors; Dudley, when forced to comment on Edward's revised statutes for the Order of the Garter, composed in impeccable Latin, admitted with some embarrassment that he could only "guess at" their merits.[6]

Yet Edward's education was intensely practical, and if he was allowed to indulge his gift for languages—he enjoyed taking notes on the sermons he heard, writing the English words in Greek characters—he was also trained to command. A solid foundation in geography was essential to a king who would in time lead armies and govern fleets, and young as he was, Edward could reel off all the bays and harbors of the French and Flemish coasts, together with the ports and coastal towns that overlooked them. He knew too the tidal patterns of the major rivers, and what size ships could negotiate them, carrying what number of men. Arms and armaments were given careful study—in the abstract, for the king was held too precious to risk his life in the tiltyard—along with military history and strategy. And he memorized the names of his leading subjects, the nobles and gentry whose contingents of fighting men were mustered in time of war to form the royal armies.

Every effort was made to surround Henry VIII's successor with the formality and decorum his father had demanded. There were the same elaborate spectacles, the tilts, masques and plays that had dazzled visitors to the court of King Henry. There was the same numerous royal household, from the French cook to the court painters, the corps of medical men— fifteen in all—and the dozens of musicians that provided dance music while the king dined and filled the privy chamber with soft ballads when he sought solitude. Exaggerated deference was paid to the king's person. Where Elizabeth had bowed three times to her father, she bowed five times before her brother, who barely acknowledged her obeisances and excluded her—as he did all his relatives—from sitting with him under the canopy of royalty. Yet despite all this, the little king was in truth a somewhat ridiculous figure in his brilliant plumage and glittering jewels. The reverence paid to him was artificial; his court held the illusion of rule, not its substance. For no one forgot that, wherever the king went, the Protector went with him, and in truth it was Edward Seymour's word that governed all.

The Protector and his haughty, prepossessing wife occupied the palace apartments normally reserved for the queen. This suited the duchess well (Edward Seymour had taken the title duke of Somerset when his brother Thomas became Baron Seymour of Sudeley), for she claimed a tincture of Plantagenet blood and thought it only natural that her rank should reflect her husband's supreme position in government. The Protector too found the accommodations appropriate, though while his wife was obsessed with status his own obsessions were with subduing the Scots and tightening his hold on the direction of affairs.

His overriding drive was to bring Scotland fully and finally under English control. Henry VIII had begun the task of subduing the autonomous Scots kingdom once and for all in the earlier 1540s, hoping to end Scotland's traditional strategic role as a "back door" for the invasion of England. For centuries the French had manipulated Scots politics to their advantage, making certain that they could at will use the country as a staging area for invasion or as a decoy when there was war between England and France on the continent. Henry had tried to end that danger, first by diplomacy and then, when his diplomatic arrangements broke down, by force.

The Protector had been Henry's vengeful emissary of war, burning Edinburgh and laying much of the surrounding countryside in ruins. Now was the time to make his final assault, for Scotland, like England, had a child for a sovereign and was weakened by faction. The young queen, Mary Stuart, had been betrothed to Edward VI but the Scots had repudiated the agreement; this, plus the everpresent danger represented by overriding French influence at the Scottish court and the monarchy's stubborn Catholicism, gave ample excuse for conquest. In the view of the Lord Protector nothing must be allowed to obstruct this purpose—not the threat of invasion from Charles V, whose power had never been greater and whose victory over the German Protestants at Mühlberg made him more of a danger than ever, not the ominous rumblings of rebellion in the countryside, above all not the rash whims of an irresponsible younger brother, hungry for power.

"My brother," Thomas Seymour remarked, "is wondrous hot in helping every man to his right, saving me." The Protector acquired an undeserved reputation for idealistic concern with the common people (he gave away all his lands around Hampton Court to farmers and smallholders), yet his humanitarianism was more apparent than real. In truth he was a ruthless autocrat, avid to dominate the council and determined to let nothing hinder his preeminence. "Angry and snappish" toward his fellow councilors, his sharp temper stung so deep it reduced even his thick-skinned colleagues to tears on occasion; he was a "dry, sour, opinionated man," unlovable and unloved.[7]

Elizabeth, sister to the king and second in line for the throne, lived in the eye of the political hurricane throughout 1547 and 1548. Outwardly her life changed little. There were the hours of study, the practice in handwriting and music and needlework, the infrequent visits to court. No doubt adolescence brought inward turbulence, but scant record of it remains. On one issue alone she tested her leverage with her stepmother and Seymour, and won.

In January of 1548 her tutor Grindal died of plague. The shock of his death, compounded by the horror of the plague itself, whose every visitation spread fear, unsettled the household for a time but in a few weeks the issue of Grindal's replacement arose. A relative, also named Grindal, was proposed; Catherine and Seymour favored another candidate. Elizabeth preferred Ascham, whom she knew to be congenial and whose uniqueness of mind she may well have perceived. On her own initiative she spoke to him, then to her stepmother and her husband. The confrontation was swiftly resolved—perhaps with the intervention of Cheke, who favored Ascham—and Roger Ascham left Cambridge for Chelsea.[8]

The contretemps over the choice of a tutor was symptomatic of the atmosphere of personal drama that was emerging at Chelsea. A love triangle was rapidly developing between Catherine, Elizabeth and Seymour, and the episode and its aftermath were to be the central turn of events of Elizabeth's girlhood.

It seemed harmless enough at first. As soon as he moved into his wife's house, Seymour began coming into Elizabeth's bedchamber very early in the morning, before she was fully dressed. As she gasped in surprise he would shout out a hearty good morning and ask her how she was, then "strike her upon the back or on the buttocks familiarly" while she struggled, red-faced, into her petticoats. He took to coming even earlier, before she was up. He would burst into the room, throw open the bedcurtains and jump at the girl (who was very likely naked, nightclothes being a rarity in the sixteenth century for anyone out of childhood), making her squeal in delicious fear and dive down under the bedclothes. Once he tried to kiss her while she was in that vulnerable state, and Kat Ashley (who slept with her), seeing that he was going too far, "bade him go away for shame."[9]

But she may well have been laughing when she said it, for Kat had a soft spot for Seymour and found him more amusing than dangerous. Before long Elizabeth regained the upper hand by getting up even earlier than usual, so that Seymour arrived to find her dressed, composed, and ready to wish him a dignified good morning. But twice, Kat remembered later, the admiral and his wife had come in together and, finding Elizabeth and Kat still in bed, had tickled Elizabeth until she shrieked with helpless laughter.

There was a strange incident in the garden after the household had moved from Chelsea to Hanworth. The three were together, and Seymour, whether in earnest or out of malicious playfulness, began shouting at Elizabeth and scolding her, and taking out a knife or dagger, slashed at the black gown she was wearing—she was in mourning for her father—until he had cut it to ribbons. Elizabeth tried to run from him but Catherine held her while he finished the job. Then, when the gown was "in a hundred pieces," she let her go, and Elizabeth ran to Kat and told her what had happened. Whether Elizabeth was frightened or merely annoyed by the incident Kat did not say; all she remembered was that her young mistress explained that she couldn't help what happened, "for the queen held her, while the lord admiral cut it."[10]

As the months went by Seymour became more provocative, and the game grew more elaborate. He took to coming to Elizabeth in his scanty dressing gown, "barelegged in his slippers," and pestering her while she was studying. When Kat complained to him that "it was an unseemly sight to come so barelegged to a maiden's chamber," he lashed out at her angrily, then went away without making more of it. But when one morning he besieged Elizabeth and all her waiting maids, who took refuge together behind the bedcurtains, and refused to leave until Elizabeth came out, there was such commotion that the servants shook their heads over the gross impropriety and complained vociferously to Mistress Ashley.

The scandal broke. The gentlewomen heard all from the waiting maids, and the gentlemen from the gentlewomen. Seymour's intentions were obvious; his reputation made them plain. And Elizabeth, it was said, was so infatuated with him that she was shameless before him, and was more pleased at his boldness than affronted. Anyone could see that she "bore affection" to him, that she blushed when his name was spoken and forgot all her lessons in modest behavior. If Seymour's indiscretions were allowed to continue the worst might happen. After all, Elizabeth was attractive and nubile, and she was, presumably, her mother's daughter. Perhaps the worst had already happened. The whispers became more suggestive.

Much as she disliked it, Kat decided to confront the admiral once and for all. She met him in the gallery at Chelsea, and told him plainly that the house was full of scandalous gossip, and that the servants of the saintly queen, accustomed to her piety and decorum, were offended by the indecencies in Elizabeth's bedroom. Elizabeth herself was being accused of unchastity; her reputation was suffering.

Seymour exploded. "God's precious soul!" he swore, he would not have such tales spread. He would complain to his brother the Protector how he was slandered, and things would go on exactly as they were, for he "meant no evil."

But instead of subsiding, the scandal grew, augmented now by the queen. Why Catherine could not intervene to restrain her loutish husband is a mystery. But even if she feared to provoke him she could have talked privately to Elizabeth, or, if all else failed, sent her to another house. Instead, possibly because she felt she had already lost out to Elizabeth in the battle over the admiral's favor, she preferred to cause further trouble for her stepdaughter.

She told Kat Ashley a suspicious story. Seymour, she said, "looked in at the gallery window, and saw my Lady Elizabeth cast her arms about a man's neck." Alarmed, Kat rushed to Elizabeth's chamber and accused her. She burst into tears and shook her head in denial, and when she could speak she swore she was innocent, and called all her women to witness on her behalf. They backed her up, and Kat, on reflection, decided to believe them. After all, no men came into Elizabeth's quarters besides Seymour but her schoolmasters, and they were certainly no seducers.

After thinking it over Kat saw through the queen's ruse. Catherine was jealous, much as she hated to admit it. She would not lower herself to ask Kat to spy on her husband, but she knew that if she cast doubt on Elizabeth's chastity Mistress Ashley might guard her more closely, and so prevent misconduct.[11]

As the web of intrigue tightened around Elizabeth her training in womanly modesty went forward. She had reached the age when such training had immediate relevance. As a child she had learned to mimic the walk, speech and courtesy of a virtuous woman; now the mimicry merged, albeit imperfectly, with authentic habit. At thirteen and fourteen sex loomed as an everpresent temptation, infatuation as a deluding pitfall, honorable marriage as a young woman's apotheosis.

Women who died virgins, ran the words of a sixteenth-century song, were doomed to "lead apes in hell." Yet to lose one's virginity before marriage was the most dreaded of tragedies. The Spanish humanist Vives, who had tutored Catherine Parr in her youth and whose treatises for young girls Elizabeth no doubt read, was expansive on the tormenting climate of suspicion a tarnished reputation produced. Once a girl loses her virginity, he wrote, everyone continually gossips about her, and men who might otherwise have offered to marry her—among them good, affectionate potential husbands—avoid her completely. She cannot hope to marry; worse still, she brings shame on her parents, who are inevitably blamed for her weak character. So deep is her humiliation that she becomes afraid to look anyone in the face, and even when she is alone the nightmare continues, for she is "ever vexed with the scourge of her own conscience." Imagined injuries compound actual ones. "If anybody speak softly," Vives warned, "she shall think they speak of her. If she hear talk about loose women, she shall think it meant for her." Of course, men who live unchaste lives suffer in the same way, "but women fare worse," Vives wrote solemnly, "because they be more timorous of nature and their offenses be reckoned fouler."[12]

Lest any young woman think herself immune from the temptations of the flesh let her never forget that sentiment, not lust, is most women's downfall. She allows fond liking for a man to gain possession of her thoughts. Yearning overcomes her; she forgets herself, she grows giddy in the presence of her beloved, and speaks immodestly to him, out of others' hearing. Then, without realizing it, she slips into sin. Love, Vives taught, "confounds and blinds her wit and reason, so that she shall not see or know what is done, but suffers herself to be wholly led and drawn at love's pleasure."

"This affliction of love strikes everyone," Vives went on, "but especially women. Therefore they need to take the more care that it should not steal upon them. For mostly it comes unawares, when the woman neither cares nor minds what is happening, and receives it as a sweet and pleasant thing, not knowing what and how perilous a poison lies hidden under that pleasant face."[13]

Unless a young woman is on her guard constantly against infatuation she will be lost. For most girls the penalties were grave: sickness, begging, the street. Why, Vives asked, do so many girls "willingly drown themselves in this great sea of wretchedness, from which come so many brothels and so many harlots, yea, and from honest families too?" But even the king's sister was not above such suffering, for her disgrace, should she lapse, would be all the greater because of her rank and responsibilities. A woman of Elizabeth's station above all should avoid even the most innocent encounters with men, knowing the risk she ran. Infatuation itself, as Vives saw it, was a form of unchastity; if a woman allowed herself to fall in love she had already tainted her purity. "A maid should not be proud because no man hath touched her body," he wrote, "if many men have pierced her mind."

Such precepts warred with Elizabeth's feelings for Thomas Seymour, whose boisterous roguery laid siege to her fragile defenses. Compounding the conflict were the admiral's ambivalent affections: though married to Catherine, and bound to love her, he preferred Elizabeth—or so Kat Ashley told her often enough—and would marry her if he could. That his heart was committed to her, even though his vows had been made to her stepmother may have given Seymour more the character of a suitor than of a potential seducer in Elizabeth's eyes. Catherine's evident jealousy reinforced this view, and in a way the rivalry and strain between the two women may have acted to legitimize Elizabeth's feelings for Seymour.

Yet his feeling for Catherine was not negligible, so the servants believed. A story circulating in the household led them to say that he was the most jealous of husbands. He had been coming up the stairs to see his wife one day, and as he approached the closed door leading to her apartments he saw one of her grooms come out with a coal basket on his arm. He made a great show of anger, roaring out his displeasure that the groom and Catherine had been behind the closed door together while he had been outside, and pretending to be beside himself with jealousy. But it was all bluster, said half in amusement, Kat told Parry later; no one who knew the admiral well took him literally.[14]

Early in 1548 a new complication arose. Catherine became pregnant. Her age (she was in her mid-thirties) gave some cause for concern, but the child might well strengthen the marriage and turn Seymour's affections back on course. When his son and heir was born Elizabeth would become less important, almost an intruder, in fact, in the Seymour family circle. Or so Catherine may have hoped.

Yet jealousy and doubt ate at her. As her pregnancy advanced Seymour seemed to be spending more time in Elizabeth's company, not less. Kat could not be relied on to chaperone them; mortifying though it was, Catherine made up her mind to be her own warder. "Suspecting the often access of the admiral to the Lady Elizabeth's Grace," Kat said to Parry afterward, Catherine "came suddenly upon them, where they were all alone."

What she saw undeceived and pained her, and after a moment made her violently angry. Seymour had Elizabeth in his arms.

7

It was a maid of Islington
and her wheell ran very rounde;
And many a wanton web she spun
and it cost her many a pound.
Alas! said she, what hap had I,
run round, run round, my whele!
I fere a mayden I shall die,
before my web I rele.

The sight of her husband embracing her stepdaughter so unnerved Catherine that she was beside herself. She shouted at Seymour, at Elizabeth, and at Kat Ashley too when she found her. The household was in turmoil, with the young redheaded girl at the center of it all. Before long Elizabeth and her servants left for Sir Anthony Denny's house of Cheshunt —possibly at Catherine's insistence, or possibly because Elizabeth took the initiative and "parted from the queen," her outward dignity served.[1]

In what emotional ferment Elizabeth left can only be imagined. She had disgraced and compromised herself, and she had probably fallen in love. Catherine, who had served as a mother to her, had been alienated utterly; there could never again be trust between them. As for Seymour, just as what passed between him and Elizabeth cannot be known for certain, so his reaction to their parting is undiscoverable. If he wrote in amorous terms to Elizabeth after she went to Cheshunt there is no surviving record of it. They may have communicated nonetheless. Kat admitted later having talked with Seymour on the way to Cheshunt, though she claimed she could not remember what was said.[2]

All this happened in the late spring of 1548. Through the summer, in the quieter atmosphere of Cheshunt, Elizabeth could turn her full attention to her studies. Until now there had been too many distractions. She had worked dutifully under Ascham's tutelage for several months, but her thoughts were elsewhere. Now, only too glad to throw herself into mental labors, she began to benefit fully from the guidance of her remarkable teacher.

A pen-and-ink sketch of Roger Ascham shows a beefy, hearty man with curling black hair and beard, full lips and cheeks, and intelligent eyes. He was a Yorkshireman from the tiny village of Kirby Wiske in the remote North Riding, and though his years at St. John's College made him an erudite classicist he retained the air of an ingenuous countryman all his life. Ascham was by nature an affable, mellow man, accepting of others and generous with his praise. Intellectually he was opinionated but unassertive, preferring comfortable moderation to driving accomplishment, and his works, though sane and rich with nuanced observations on human nature and his times, lacked originality.

He was truly at home with the ancients, referring to "my old masters Plato, Aristotle and Cicero," and liked nothing better than to reread their works with a quick-witted student at his side, taking his time and devoting patient hours to unraveling the secrets of their style and matter. His was not an aesthetic temperament. The subtleties of the poetic imagination were beyond him—"I had never poetical head," he confessed, and his extant poems confirm it—but so was the contentiousness of the intellectual combatant. Theological controversy in particular he deplored as a waste of mental energy. Of a contemporary who was continually enmeshed in debating points of belief he wrote that he was "sorry to see so worthy a wit, so rare eloquence, wholly spent and consumed, in striving with God and good men." If only the scholar would put his time into translating Demosthenes, his eloquence would become sublime.[3]

Ascham's own recent experience had brought a departure from this peaceable attitude, however. Early in Edward's reign the pulse of religious reform quickened, and at Cambridge a lively debate began over a crucial reform issue: the Roman mass versus the Protestant lord's supper. Ascham wrote an irreverent satire upholding the Protestant view, denouncing contrary doctrines as "filths of the Roman cesspool" and turning the language of the mass against itself. "Behold the mass of the pope," he wrote, "that taketh away the supper of the lord. Behold the foxes of the pope, that devoureth the lamb of God. Behold the heathen idol of the pope, that addeth to the sins of the world."[4] The agitation backfired, and Ascham was disciplined by the master of St. John's. A more contentious man might have been fired to stronger assaults, but Ascham was crushed. The chastisement, he wrote to the master, "caused me greater bitterness of mind than either you can conceive or I can describe."[5] Within weeks he had left the college to take up his position in Elizabeth's household. He made no further forays into the theological arena.

Compared to Cambridge, Ascham found in the society of Kat and John Ashley a haven of congeniality. With the latter—himself a scholar—he read Aristotle and Livy, while the three of them, perhaps joined by Elizabeth on occasion, spent hours "in free talk, mingled always with honest mirth." For all his straitlaced moral views Ascham was an easygoing companion. By his own admission he liked "a merry, pleasant, and playful nature," and found the "friendly fellowship" of the Ashleys much to his liking. Nor was the talk all lighthearted. The instability of the times—political and social unrest, the court and its intrigues, religious change—was often discussed, and Ascham later reminded John Ashley of "our trim conferences of that present world, and too true judgments of the troublesome time that followed."

But Ascham's chief delight was in his royal pupil. In the morning they read the New Testament together in Greek, then the orations of Isocrates and Demosthenes, and the plays of Sophocles. All these texts Ascham chose with care, as "best adapted to supply her tongue with the purest diction, her mind with the most excellent precepts, and her exalted station with a defence against the utmost power of fortune." Then came religious instruction—the Bible, the works of Saint Cyprian and of Luther's disciple Melanchthon (who on Anne Boleyn's death had declared himself convinced of her innocence). Finally they read together Ascham's beloved Cicero and "a great part of Livy," followed by Italian and French texts. As Elizabeth's capacities expanded she became more and more adept at the narrow art of double translation—turning Greek and Latin into felicitous English, then back again, in an effort to arrive once more at the original wording—highly exacting proof of stylistic mastery.

Elizabeth surprised him by the rigor of her mind, "exempt from female weakness," and especially by its "masculine power of application." "No apprehension can be quicker than hers," he wrote, "no memory more retentive." Her Italian and French were as fluent as her English, her Latin excellent and considered, her Greek moderately good. Her handwriting was truly outstanding. Ascham perfected her command of the Italian, or italic, script—the romanesque-based humanist style which was beginning to supersede the secretary, or gothic, style—and surviving examples of her writing show real artistry.

To Ascham eloquence was the touchstone of true learning, and he took much satisfaction from his pupil's literary discrimination. She was a good judge of tone, and could pick out cliches and poor expressions at a glance. She "greatly admired metaphors, when not too violent, and antitheses when just, and happily opposed," and so strong was her sense of quality that she knew unerringly which texts ought to be rejected with disgust and which welcomed and savored.[6]

There is no doubt that Ascham was proud of Elizabeth's learning, and respected her capabilities. Yet his praise ought to be set in context. In fact Elizabeth was only one among several highly intelligent students he encountered, and she took second place to Mildred Cooke, who Ascham said "understood and spoke Greek like English," and even to the wan and diligent Jane Grey with her cherished Plato. All the children of Henry VIII were strikingly intellectual, Mary in particular, and though Elizabeth followed in her sister's footsteps she did not overtake her. Elizabeth's mature writing style, moreover, was heavy-handed and pedantic, full of labored, overelaborate metaphors and weighed down with long words. She had little affinity for music (though she "composed measures" for dancing and played them on the virginals) and probably lacked the finely tuned ear that often makes a gifted musician a graceful writer and clever linguist as well.

Above all Ascham, however sincere and well intentioned toward his royal pupil, was inclined to exaggerate his praise, not only because Elizabeth was the king's sister but because he found her achievements doubly remarkable considering her sex. He thought of her as he did of all learned women, as a sort of freak of nature whose accomplishments were different in kind from those of learned young men. It was partly for that reason that he found his other pupil John Whitney so rewarding to teach. Whitney studied along with Elizabeth, and was phenomenally eager and apt. The shortage of sleeping accommodations made the boy and his tutor bedfellows, and they developed so close a bond that when Whitney suddenly died in August, Ascham grew despairing for a time and speculated about returning to Cambridge before long.

If the first few months of Elizabeth's study with Ascham had been hampered by the distressing domestic triangle the summer at Cheshunt was interrupted by illness. Elizabeth began to suffer from "rheums"—head colds—and other pains in the head which sometimes confined her to bed and generally reduced her capacity for concentrated study. It could be that study itself had brought them on, for she was nearsighted and may have suffered eyestrain. Or, more likely, the recent emotional upheaval had begun to take its toll.

She had not been able to put Catherine or Seymour out of her mind. Catherine's sharp rebuke was still fresh to her, along with her promise to warn Elizabeth "of all evils she should hear of her." This may well have been a threat, but Elizabeth, in a letter to Catherine, decided to look on it as a gesture of conciliation, and thanked her for it. Nonetheless, she admitted, "all men" judged them to be bitter enemies, and the most she could do under the circumstances was to say she had been sorry to leave, especially as Catherine was "undoubtful of health," and to assure her stepmother that though she had made small answer to her warning she had not taken it lightly.[7] The time of Catherine's delivery was approaching, and in another letter—its tone belying any strain between the two women—Elizabeth commiserated with Catherine, who was sickly and whose pregnancy had been a difficult one. "If I were at his birth," she said of the child, "no doubt I would see him beaten, for the trouble he hath put you to."[8]

The queen's "good hour" came, and the child proved to be a girl. Catherine languished, and as she grew weaker her mind was disturbed and she became deluded and lucid by turns. Elizabeth Tyrwhitt, Catherine's stepdaughter by her first marriage and among the most intimate of her ladies in waiting, described her final anguished hours. Shortly before her death, she wrote, Catherine told her "she did fear such things in herself, that she was sure she could not live." The bedchamber was full of attendants as she spoke, and Seymour sat beside Catherine holding her hand. Despite the evident finality of the scene Lady Tyrwhitt tried to give a hopeful reply, and said "she saw no likelihood of death in her." Then Catherine became distracted, and burst out, "I am not well handled, for those that be about me careth not for me, but stand laughing at my grief. And the more good I will to them, the less good they will to me."

"Why, sweetheart," Seymour said at once, "I would you no hurt."

"No, my lord, I think so," she replied, her tone biting even though her voice was weak. And in a whisper she added, "My lord, you have given me many shrewd taunts."

Catherine's mind was "far unquieted," Lady Tyrwhitt noted, yet this accusation was made "with good memory, and very sharply and earnestly." Then followed an hour of caustic recrimination, with Catherine accusing her husband—who was lying on the bed beside her, trying to "pacify her unquietness with gentle communication"—and blaming him for her extremity. It was his fault, she said, that she had not been able to speak at length with her physician right after her delivery—a thing that might have saved her life. Seymour tried to deny this soothingly, but before he had spoken three or four words she "answered him very roundly and smartly, saying my lord, I would have given a thousand marks to have had my full talk with [Dr.] Huick, the first day I was delivered, but I durst not, for displeasing of you."

She went on and on in the same vein, the embarrassed attendants wishing the stream of abuse would end even as they pitied poor Catherine. Lady Tyrwhitt found the grotesque scene too painful to bear. "I perceived her trouble to be so great," she wrote, "that my heart would serve me to her no more."9

Catherine's ravings ceased between three and four in the morning on September 5, 1548, two days before her stepdaughter Elizabeth's fifteenth birthday. Jane Grey, who had been living for some time in Seymour's household, performed the office of chief mourner, watching hour after hour beside the candlelit bier and making the traditional offerings of money to the alms box at the funeral. The obsequies were uncompromisingly Protestant, with psalms and the Te Deum sung in English and an admonitory sermon by the reformer Coverdale advising the worshipers not to interpret the ceremonies in the old superstitious way but as acts of commemoration honoring Catherine's life. Catherine herself had been known to hold strong views against mourning the dead. To grieve, she once wrote, was to protest God's ordinances, since the death of a loved one was part of a divine plan. "Such as have doubted of the everlasting life to come, doth sorrow and bewail the departure hence; but those which be persuaded that to die here is life again, do rather hunger for death and count it a felicity than to bewail it as an utter destruction."10

That she evidently had not welcomed her own imminent death as a gateway to eternal life only fueled the gossip that Catherine had been poisoned. The circumstances were highly suspicious. Seymour had become enamored of Elizabeth—many said that he had seduced her—and within months his unwanted wife died, cursing him for his cruelties. He was clearly preparing to marry Elizabeth; otherwise why had he kept on the queen's dozens of women—not only her personal servants but the ceremonial household of gentlewomen of the privy chamber and waiting maids—as if in anticipation of a new royal mistress? Both Lady Tyrwhitt and her husband warned Kat Ashley of the admiral's apparent designs, cautioning her to remember that no lawful marriage could be made without the council's prior assent. There was a more practical issue as well. If Kat valued Elizabeth's peace of mind, could she really see her brought to Sudeley Castle to be served by Catherine's partisans—women who, having been witness to all the turbulent events of the past year and a half, whispered that their mistress had been "hastened to her death" on Elizabeth's account and believed that Elizabeth had allowed Seymour to seduce her?

According to the widower himself, the loss of his wife had at first left him "so amazed, that he had small regard either to himself or to his doings," and it was several weeks before he could begin to sit down and work out just where he stood. He had seen to it that Catherine left him all her substantial wealth in a deathbed will, and he had plans to acquire more. He realized he could afford to keep the late queen's servants—not only the women but the hundred-odd gentlemen and yeomen who had attended her—and that in Catherine's absence his mother would look after Jane Grey with as much solicitude "as if she were her own daughter." Catherine's death, in fact, gave him a chance to show how extensive his own influence was. Now that he was no longer in her shadow his true stature would be revealed. When the earl of Rutland remarked to him that since his wife's death "his power was much diminished," Seymour scoffed. "Judge, judge," he cautioned the earl, "the council never feared me as much as they do now!"[11]

Beneath his bluster Seymour was anxious, and his anxiety lent added urgency to the bold gamble he now undertook. Not that his intended coup was unpremeditated: on the contrary, he had been building toward it for many months. But the timing caught him by surprise (always assuming he did not in fact "hasten" Catherine's death). If he was to gather his forces, marry Elizabeth, and win over the king and council then he had to act quickly, before Elizabeth was married to someone else and while he still enjoyed the protection of King Edward's favor. Above all, he had to act before his brother or Dudley realized the full extent of his ambition and challenged him with a show of force. That might come in time, but with haste enough he would be ready for it.

Soon after Catherine's funeral Seymour rode off to the West Country to rouse his sworn followers and bind others to his cause. His methods were proven and effective. He had shared them with Rutland, when he thought the earl was among his allies. "Make much of the gentlemen," he had advised, "but more of such honest and wealthy yeomen as are ringleaders in good towns." Gentlemen may waver, but yeomen never. "Making much of them, and sometimes dining like a good fellow in one of their houses," Seymour had said, would "allure all their good will," and bind them fast.[12]

To the admiral the terrain of England was a vast campaigning ground, and he liked nothing better than to lay out a map he carried with him and sweep his hand across it, saying "All that be in these parts be my friends," "this is my Lord Protector's, that my lord of Warwick's [Dudley's]." As he reckoned it, with his own ten thousand tenants and servants, and the supporters he could count on elsewhere, he had "as great number of gentlemen that loved him, as any nobleman in England"—certainly many more than his brother and Dudley.[13] And where friendship failed, pounds and pence could buy loyalty. Seymour had an invaluable accomplice in Sir William Sharington, gentleman of the king's chamber and master of the mint at Bristol, who supplied him with the money he needed to finance his takeover. "God's faith, Sharington," the mint master recalled the admiral saying, "if we had ten thousand pounds in ready money, that were well.

Could not you be able to make so much money?" Sharington assured him he could, and the bargain was made. A few months later, when Seymour's house was searched, a great store of money was found hidden there.

In unstable times Seymour's bluff bonhomie and old-fashioned truculence were a welcomed contrast to the indecisive leadership of the Protector. The latter was believed to be an altruist, yet he dared not go among the people for fear his irascible temper would betray him. His much admired military prowess, which had made him popular in the past, had been stalemated in Scotland, where the heavy cost of occupying his conquest meant that the victory at Pinkie Cleugh could not bring the Scots permanently within English control. The admiral, on the other hand, held not only the fleet—and swore "he was as glad to be admiral as of any office in the realm, and that no one would take that office from him without taking his life too"—but stalwart men across England, and swore he had the arms and even the ordnance to equip them. (Two cannon foundries, it was said, were producing at full speed to meet his requirements.)

Realistic and sober men were inclined to dismiss Seymour as a reckless fool, who would no doubt be stopped before his plan had gone very far. Yet so precarious was England's security that a few hundred soldiers, let alone the admiral's vaunted thousands, could indeed threaten the king and the council, especially if they had mobile ordnance (which even King Henry had lacked at times) and took the initiative. What was more, Seymour seems to have had the avid interest, and potential backing, of the French.[14]

The centerpiece of the admiral's bid for power was Elizabeth, and as he went about rallying his supporters he never lost sight of his objective of marrying her. Throughout the fall he flirted with the idea, bringing it up as if rhetorically with Lord and Lady Tyrwhitt on one occasion, hinting to Catherine's brother William Parr, earl of Northampton, on another that he might even broach the subject informally to the Protector, to see what his attitude would be.[15]

Legally, Seymour could do nothing without the written and sealed consent of a majority of the council members. Under the terms of King Henry's will, if either of his daughters married without that consent she automatically forfeited all right to the succession.[16] This in itself ought to have made Elizabeth exceedingly cautious; she had a great deal to lose. Yet the admiral was not just any adventurer scheming to win her hand. He was the king's favorite uncle, and was urging his eleven-year-old nephew to assert his independence in just such matters as approving his favorite uncle's marriage to his sister. And Seymour was the Protector's brother, and had exploited this advantage of blood once before in just such a situation, marrying where he had been warned not to and getting away with it. Of course, the risk of marrying Elizabeth, who was second in line to the throne, was greater than the risk of marrying Henry VIII's widow. But Seymour was stronger now in authority and followers, and had the girl's chief keepers, if not the girl herself, firmly on his side.

Kat Ashley, Elizabeth's easygoing, uncircumspect mistress had wanted the two to marry for so long it had become almost an obsession. Nothing that happened while Seymour was married to Catherine had changed her opinion, and indeed if she heard Seymour's name slandered she rose hotly to his defense.[17] She more than anyone knew what "familiarities" had been between them, and believed firmly that, contrary to the general view, if Seymour married Elizabeth he would not treat her shabbily but would "make but too much of her."[18] (In a candid conversation with Thomas Parry, so Parry deposed later, Kat had told him about Catherine's discovery of Elizabeth in Seymour's arms, and made a tantalizing reference to further indiscretions. "She sighed, and said, as I remember," Parry deposed, " 'I will tell you more another time,' " becoming anxious afterward and swearing Parry to absolute secrecy lest Elizabeth "be dishonored forever, and she likewise undone." Clearly there was more to hide.)

Sometime during the fall of 1548 Kat was brought before the Protector and his imperious wife, and criticized for being too lax in watching over the king's sister. She had let Elizabeth "go one night on the Thames in a barge," and had allowed other ill-advised freedoms. The duchess had threatened to replace Mistress Ashley with someone more responsible, "fearing that she bore too much affection for my lord admiral."[19] Yet for the time being nothing was done, and as Seymour's plans ripened Kat became more eager for her cherished Elizabeth to marry the dashing admiral.

"What news is at London?" Elizabeth recalled asking Kat.

"The voice goes there," was the reply, "that the lord admiral shall marry you."

Elizabeth smiled. "It is but a London news," she said, and dropped the subject. But Kat would not let it rest. "You shall see shortly," she said sometime later, "that he that would fain have had you before he married the queen will come now to woo you."[20]

Weeks went by, then months, and by Christmas the admiral's doings were rumored all over London. He had come to the capital, and was staying at Seymour Place where his proceedings were virtually public knowledge. Elizabeth's cofferer Thomas Parry—who was judged to keep "very uncertain" books and to have "little understanding to execute his office"—went to him there frequently, and stayed an hour or more each time. It was not difficult to guess what they were discussing. Elizabeth knew for certain, for Parry came to her and described how Seymour had asked him in detail about the costs of her household, the extent of her lands and the state of the patents she held—all the questions a very practical suitor would pose. The admiral had proposed an exchange of properties, Parry said, and "went about to have her" along with them. Then Parry asked her the question Seymour had no doubt told him to ask: "whether if the council would like it, she would marry with him?"

"When that comes to pass," the cofferer recalled her saying, "I will do as God shall put my mind."

Undaunted by this equivocation, Parry persisted. Seymour, he told Elizabeth, needed his future wife's help in obtaining the council's permission. The best way would be to win over the Protector's wife, and he was counting on Elizabeth to accomplish this. She was to go to the duchess, charm her, and eventually persuade her to use her considerable influence to promote the marriage.

It was pure fantasy; worse still, the admiral had misjudged Elizabeth's reaction to his demand for help.

"I dare say he did not so, nor would so!" she said sharply.

"Yes, by my faith," Parry insisted, bewildered.

"Well, I will not do so, and so tell him. I will not come there, nor begin to flatter now!"

The duchess's hauteur rankled with Elizabeth, as did her recent threats against Mistress Ashley. Elizabeth was angry that Seymour should think her capable of such hypocrisy. She may even have exaggerated her reaction for reasons of her own.

Young as she was, flattered and infatuated as she was, Elizabeth may well have begun to sense that Seymour's venture would prove to be stillborn. He was underplaying his hand. His ultimate aims, as far as she could tell, had not changed, but his tactics had stalled. He held back from making his dramatic bid for power, from massing his men and marching them to London. He had made no political headway either—or else why rely on Elizabeth's feeble leverage to gain the council's support for their marriage? Instead of acting, he was procrastinating, shut away in his London house, waiting, it seemed, for events to favor his hopes.

Whether from fear or shrewdness, Elizabeth refused to see him or communicate with him. She may have given him secret encouragement, but if so it has remained secret. Questioned about the widespread rumor of an impending marriage, Kat Ashley—struggling hard to lie convincingly, no doubt—denied it absolutely, saying "it was never meant nor thought."[21]

83

Parry and Seymour continued to meet, but in a changed atmosphere. Seymour was sarcastic and bitter, and seemed for the first time to mistrust the cofferer. He felt totally thwarted by the Protector, and told Parry in some heat that the marriage "would not be," as "his brother would never consent to it." Then, as if forgetting that Parry was there, he began muttering angrily under his breath, stammering out the words so that the cofferer could barely make them out. "I am kept back," or "I am kept under," was as much as he could hear. After a perfunctory request to meet again the next time Elizabeth came to London, Seymour let Parry go. It was their last meeting.

Shortly afterward Seymour risked all in a foolhardy act of bravado. Having sent away the yeomen of the watch on various errands, he broke into the king's private apartments, but before he could get at the boy he alerted the entire palace to the danger by taking out his pistol and shooting the barking dog that kept watch outside the bedchamber door. The chamber gentlemen rushed to protect their master, and the rest of the servants came running. They eventually found Seymour hiding in the palace with a party of his followers. Summoned to appear before the council, he refused, demanding a guarantee of safe conduct and a hostage besides; instead of these accommodations he was given safe conduct to the Tower, and left there.

The escapade was interpreted in the most menacing light: obviously, it was said, Seymour had meant to kill the king, the Protector and eventually Mary as well, then marry Elizabeth and rule as king himself. Paget referred to him as a "great rascal" or bandit who had "more greed than wit or judgement," but made it plain that the admiral could not hope for mercy merely because he lacked the brains of an archcriminal.[22] His accomplices were sought out, his associates questioned, and a long list of treasonable charges was amassed against him. Seymour and everyone linked with him came under grave and fateful suspicion.

Within days of his apprehension a party of men came riding to Hatfield, clearly bent on weighty business. The cofferer, hearing of their arrival, rushed like a hunted man to his living quarters, his hands trembling and his face white with fear. A servant remembered later that he looked "very pale and sorrowful," and began wringing his hands, saying to his wife "I would I had never been born, or I am undone." Parry had no doubt that the men had been sent for him, and he was frightened for his life. He managed to grab the chain of office from around his neck and to yank the jeweled rings from his fingers before he was taken; his wife fled to London, probably taking these and other valuables with her.

Before they could save themselves, before they could appeal to their mistress or speak a word to one another, Parry, Kat Ashley and another servant were spirited away by the grim-faced guardsmen, who sped off in great haste along the high road to London.

8

No croked legge
No blered eye
No part deformed out of kinde
Nor yet so ouglye
Half can be
As is the inward suspicious minde.

The inquiry—it was not yet an interrogation—began at once. Elizabeth was asked about her dealings with Seymour even as Kat Ashley and Parry were being taken into custody, and she answered briefly, too startled to do more than deny any contact between them. Later, after the men and their prisoners had gone, she became apprehensive, and the next day her worried surmises were confirmed.

Robert Tyrwhitt, the shrewd and cynical investigator sent by the council to Hatfield to extract the truth from Elizabeth, opened his campaign with a ruse. He saw to it that a letter, ostensibly sent to one of Elizabeth's women by a friend but in fact composed by Tyrwhitt himself, came into Elizabeth's hands. In it she read her servants' fate: both Kat and the cofferer had been committed to the Tower.

Lady Browne, a familiar figure in the household who had Elizabeth's confidence, watched her read the fearsome news and reported her reaction to Tyrwhitt. She was "marvellous abashed," and burst at once into tears. After weeping "very tenderly a long time," she recovered herself enough to ask Lady Browne the crucial question: Had Ashley or Parry confessed anything?

Most likely Lady Browne claimed not to know, and Elizabeth, her mind alive with conjecture despite her distress, tried to decide what innocuous incidents her servants would most likely have revealed. She sent for Tyr-whitt so that, on a pretense of full disclosure, she could confirm what she believed Ashley and Parry had said.

When he came to her she volunteered two inconsequential bits of information. First, that she had once added a postscript to a letter written to Seymour asking him to "credit" Parry in all things. But this referred not to any secret design between them, she said, merely to a minor matter of her housing in London. And second, Mistress Ashley had once written to the admiral warning him not to come to Hatfield "for fear of suspicion." But Elizabeth had been displeased with her for even acknowledging that such "suspicion" existed in the minds of others, and in fact the reference implied no guilt.[1]

To Tyrwhitt Elizabeth's tactics were obvious, and he cut straight through to the chilling reality of her situation by reminding her "to con-sider her honor and the peril that might ensue, for she was but a subject." Then, taking his cue from her reference to Kat Ashley, he spoke at length about what an irresponsible and sinful woman Mistress Ashley was, not only indiscreet and foolish but morally unfit, adding that Parry was no better. If only Elizabeth would confess everything, he said, he was sure that, "her youth considered," all the "evil and shame" would be ascribed to them.

But Tyrwhitt had seriously misjudged Elizabeth if he thought she would grasp like a child at the opportunity to blame others, especially her beloved mistress. "I do see it in her face that she is guilty," he reported to the Protector, yet she persisted in denying that Ashley and Parry had had any secret understanding with Seymour. Furthermore he sensed that it would take much more than irate speeches and threats to break her. "She will abide more storms," he wrote, "ere she accuse Mistress Ashley."

But he went on storming at her for hours, "deliberating" many matters, eventually abandoning the direct assault and trying a variety of other tones, searching for her soft spot. He found it. "Gentle persuasion" worked where angry confrontation had failed, and Tyrwhitt believed that through gentle-ness he was "beginning to grow with her in credit." In fact she made a substantial confession, telling Tyrwhitt about her long conversation with Parry in which he asked her whether she would marry Seymour if the council gave consent. "This is a good beginning," Tyrwhitt recorded. "I trust more will follow."[2]

For three days the questioning went on, but by the fourth Tyrwhitt was losing his sense of mastery. It wasn't that Elizabeth was uncooperative; on the contrary, she had become almost friendly—"more pleasant than she has been at any time since my being here," he wrote—since he showed her a letter from the Protector. (The letter was another ruse; though it was

87

written for her to see Tyrwhitt showed it to her "with a great protestation that he would not for £1,000 to be known of it." She considered it "a great kindness," so he thought.)

Yet it was becoming clear that Elizabeth would disclose only as much as she chose to, and no more. "I do assure your grace," Tyrwhitt wrote to Edward Seymour, "she hath a very good wit, and nothing is gotten of her, but by great policy." Try as he would he could not penetrate her reserve beyond a certain point. Uncertain what else to do, he wrote to the Protector asking for help and advice, and asking, too, for Lady Browne, who had left Hatfield soon after his arrival. "There is no body may do more good to cause her [Elizabeth] to confess the truth than she," he said of Lady Browne, praising both her "wise counsel" and her dedication to persuading Elizabeth to hold nothing back. It was not the first time that Lady Browne's influence with Elizabeth had been sought and prized. Seymour too had tried to use her to speak favorably of him in Elizabeth's presence, finding her, in the words of one of his servants, "wise and able to compass matters."[3]

In fact Elizabeth seems to have been gathering strength as, day after day, she stood up to the onslaught of questioning. In addition she found, to her relief, that Kat had not been condemned to lie on filth in a stinking, lightless Tower cell but was being held in less harsh confinement. There might be hope for her release, if only she, Elizabeth, could remain resolute and argue convincingly that though Parry had mentioned marriage with the admiral, Kat had "never advised her to it," and had never even touched on the subject except to caution Elizabeth in the most responsible fashion that she could never marry anyone without the council's consent.

After a week of constant demands and queries Elizabeth was rising resilient to the challenge. Steadfast denials had given way to righteous indignation, which flared when she learned—Tyrwhitt told her, to goad her —that farfetched rumors were circulating among the people, deepening the stains on her reputation. She wrote to the Protector, thanking him for his "great gentleness and good will" and, after repeating what she had already told Tyrwhitt, came to her main purpose for writing.

"Master Tyrwhitt and others have told me that there goeth rumors abroad, which be greatly both against my honor, and honesty (which above all other things I esteem)," she wrote, "which be these: that I am in the Tower, and with child by my lord admiral."

In truth the rumors went further. A midwife, it was said, had been brought from her house blindfolded to attend a mysterious birth. She came into a candlelit room, and saw on a bed "a very fair young lady" in labor.

In the darkness she could not tell whether she was in a palace or a hovel, or whether the beauteous young lady was Elizabeth or not, but it was said that the child she delivered was "miserably destroyed" afterward, and because of the mutterings about the admiral and the king's sister, she drew her own conclusions.[4]

Nor were the mutterings confined to taverns and parlors. Hugh Latimer, former bishop of Worcester and the most outspoken popular preacher of the day, thundered so forcefully from the pulpit against the sinful doings of Thomas Seymour and Elizabeth that his condemnation lent credence to more fanciful rumors, and made some formal response from the Protector or council all but imperative.[5] Elizabeth was in no doubt about what form her response should take.

"My Lord," she went on in her letter, "these are shameful slanders, for the which, besides the great desire I have to see the king's majesty, I shall most heartily desire your lordship that I may come to the court after your first determination, that I may show myself there as I am."[6]

Before the Protector could reply to this bold request, however, the interrogators at the Tower stretched Parry's endurance to the breaking point, and it snapped. Silent until now, he finally broke down and confessed to his meetings with Seymour, their conversations about Elizabeth's properties, his asking Elizabeth about her willingness to marry the admiral. He admitted too what he knew about the familiarities between the two while Catherine Parr was alive, telling much that Kat Ashley had made him swear on his honor—"I had rather be pulled with horses, than I would," he had promised—never to reveal.

Kat was confronted with the cofferer's written testimony, but refused to either confirm or deny it until she and Parry were brought face to face. Then, seeing that he asserted it in her very presence, she exploded in fury. "False wretch!" she cried. He had promised "never to confess it to death!" Though she must have balked at the thought of repeating the cofferer's treachery, the confrontation had broken her will to resist further, and she too wrote a detailed confession.

Both documents were rushed by swift messenger to Hatfield, where Tyrwhitt gave them to Elizabeth to read.

Kat's confession at first unnerved her completely. She was "much abashed," Tyrwhitt noted with satisfaction, "and half breathless, before she could read it to an end." Could it be forged? She looked at Kat's signature, and Parry's. Both were genuine; she knew them "with half a sight." Her heart pounding, she completed her reading, realizing as she did so that, embarrassing and dishonoring though the revelations were, they did not make her a traitor. Neither Kat nor the cofferer had incriminated her, nor had they accused one another of anything more grave than bad judgment and thoughtlessness.

Tyrwhitt was telling her how Kat had resisted until the last moment, how she had called Parry a "false wretch" and claimed he had betrayed her. No doubt he expected an outburst from Elizabeth as well. Instead, having mastered herself, she answered coolly. "It was a great matter," she said, weighing her words as if reciting before her tutor, "for him to promise such a promise, and to break it."[7]

In the end Tyrwhitt and those who were interrogating Ashley and Parry decided, or were ordered, to be satisfied with what revelations they had forced into the light. Elizabeth wrote a confession that dovetailed neatly with those of her servants, convincing Tyrwhitt that all along there had been "some secret promise" among the three "never to confess to death." "They all sing one song," he wrote irritably, "and so I think they would not do, unless they had set the note before."[8]

Maybe they had agreed among themselves on exactly what to say and what to conceal; maybe there had been a well-developed conspiracy or plans for one, with Elizabeth agreeing to gamble her future on Seymour's hoard of money and soldierly appeal. At the very least the two servants cannot have been overly scrupulous in reiterating the need for the council's approval in any suggestion of marriage, and were probably guilty of enticing Seymour to marry Elizabeth in order to enrich and advance themselves. How much Elizabeth was an actor in all that had gone on, and how much a prudent spectator, cannot be known, but her key role in safeguarding herself and Kat Ashley—and Parry too though to a lesser extent—ought not to be underestimated. At fifteen years of age Elizabeth had held out for weeks against the relentless, probing examination of a highly skilled interrogator, with no one to advise or support her, knowing that the fate of the woman she loved best in the world might turn on the answers she gave.

And what of Seymour? Did she worry over him as well or did she assume, wrongly, that either his brother or the king would spare him? If so she found she was mistaken about the middle of February, when she heard that his properties were being dispersed. The news made her noticeably disconsolate, and now for the first time since the crisis began she allowed herself to show some feeling for the admiral. When he was criticized in her hearing she was "ready to make answer therein," and came quickly to his defense.

But her loyalty could not aid him now. Toward the end of February a bill of attainder was brought against him, among its accusations the charge that he had sought the king's sister in marriage contrary to law. He waited in his Tower cell, expecting a delegation from the council to appear to hear his defense. But none came; instead there was only his jailer, who listened patiently and somewhat sympathetically to Seymour's grandiloquent affirmations of innocence. "There was never poor knave truer to his prince than I am," he swore, "and to all his succession, both my lady Mary and my lady Elizabeth." All that was said against him was falsehood and fabrication, and none of it could be proved. "If there be any man in all England to accuse me," he insisted righteously, "that I should be a false knave to the king or his succession, or to the realm, I will wish no life. For if I had, I thought the stones will rise against me."[9]

Meanwhile Elizabeth's punishment had been meted out—minor punishment, in view of the danger she had stood in until recently, but exceedingly irksome to her even so. A letter arrived from the council, announcing that because Mistress Ashley had "shown herself far unmeet" to supervise the "good education and government" of a king's sister, a new mistress had been appointed: Lady Tyrwhitt.

Elizabeth rebelled. "She had not so demeaned herself, that the council should now need to put any more mistresses unto her," she said. Kat Ashley was her mistress; no other was necessary.

Having accepted Mistress Ashley, Lady Tyrwhitt responded, Elizabeth "need not be ashamed to have any honest woman" to be in charge of her.

But Elizabeth would hear none of it. She grew morose, then hopeless. She wept all that night and was sullen and moody the next day. Two things weighed on her, Tyrwhitt judged. First, she clearly hoped that, when the crisis was fully past, she could have Kat back as before. ("The love yet she beareth her is to be wondered at," he wrote in an aside.) And second, she was distressed for what was left of her good name, telling Tyrwhitt that "the world would note her to be a great offender, having so hastily a governor appointed her." (And Tyrwhitt added that in his opinion she needed two governors rather than one.)[10]

And there was another cause of anxiety. Lady Tyrwhitt, Catherine Parr's stepdaughter and confidante, had watched the late queen's happiness slip away as her husband became preoccupied with Elizabeth. She had seen Catherine through her endless, painful pregnancy, then through her final agonizing hours when, near delirium, she had made Seymour's cruelties public. She was not likely to prove a sympathetic or well-disposed mistress for Elizabeth, and the prospect of spending her days under Lady Tyrwhitt's contemptuous eye must have been exceedingly unpleasant.

Soon after Lady Tyrwhitt's appointment Elizabeth wrote to the Protector again, explaining succinctly why she found the prospect humiliating ("because that I thought the people will say that I deserved, through my lewd demeanor, to have such a one") and replying, in remarkably argumentative language, to the Protector's charge that she put too much faith in her own judgment.

"And as concerning that point that you write, that I seem to stand in mine own wit, it being so well assured of mine own self, I did assure me of myself no more than I trust the truth shall try," she insisted. It was not that she wanted to "rule herself," merely that she was following the Protector's own expressed desire that she "be plain with him in all things."

Her letter was full of counterargument and reasoned, orderly self-justification. And bold requests—for a proclamation to be issued to "refrain the tongues" of the talebearers who were spreading lies about her, and for the council to "be good" to Kat Ashley, for Elizabeth's sake.[11] In time both requests were granted. A proclamation went out denouncing the rumors concerning Elizabeth as slanderous and the rumormongers as culpable, and finally, in a gesture of vindication, both Ashley and Parry were released and returned to her service.

With the eclipse of Seymour's electrifying yet baleful influence the episode was finally closed. On March 19, 1549, he went to his execution, unreconciled to death and disconcerted that his final scheme—treasonous letters to Elizabeth and Mary written from prison—had been discovered and foiled. He died "very dangerously, irksomely, horribly," Latimer told his congregation. "Whether he be saved or no, I leave it to God, but surely he was a wicked man, and the realm is well rid of him."

Nine months later, in mid-December, Elizabeth was received at her brother's court "with great pomp and triumph." Her arrival was widely heralded, and crowds gathered to watch her as she passed into the court precincts, a regal yet ladylike figure, proud without being aloof, whose understated dress made her translucent white skin and flowing red hair doubly striking.

Her appearance, and the evident regard in which she was held by the king and his courtiers, did much to confound the recent murmurings against her. Was this unadorned, maidenly young lady with the sweet face and pure, milk-white hands the one accused of being Thomas Seymour's wanton mistress and the mother of his child? She was too chaste, too obviously virginal for that, and though she looked out over the crowd with the attractive, level-eyed gaze of a princess she had the air of the gospel about her as well.

In fact Elizabeth was cultivating an image of innocent, sober piety both to counteract the recent slanders against her and to align herself unmistakably with the new, zealously Protestant tone of Edward VI's court. She was cultivating a reputation for devout simplicity, for shunning adornment in order to rise above the transitory vanities that ensnared young women. At a court where women curled and double-curled their hair, or plaited it in elaborate coils, Elizabeth wore hers long, thick and free, as her mother had years earlier. In place of the fretted golden cauls and bejeweled "biliments" that framed the face she wore only the plainest of headdresses, or none at all. Her simply cut gowns, often of black velvet, put the rainbow silks of the other ladies to shame, while her natural coloring seemed more attractive than the over-ruddy painted lips and leaden-white complexions produced by cosmetics.

It was said that Elizabeth's aversion to extravagance in dress had made her scorn her inheritance. "The king her father," wrote the churchman John Aylmer, Jane Grey's tutor, "left her rich clothes and jewels, and I know it to be true that in seven years after his death she never, in all that time, looked upon that rich attire and precious jewels but once, and that against her will; and that there never came gold or stone upon her head."[12] This austerity had an influence on the more godly of the young women at court, though others continued to be "dressed and painted like peacocks." Jane Grey, Aylmer wrote, belonged to the former group, rejecting color and glitter for the simplicity of "my lady Elizabeth, which followeth God's word."

For as long as she stayed at court Elizabeth continued to be feted and honored, and was said to be continually with the king. "It seems," the imperial ambassador wrote, "that they have a higher opinion of her for conforming with the others and observing the new [religious] decrees, than of the lady Mary, who remains constant in the Catholic faith, and stays at her house twenty-eight miles from here without being either summoned or visited by the council."[13] In fact, Mary too had been invited to court for Christmas, but had refused, knowing that Edward would have insisted that she attend Protestant sermons and forgo the mass. "I would not find myself in such a place for anything in the world," she said flatly, and excused herself on account of indisposition.[14]

Mary, who like Elizabeth was identifying herself more and more staunchly in confessional terms, saw the situation through a biblical lens. "He hath hardened the hearts of the councilors as he did Pharaoh's," she commented dourly, and fortified herself for the religious struggle she foresaw by increasing to three or four the number of masses she heard each day in contravention of official Protestantism.

The atmosphere of renewed religious dedication was only one sign of a more fundamental shift in political power. In recent months the protectorate—and, for the moment, the Protector—had been swept away, and Dudley had emerged as actual, though untitled, ruler of the council and the king.

The challenges to rulership Edward Seymour had faced as Protector were unparalleled in scope. In the countryside, a variety of forces had converged to produce widespread poverty and the perception of catastrophe. Common fields and parklands used by the peasants for centuries had been fenced off, or "enclosed," by hard-pressed landowners who could no longer live on their rents and were forced to turn to sheep-raising. At the same time, the vast expanses of land once owned by the monasteries were being turned over to noblemen determined to make profitable use of the spoils of the church, no matter what dislocations resulted.

By the 1540s the familiar landscape of agrarian England had been permanently altered, and villages which had once housed a hundred laborers and their children now held ten or fewer. Many were entirely deserted, their roofless huts in ruins and their gardens overgrown, their fields overrun by the hated sheep. To the thousands displaced by these changes the Protector's attempt to halt enclosures, while welcome, came too late and brought little real relief. Nightmare inflation put even the coarsest bread beyond their means, while the few coins that came to them were made almost worthless by Seymour's ruinous decision to continue Henry VIII's policy of debasement.

To this economic ferment was added religious instability on an unprecedented scale. The unsettling of the traditional faith by King Henry in the 1530s, and the subsequent alterations in doctrine—the most recent of these the introduction in 1549 of the Book of Common Prayer, a rendering into English of the missal and ritual of the Catholic breviary—brought relatively moderate doctrinal change. But they ushered in a climate of radical theological speculation and rampant hostility to the old faith that took public and violent form. Edward Seymour, who tended toward the more radical of the reformed doctrines, repealed Henry VIII's doctrinal legislation, inviting noisy controversy over the nature and meaning of the sacraments, and reformers from the continent came to England in large numbers in expectation that the realm's official faith would soon move further to the left. Radical preachers sprang up to harangue excited audiences, and ballads, pamphlets and printed argument in every form poured forth from the London booksellers.

"Lent is buried in rhyme," Bishop Gardiner complained, and mockery soon gave way to anger, then destruction. In a fury of anticlericalism every sort of ecclesiastical fixture was thrown down—statues smashed and broken, chalices and pyxes melted down, carved crucifixes burned. Paintings and tapestries were slashed, and the vestments, liturgical books and illuminated manuscripts of the clergy were seized and torn to shreds. Churches were scenes of devastation, spiritual battlefields where in their zeal to purge idolatry the reformers wrecked much fragile, irreplaceable medieval art.

And with violence in the name of faith came the nameless lawlessness of crime. The savage restraints against disorder which had held the country dwellers in check under Henry VIII were relaxed by the Protector for the sake of humanitarian rule; the result was enthusiastic lawbreaking. Every district suffered, but the northern borderlands were especially hard hit. "For want of justice," a royal official wrote from Berwick, "robberies [are] being committed without restitution, murder without punishment, open lechery without shame." "The country is in such murmur and disobedience," he concluded, "that it is exceeding needful to be reformed."[15]

Then in the summer of 1549 nearly half of England broke into open revolt. In the west, there was armed resistance to the new prayer book and demands for a return to the mass and for restoration of the old images and symbols. Devon and Cornwall were out of control, and rioting in Wiltshire, Dorset, Hampshire and elsewhere in the south threatened to kindle into a general rising against the crown. There was rebellion in Yorkshire, and scattered turmoil in other areas as well, but the most serious unrest was in East Anglia, where rebels by the thousands broke down the hedges and fences that enclosed the common lands and gathered in a huge encampment on Mousehold Heath two miles from Norwich.

At this dangerous juncture the underlying weakness of the Protector and his government had become clear. The county levies entrusted with the task of restoring order were too few in number to suppress such widespread disorder; paradoxically it was the foreign mercenaries Edward Seymour had assembled in England to fight the Scots that prevented massive, unified revolt. The Protector himself failed to take the initiative, and left it to the military men on the council to direct the resistance. With a core of tough, experienced Italian mercenaries Lord Russell put down the western rising while Dudley, his men backed by fearsome German landsknechts, crushed the rebels on Mousehold Heath and left more than three thousand dead. At the height of the revolt a troop of German cavalry had to be brought to court to guard the king—and so distrustful were they of the solvency of the regime that they demanded to be paid in advance.[16]

In the aftermath of the rebellions the men who had led the armies inherited political leadership as well. Seymour had proved himself incapable. In October he was committed to the Tower, and when Elizabeth made her conspicuous return to court the following December Dudley, the "faithful and intrepid soldier of Christ," was firmly in command of the council and the protectorate was no more.

From now on there would be a new alignment of forces. Dudley, not

Seymour, would rule through the twelve-year-old king, and Elizabeth would come more and more into prominence as the king's favored sister. With the tensions and harrowing strain of the past two years behind her, Elizabeth was once more finding her equilibrium, fitting herself for the role she was expected to play. "Sweet sister temperance," Edward called her, and from now on she would incarnate staid moderation in all things, her life a model of poise and judicious self-control. Yet the lessons of the recent past would inform her every move on the chessboard of court politics, and beneath her sedate exterior would roil the cunning wit of a burgeoning politician.

9

'Tis known I am Fair,
And Brisk as the Air;
Not one in a thousand
With Me can Compare.

The boy-king Edward was proving to be none too hardy. Dudley was toughening him by letting him ride and wrestle and run at the ring—sports Edward Seymour had never permitted—but he took such a jolting in the saddle that his delicate physique looked as if it would fly to pieces, and his boyish grimace of determination made him seem all the more vulnerable. In November of 1550 he was very ill, and though the episode was kept as secret as possible one ambassador learned soon afterward that he had been near death, and that even his doctors had given up hope.[1]

If Edward should die before marrying and begetting an heir the presumption was that Mary, as the elder sister, would succeed him, despite her opposition to the prevailing faith. Yet Mary was sickly, and had been since adolescence. From time to time she slipped into deep melancholia and coma-like immobility, her skin drained of color and her face haggard and aged. Mary's chronic illness struck each year at the "fall of the leaf," and sometimes oftener. Her survival could not be counted on. "My health," she wrote to the council early in 1551, "is more unstable than that of any creature."[2]

Next in line, surely, was "the right excellent princess the lady Elizabeth her grace." Such was the exalted style by which she was known at court;

the people too called her princess, fully sensitive to the implications of the title.

Overshadowing the mortality of King Edward and both his sisters was the dark menace of the sweating sickness. In the summer of 1551 the deaths began, a few in the first days, then dozens, then hundreds. It had been nearly a quarter of a century since the last virulent epidemic of the sweat had driven Londoners into the countryside in panic in an effort to flee the contagion. That had been in 1528, a year memorable for terrible loss of life and for the mantle of sickening fear that closed in as the corpses multiplied. Now in 1551 the visitation returned. As if struck by the angry hand of God men and women staggered and cried out, suddenly disoriented and terrified. Their heads throbbing, burning with fever and exuding a stinking sweat, they were overcome by a desire to sleep yet dared not sleep, for if they did they became delirious and died within hours raving mad.

Old people who had survived the last epidemic were agreed that this one was worse—"more vehement than the old sweat"—and got away as quickly as they could. The king braved it out for a time, but when the daily death toll in London reached a hundred and twenty he too fled. "One of my gentlemen, another of my grooms fell sick and died," Edward wrote dispassionately in his journal. "I removed to Hampton Court with very few with me."[3]

The long summer dragged past, a summer of tolling bells and shuttered houses, with creaking wagons bearing cartloads of the dead through the deserted streets. And even as they stood in the shadow of death the disaffected English did not forget to rail against the merchants, who had "suddenly raised the prices of all things to a marvelous reckoning," to rebel against the payment of tithes and the plunging value of coins, above all to denounce the councilors, especially Dudley, for their corruption and misgovernment. Troops of horsemen were sent out into the countryside by the council as a show of force, yet the loud denunciations could not be stilled. And the king, though he escaped the sweat, succumbed to his own frailty. During the late summer and fall he became "very thin and weak," causing Dudley and the others to fret once more over the succession and turn over in their minds the counterbalancing merits of the king's two sisters.

Elizabeth, meanwhile, turned her attention to the running of her great household at Hatfield. The house was hers now; Dudley, who got it from the king, had made it over to her, at the same time securing to her the rest of her lands—the lands Thomas Seymour had been so inquisitive about. It must have been comforting to Elizabeth to know that the house which had been her home for so much of her life would now be hers forever, its vast green parks, "replenished with wood of great age," its gardens and orchards, its "very stately lodgings" a permanent sanctuary amid uncertainty.

A book of household accounts kept at Hatfield in these years tells a little about her life there. Its rubric indicates her regality: a rosebush was intertwined with the opening letters, with the red and white roses of her Tudor and Plantagenet grandparents and her own initial E overlaid. At the bottom of each page was the chamberlain's name and Elizabeth's own bold signature, with its elaborate scrollwork and flourishes; Thomas Parry had resumed his office of cofferer, but the detailed accounting was now out of his hands.[4] Wages for the servants indicate a very large and active household, with thirteen liveried gentlemen and a number of ladies and gentlewomen constituting a minor court and dozens of yeomen, grooms, chamber women and kitchen servants laboring to warm and clean the rooms, cook the food, look after the clothes and tend the animals and grounds for the grander staff. The Ashleys were on the household rolls along with Thomas Parry, and Blanche Parry, who was far into her second decade of service to Elizabeth and had decided to go on serving her, forgoing marriage for her mistress's sake.

One familiar name was missing from the rolls: Roger Ascham. He had left her service sometime in 1549 or early 1550, "shipwrecked" by a storm of "recent violence and injury at court." It had been Elizabeth's steward and not Elizabeth herself who had sent him away; she had shown her continued good will by reinstalling him at Cambridge through her patronage. Yet it rankled with Ascham that still another of his hopeful beginnings had ended in bitterness and bad luck, and as he returned to the scholarly life he took solace in his favorite diversions of archery and cockfighting, and gambled away his earnings and what remained of his youth.[5]

Hatfield was many things—a great house, a country estate, and a working farm whose fields and pasturelands yielded an abundance of food. Beef, mutton and veal for the long tables in the great hall came from cattle and sheep that grew fat on the grazing lands of the estate; suet from the butchered animals yielded tallow for candles and soap; their wool made cloaks and tunics and their leather, a multitude of things. There was abundance enough, in 1551 and 1552, to supply most household needs and to provide mutton, candles, wood and fresh fish to the court of King Edward as well.

The rhythm of life at the manor followed that of the agricultural year, with plowing, weeding and the felling of timber in the spring, shearing in June, then the climax of the cycle, the high season of summer when wagonloads of newly harvested hay and grain choked the manor courtyard and purveyors of foodstuffs and other necessities came to sell goods to be laid up for the winter. On through the fall the heightened activity continued, with laborers picking fruit and chopping and stacking logs and gathering fresh rushes to store against the cold season to come. Then at last, with the onset of the autumn frosts, the chimneys were cleaned and the strawberries and flowers covered, and the household settled in around the hearth to celebrate the holidays and wait for the spring thaw.

In her accounts Elizabeth showed a countrywoman's frugality. Nothing was wasted. Oxhides and calfskins and the entrails of the cattle were sold. Sheep yielded high profits in woolfells—at least until 1551, when in response to severe devaluation the demand for English wool dropped sharply —and the Hatfield account book records that even the remains of diseased animals were turned to profit. Along with the income from wool of various grades is an entry for "mutton skins which died of the rot." But parsimony did not preclude charity. Among the payments are subsidies to poor scholars at Oxford and Cambridge, and to "a poor woman that came out of Ireland," and alms whose recipients were not described. Relatives were generously rewarded. Seventy pounds was paid to "Edmund Boleyn, her grace's kinsman," and gifts of money were made "at the christening of Mr. Carey's child" and again "to Mistress Carey at her departing from Hatfield"—possibly, though not certainly, George Carey, son of Mary Boleyn and Elizabeth's first cousin, and his wife.

The household accounts preserve something of the flavor of daily life. There are charges for the care of Elizabeth's two geldings, for lute strings, and for the flowers and herbs she used to freshen her chamber and other rooms in the house. The bills from Warren the tailor list such plain fabrics as fustian and cotton alongside the sober black velvet that went into her robes and hoods, and the two Bibles she ordered echo Elizabeth's newfound image of godliness. Other entries are reminders of her rank—costly New Year's gifts formally received from courtiers and others she ordered from a goldsmith to be sent in return, rewards to the footmen, grooms, and minstrels of Edward's court when she visited St. James's in 1552, payments to the companies of boys who presented plays before her, and to the playwrights.

Life at Protestant Hatfield was tranquil indeed compared to Mary's Catholic establishment, where a siege mentality gripped both Mary herself and the embattled coreligionists who had enrolled themselves in large numbers in her service. Since the start of the reign Mary's relations with the ruling group had grown steadily worse; King Edward was persuaded that her faith put her at odds with him, while the Protector and, later, Dudley saw her Catholicism not only as a peril to her soul but as a danger to the security of the kingdom.

Mary had lately shown just how great a danger she represented. In June of 1550 she had tried to escape. Charles V had sent an expedition to rescue her: a flat-bottomed grain ship slipped into an Essex harbor, waiting to take her aboard in disguise and carry her to Flanders. A last-minute confusion of events made escape impossible, but Mary's determination to risk all was never in doubt, and if she had been able to get away the consequences might have been far-reaching. The emperor, it was said, had planned to marry his cousin Mary to his son Philip, who would then inherit Mary's claim to the throne. Philip would invade England, setting King Edward aside as a schismatic and bastard, and ruling in his wife's name but in the Hapsburg interests.[6]

The contrast between the king's sisters was becoming more and more pronounced. Londoners were growing accustomed to watching their imposing, handsomely appointed retinues pass through the streets on their way to and from court, and to noting the size and character of their escorts. When Elizabeth entered London to spend the Christmas season with her brother careful note was taken of the "great suite" of gentlemen and ladies that accompanied her, and of the hundred horsemen of the royal guard provided by the king. The conspicuous respect shown her by the council on her arrival was also observed with interest; the councilors "acted thus," the imperial ambassador wrote, "to show the people how much glory belongs to her who has embraced the new religion and is become a very great lady."

Epiphany was celebrated with a sumptuous banquet, with Elizabeth in the place of honor below her brother, and after the feasting the king and princess were taken to see bear-baiting and other entertainments. Elizabeth was just seventeen, Edward thirteen; as they sat together, alike in coloring and in the delicacy of their features, they might have been any well-born brother and sister watching a holiday performance. Dudley, who sat nearby, deep in conversation with the French ambassador, might have been a benevolent guardian and not the feared power behind the throne.[7]

But Mary too could show what a "very great lady" she was, with or without the council's support. Two months later she rode into the capital with a huge train of followers. A liveried guard of fifty preceded her, and eighty gentlemen and ladies rode behind—the council provided no escort —but the parade was swollen in size by the hundreds of ordinary citizens who had gone out from the city to greet her and accompany her to the palace. All the mounted riders, and no doubt many of those who followed on foot, wore large rosaries, making this as much a religious procession as a state entry. The event had an aura of sacred drama. Spectators reported seeing visions in the sky—armored horsemen, miraculous suns glowing with otherworldly fire—as Mary and her supporters passed, and feeling the earth shake beneath them with awesome force.

It was no wonder Dudley feared Mary, for she commanded wide popular support and incarnated both the old faith and the old ways of more settled times. So far, despite persuasions and threats, he had not been able to force her to give up the mass, or even to keep her worship private, restricting her large and influential household from joining in. Dudley "governed absolutely," it was said; with his allies William Parr, marquess of Northampton, and "that mad, fighting fellow" William Herbert, soon to become earl of Pembroke, Dudley so overawed the council that none dared oppose him. Yet Mary stubbornly resisted, and Dudley had not yet found a way to break her as he had all other opposition.

He was about to complete the destruction of his only potential rival, Edward Seymour. The former Protector, released from imprisonment in the Tower early in 1550, had inched his way back toward membership in the council and in a gesture of submissive reconciliation had married his daughter to Dudley's eldest son. But by spring, 1551, he was conspiring to maneuver the arrest of Dudley, Northampton and Pembroke, and though before long he decided the scheme was unworkable, several of his co-conspirators could not be held in check; through their blundering he was arrested and eventually convicted on a charge of felony.

The day Seymour was arrested Dudley inaugurated such security precautions as had not been seen since the great rebellions of 1549. All approaches to the capital were blocked by mounted guards; a night watch was set; vagabonds and suspect persons with no responsible citizen to vouch for them were expelled. To forestall a public outcry when news of the arrest spread the officers and wardens of the livery companies were told the official account of Seymour's activities. He had meant to seize the Tower, then to "have destroyed the city of London, and the substantial men of the same." There was much resentment, but no uprising, when Seymour was executed the following January, the words "Lord Jesus, save me" on his lips.[8]

Dudley's apprehension and overarmed safety measures were indicative of his paramount fear: that the underlying weakness of his rule would be detected, and that the floodgates of rebellion would open in a final apocalyptic burst. The only hope lay in the semblance of power, and in the immediate and savage suppression of even the slightest disorder. Convinced that he had to act quickly, Dudley entrenched himself behind a semi-permanent army of mercenaries and private troops led by trusted councilors and peers licensed to maintain them at state expense. These "lords lieutenants," he hoped, would hold the country together while King Edward's minority lasted, which he expected would not be too much longer. In this year of 1551 he brought Edward into the council meetings and encouraged him to employ his excellent education in writing long analyses of governmental issues—copied from drafts prepared by others— in elegant Latin. The young man was gaining a solid grasp of affairs, and lacked only strength and size—and health—to make a promising king.

But Edward's health was in the hands of fate, and as he grew older it began to seem that fate would be cruel. For several years courtiers had been saying privately that the king was not likely to live long; his astrology foretold an early death. In the fall of 1552 he was visited by Girolamo Cardano, a physician and medical astrologer. Cardano found the contrast between Edward's unusual physical beauty and mental endowments and his inherent frailty tragic. He agreed with the appraisal of a visiting French nobleman that the king was "an angel in human form," his face and figure as beautiful as could be imagined. Yet his vital powers were irremediably weak, Cardano judged, and there was "an appearance on his face denoting early death."9

His final illness began as a rasping cough which racked his slender frame and seemed to drain his spirits as well. Before long he had begun to spit up corrupt matter from his lungs, some of it "pink like the color of blood," and his thin arms and legs grew thinner and his muscles too weak to support him. The outcome was clear, and the physicians admitted it, though Londoners who spread rumors that their king was dead or dying had their ears torn off in punishment.

By mid-May there was no longer any question of whether the king would die; there was only the question of when. Ulcers broke out on his fevered body, and his swollen belly—swollen from malnutrition, as he could eat nothing and was subsisting on the reeking compounds prescribed by his apothecaries—made a grotesque contrast to his shrunken limbs. He coughed continuously.

There was wild speculation about the succession. It was hardly conceivable that the Catholic Mary, designated heir under the 1544 Act of Succession and Henry VIII's will, would be crowned queen when Edward died. Quite apart from the issue of her sex, and her unmarried status, she would undo the reformation in England, which only in the last year had taken full form with the passage of the second Act of Uniformity and introduction of the revised Book of Common Prayer. The communion service in the new prayer book had no resemblance to the mass, and was at base a commemoration rather than a miraculous reenactment of Christ's sacrifice. Mary

would undoubtedly sweep this away, along with every other piece of ecclesiastical legislation enacted over the last twenty years, and such a thoroughgoing change would threaten far more people—prominent among
them the holders of former monastic lands—than would welcome it.

And if Mary was unsuitable, then the natural choice would be Elizabeth.
Rumor had it, in fact, that Elizabeth would soon be in London, and that
Dudley's eldest son John intended to put aside his wife and marry her. The
story was not entirely implausible, though Dudley's younger son Robert
would have been more to Elizabeth's taste. Her childhood companion,
Robert Dudley had continued his close ties to Elizabeth in adolescence;
Ascham had tutored them both. In 1551 Robert had married a Norfolk
heiress, Amy Robsart, but the marriage had been childless and the couple
had become estranged. If any Dudley was to be linked with Elizabeth, it
would most likely be Lord Robert.

Yet the elder Dudley did not seem well disposed toward Elizabeth in
Edward's final months. He kept news of the king's worsening condition
from reaching her as best he could, and when she attempted to visit her
brother she was intercepted before reaching London and told to turn back.

Clearly the council was taking steps to strengthen defenses in the event
of a crisis. Money was being amassed by Dudley and his supporters, and
the sale of church ornaments hastened in order to provide further funds.
Meanwhile the chief fortresses, such as Windsor, were made ready and the
lords lieutenant alerted for possible service.

At this juncture, in about mid-May, a document was drafted in Edward's
handwriting which excluded both Mary and Elizabeth from the succession
and, in its final, amended form, designated Jane Grey as heir. Whose the
initiative was in the drafting of this document is uncertain, yet it effected
both the king's primary desire—to preserve the Protestant settlement by
barring Mary's accession—and Dudley's goal of maintaining power in the
next reign. The device represented the convergence of their interests, yet
was profoundly unrealistic, as the sequel showed. Probably neither the king
nor the duke—Dudley had taken the title duke of Northumberland after
Edward Seymour's arrest—had the energy to think through the full implications of the dynastic revolution they were attempting. Edward was
debilitated by illness, while Dudley, his own health faltering, was overcome
by melancholy. "I have entered into the bottom of my care," he confided
to friends; now that the king was dying he went to bed often "with a careful
heart and a weary body."[10]

A vital step in implementing the transfer of power was the marriage of
the designated heir, Jane Grey, to Dudley's only unmarried son Guildford.
The wedding was a magnificent affair, held at Dudley's London house, but

the rejoicings were incongruous in view of the suffering and humiliations of Jane's childhood playmate, the king. In recent days Edward's head had begun to swell to a melon shape; all his hair was shaved off, and plasters were applied to the naked skull. It was taking him too long to die. Such putrefaction from within, people said, was unnatural. It was a sure sign of poison.

The marriage of Jane Grey and Guildford Dudley took place on May 21. Six weeks later Edward's agony still continued. He lay corpselike in his high regal bed, hardly able to breathe, his useless body covered with scabs. The physicians and apothecaries had yielded place to a gentlewoman who claimed she could cure the boy if only she were given a completely free hand. Under her ghoulish ministrations he fell into "desperate extremities," his "vital parts mortally stuffed," his pulse failing and his skin changing color.

Elizabeth, at Hatfield, knew that her brother was dying but was spared the sight and, it may be hoped, detailed knowledge of his slow decay. She must have known something of the succession scheme, and news may have reached her from London that it was now being said Dudley meant to divorce his own wife and marry her.[11]

Mary remained at Hunsdon, as yet undisturbed, though Dudley could hardly afford to allow her to go free much longer. Once Edward died he would move quickly to proclaim Jane queen and to crush all opposition; he could not afford to take the risk that Mary might resist, and would have to take her and keep her under guard. Mary's danger was clear to her, though she may or may not have heard how both the judges and the councilors argued against the altered succession and had to be coerced—by Edward's hoarse deathbed whispers and Dudley's most savage bullying —into signing the formal version of the document. She believed that there were many in the kingdom who would rally to her as soon as Edward died, some from loyalty to the church of Rome, some because they hated Dudley, many out of simple, strong allegiance to the legitimate Tudor line. To these legitimists, Jane Grey, though she was a great-granddaughter of Henry VII, was not the rightful heir. Mary, whatever her faith, was their liege. As events were to prove, a generation of ever widening religious divergence had not dislodged Englishmen's adherence to the time-honored order of succession.

Several days before Edward's death Mary was warned to move to safer quarters. At about the same time both she and Elizabeth were summoned to Edward's bedside. Elizabeth did nothing; Mary at first moved cautiously toward London. Then word reached her late on the evening of July 6 that her brother had finally expired, and at once she called for her small escort and rode northward through the night toward Suffolk, where she had firm supporters among the gentry.

Over the next two weeks Elizabeth waited at Hatfield while her sister and Northumberland contended for the throne. The duke had nearly every advantage. He held the Tower, arsenal of the kingdom and castle and court of the newly proclaimed Queen Jane. The treasury was his, and all the military forces of the kingdom; his men, ships and artillery seemed invincible. Yet Mary had the people's loyalty, and her own remarkable courage. From her headquarters at Framlingham Castle she rallied dozens, then hundreds, then thousands to her cause. Day after day nobles rode into her camp with their own private bodies of horsemen and footsoldiers. Provisions were contributed, and money, and arms; at the core of the gathering host were "innumerable companies of the common people."

Dudley had miscalculated. He had sent his son Robert with three hundred men to seize Mary, but she had eluded him. Now an army had to be sent against her. On July 14 the duke himself rode out of London at the head of a hastily assembled force, full of misgivings about the disloyal Londoners and quarreling councilors he was leaving behind. He had not gone far before they betrayed him. News reached the council that Mary commanded a mighty force of men, and that sailors on the ships Dudley sent to guard the Norfolk coast had defected to her side. With no strong leader to take command, the councilors panicked, and began to imagine how the victorious Mary would treat them once she confronted them as queen. With Dudley and his army in Cambridge, hesitant to move farther toward Framlingham, on July 18 the council issued a reward for the duke's arrest, and the next day proclaimed Mary queen.

What Elizabeth knew of this swift, bloodless rebellion no evidence records. She may have heard of the proclamation—unwelcomed by Londoners—of her sixteen-year-old second cousin Jane as queen, and of the fiery preacher Latimer's denunciation of herself and Mary as unfit to rule. She may have marveled at her sister's fortitude and eventual triumph as Dudley's supporters melted away around him. She may well have feared for Robert Dudley, whose abortive effort to capture Mary had been a key part of his father's venture and who was certain to suffer now that it had failed.

Whatever her private thoughts, as soon as she knew that Dudley had capitulated in Cambridge and that Mary was on her way to claim her throne Elizabeth acted at once to show her loyalty. She wrote Mary a letter of congratulations, and prepared to meet her and ride with her in her triumphant state entry into the capital.

In the cool of an August evening the new queen came to London, her steadfast soldiers rank on rank around her, her jubilant subjects singing and shouting and throwing their caps in the air for joy. She was all in regal purple, and her robes and baldric and headdress glowed with jewels. After more than twenty years of anguish, frustration and intermittent persecution Mary was queen, and there was an unmistakable glint of steely gloating in her eyes as she passed slowly, smiling, amid the crowds. More dangerous, from Elizabeth's point of view, was Mary's absolute conviction that God alone had preserved her for this moment, shielding her from harm and breaking her enemies so that she might restore his Catholic church in England. She whom miracles had brought to power would expect superhuman accomplishments of herself. What might she expect—or fear—from her clever, popular Protestant sister and heir apparent?

In the dusk Elizabeth rode with her large train of attendants behind Mary, acknowledging the cheers that greeted her, turning to right and left to show off her handsomeness to advantage. She must not take too much attention from Mary on this day, she knew, yet it could do no harm to let the people see her at her best.

10

My fortune hangs upon her brow;
For as she smiles or frowns on me,
So must my blown affections bow.

Queen Mary began her reign in a fever of dedicated labor. She was up by daybreak each morning, and after dressing and hearing mass she went at once to her desk and began the long day's work of government. She worked straight on through the morning, never stopping to eat or drink, on through the early afternoon. At one or two o'clock she paused for a light dinner, then resumed her tireless perusal of the letters and warrants and other documents that accumulated throughout the day, conferring from time to time with foreign ambassadors, with her councilors and in particular with her chancellor Stephen Gardiner, bishop of Winchester. Fighting off headaches, heart palpitations and what she called "her natural melancholy," she worked doggedly on through the evening, squinting at her papers in the candlelight, until it was time for vespers. Then, having heard the service and attended to her private devotions, she called in her chamber women to undress her and put her to bed.

What fueled Mary's determined efforts was her conviction that she was doing God's work, not her own; she committed her hours of work, as she had long ago committed her heart and spirit, to the divine master who had brought her to the throne. Her one overriding goal was to make England a Catholic realm once more, as it had been in the untroubled days of her childhood. The mass, the sacraments, the religious customs embedded in popular folklore had all to be restored. Most important, England had to return as an erring penitent to the fold of the pope in Rome.

Mary's purpose inflated her pride. The ambassador who knew her best, the perceptive, shrewd if somewhat jaundiced envoy of Charles V, Simon Renard, observed that she was "inclined to talk about her exalted station," and that her natural greateartedness and magnanimity went along with a ferociously regal self-assurance. In appearance too she was flamboyantly, almost overwhelmingly regal, her thin figure swathed in thickly embroidered velvets and heavy, jewel-encrusted cloth of gold and silver, her neck and fingers ablaze with gems. Visitors to court were dazzled by her array of jewels, yet according to the Venetian ambassador she would have bought many more had her treasury not been all but empty.

As queen Mary enjoyed more personal liberty than she had ever known, and this too made her surgent and kept her at her labors. To be sure, she was surrounded by councilors and statesmen who sought to control her opinions and decisions—and none of whom, in this fall of 1553, seriously believed that she was capable of governing. But to this veteran of helpless suffering and deep sorrows, who by her own admission "had never known what it was to be happy," queenship came like a second birth, a new and auspicious beginning. It was her long-awaited chance to right former wrongs, to set straight what had gone awry, to serve God's purposes. And in serving his purposes she would heal her own wounds; for the first time, she would make her own happiness.

To Elizabeth the spare, spinsterly queen with her manly voice and myopic frown must have seemed at once fragile and dangerous. Elizabeth had known Mary in many roles: as a bitter, disinherited elder sister, as a generous benefactress who gave her necklaces and brooches, yards of satin for gowns, money to gamble with at cards, as an anxious, beleaguered opponent of her brother and his councilors, as a would-be fugitive, driven in desperation to attempt escape from England. She knew Mary to be in very poor health—although in her early months as queen she seemed to abound in vitality—and to be highly strung and prone to nervousness and, so the men around her said, to hysteria. Yet she knew also that her sister had been immeasurably strengthened, at least in spirit, by her adversity and that she was so fixed in her convictions that to oppose her on matters of faith could be fatal.

Elizabeth was to find Mary implacable, but not pitiless. She would rely more and more on that saving margin of pity in the months ahead.

According to the Venetian ambassador Soranzo, Mary had indicated by "very clear signs" during Edward's reign that she did not love her sister. Once she became queen her lack of love became more pronounced, heightened by her immediate danger—she was menaced by assassination threats, which she outbraved by continually showing herself in public—and by the dire warnings of the foreign ambassadors at her court. The French ambassador Noailles, opposed to Mary's pro-Hapsburg regime, tried to stir up the queen's suspicions against her sister as often as he could. Noailles was especially hospitable to English Protestants with plots against the Catholic crown, though he thought little of the schemes they devised, and never ceased to remind Mary that her Protestant subjects looked to Elizabeth as their chief hope. They meant to kidnap the princess, he told Mary, and marry her to some powerful nobleman who would then take up arms on his wife's behalf and put her on the throne in Mary's stead.

But the French ambassador's warnings were slight compared to the admonitions of Renard, who as the envoy of Mary's imperial cousin Charles V was swiftly becoming the queen's most intimate consultant. Mary had four "certain and open enemies," Renard told her: the Protestants, Dudley's adherents and other rebellious malcontents, the French king, and her sister Elizabeth. That Elizabeth would make common cause with the Protestants created an especially potent danger, but the princess was dangerous enough in her own right. Renard perceived a quality in her—he called it "a power of enchantment"—which gave Elizabeth a strong hold over others and made them do her will. She was, quite simply, charismatic; like her father, she possessed an authority beyond the natural authority of royal lineage and self-confident temperament. She was mesmerizing, and her mesmerizing personality in combination with her shrewd and subtle mind made her dangerous indeed.[1]

What was equally disturbing, Elizabeth clearly had a mind of her own when it came to religion, and was accustomed to the give and take of theological argument. She "not only knows what the true religion is," wrote an ecstatic Protestant contemporary, "but has acquired such proficiency in Greek and Latin, that she is able to defend it by the most just arguments and the most happy talent; so that she encounters few adversaries whom she does not overcome."[2] To Mary, whose chief desire was to bring back the religion England had lost, Elizabeth's readiness to champion the reformed faith in argumentative debate was an unwelcome obstacle. It was bad enough that, for the time being at least, the daughter of Anne Boleyn should be heir apparent, and should share her mother's casual morality (as Mary persisted in believing); it was almost perverse that she should be a tenacious upholder of heresy as well.

Elizabeth was given the place of highest honor in Mary's coronation procession, riding in a gorgeous litter along with Anne of Cleves. She wore a gown of cloth of silver, which no doubt set off her fresh beauty, and made her easy to distinguish among the dozens of other female attendants, all of whom wore red. There was no hint, either at the coronation festivities or at the coronation itself, that the queen's sister was under any suspicion or out of favor. She dined at the royal table at the banquet on coronation night, watching with impassive interest when Mary's champion, following old custom, rode into the banqueting hall and threw down his gauntlet, challenging all present to dispute the reigning monarch's right to her title. She took her place at court, fulfilling her ceremonial duties while at the same time joining in the gossip (chiefly about whom the queen would marry) and making alliances among the women.

Yet inevitably Elizabeth stood out, inevitably she was herself the subject of constant gossip, as well as of much deep discussion among the councilors and ambassadors. "That heretic and schismatic sister," a papal envoy to England wrote of Elizabeth, "is in the heart and mouth of everyone."

Her position, in fact, could hardly have been more perilous. As heir to the throne Elizabeth was at the mercy of any conspirator bold enough to act, yet she could do nothing to prevent such action nor to protect herself from becoming involved. Anyone could move, as Thomas Seymour had done, to exploit her; anyone could force her to challenge Mary's authority —as Northumberland had forced Jane Grey to do—and if he failed, as Northumberland had failed, Elizabeth would join Jane Grey in the Tower. It could happen at any moment, without warning. Elizabeth became accustomed to living with dread.

Then one evening her nightmare became real. She was walking with Mary and a number of other courtiers down a long, dim gallery. They were on their way to vespers, and as they were within the protecting confines of the palace compound they were not accompanied by armed guardsmen. Suddenly they heard a loud voice cry "Treason!" and in an instant the courtiers ran off in all directions, no doubt thinking that it was an assassin's voice they had heard.

Expecting to hear an arquebus fire next, or to see a body of desperate men come running into the gallery, Elizabeth panicked and stood where she was, trembling violently, her terror visible on her white face.

Mary, who had developed something of the reckless courage of a combat soldier convinced that he cannot be killed, walked on unperturbed into the chapel to hear the service. After a time, when no further disturbance erupted, the courtiers crept back to their places around the queen. (The alarming cry, they found out later, had been directed to Mary's chancellor Bishop Gardiner and not to the queen herself.) Elizabeth, though, "could not compose her countenance"; her chest heaved from fright and her knees were weak. Mary's leading gentlewoman Susan Clarencieux, who had had much experience over the years in calming Mary, came up to Elizabeth and began massaging her stomach. Gradually she relaxed, the color came back into her cheeks and she rejoined the others.

No doubt her panic gave rise to further gossip. Why, unless she was guilty of plotting, had the cry of treason frightened her so badly? Or was her overreaction a ruse, intended to make her look weak and vulnerable when in fact she and her co-conspirators were about to strike?

No one among the queen's advisers knew quite what to do with Elizabeth. Some thought she should be sent away from court, for even though this might give her greater scope for treachery she could be kept under surveillance and might even serve as bait to lure other traitors into the open. Others thought it safer to keep her nearby, just in case something happened to Mary. Still others believed it would be safest to marry her to the man who, since the start of the reign, had been urged as the most suitable potential consort in the kingdom: Edward Courtenay.

Great-grandson of Edward IV, Courtenay's pedigree could be matched only by that of his relatives Reginald and Geoffrey Pole, grandsons of Edward IV's brother George, duke of Clarence—and neither the former, a cleric, nor the latter, who was of weak character and more than a little deranged, could be considered as a husband for the princess. Courtenay certainly thought himself worthy of Elizabeth's hand—and of Mary's too, for that matter—though his aristocratic handsomeness was combined with an unfortunate personality. Renard found him "proud, poor, obstinate, inexperienced and vindictive in the extreme," and his peculiar upbringing (he had spent his life since childhood in confinement in the Tower, where his father Henry Courtenay, marquess of Exeter, had been executed by Henry VIII) had not fitted him for public life. Still, he was popular with the people, and perhaps with Elizabeth as well.[3] He was also staunchly Catholic; as Elizabeth's husband he might be expected to lend his weight to her recent conversion—a conversion many suspected of being shallow and expedient, if not completely cynical.

The problem was the mass. Elizabeth dutifully attended, but was less than convincing in her devotion. During a painful audience with Mary she had sworn tearfully that she had in all good conscience adopted the Catholic usages from conviction and not out of "fear, hypocrisy or dissimulation." Mary was inclined to be convinced of her sincerity—after all, she spoke very timidly, and trembled fearfully at every word. Yet somehow she instinctively distrusted Elizabeth, and "begged her to speak freely and declare what was in her mind." Mary was confused. The pure, unlined face Elizabeth turned up to her was surely too innocent to be capable of guile. Yet it was Anne Boleyn's face—and Mark Smeaton's—and it had attracted scandal and suspicion for years. Mary could not conceive of lying about her faith, yet she had learned well what it was to scheme, to plot deception when forced to it by circumstances. On balance, it was wiser to reserve judgment about Elizabeth's sincerity, meanwhile keeping close watch on her activities.[4]

Mary's distrust corroded what goodwill there had been between the sisters, and early in December, 1553, Elizabeth was allowed to leave the court. She set off for her house at Ashridge, accompanied by an imposing escort of five hundred mounted gentlemen. To preserve at least the appearance of affection Mary gave her parting gifts—a costly sable hood and two pearl necklaces—and Elizabeth, in turn, urged Mary not to listen to what others said about her, but to trust in her loyalty and sincerity, at least until she had a chance to defend herself against any accusations in person.

So they parted—with deep misgivings on both sides. Mary was becoming convinced that she ought to marry her sister to Courtenay. She was about to announce her own betrothal to Prince Philip of Spain, son of Charles V, and though she could not have been more joyful about the coming marriage she knew that her subjects would be incensed at the thought of a Spanish king. Marrying Elizabeth to Courtenay would mollify them, and she knew he would be willing. Yet she had to know the emperor's opinion of the match before she did anything further. Meanwhile she was letting her sister out of her grasp.

Elizabeth too was anxious. The vague plottings were crystallizing, taking firm shape. She knew at least something—it is uncertain how much—of an ambitious plot to take up arms against the queen on Palm Sunday, March 18 (when Prince Philip was expected to arrive). Most likely she refused to play any active role in the rising, yet by its very existence the conspiracy put her life in danger and gave Mary the excuse she needed to order Elizabeth's execution.

As she rode out of London Elizabeth's worries ate at her, making her head ache and bringing on the first symptoms of illness. How could she preserve at least an image of innocence and trustworthiness in the queen's mind? Ten miles out of the capital she signaled for her party to halt. She had become too unwell to ride, and sent a messenger back to the palace to borrow a litter from Mary. And at the same time she instructed the messenger to ask Mary for chapel ornaments—copes for the priests celebrating mass, crosses to be borne before them in procession, chalices for the altar she would set up at Ashridge—everything needful for observance of the Catholic faith. It was a dramatic gesture and it left its imprint. Mary sent on all that was asked for—as usual, somewhat puzzled and doubtful yet not quite ready to give up hope for her enigmatic sister.

During January of 1554 popular opposition grew to the queen's announced betrothal to Philip of Spain. Slanderous tales were spread about the prince, and about Spaniards in general, and many of the English swore they would die rather than allow Philip and his wedding party to set foot on English soil.

The impending Spanish marriage congealed conspiracy, but the conspirators were in no clear agreement about their aims. Mary was to be removed from the throne, and her shadowy fiancé along with her. But how? Not by assassination: several of the plotters "detested the horribleness of the crime." Simply by supplanting Mary with Elizabeth and Courtenay, then: but Courtenay had lost his nerve, and was telling all he knew to the chancellor even before the rising began. By sheer force? But that would mean massed fighting men, armed and led from the country districts. Very well then, there was no alternative. Peter Carew would raise the west, where Courtenay's followers were. James Crofts would command in Herefordshire, Thomas Wyatt in Kent, the duke of Suffolk in Leicestershire. Help could be expected from Noailles and the French. Hinting strongly that Elizabeth would cooperate if she saw that the coup was succeeding, Crofts assured Noailles that the planned revolt had "a foundation."

But in reality Elizabeth, whatever her assessment of the undertaking, was in no condition to further it. She had begun to suffer seriously from a painful swelling of her face, arms, and eventually her whole body. The affliction weakened her and made her "very evil at ease"; that it may have been at least partly psychosomatic only increased its trauma. She lay at Ashridge, fearful of the expected rebellion, perhaps even more fearful of her dropsical body, for her brother's fatal illness had also been marked by swelling of the arms and legs and head. Victims of poisoning often swelled to bursting before they died.

Then word came from the capital, where late in January every city gate was guarded by armed men prepared to turn back rebels should they try to enter the City. Elizabeth was summoned to court. She sent a reply saying she was too ill to make the journey, and backing up her assertion by inviting Mary to send a physician to examine her.

Elizabeth might be ill, but she could hardly be innocent. Mary found out that one of the conspirators had written to the princess, advising her to "get herself as far from the City as she could, the rather for her safety from strangers." It was an ambiguous message, and her verbal reply—throughout the rebellion she committed nothing incriminating to writing—was even more ambiguous. She sent word by way of Sir William Saintlow "that she did thank him much for his goodwill, and she would do as she should see cause."[5] But there was more. A diplomatic pouch bound for France was seized and its contents examined. Inside was a copy of Elizabeth's last letter to Mary. How could it have got there without Elizabeth's cooperation? More important, what would it mean to the French unless they were relying on Elizabeth to take an active part in the revolt?

Renard elaborated on the gravity of the discovery. The French, he said, were sending arms, artillery and provisions into Scotland, intending to invade England from the north. At the same time French ships were being readied to carry an invasionary force across the Channel, and in Normandy, twenty-three infantry companies were being massed along the coast. The letter proved to Renard's satisfaction that Elizabeth had an understanding with the French, and that the purpose of the military preparations was to put her on her sister's throne.[6]

Mary barely had time to send her physicians to Ashridge before the capital was engulfed in rebellion. Of the four regions expected to ignite into revolt only Kent, Thomas Wyatt's county, generated a real rising, but Wyatt's followers formed a dangerous core of rebels and by early February they were marching on London. There was real fear that Mary's government might not be able to resist them. The queen's councilors bogged down in self-absorbed squabbling; she had no standing army, only men mustered for this emergency, led by that sour relic of her father's reign, the eighty-year-old duke of Norfolk; she had reason to suspect treason among even her closest advisers.

With London in an uproar her councilors begged Mary to escape upriver to Windsor in her barge, or at the very least to take refuge in the Tower. Instead she made her way through the City, along streets full of "much noise and tumult" and congested with horses and men-at-arms and freshly mustered soldiers wearing the white coats of the queen's guard. At the Guildhall she paused to address a crowd of citizens, calming their fears about her marriage and appealing to them to stand with her now, as they had stood with her against Northumberland.

"I cannot tell how naturally the mother loveth the child," Mary told them, "for I was never the mother of any, but certainly if a prince and governor may as naturally and earnestly love her subjects, as the mother doth love the child, then assure yourselves that I, being your lady and mistress, do as earnestly and tenderly love and favor you."

Standing before them with her head held proudly, her low voice ringing out through the lofty hall, Mary touched her subjects' hearts.

Pluck up your courage, she told them. "Stand fast against these rebels, both our enemies and yours, and fear them not, for I assure you I fear them nothing at all!"[7]

Queen Mary's rousing speech rallied the Londoners for the coming invasion of the Kentishmen, and when Wyatt and his men finally made their assault on February 3 they found they lacked the numbers to overcome the royal forces. For most of that day there was skirmishing throughout the City and suburbs, though, and at Whitehall, where Mary and her courtiers waited for news, rumors of ruin and treason sent the court into panic. The palace was filled with "such a screeching and noise as it was wonderful to hear," an observer wrote, yet through it all the queen was calm and steadfast. God would not desert them, she told her fearful servants and crying gentlewomen. "Fall to prayer!" she urged. "And I warrant you, we shall hear better news anon."

Then at last toward evening Wyatt surrendered, having found that he and his men were trapped within the encircling girdle of the queen's bands. He was led to the Tower. His confederates were taken, his followers herded off to await trial and to pray that the queen would be merciful. And with the immediate danger past, the grim process of retribution could begin, a process that in time would touch everyone implicated in the plot, especially the queen's sister.

Mary's doctors had probably reached Ashridge late in January. They found Elizabeth to be in poor health, but believed that, provided every consideration was shown to her, she could make the journey to court. Yet though they "travailed very earnestly" with her for some days—no doubt exacerbating her condition—they could not persuade her to leave Ashridge, and it was not until Mary summoned her formally on February 10 that Elizabeth reluctantly agreed to go.

The three councilors who delivered the summons conferred first with the physicians, then with the patient herself. They saw at once how ill she was, "so sick in her bed, and very feeble and weak of body," yet they hardened themselves to her whispered remonstrances that a journey would endanger her life, and next morning they "had her forth as she was, very faint and feeble." Although she was "ready to swoon three or four times," they saw her carried to the litter Mary had provided for her to ride in, and bundled in furs against the cold.

The easiest possible itinerary had been scheduled, with only seven or eight miles to be covered in a day. But even the most moderate exposure to the damp, chill February air was hazardous in Elizabeth's condition (the physicians had specifically requested that she be housed in dry and warm quarters once she reached the palace), and before she had gone more than a few miles she was "all sick in the litter," and could not hold her head up from dizziness and pain. When the party reached St. Albans it was evident that the strain was weakening her still further; at Highgate, only five miles from Westminster, she collapsed completely and had to remain bedridden for an entire week before she could go on.

Illness and dread commingled to prostrate Elizabeth. What awaited her in the capital she could easily imagine, given the course of recent events. The queen, having won new respect from her councilors and advisers for her stony courage, had abandoned pity for stern punishment. "She is absolutely determined to execute severe and exemplary justice," Renard reported, "and thus secure herself by force." She had made up her mind, or so it seemed, to annihilate all claimants to her crown, even those who, like sixteen-year-old Jane Grey, were personally innocent of intrigue. New signs of her wrath were visible daily. "There is no other news than that every day someone is condemned to death," Noailles wrote. "This one has been executed; yet another has been taken prisoner," and so on. There was general agreement that, when Elizabeth finally reached the city, she would become the next victim.

At last, on February 22, she roused herself for the last stage of her anguished journey. She had her swollen body draped in purest white on this last day, and ordered that the curtains of her litter be drawn back so that the crowds in the City might see her as she passed. There had been rumors of her illness for weeks, and the usual speculations to go with them: she was pregnant; she was near death, and nothing could revive her; she had been poisoned. In any case, whatever her condition, Mary would never let her live.

Renard was among those who watched the royal litter pass on its way to Westminster. Elizabeth's body sagged weakly against the soft cushions but her pale face, grotesquely bloated and hollow-eyed, was defiant. She was "proud, lofty, superbly disdainful," the ambassador said, supposing, as usual, that she was trying to disguise her guilt and humiliation. Others felt only compassion for her. "She is so distended and exhausted that she is a sad sight to see," wrote one; another said simply that "those who have seen her do not promise her long to live."[8]

The people, dazed first by the tumultuous excitement of the rebellion and now by the lurid spectacle of dozens of public executions, stared at Elizabeth in blank wonder. She was unreal, wraithlike, as white as the new corpses that hung conspicuously from the gibbets by the roadside. In silence they let her pass.

At Westminster the palace gates swung open to admit the princess and a bare dozen of her attendants, then swung shut again. The rest of her suite, she was told, would have to find lodging in the City. Her reception was ominously cold. There were no ceremonial guards, no footmen, no fanfare to signal the arrival of the heir apparent. And the queen, her unloving sister, was nowhere in sight.

11

Life is a Poets fable
and al her daies are lies
stolne from deaths reckoning table.

For three weeks Elizabeth lay in the palace, ill and in isolation, waiting for word from Mary. None came, nor did anyone enter her rooms save the chamberlain John Gage and the vice-chamberlain Henry Jerningham, who stood at the doors, less in attendance than as silent warders watchful against escape.

She had been purposely lodged in a remote quarter of the palace, which neither she nor the few servants allowed to stay with her could leave without passing a cordon of guards. Though no one spoke it, there could be no doubt that her liberty was being restricted; that Mary had forgotten, or ignored, her request for quarters far from the river for the sake of her health made her ill at ease, and fed her worst expectations.

Shut off as she was from the activity of the court Elizabeth could learn nothing of her sister's present mood, but she could imagine it without much difficulty. Mary, she knew, would be agitated, pulled in many directions at once by the force of her own newfound authority, her treasured hope of marriage to Prince Philip, her quarrelsome, insistent advisers, who were themselves of several minds about what course the queen should pursue. Left to make her own judgment, Mary might, after much inner deliberation, come down on the side of clemency toward Elizabeth. Surrounded as she was by clamorous councilors, many of them calling loudly and emphatically for the princess's execution, she might give way and satisfy both their demands and her own long-buried urge to revenge.

In fact Elizabeth had little reason to expect clemency. She had been in communication with the conspirators; they had written to her and had received verbal messages in reply; two of them, James Crofts and Nicholas Throckmorton, had come and gone freely in her household. Little further pretext for her execution was needed, yet there remained, of course, the ultimate justification: the rising had been plotted, designed and carried out in Elizabeth's name, its avowed purpose to put her on the throne.

The forceful, opinionated chancellor Gardiner had been demanding since early February that the princess be tried for treason. Simon Renard, whose views weighed heavily with Mary and whose cool diplomatic judgment was largely unalloyed by compassion, concurred. To allow her to live, he calculated, could lead to further rebellions, and would certainly make the imminent landing of Prince Philip and his Spanish retinue even more hazardous than it was already likely to be. There was no realistic alternative. Elizabeth would have to be ruthlessly sacrificed to protect Spanish interests in England.

But other voices demurred. One was that of Paget, seasoned councilor of Henry VIII and Edward, who opposed the over-hasty elimination of the heir to the throne and argued that, given Elizabeth's popularity, her execution might rather guarantee rebellion than forestall it. Another was the booming, good-natured voice of Lord William Howard, Elizabeth's great-uncle, who had won Mary's undying gratitude (and a barony) for his heroism during the rebellion. A mettlesome soldier and diplomat and currently admiral of the fleet, Howard's protests against harsh treatment of Elizabeth could hardly be ignored—especially not now when every royal ship was needed to safeguard the wedding fleet that would soon be on its way from Spain.

So, as Elizabeth waited at the palace, the debate over her life continued, while the chancellor did his best to extract incriminating confessions from his prisoners and his agents scoured their goods and estates for some scrap of written evidence of Elizabeth's guilt. Gardiner was an excellent lawyer; by an irony of history he had been Henry VIII's principal advocate at the papal court in the days when the king was attempting to annul his marriage to Katherine of Aragon so that he could marry Anne Boleyn. But three weeks of ransacking and interrogation and torture brought to light no proof of Elizabeth's complicity, and even Gardiner's expertise was inadequate to create evidence where there was none. The circumstance that had made Elizabeth look worst—the discovery of her letter in the diplomatic pouch of the French ambassador—the chancellor could not afford to emphasize, for reasons of his own: the ambassadorial dispatch had described a compromising meeting between Gardiner himself and Edward Courtenay.

Winnowed to its essence, the case against Elizabeth was slight. Some of her familiars were conspirators, but all denied her involvement in their conspiracy. To the messages she received from the ringleaders—messages she could hardly have prevented from reaching her—she had given courteous but utterly undirected replies. Even under torture Wyatt himself, who might have expected he had everything to gain by telling the royal examiners what they wanted to hear, refused in the end to implicate Elizabeth. (Contrary evidence given at a later Star Chamber hearing has never been substantiated.) "I assure you," Wyatt said to the crowd when he had mounted the scaffold on the day of his execution, "that neither they [Elizabeth and Courtenay] nor any other now in yonder hold of durance [the Tower] was privy to my rising." A shouted attempt by one of Mary's advisers to twist Wyatt's last words angered the crowd. The traitor had told them what they needed to hear, that the queen's sister, their favorite, had preserved her honor intact.

Long afterward Elizabeth wrote her own epilogue to this dangerous passage. She admitted having "tasted of the practices against her sister," having "had great occasion to hearken" to the designs of the conspirators, whose full "knavery" had never been revealed. Evidently there was more to Wyatt's rising than the royal judges ever discovered, and Elizabeth carried it on her conscience throughout her ordeal, knowing the full gravity of her burden. "I stood in danger of my life," she said simply, "my sister was so incensed against me."[1]

By mid-March a decision had become critical. Mary was due to leave for Windsor for the Easter holidays, then to go on to Oxford where her second Parliament would be held. Weeks of debate had not led to a consensus among the council; on the contrary, alignments were shifting and new factions forming in the aftermath of the rebellion, leaving even that astute judge of political maneuver, Renard, baffled as to the motives and goals of the courtiers. Once the queen left the capital there could be no question of leaving Elizabeth in informal custody in one of the royal palaces; the danger of a rising was too great. Once Mary left, London would be vulnerable, for the royal army consisted chiefly of the bands of fifty or a hundred soldiers that each of the councilors had under his command, and the council would follow the queen. Mary had promised to "make strict order and provision for the safety of the Tower" before she left, but what was she to do with her sister?

Renard suspected Gardiner of ambivalence, if not duplicity, in his handling of Elizabeth and Courtenay. Certainly Courtenay was "most gravely implicated and guilty": he had been an active conspirator, he had intrigued with the French king, and had sent treasonable messages by means of a "cipher cut upon a guitar." Yet the men Gardiner had chosen to be his keepers in the Tower were the earl's known partisans Southwell and Bourne, with the result that he was given special privileges and even a large and relatively comfortable room—without the council's approval.[2] And Gardiner seemed to have grown cool about Elizabeth's punishment, leading Renard to suspect that the chancellor now hoped she would not have to be put to death after all.

Yet what reason could Gardiner have—other than to foment unrest—for sparing the princess? The restive Londoners were eager for an opportunity to show their preference for her. Any clever rabble-rouser could draw them into the streets by the thousands. Early one morning, while the council deliberated and Renard knitted his brows over the unpredictable English, a tumult arose in the city. Word spread among the people that in one of the great houses a man and a woman were in direct communication with an angel.

The angel spoke through a wall, and could not be seen, but its oracular utterances proclaimed it divinely inspired—and Protestant.

"God save Queen Mary!" the man and woman cried out to the wall. No answer came.

"God save the Lady Elizabeth!"

"So be it," was the solemn reply.

"What is the mass?" the two interrogators went on.

"Idolatry," said the angel—to the cheers of the crowd gathering outside the house.

By mid-morning the phenomenon had drawn thousands of people, and Admiral Howard, together with Paget and the captain of the guard, had to bring a troop of horsemen to keep the crowd from becoming a mob. The man and woman who had claimed to communicate with the angel were seized, and with that the voice too silenced itself. It seemed clear that the instigators had hoped to agitate on behalf of Elizabeth and Courtenay, and to "excite the people against the queen, raise the heretics, and trouble the kingdom." Elizabeth knew of it, saw its obvious purpose, and hoped, though hope now dimmed, that Mary would not be irrevocably turned against her.[3]

The time for Mary's departure had come. Elizabeth must, at least, be taken into private custody by one of the nobles. To a man the councilors shrank from the task. She was too powerful a magnet for treason. No one could guard her and come away unscathed. After impassioned discussion the choices narrowed to one: Elizabeth must be imprisoned in the Tower.[4]

There was no formal charge of treason—indeed, there was no formal charge of any kind—but when the news was brought to her it must have been nearly as fearsome as news of a sentence of death.

Gardiner himself came to make the announcement, flanked by nineteen others of the council. He began by laying before her what circumstantial proof there was that she had been entangled in the plot, while she, remarkably resilient after three weeks of stress and illness, asserted her complete and unclouded innocence of every accusation he made. Then, "after long debating of matters," he informed her that it was the queen's will and pleasure that she should be taken to the Tower.[5]

She protested, even as the waves of shock passed over her, making her heart beat violently and her chest constrict. She was a true woman, she said. She trusted her highness would not conceive her to be otherwise, and given her high station and her honor, she did not deserve to have her fidelity rewarded so ungraciously.

There was no remedy, she was told. The queen was adamant; she should be taken to the Tower. The delegation left, "with their caps hanging over their eyes."

The machinery of degradation in rank went immediately into effect. Four of the councilors herded Elizabeth's servants into one room and sealed them there under guard. Six of them were allowed to continue to serve her —along with six new attendants hand-picked by the queen—but the rest were forbidden to go near their mistress, and were soon dismissed.

Guards poured in from all parts of the palace, taking up their stations in her apartments, watching her servants, installing themselves throughout the gardens and grounds. That night, as Elizabeth waited for the final summons to imprisonment, an enormous fire blazed in the great hall, warming the soldiers who had gathered there, while outside the windows a hundred guardsmen in white coats—tall, burly northerners—stood in their long rows to keep watch over the princess until she could be removed to her imprisonment the next day.

In the morning two councilors, Winchester and Sussex, came to escort her to her dread destination. In the long night hours she had had time to think. Had this been Mary's doing, or had her sister merely given in to the soft-spoken, dangerous ambassador of Charles V or, more likely, to the overbearing chancellor? She needed to see Mary, to confront her, tenderhearted as she knew her to be, with the enormity of what was being done in her name.

When the two councilors announced that the barge was waiting below and the tide ripe, Elizabeth surprised them by asking to be taken to the queen instead. Mary could not possibly know of this cruel and unjust order;

it had to be Gardiner's doing, motivated by spite and anger. The request was refused. Well then, Elizabeth said, if she could not see her sister, she must write to her. Winchester denied this request too, but Sussex, who through his Howard mother was Elizabeth's uncle, was lenient. Pen and paper were sent for, and the slow procedure of drafting a readable letter in a courtly hand got under way.

Historians have always pointed to the cleverness Elizabeth showed in composing this letter so slowly that, by the time she ended it, the river had fallen to its ebb and the bargemen waiting to convey her downriver to the Tower would not hazard the rushing waters under the bridge until it rose again with the next tide. But delaying, if possible, her delivery to the Tower was at most a minor goal; a few hours' postponement meant little in view of the peril she faced.

To emphasize the small triumph of the delay is to miss the larger purpose of the letter, which was to persuade Mary to see her, and to spare her life. All the carefully honed articulacy of her education was tested now as Elizabeth prepared her pen and, with the two councilors looking on, composed her first sentences.

"If anyone ever did try this old saying," she began, " 'that a king's word was more than another man's oath,' I most humbly beseech your majesty to verify it to me, and to remember your last promise and my last demand —that I be not condemned without answer and due proof." She meant to call to Mary's mind their last meeting, when on leaving for Ashridge Elizabeth had made Mary promise never to believe anything said against her sister without first giving her a chance to defend herself in person. It was a strong appeal to Mary's fair-mindedness, and to her conscience. "Without cause proved, I am by your council from you commanded to go unto the Tower—a place more wonted for a false traitor than a true subject —which though I know I deserve it not, yet in the face of all this realm appears that it is proved."

The injustice of her situation stung the more sharply in view of her complete innocence, which she asserted in the most heated terms. "I never practiced, counselled, nor consented to anything that might be prejudicial to your person any way or dangerous to the state by my means," she insisted. "I pray God I may die the shamefullest death that ever any died before if I may mean any such thing." God would judge her veracity, she wrote—and Mary could as well, by letting her answer in person the accusations brought against her—"and that before I go to the Tower, if it be possible."

"If it be possible"—there was wistfulness mixed with her assertive tone, and midway through the letter it occurred to Elizabeth that her sister might take offense at her forthright, argumentative language. "Let your conscience move your highness to pardon this my boldness," she went on, "which innocency procures me to do." Mary was too kind, she knew, to allow her to be "cast away" undeserving—yet how could she judge her deserts if she heard only one side of the story? A recent parallel came to mind—a particularly painful one.

"I have heard of many in my time cast away for want of coming to the presence of their prince; and in late days I heard my lord of Somerset [Edward Seymour] say, that if his brother had been suffered to speak with him he had never suffered. But the persuasions were made to him so great that he was brought in belief that he could not live safely if the admiral lived, and that made him give his consent to his death." The similarities were indeed striking: brother turned against brother, as sister was turned against sister now, the nagging councilors, exaggerating danger, inventing guilt, working relentlessly on the better nature and compassion of the ruler.

And yet Thomas Seymour had gone to his death, and Elizabeth might soon go to hers.

There was little left to say. Deflated, perhaps, by the grim recollection of Thomas Seymour's fate she fell back, for her final paragraph, on phrases she had learned in early childhood, formulas of submission meant to appease a parent's displeasure.

"Therefore, once again, kneeling with humbleness of heart, because I am not suffered to bow the knees of my body, I humbly crave to speak with your highness, which I would not be so bold as to desire if I knew not myself most clear, as I know myself most true."

Almost as an afterthought—and realizing, even as she wrote, that there was only a slight chance that Mary would agree to see her—Elizabeth added a brief response to the two most serious allegations of her guilt. Wyatt, she said, might have written her a letter, but she never got it; as to the letter found in the French ambassador's bag (which Gardiner had decided to suppress, claiming it had been mislaid), she had no idea how it got there, having never sent the ambassador any word or message of any kind.

The letter covered all of one sheet and part of a second. Rather than leave a blank space, she filled the blank area with diagonal lines. There must be no malicious tampering with this document, no attempt to turn an exoneration into a confession. She handed it to the councilors, who left to deliver it and, by failing to return soon, confirmed her hope that she had, after all, managed to outlast the tide.

Once the letter reached Mary there was an explosion of royal anger. How could the spineless councilors have let Elizabeth manipulate them so cleverly! Furious that her authority had been thwarted—and furious too, no doubt, that the distasteful order committing her sister to the Tower had to be given once again—Mary chastised Winchester and Sussex like wayward children. They would never have dared to disobey this way if her father were still alive, she declared angrily. She would not tolerate it any more than he had.

The eloquent, carefully worded letter lay unread during this tirade, its persuasions powerless in any case to mellow the queen's temper. Unfortunately for Elizabeth, far from moving Mary to pity her tactic had fed her sister's deep distrust, the unshakable distrust of a literal-minded, gullible and honest woman for a cleverer and far less scrupulous one. Mary had learned something of dissimulation (and a good deal about tides) during her brother's reign, when she had schemed to escape by sea and had suffered all the persecution that went with being the second person in the kingdom. In those days she herself had learned such trickery as Elizabeth was relying on now, and had reacted with sarcasm and assertive hauteur when confronted.

It was all familiar—and sordid. There would be no reconsideration. The two councilors were ordered to return the next morning and carry out their responsibility. (It was decided not to take advantage of the midnight tide; in the dark, with the riverbanks deserted, it would be too easy for the queen's enemies to kidnap Elizabeth.)

The next day, Palm Sunday, dawned dark and cheerless. There were religious solemnities throughout the city, the people having been ordered to "keep to the church, and carry their palms" to divert attention from the passage of the royal barge. But the palm fronds wilted in the rain, and the queen, who was taking part in one of the processions, had her pleasure spoiled by the weather.

This time Elizabeth went with Winchester and Sussex without argument, entering the barge at the water stairs along with the servants in her diminished household. As the boat moved downriver London Bridge loomed ahead, its expanse of shops and houses broken at intervals by poles surmounted by the decaying heads of traitors. Because of the rain the river was more hazardous than usual, the swift current frothing into treacherous rapids between the bridge's nineteen broad piers. The bargemen hesitated, backing water, fearful that their fragile craft would be overturned or sucked under or dashed to pieces as they shot the narrow passage. Finally they attempted it—only to find themselves in peril. "The stern of the boat struck upon the ground, the fall was so big, and the water was so shallow, that the boat being under the bridge, there stayed again awhile." But they negotiated their way through at last, earning the bonus that was always awarded "for a barge beneath the bridge."

To Elizabeth, dejected by frustration and by her sister's tacit rejection of her appeal for clemency, drowning might have seemed preferable to the imprisonment she faced. At twenty she was retracing the sorrowful way her mother had taken at twenty-nine, living out the unhappy fate frowning courtiers had predicted for her in childhood. That she had not been able somehow to outwit the enmity of the queen and her council made Elizabeth miserable, and robbed her of the courage to make a dignified entrance into the Tower.

The barge stopped before the water stairs of the fortress, where it had stopped, seventeen years earlier, to let Anne Boleyn disembark at her last moment of freedom. The servants and warders of the Tower were assembled to watch the princess's entrance, and some of them, the Protestant hagiographer John Foxe wrote, wept to see Elizabeth there and knelt and prayed for her preservation. According to Foxe, she deflated the solemnity of the occasion by complaining peevishly about wetting her shoes on the stairs, and then by sitting down in the rain and refusing to go farther, observing snappishly to her custodians that "it was better sitting here, than in a worse place, for God knows, I know not whither you will bring me."[6]

But her chagrin matched the finality of the proceedings, and could not disguise her dread. Once inside, with the massive iron doors locked and bolted behind her, she was "not a little discomforted and dismayed," as if the clanging metal tolled the hopeless passing of the life she had known.

12

The spring is past, and yet it hath not sprung;
The fruit is dead, and yet the leaves be green;
My youth is gone, and yet I am but young;
I saw the world, and yet I was not seen;
My thread is cut, and yet it is not spun;
And now I live, and now my life is done.

Soldiers, guardsmen, black-robed officials and prisoners on their way to trial or execution filled the Tower compound in the last week of March, 1554. Armorers at the White Tower attended to the heavy guns and harness that had been brought out for use against Wyatt and might at any moment be needed again. Carts laden with ordnance, shot, or provisions for the soldiers and their horses rumbled over the stones, their clatter competing with the ringing of carpenters' hammers and the shouts of workmen making repairs.

No one could remember when the Tower had held so many prisoners. Hundreds of Wyatt's followers had been arrested, dozens of them executed. Conspirators from Devon and elsewhere who had not marched on London were being hunted down and brought to justice daily, along with witnesses who could speak against them. Many of the chief plotters, among them Crofts and Throckmorton, who had had direct dealings with Elizabeth, and Wyatt himself, still lay in confinement awaiting judgment. The number of prisoners, though, had been reduced by two. Guildford Dudley, Northumberland's son, had been executed shortly after Wyatt's entry into London; his brothers, including Elizabeth's childhood intimate Robert Dudley, still lay at the queen's mercy. And Guildford's wife Jane Grey, a proven danger to Queen Mary, had also been judged too dangerous to live.

A special scaffold had been erected on Tower Green for Jane's execution, on the site reserved for royalty where Anne Boleyn and Catherine Howard had suffered in Elizabeth's childhood. Jane had died piously, pitiably; Mary had not pardoned her. Had the scaffold been taken down, Elizabeth asked anxiously, or was it still in place, ready for the queen's sister?

For the next two months Elizabeth was confined with her ladies in a damp, airless stone chamber in the Bell Tower whose high painted windows let in more cold than light. Once again she had been placed near the river, prey to the mist and fog that the physicians had advised her to avoid, and the fire in the high stone hearth (when she was allowed a fire) could not drive back the chill. Twenty years earlier Henry VIII had confined the aged Bishop Fisher in this room, and the old man had lain here, ill and neglected, until his clothes were in rags and his body a wraithlike waste. In the room immediately below Thomas More had spent his imprisonment, passing his hours praying for his misguided sovereign Henry, who had decided to proclaim himself head of the church so that Anne Boleyn's child and not Katherine of Aragon's should be heir to the throne. Both Fisher and More had died on Tower Hill, yet Katherine of Aragon's daughter had after all become queen; would Anne Boleyn's child now suffer as her mother had?

In those grim quarters, a prisoner among doomed prisoners, certain now that she had failed to move the queen to clemency, Elizabeth must often have thought on death. No doubt she turned the concept in her mind, recalling passages from Cicero or Jerome or the Bible, remembering classical metaphors, exhausting the store of teaching her tutors had instilled in her before she allowed herself to feel at the pit of her stomach the chilling reality of her danger. Then, her imagination engaged, she must have called up images of death: of condemned criminals mounting the scaffold, of last thoughts, last looks, of headless bodies, of eternity. Years later she confided to a French nobleman that the thought of the headsman's axe biting with butcherly strokes into her neck had so alarmed her that she made up her mind to request a French executioner, as her mother had, who would slice through her neck with one clean stroke of a sword.

But of course she might not die. She might simply be allowed to live on in perpetual confinement, for as long as Mary lived and longer, if Mary had a child. This dank room and the stinking garderobe with its three latrines might become home to her, until she learned to chart the months and seasons by the way the shadows fell across the walls and to ponder her passing youth as she waited, day after empty day, for the queen to die or the Spaniards to invade or another rebellion to break out in her name.

These speculations aside, there was little to occupy her thoughts. There were no visitors, and no news came. No books or letters got past her jailers, and if she asked old John Gage, the chamberlain and her immediate custodian, for any favor or privilege that might break her monotony she got nowhere. Gage, she judged, was "a good gentleman, yet by age and other his earnest business, he hath occasion to forget many things."[1]

After several weeks Elizabeth received an unexpected boon. She was given permission to walk along the battlements between the Bell Tower, where she was confined, and the Beauchamp Tower. The walkway was three feet wide and some seventy feet long, and offered the most dismal of views: Tower Green. Yet it meant fresher air and sunlight, and exercise. As often as it was permitted, Elizabeth paced the narrow leads in thoughtful silence, preceded and followed by the guards who never left her, taking watchful note of all that went on below her and trying to guess the meaning of what she saw.

There were executions. Wyatt died on April 11, Lord Thomas Grey, Jane Grey's uncle, on April 24. In May William Thomas, a scholar and writer whose works, in particular a history of Italy, Elizabeth had read as a young girl, was beheaded for plotting to assassinate the queen. But many of the other leading conspirators still lived, or so Elizabeth had no reason to doubt, among them her own servants and familiars. One of these, Nicholas Throckmorton, had actually been acquitted. To the astonishment of the queen and her councilors the jurors ("all heretics," Renard said) brought in a verdict of not guilty, and when Throckmorton was brought back to the Tower after his acquittal "the people with great joy raised shouts and threw their caps in the air," cheering not only for Elizabeth's servant but for Elizabeth's cause.

The triumph was not without its aftermath. "Proofs of collusion and ill affection" were discovered against the jurors, who were jailed for six months and heavily fined.[2]

But the tide of vengeance was turning. Renard might continue to frighten Mary with warnings of danger to her Spanish fiancé and predictions of a new rebellion, stouter than the first—he gave her Thucydides to read, in French, to toughen her attitude toward the rebels—yet during Holy Week she yielded to the entreaties of some council members and pardoned more than a dozen of the gentlemen who had taken part in the rising, and shortly afterward it was noted that Elizabeth's portrait, taken down at the time of her disgrace, had been restored to its place beside the queen's own.[3]

Barring new evidence, or a more widespread rebellion, it now seemed certain that Elizabeth would not be put to death, even though Mary had reason to believe, from the most recent reports of her unsparing interrogators, that her sister had actually gathered arms and provisions at a fortified house "for the purpose of rebelling with the others."[4] There were new proposals for putting Elizabeth out of the way, removing her as a threat to Prince Philip while avoiding continued harsh imprisonment: she should be sent to the court of Charles V's tough, athletic sister Mary, regent of the Netherlands; she should be sent to Pontefract Castle in far-off Yorkshire, scene of the imprisonment and murder of Richard II; she should be married, either abroad, as Renard urged, or in England, to Courtenay, who had been freed from imprisonment in May and taken under guard to a castle in the north, distant from London.[5]

In the second month of Elizabeth's captivity Mary's authority collapsed as a vocal minority of her people began unmercifully to mock her and open warfare broke out among her councilors. Angelic voices supporting the Protestants, seditious pamphlets in the streets (one flung into the palace kitchens), loud and violent outcries over the restoration of the mass and continued mutterings that Elizabeth would be preferable to her sister—all these helped to reduce the queen "to a state of perplexity." Wyatt, despised and reviled when he was brought in chains to the Tower in February, had become a macabre hero since his death. People ran forward to dip their handkerchiefs in the blood that flowed at his beheading, and afterward, when his head was set up for display with those of his convicted fellow-conspirators, someone snatched it from its pole and spirited it away, in defiance of the queen's command.

At the council table all trace of unity had evaporated. Mary's explicit orders were stiffly carried out; for the rest, all the needful work of government was forgotten amid private quarrels. Paget and his allies were arming themselves, and scheming, so Renard heard, to kidnap their bitter enemy the chancellor. Gardiner, for his part, was trumpeting danger and insisting that Mary send Paget and the others to the Tower, meanwhile (as rumor had it) raising an armed force of his own and turning one of his castles into a fully armed fortress. Day by day soldiers of indeterminate allegiance rode into the capital, took lodgings, and strode up and down in the streets as if waiting for an imminent call to war. They were not the soldiers of the queen; whose they might be, and what havoc they might create, gave Mary much distress.[6]

Then in mid-May someone at last was found to take private charge of Elizabeth. He was Sir Henry Bedingfield, governor of the Tower, knight marshal of the army, captain of the queen's guards and a privy councilor as well. Loyal, stolid, completely unimaginative, Bedingfield was a reliable soldier and an old-fashioned Catholic gentleman besides. Mary had done much for him, for in addition to his offices he had been given some of the lands Wyatt had forfeited on his imprisonment. Clearly Bedingfield owed the queen a favor, yet when Gardiner approached him to ask that he undertake the heavy responsiblity of guarding the heir to the throne he hung back. It took all Gardiner's persuasiveness and glib eloquence— markedly inarticulate himself, Bedingfield was much in awe of those who spoke well—to win him over. But in the end, Bedingfield wrote later, "by words of marvelous effect, comprising both the queen's commandment that I should enter into it, and his earnest request," Gardiner won him over, and on May 19, nearly two months after she entered the Tower, Elizabeth left, escorted by a hundred of her keeper's blue-coated guardsmen.[7]

Though exceedingly deferential in manner toward the princess Bedingfield kept a nervous eye on her from the moment they embarked for Windsor, where they were to rest on the first night of their journey. They traveled by water in order to attract as little attention as possible, yet no sooner had they started upriver than a deafening explosion shattered the quiet and sent Londoners running out into the streets to see what was going on. It was the gunners of the Steelyard signaling their support for Elizabeth by the most disruptive means at hand, and it had the result of turning the unobtrusive, unannounced exit of the princess from the Tower into a noisy parade.

To Bedingfield's dismay, the festive atmosphere grew in intensity the farther they got from the capital. Elizabeth rode in an open litter, and as she passed along the country lanes, bordered by flowering hedges and sweet-smelling May roses, crowds gathered to watch her pass by. Villagers harvesting hay in the fields paused in their labor and came eagerly to see the princess. Only the boldest shouted "God save your grace!" in open defiance of Bedingfield and his soldiery, but the ringers in nearly every village pulled a joyous peal of bells and everywhere people came forward with gifts in great abundance: flowers, sweets, cakes and sugary biscuits. At Rycote, where Lord Williams of Thame showed Elizabeth and her party hospitality, there was feasting and celebration more suited to a reigning monarch than to a suspected conspirator on her way to further confinement. Bedingfield glowered disapprovingly, but did not interfere. It was for the queen's councilors to dictate the restrictions on her sister's activity, and they had not foreseen this; he would write to them about it, but nothing more.

At last they reached their destination: the dilapidated medieval palace of Woodstock, a monument of crumbling stone and creaking casements rising from a marshy riverbed.

It was an historic place, a hunting lodge for the Norman kings and the site of a famous romance. Henry II had kept his mistress Rosamund

Clifford at Woodstock, and the ruins of Rosamond's Bower—"many strong and strange walls and windings, and a dainty, clear, square-paved well," as one seventeenth-century visitor described them—were still to be seen in the palace grounds. But Woodstock was as undesirable as it was old. "The place is unwholesome," Robert Cecil wrote half a century later, "all the house standing upon springs. It is unsavory, for there is no savor but cows and pigs."[8] The unique distinction of the site, a prodigious echo which could boom back two shouted lines of Vergilian poetry (or half a round), was no compensation for the mud and swamp grass and stench. Bedingfield must have blanched slightly at the sight of the old lodge. How would he make the imperious princess comfortable here?

More important, how would he make her safe? If he was her keeper, ensuring her continued captivity, Bedingfield was also Elizabeth's guardian. She was as vulnerable to assassination or other harm as the queen was, and it troubled Bedingfield that in all the house he could find only four heavy locks to fasten to the doors.

The palace itself proved to be so far decayed that it could not be used. Only the gatehouse, built in the reign of Elizabeth's grandfather Henry VII, was fit to house her. Of its three rooms besides the chapel, one was taken by guardsmen, leaving only a decorated gothic council chamber and one other room for Elizabeth and her servants. Here, amid furnishings and tapestries supplied by Queen Mary, under an ornate carved ceiling of Irish oak, painted blue and gilded, like the ceiling of the great banqueting hall at Hampton Court, Elizabeth was to spend an indeterminate—and seemingly interminable—imprisonment.[9]

Her day began as the morning light fell on her sister's tapestries and lit the gold stars painted on the ceiling. She rose, was dressed, attended a morning service in the chapel and then sent for either Bedingfield or his deputy Lord Chandos to guard her as she walked in the garden. Her dinner —the main meal of the day—was brought in at mid-morning, and eaten in some state, though when her gentleman usher Cornwallis asked Bedingfield for permission to drape a cloth of estate (symbol of royalty) over her dining table the keeper refused. There had been no word about a cloth of estate from the privy councilors.

During the long, often wet afternoons Elizabeth talked with her attendants, especially Elizabeth Sands, a favorite companion who had been with her in the Tower and now shared her restricted life at Woodstock. Then she read (though very few books passed Bedingfield's suspicious scrutiny), or did embroidery, or retreated into private thoughts. Contemporary tradition records that in her idleness, brooding on the queen's lack of evidence against her, Elizabeth took a diamond and scratched out a couplet on a windowpane:

> Much suspected, by me
> Nothing proved can be
> Quoth Elizabeth, prisoner

But though nothing could be, or had been, proved against her as yet she had not been found innocent either, and bore the weight of suspicion. At the very end of the sixteenth century, when the story of Elizabeth's captivity had entered into the popular mythology of her reign, a German visitor to England recorded some Latin lines in sonorous dactylic hexameters— Vergilian meter—which, he was told, Elizabeth had written on a shutter. They bemoaned "wavering fortune," which had snatched all joys from her and left her in wretched bondage. She, though guiltless, had no liberty while others, criminals deserving death, ran free. The last line was a challenge, almost a curse: Father Jove, she prayed, blunt the weapons of my enemies, and let them feel the sting of my lance in return![10]

An English translation of Saint Paul's Epistles that belonged to Elizabeth at Woodstock has been preserved. In it, in a blank space, she wrote a passage that gave a glimpse of her meditative life. "I walk many times into the pleasant fields of the holy Scriptures," she wrote, "where I pluck up the goodlisome herbs of sentences by pruning, eat them by reading, chew them by musing, and lay them up at length in the high seat of memory, by gathering them together. That so having tasted the sweetness, I may the less perceive the bitterness of this miserable life."[11] On the silken corners of the book mottoes are embroidered in gold thread: "Heaven my Fatherland," "Christ the Goal of Life," "Blessed is He Who, Reading the Riches of Scripture, Turns Those Words into Deeds." On one side a star has been worked in gold, and in a circle surrounding it, the words *"Vicit omnia pertinax virtus E.C. [Elisabetha Captiva]."* "Tenacious Virtue Overcomes All. Elizabeth the Captive."[12]

At five each afternoon it came to be Elizabeth's custom to summon Bedingfield and walk in the garden or orchard again, he keeping a respectful distance while she strolled, sometimes moodily, sometimes with a preoccupied air, through the grounds. On her return from her walk Elizabeth ate a light meal and, most likely, attended vespers. Then she retired for the night, her women setting aside the underclothes she had worn that day for the laundress. (The princess's underwear was the only thing to enter or leave the gatehouse that was not "viewed and searched" by Bedingfield or one of his brothers, who formed part of the guard. The regulations called for "all linen brought to her grace clean by the laundress to be delivered to the queen's women. And they to see all the foul linen delivered to the said laundress."[13])

In the first days of this regimen danger disrupted the entire household. A fire broke out in the ceiling of the chamber immediately below Elizabeth's, and though her grooms rushed to put it out, and no harm was done, Bedingfield became alarmed. Had an arsonist got past his guards? A "worshipful knight of Oxfordshire" who happened to be present thought so, and the keeper took warning.

There was reason enough to be concerned, for it was not possible to seal the princess off entirely from the outside world, and no one who came and went from the gatehouse could be trusted absolutely. A former servant of Elizabeth's arrived with a gift of freshwater fish from a nearby estate. He came again, this time bringing pheasants. Both times he stayed so long talking with the other servants that Bedingfield sent for him and questioned him closely about his activities, telling him not to come again or to send any more presents, and sent him away.

Another incident caused more concern. John Fortescue, son-in-law of Elizabeth's cofferer Thomas Parry and an Oxford scholar, sent the princess some books and letters, and Bedingfield, thoroughly distrustful (books and letters being ideal vehicles for ciphered messages), refused to let Elizabeth have them. Furthermore, Fortescue's letters used puzzling phrases "which seem to us to be ambiguous and to have some secret meaning in them," the keeper wrote to the councilors, and when the queen heard of this she sensed intrigue.

Mary ordered Bedingfield to send to Oxford for Fortescue and to grill him about the precise meaning of those ambiguous words—and then to give him "a sharp check for his presumption." The keeper did as he was told, only to find that the impudent Oxford man talked rings around him, leaving him flatfooted and befuddled. Bedingfield did his best, but found "certain diffuse words uttered by the same Fortescue" to be "so much in the Latin phrase that they passed his Norfolk understanding." In the end he had to let the suspect go with a plain warning, and the meaning of the strange phrases remained hidden.

That Fortescue was related to Parry made him automatically a doubtful character in Bedingfield's eyes, for the cofferer was making trouble of several kinds. He was not reimbursing Bedingfield for his expenses, he was keeping company with such disloyal men as Francis Verney, Elizabeth's former servant and a born conspirator, and he was conducting himself indecorously at the Sign of the Bull in Woodstock, the tavern where he was lodged. "By anything that I can learn," Bedingfield wrote judiciously, "I am not persuaded to have a good opinion of him."[14]

In all the skepticism and concern the books themselves were nearly forgotten. Elizabeth languished with nothing to read, nothing to challenge her wits or improve her mind. She thrived on intellectual stimulation; more than just a taste, she had acquired a thirst for classical literature. Deprived of study she fretted, her hours as empty as they were long. Then Mary, who in her father's reign had made her own sorrow and bitter isolation more bearable by reading the classics late into the night, decided to extend the same privilege to Elizabeth. Books sent by outsiders were to be looked on with apprehension, but if Elizabeth herself asked Bedingfield "for the having of any book that is honest and sufferable to read or pass her time withal," she was to have it. Parry's books—a volume of the Psalms and other "hymns of the church" and Cicero's stoic reflections on duty, *De Officiis*—were left in limbo.[15]

The summer proved to be wet and miserable, "the greatest rain that came these two months in these parts." Torrents of rain made the orchards and gardens an unhealthy bog, and Elizabeth spent her entire day in the dark gatehouse, troubled now by a flareup of the chronic swelling of her face. Upsets in her household staff were vexing. Her gentleman usher Cornwallis developed an "unclean leg" and had to curtail his duties. Replacements were sought, but one after another they proved unsuitable; one was even more ill than Cornwallis, another was deaf (and enfeebled, Elizabeth confided to Bedingfield privately, "with a pitiful disease which I will not name"), a third was already in service to an important lady of the court. Diseased leg or no, Cornwallis had to be kept.

Changes in the princess's serving women, though, were much harder to bear. Mary had given orders that her sister be served at Woodstock "in such good and honorable sort as may be agreeable to our honor and her estate and degree." Finding one of the women, Elizabeth Sands, to be "a person of an evil opinion, and not fit to remain about our said sister's person," Mary abruptly ordered her dismissed. No appeal was possible, and at two o'clock one afternoon the princess was forced to part from her favorite companion. They said their goodbyes, "not without great mourning both of my lady's grace and Sands," and the spirited young gentlewoman was delivered to Thomas Parry, who had promised to see to it that she was put into the custody of relatives.

Bedingfield had disapproved of Elizabeth Sands, and even after she left he feared her. He wrote to the queen's council about her, calling her "a woman meet to be looked unto for her obstinate disposition." So mercurial and volatile a personality as Elizabeth Tudor's required placid, good-natured gentlewomen around her—or else those who shared the queen's sympathies intimately. The princess took the initiative in suggesting two women to replace the friend she had lost. Mary refused them. Then could she at least have one of them? Elizabeth asked. No, came the reply: she was to have Elizabeth Marbury, Mary's particular choice and one that was "clearly against her [Elizabeth's] desire."[16]

Frustrated and lonely, increasingly "vexed with the swelling in the face and other parts of her body," Elizabeth confronted Bedingfield with angry accusations.

Responding to her summons, the keeper found her "in the most unpleasant sort that ever I saw her since her coming from the Tower."

"I have at divers times spoken to you to write to my lords [of the council] certain of my requests," she said sharply, "and you never make me answer to any of them. I think you make none of my lords privy to my suit, but only my lord chamberlain"—John Gage, whose forgetful ways she had learned to know in the Tower.

Bedingfield asserted, as deferentially as he could, that he always wrote to the full council and not to any individuals privately, and reminded her that the councilors were at present preoccupied with the coming of Prince Philip and might have to be approached more than once before they gave a reply.

"Well," she said, "I require you to do thus much for me, to write unto my said lords and to desire them on my behalf to be means unto the queen's majesty, to grant me leave to write unto her highness with mine own hand. And in this," she added peremptorily, "I pray you let me have answer as soon as you can."

"I shall do for your grace that I am able to do," Bedingfield said gravely, "which is to write to my said lords, and then it must needs rest in their honorable considerations whether I shall have answer or none."

So Bedingfield reported their conversation. Within a few days he received word that Mary would allow her sister to write to her, "according to her desire."

At this juncture, Elizabeth's powers of charm and ingratiation failed her utterly. Instead of appealing to Mary's charity, soothing her fears and disarming her with soft and subservient language, Elizabeth wrote a letter that was harshly argumentative, cerebral and legalistic. She tried again, as she had in the "tide letter" written on the day she was to be taken to the Tower, to refute all that the conspirators had confessed against her.

But as she might have predicted, this approach brought the same reaction from Mary that the earlier letter had. Far from being persuaded by her sister's raw denials Mary felt offended and ill used. Elizabeth had not only insulted Mary's intelligence by her crude refutations, she had shown ingratitude for the "clemency and favor" Mary had so far shown her—

clemency far greater, Mary claimed, than was customary under the circumstances. After all, Mary did not need "plain direct proof" to be convinced of her sister's guilt; she already had "probable conjectures and other suspicions and arguments" enough.

Further letters from Elizabeth would be futile, Mary wrote to Bedingfield, until she had squared her conscience with God and ceased to entrench herself further in defensive lies. "Wherefore our pleasure is not to be hereafter any more molested with such her [sic] disguised and colorable letters."[17]

The keeper's heart must have sunk as he read the queen's letter. He would have to deliver Mary's icy reply, and he could imagine Elizabeth's stormy reaction. To protect himself he copied out Mary's letter, word after difficult word, in his own crabbed handwriting, and when he went to read it to Elizabeth he took along his better educated servant Tomio, just as he had when he faced the supercilious Fortescue.

Together they knelt before the princess, and Bedingfield read the letter in full.

Elizabeth cried out in dismay, and asked him to read it again. Still on his knees, he did so.

The final sentence stung. "I note especially," Elizabeth remarked ruefully, "to my great discomfort (which I shall nevertheless willingly obey) that the queen's majesty is not pleased that I should molest her highness with any more of my colorable letters, which, although they be termed colorable, yet, not offending the queen's majesty, I must say for myself, that it was the plain truth, even as I desire to be saved afore God almighty, and so let it pass."

Having uttered this rather ragged counter-refutation, Elizabeth asked Bedingfield to take down in writing her verbal reply to the privy council, and when he begged to be excused, she exploded.

Even the prisoners in the Tower were allowed to send word to the council, she insisted angrily, yet he had the audacity to refuse. They were at an impasse, and the keeper, having had enough of his unpleasant duties for one day, made an excuse and left.

But Elizabeth would not leave him be. The next morning, even though the sky was heavy with rain clouds, she summoned him to escort her on her morning walk. She had a speech ready.

"I remember yesterday you refused utterly to write on my behalf unto my lords of the council," she began, "and therefore if you continue in that mind still, I shall be in worse case than the worst prisoner in Newgate, for they be never gainsaid in the time of their imprisonment by one friend or other to have their cause opened and sued for." She went on, ticking off her points one by one as she made the rounds of the sodden garden with Bedingfield in tow. It was beginning to rain, yet she argued on, emphasizing that without the keeper's advocacy she would be bereft of help.

"I must needs continue this life without all hope worldly, wholly resting to the truth of my cause, and that before God to be opened, arming myself against whatsoever shall happen, to remain the queen's true subject as I have done during my life."

Both Elizabeth and the long-suffering Bedingfield were getting damp, and she seemed to be getting nowhere.

"It waxeth wet," she said, impatiently and abruptly, "and therefore I will depart to my lodging again." Without making a reply, he escorted her back to the gatehouse.[18]

On through the summer Elizabeth went on wrestling stubbornly with her obstinate keeper and her mistrustful sister, refusing to resign herself to what was becoming a semi-permanent captivity. She was not accustomed to staying in one lodging for very long; normally the household moved on at intervals of a few weeks so that the palace or manor could be sweetened by a thorough airing and a fresh carpeting of rushes. By early fall the gatehouse must have reeked like a London street—only worse, for the house was shut as tightly as possible against the rain and the occupants had nowhere else to go. To Elizabeth, who hated stale air and bad odors, the stench was a cruel punishment. She redoubled her efforts to free herself.

She persuaded Bedingfield to write on her behalf, in a more fervent, personal tone, beseeching the council "upon very pity, considering her long imprisonment and restraint of liberty," to either grant her a formal trial with specific charges or to allow her to see the queen. She arranged an impressive display of piety, calling Bedingfield into the chapel and swearing in his presence, before receiving the sacrament, that she had never taken part in any scheme dangerous to Mary's person. She had her chaplain Young declare to Bedingfield that her religious observances were Catholic in every respect, and her love for the mass beyond question.

For a time, Elizabeth allowed herself to be—or to seem—optimistic. Bedingfield reported that she was "in quiet state," and that she told him she had hope that Mary's "clemency and mercy toward her" would soon bring a reprieve. But though the queen unbent slightly and allowed her sister to write to her, another source of irritation soon arose. Elizabeth's chaplain, Mary discovered, was repeating the litany in English instead of Latin; this unorthodox practice must stop. Still, in all, Mary did appear to be mellowing slightly, made more compassionate, it seemed, by her happiness as a new bride. She was "not unmindful" of Elizabeth's cause, Mary wrote, early in October. If Elizabeth's deeds bore out her words of fidelity and religious devotion, there would be a "further consideration" of her current plight.

By this time, though, Mary's own deeds were belying her words. She had given orders that Woodstock be provisioned for the winter. She was looking after the fuel supply (wood in sufficient quantity to warm the servants and soldiers was simply not to be had in the immediate neighborhood of the palace, whatever the cost), and had agreed to undertake badly needed repairs to the gatehouse. Clearly she meant her sister to remain in this uncomfortable establishment for many months to come.

The nights were now so long and cold that the soldiers could not stand watch as they had during the summer. Elizabeth and her servants shivered in their lodgings, even during the day, for the wind gusted through the tattered roof and broken windowpanes until "neither she nor any that attend upon her could abide for cold." At times, she confessed, her fingers were so chilled she could not seal a letter.

The harsh weather did nothing to help her swollen face and limbs. The disease had become unusually troublesome during the summer, but Mary's physician Dr. Owen had recommended nothing more than a carefully restricted diet, summer being the wrong season for administering medicines. In October she had been bled from her arm and foot, but she continued to suffer. The longer she was exposed to the chill, the doctors said, the longer her "cold and waterish humors" might be expected to vex her.

In November a cri de coeur from Woodstock arrived at Mary's court. Bedingfield, who had long since begun to ask that he be relieved of his responsibilities, begged for aid. He had hardly left the palace for more than a few hours since his service began, and needed badly to get away. Besides, the job threatened to bankrupt him. The soldiers had not been paid for nearly three months, and the people of Woodstock who were quartering them, "being very poor persons," could not feed them on their own; Bedingfield had been paying the town victualers out of his own pocket, and had recently begun to borrow from a London moneylender. The weather was becoming worse and the entire establishment was a shambles. The thought of spending an entire winter there must have increased Bedingfield's "care of mind and travail of body" tenfold.

Elizabeth added her own message to the keeper's despairing letter. Could Mary not move her, she pleaded, to a palace nearer London, or to one of her own houses where she might be kept under guard? If not for her sake, then for the sake of "the poor men which are daily sore travailed with extreme long journeys this winter weather and days, in making the carriage of provisions to serve here."[19] One severe storm and there would be flooding so great no carts could come through at all.

The need was urgent. What would happen if one day the provisions ceased? But Mary, miles away in the milder southeast, had even more pressing thoughts. After twenty years of apostasy, England was being reunited with the church of Rome. And after four months of blissful marriage, she herself was about to become a mother.

13

When I was fair and young and favour graced me,
Of many was I sought their mistress for to be,
But I did scorn them all and answered them therefore,
Go, go, go, seek some other where,
  Importune me no more.

All was happy confusion at Hampton Court when Elizabeth arrived "very privately" at the end of April, 1555. The palace was filling with ladies and gentlewomen, summoned to be present at the queen's delivery, and each of them brought with her personal servants, maids, lapdogs, and trunks of voluminous finery. Above the hubbub of female voices came the urgent sounds of household servants carrying linens and candles and other necessities for the guests and for the royal nursery; the storehouses and attics of the palace had been ransacked to provide enough chests and tables and candlesticks that were not "old and broken" to make the ladies comfortable.

The queen's time was near. She had made her formal withdrawal from court weeks earlier, and had taken to her bed (with brief periods of exercise allowed each day) to rest and pray for a liveborn son. In the opinion of the midwives—whose opinion, suddenly, had become more precious than gold—the child would assuredly be born before the ninth of May.

There was no question why Elizabeth had been brought to court. Her status as heir to the throne, her vulnerability as the object of rumors, plots and counterplots lent great consequence to her presence. Yet amid all the excitement surrounding the queen's impending delivery Elizabeth's arrival was unheralded, and with her tiny retinue of three or four women and the same number of menservants she settled into her assigned apartments—which happened to be those of the duke of Alva, King Philip's mentor, then away in London—to await, with everyone else, the birth of the prince.

She saw no one at all, not even the resident of the neighboring apartments, her cousin Reginald Pole. They had never met, Pole having been out of the country studying and then in exile since long before Elizabeth was born. Yet their lives were closely intertwined, for it was through Pole's opposition to Henry VIII's marriage to Anne Boleyn that the cardinal had lost his brothers, his aged mother, even his innocent young nephew to imprisonment or the executioner's axe. It was no wonder Pole avoided Elizabeth; she, on the other hand, may well have been curious to see the celebrated cousin whom Queen Mary counted on to bring the English back to the Roman faith. For he was very much a celebrity, whose melancholy features, tinged with beatific simplicity, were well known in humanist circles. He was also, so many said, a living saint, and had missed becoming pope by the narrowest of electoral margins.

Yet if Pole was avoiding Elizabeth, so were the dozens of councilors, royal officials and other courtiers who congregated nervously in anterooms to exchange news and to speculate about the queen's condition. They had become accustomed to the presence of the Spaniards—though resentment continued to flare, and swordfights were not infrequent—and to having a Spanish consort for their queen. Yet they were still wary of foreign tyranny, and even as they fawned on Philip they gathered in fevered knots to hatch plots against him; the boldest among them had from time to time cherished hopes of marrying their sons to Elizabeth, in case chance should after all bring her to the throne. Mary's pregnancy had disconcerted these hopes, and though their plotting continued, the courtiers, taking their cue from Pole and from the notable absence of ceremony and attention paid to Elizabeth, kept their distance from the princess.

Their wariness was well advised. A new and oppressive religious climate was abroad in England in the spring of 1555, and marital and political alignments with Protestants (or crypto-Protestants, as Mary believed Elizabeth to be) came under added scrutiny. For if some welcomed the rigorous and brutal suppression of Protestant heresy, as they did the imminent arrival of a Catholic heir to the throne, as the consummate vindication of Mary's reign and of her faith, others felt chill anger as the dark pall of religious violence descended.

In February the first burnings of Protestants had begun. Men and women who disputed the teachings of the Roman church and denied the authority of the pope were brought from prison, tied to stakes, and burned alive as crowds of onlookers watched in horrified sorrow. Most of the victims were young—a few far too young to fully comprehend the opinions they were accused of holding—yet many of them died, so their coreligionists said, with a transcendent dignity that made the tragedy of their deaths sublime. Nothing, not the slow agony of death by fire, not the spectacle of blackened limbs and charred faces, not even fearsome torture could tarnish the sanctity of these martyrs. And the longer the burnings continued, the more staunch English Protestantism became.

And it was no secret that the Protestants looked to Elizabeth as their ultimate deliverer. Pamphlets proclaimed her the rightful queen, and denounced Mary for her persecution of the true church. Ballads, scurrilous libels, broadsheets and political writings of every kind set forth the usurped power of the queen and her husband and prayed earnestly for Elizabeth's delivery from her captivity at Woodstock. Nightly meetings were held at which, after the performance of "heretic rites," believers would "pray for Elizabeth's freedom and prosperity."[1] The believers were seized and imprisoned, yet the meetings continued, and as the queen's pregnancy approached its term the Protestant campaign increased in intensity and shrillness.

The streets of the capital were littered with printed indictments of Mary —portrayed as a monstrous matron suckling a brood of parasitical Spaniards —and optimistic poems anticipating Elizabeth's accession.

False rumors were given out: that Mary was dead, that King Edward was still alive and had been seen in Kent or Surrey, that the queen was not pregnant after all, or that her ill-omened pregnancy had come to a grotesque end, with the delivery of a lifeless "mole or lump of flesh" too gruesome to be described.

The propaganda (and the burnings) bred seditious talk, and not talk alone but violence, for there were assassins and arsonists among the Protestants as well as martyrs. As always, Elizabeth was implicated, for one of the most widespread of the libelous pamphlets was attributed to her Italian master Castiglione, a resolute opponent of Queen Mary who had been imprisoned at least once before for a similar crime. A thousand copies of this pamphlet had been gathered in the city and brought to the lord mayor, and suspicion pointed to the Italian, and through him to Elizabeth's circle of servants and confidants, and finally to the princess herself.

All this and much more weighed on Elizabeth as, within a day or so of her arrival at court, word spread that her sister had been delivered. Almost before the news reached the courtiers it was known in London, where cheering crowds built bonfires in celebration and the bells of the city rang an enthusiastic welcome to the prince. In their eagerness to believe the report even the royal officials were quick to confirm it—though none of them had actually seen the queen or her child—and by midday the clergy of London had begun to process through the streets singing hymns of thanksgiving, while ships embarking for Flanders carried the good news to the imperial court.[2]

It was all a mistake, of course—not a hoax, exactly, or if so not a hoax emanating from the queen's chamber or her council board. The false rumor was corrected, and the truth spread slowly through the court and capital, leaving the celebrants long-faced and irritable. The waiting began again.

For Elizabeth the stress, the unsettling excitement of the false rumor was compounded in the following week by other pressures. She was the subject of much discussion among the queen's councilors, who urged her, as much (they said) for her own safety as for the good order of the realm, to leave immediately for Flanders. Her continued presence in England could only give rise to further trouble, for once Mary's child was born the Protestants, robbed of their hope for Elizabeth's accession, would surely rebel.

Prince Philip, though, thought otherwise, wanting Elizabeth near at hand in case Mary died in childbirth or in case the baby was born dead or defective. Whatever happened, she was more useful to him nearby, with the hundreds of guardsmen at the palace and in the vicinity as a cordon between her and the rebels.

Philip's view prevailed, though what might happen after Mary's delivery was much in doubt. Glad as she was to be released from captivity (as was her captor Bedingfield, who called his discharge "the joyfullest news he had ever heard"), Elizabeth must have been fearful of the reasoning behind it. Had she been brought to court merely as a means of keeping her out of rebel hands until the Catholic succession was assured, only to be returned to straiter imprisonment, perhaps in the Tower, once the queen and her child were out of danger? Should she flee to the continent (as many of her supporters were demanding of her), joining the widening stream of Protestant exiles leaving England and trusting that, once she was out of sight, Mary might grant her a tacit pardon?

Or was all hope vain, in light of what had gone on at Woodstock in recent months? Since January the dilapidated old hunting lodge had been riddled with conspiracy. Every month a servant of Elizabeth's was arrested for plotting or seized for questioning about "seditious words" or suspicious behavior, and spies, agents of the French and other nefarious personages haunted the vicinity. Elizabeth did her best to maintain an appearance of pious, maidenly innocence as plots swirled about her, attending mass faithfully every day, obtaining the papal indulgences made available to the faithful of England by the pope after the reunion with Rome, and spending long secluded hours in prayer. Yet as Bedingfield reported, her solitary devotions offered a pretext for secret conferences with her treasurer and purveyor, through whom, he felt certain, she maintained close contact with those who sought to overthrow the queen in her name.[3]

Until now, Elizabeth knew, she had enjoyed some measure of immunity by the mere fact that Mary had no other apparent successor. But once a son was born to Mary—or even a daughter, with the hope of sons to come in the future—Elizabeth would lose all protection. She would become expendable. More than that: she would become a dangerous rival to the royal infant, a rival who would have to be eliminated.

The days passed, and the midwives and physicians shook their heads in disbelief. The ninth of May, the latest day they had predicted for the birth, came and went uneventfully, and they hurried to make fresh calculations. Evidently there had been an error. The child, they said now, would be born either on May 23 or at the time of the new moon on June 4 or 5.

Pale and sickly, Mary sat on a cushion on the floor of her chamber for hours at a time, unwilling to see any but her attendant women, dejected by the peculiar course her pregnancy was taking. She had all the usual signs of approaching motherhood, yet now her belly was beginning to deflate, and though one of her doctors assured her that this too was normal, and meant that delivery was near, doubt began to nag at her.

Meanwhile Elizabeth lost no time in cultivating her princely brother-in-law, knowing, or guessing, that her best chance of protection against her sister lay with him.

After nearly a year in England Prince Philip of Spain had resigned himself to the drawbacks of his adopted kingdom: to his delicate role as prince consort, to the English nobles and courtiers, who seemed to him by turns churlish and groveling and treacherous, to the coy spinster he had married and somehow managed to impregnate. He bore these indignities —as he did the painful bowel disorders that harassed him nearly every day —with little outward complaint, but there was a melancholy cast to his fine features, and the inordinate delay in his wife's delivery was trying his patience sorely and upsetting his sour stomach.

The pleasing company of his attractive, redhaired sister-in-law was a delightful diversion for Philip as he waited for news of the queen's labor. At twenty-one Elizabeth was nearer his own age of twenty-eight than his careworn, middle-aged wife, and though he took full cognizance of her cleverness and capability for deceit, Philip allowed himself to savor the charm which she, in turn, lavished on him and on his Spanish favorites.[4]

For even to Philip's dull eyes Elizabeth seemed unique. Mercurial, waif-like in her slightness and in the faint look of alarm that hovered around her eyes, she was at the same time a hoyden, an imperious royal brat of incorrigible arrogance. She was blunt, unladylike, impatient with the rounded edges of gentility. Yet she was anything but unfeminine; she had a grace and sensuality all her own, focused in the long, fine hands and thin fingers she wafted about conspicuously as she talked.

Her face had too much character, too much alertness to be called beautiful, yet so strong was her fascination that the pliant, unimaginative beauties of the court paled beside her. One imperfection marked Elizabeth's appearance throughout her sister's reign. Her smooth complexion took on a yellowish tinge—a sign of the jaundice which plagued her—and the Venetian ambassador Michiel called her "olive-skinned."[5]

But the defect was forgotten as soon as she spoke, for then the full force of her intellect was revealed, dazzling in its virtuosity and startling in its breadth. Unlike Mary, who had channeled her outstanding mental gifts, as she had all her other energies, along personal and confessional lines, Elizabeth had never ceased to cultivate her mind, and the schoolgirl pedant she had been was becoming replaced by a brilliantly learned young woman.

Elizabeth's exceptional attainments as a linguist were beyond the understanding of the thick-tongued Philip, whose only fluent language was his native Spanish and whose few lumpish words of English drew wan smiles from the English courtiers. But he could see as clearly as anyone how easily and how well she spoke Italian, and how "from vanity" she invariably addressed Italians only in their own tongue. And he had it on good authority that Elizabeth's Greek, which she studied assiduously, was on a much more advanced level than the queen's.

But what most struck Philip, and indeed everyone who saw the princess, was her resemblance to her father Henry VIII. "She prides herself on her father and glories in him," Michiel wrote of Elizabeth in 1557, and she loved to hear people say (as they often did) that she was much more like him than Mary was.[6] Likenesses of the old king were everywhere—in portraits, in images painted on jewelry or furniture, or woven into hangings, in the nostalgic recollections of the courtiers who had served him. Hampton Court was his monument; so were Greenwich and Richmond and, in its overturreted way, so was Henry's last palace of Nonsuch, which Mary avoided. A decade after his death the bloody horrors of his later reign were fading into myth, while the confusions and hobbled leadership of his successors made him seem enviably strong and decisive by comparison.

In associating herself closely with her father Elizabeth was tapping a popular longing. Throughout her childhood the English had loathed Henry VIII; now they yearned for him, or for the mellowed image of him they carried, and when they looked at his strong-willed tall daughter they thought they saw a way to bring him back.

Elizabeth's proud association with her father served another purpose. It gave her a firm identity, counteracting once and for all the uncertainties about her parentage that had shadowed her early childhood. A new version of her childhood story arose. King Henry, it was said, always liked Elizabeth, however he might have hated and mistreated her mother. For this reason, and because of her resemblance to him, he had given orders that she be brought up as a king's daughter and not as the daughter of the dishonored traitor Anne Boleyn. In his will he had left her well provided for; had the engorging inflation of Edward's reign not eroded her annuity, she would be well provided for still.[7]

Elizabeth had also come to terms, at least on the surface, with what it meant to be her mother's child. She affirmed to whoever would listen that she was no less legitimate than Mary was, and of equal rank in blood. As for the potential stigma left by Anne Boleyn, there was none; Anne, she felt certain, would never have lived with King Henry except as his wife, "with the authority of the church, and the intervention of the primate of England." Anne's conscience had been clear, and in the last analysis nothing else mattered. She had acted in good faith, as the king's true Protestant subject; even if she was deceived about the validity of her marriage (as adherents of the Roman faith were quick to claim), the fact that she had lived and died in the church which had legitimized it left her blameless. And left her daughter Elizabeth, born into that same church, without any taint of bastardy.[8]

By mid-June the midwives were sulking. The royal chaplains led solemn processions around the palace grounds each day, as they did in times of plague or drought, begging God to relieve the queen of her burden and to give her kingdom a prince. Councilors and court officials processed along with the clergy, pausing below the windows of Mary's chamber to acknowledge her gracious bows and smiles of thanks. Yet their earnest prayers went unanswered, and to heighten the tension the burnings of Protestants escalated, with eight more men and women executed by fire in the first two weeks of June. The queen, it seemed to some, had decided that her child could not be born until every Protestant in prison was burned alive.[9]

For Elizabeth each day of delay was another opportunity to cultivate the Spaniards, whose growing uncertainty about Mary's condition made Elizabeth herself seem all the more important. A new strategy was in the air. Should Mary die, the Venetian ambassador wrote, Philip might "not improbably" marry Elizabeth, and she might just possibly accept him.[10]

The thought must have been present in both their minds as they met and exchanged the curtsies, bows and kisses that courtly ritual demanded. They would have made an odd pair, he short and compact, with the natural languor of a sometime invalid, she tall and slender and uncommonly vigorous. Both were more than capable of calculating the political usefulness of the match; as to the chemistry between them, we have only Elizabeth's boast in later years that during his stay in England Philip had been in love with her.

The thought that her husband might marry Anne Boleyn's daughter must have darkened Mary's spirits as her doubts about her fruitfulness continued to grow. She sat on her cushion, her knees pulled up to her chin, squeezing her deflated abdomen. Her chief consolation was her worn prayer book, with its prayer for the safe delivery of a woman with child; the page was stained with the mark of her tears.

Philip had been a courteous, dutiful husband to her, a grave and gentlemanly presence at her side at daily mass and vespers, an amiable, if not exactly jovial, companion at banquets and jousts, a correct and occasionally tender spouse. But if she was unable to present him with a son, duty would oblige him to subordinate his marriage to interests of state. Elizabeth would become the all-important figure at court. Either Philip would have to find a suitable husband for her, or, if he should become a widower, marry her himself.

July was cold and rainy, and the ladies who had come to Hampton Court cheerful and hopeful in April were bored and housebound, and wished they could go home. Like the diplomats and councilors and midwives—and the people at large—they had given up all speculation about the birth and simply waited for a miracle.

The French ambassador Noailles found the situation ludicrous. One of his spies claimed to have wormed the truth out of two of Mary's female intimates: the queen, they admitted, was deceived about her condition, and the other midwives were too fearful to tell her that she was not pregnant after all.[11] Elizabeth had been from time to time in communication with the French, and may well have heard this story. If it was true, it added one more fold to the involuted mystery.

For three months the court had been suspended in time, while the queen waited for a miracle that never came. By the end of July the overcrowded halls and chambers of the palace stank of unclean floors and rotted expectations. Philip and his retinue of intimates were making ready to embark for Flanders, and the business of government, which had never entirely ceased, despite Mary's seclusion, now required her constant attention.

The announcement came without fanfare: the court was moving to Oatlands, so that Hampton Court could be cleansed. This gave tacit permission for the courtiers to depart for their homes in the country, for there was no room for them at Oatlands. Though the myth of Mary's pregnancy was never officially dispelled, the message was clear, adding the sting of humiliation to the queen's deep and inconsolable sorrow. Somehow she had lost the child she had mistakenly hoped for, and soon she would lose the company of her beloved husband. The one person she could not seem to lose was her despised sister, who stood arrogantly by, waiting for her opportunity to supplant Mary. Only a few weeks earlier a group of Elizabeth's partisans had been discovered in London, making the most of popular bewilderment about the queen, and no doubt helping to spread the rumor that she was dead. The plotters had been threatened and dispersed, yet in Mary's more fearful moments it seemed as if each nest of conspirators she uncovered somehow brought Elizabeth one step closer to her throne.

Elizabeth queen! The thought was almost too bitter to be borne, yet Mary knew she had to endure it for a few weeks longer, until Philip left. Then she would see what could be done with her unworthy sister.

At the end of August Mary and Philip rode together through the streets of the capital to Tower Wharf, where they would embark in the royal barge for the short ride downriver to Greenwich. The queen chose to be carried in an open litter, flanked by her husband on one side and by Cardinal Pole on the other, and at the sight of her the people surged forward in curiosity and amazement. Satisfied that it was indeed Mary, alive and in at least reasonable health, they applauded their sovereign and, for the moment, forgave her for thwarting their expectation of a prince.

But when they heard that Elizabeth had been seen on the river, on her way to Greenwich in the shabby barge her sister had assigned her, with only a few attendants to pay honor to her rank, they were "much displeased. They blamed Mary, as they blamed her for the inhuman burnings, the stunted crops, even the chill summer weather. They knew that Mary had intended to deprive them of the sight of Elizabeth, their next queen, "which they greatly desired."

14

Up, said this God with voice not strange,
Elizabeth, thys realme nowe guyde!
My wyll in thee doo not thou hyde,
And vermine darke let not abyde
*   In thys thy land!*
Straightway the people out dyd cry,
Praysed be God and God save thee,
*   Quene of England!*

T he public hunger for the sight of Elizabeth was fed some weeks later when Mary, lonely for Philip and finding Elizabeth's presence at court distasteful, allowed her to return to Hatfield.

When the princess and her modest retinue passed through the capital they caused a commotion. "Great and small followed her through the city," wrote an eyewitness, "and greeted her with acclamations and such vehement manifestations of affection that she was fearful it would expose her to the jealousy of the court." The cheering and clapping and stomping could be heard some distance away, carried on the crisp autumn air; as she rode past, tall and regal on her prancing horse, recalling her father with her fine features and blond-red hair, Elizabeth called forth a deafening burst of acclaim.

Much as she warmed to the Londoners' support, though, she knew she must try to check it for fear of her sister's resentment. Turning her horse she rode back through the ranks of her liveried attendants and fell into place behind some of her household officers, remaining there, "as if unwilling to attract public attention and applause," until the traveling party had passed through the city and started up the high road toward Hatfield.

Once installed in the old manor house—which she had not seen for a year and a half—Elizabeth reassembled a staff of servants and officials, choosing judiciously from among the eager candidates offering to serve her, always careful to avoid selecting anyone who might offend the queen. She had to disappoint many, yet she turned their disappointment to advantage by excusing herself on grounds of poverty. She simply could not afford to keep a large establishment, she explained; the ten thousand crowns her father had left her was too meager to permit an abundance of servants. In truth, of course, she did not dare to live ostentatiously, for the same reason that she had to dampen the cheering crowds that greeted her wherever she went. But by pleading poverty she won sympathy, and at the same time made Mary look mean for keeping the second person in the realm in such reduced circumstances.[1]

There was money enough, to be sure, to keep on the beloved servants of her childhood and youth, Blanche and Thomas Parry and Kat Ashley—whose husband John was away during Mary's reign, studying in Padua. And there were newer intimates: the embattled, intrigue-loving Piedmontese Castiglione, who taught her Italian, and the young mathematician and philosopher John Dee, only recently released from imprisonment and fearing for his life.

Dee had had the misfortune to calculate the nativities of the queen and king and Princess Elizabeth; he was suspected of attempting to enchant the queen, just at the time when her fruitless pregnancy was reaching its nerve-racking climax. He was eventually released, but only after enduring the terrors of imprisonment. His fellow prisoner Barthlet Green, who shared his cell and wretched sleeping pallet, was burned at the stake.[2]

And there was Roger Ascham, who had returned to court to serve Mary and Philip as Latin secretary and to resume his tutelage of the adult Elizabeth.

On his dismissal from the princess's household some years earlier he had traveled to Germany in an ambassadorial party, then returned to Cambridge—where he was miserable—and finally he had received his court appointment. With this had come financial solvency and the lease of a farm in Essex, and Ascham badly needed both, for he had just married a gentlewoman, Margaret Howe. His Protestantism was, surprisingly, no hindrance at Mary's court; she favored him in spite of it, and Cardinal Pole treated him "familiarly," their bond as humanists stronger than the doctrinal views that divided them. All in all he had never been happier; his life was complete. "I would not change it," he wrote a close friend, "so help me Christ, for any other way of life that could be offered me."[3]

And as before, a particular joy in Ascham's life was reading Greek with Elizabeth. They were working their way through Demosthenes' oration *On the Crown*. "She reads it first to me," Ascham wrote in a description of their hours together, "and at first sight understands everything, not only the peculiarity of the language and the meaning of the orator, but . . . the decrees of the people, the customs and manners of the city, in a way to strike you with astonishment."[4]

Elizabeth's political insight was becoming keener year by year, sharpened by her experience living on the razor's edge of Marian politics. She had never been trained to govern, yet her reading of the classics taught her a good deal about the workings of ancient governments and societies, while her searching observation of her sister's rule and court was a sobering, practical lesson—albeit a negative one—in queenship.

Mary, she noted, had begun her reign in a frenzy of conscientious labor, yet her efforts had been undermined by others' perceptions of her as womanly and therefore weak. She had underscored those perceptions by marrying, and by treating her husband with elaborate deference, almost abdicating her authority to him even while continuing to bear a heavy burden at her desk and at the council table. And she had been subjected to all the humiliations and privations of a royal wife—which had undermined not only her appearance of majesty but her sane temper and self-confidence as well.

Ascham took full cognizance of the refinement of Elizabeth's political sophistication even as he praised her linguistic accomplishments and, inseparable from these, her oratorical skill. Years later she herself was to look back on these years and remark that by the time she reached her mid-twenties "she knew six languages better than her own."[5] She was, quite simply, a marvel. Responding both to her learning and to her commanding presence at about age twenty-two, a visiting scholar whom Ascham referred to merely as "Metellus" wrote that "it was more to him to have seen Elizabeth than to have seen England."[6]

At Hatfield, surrounded by her most trusted servants, Elizabeth might have been tempted to savor the illusion of freedom. But it was only an illusion; Mary's spies were everywhere. Guards and royal agents patrolled the roads and haunted the villages in the vicinity, keeping watch on everyone who came and went, and reporting all that they saw and heard to the queen. Elizabeth had not after all been freed, merely transferred to a larger prison, and her jailer, Mary, looked in more than once to check on her during the fall.

Early in the new year 1556 the most widespread and potentially dangerous of the plots against the queen began to come to light, its central aim the forcible removal of Mary, with Elizabeth to take her place. As before, no matter how damning the circumstantial evidence the princess could not be directly implicated. Her rebellious supporters might cry defiantly that

Elizabeth was "a liberal dame, and nothing so unthankful as her sister," and look to "their neighbor of Hatfield" to restore their lands and show gratitude for their service. But no one produced treasonous letters she had written, or repeated messages in which she had betrayed her sister.

The danger lay not so much in Elizabeth herself as in the escalating popular support she commanded. With Mary apparently barren, and presiding, in bitter cruelty, over a reign of fire her subjects were deserting her and looking eagerly toward Elizabeth's accession. Some thought Elizabeth now had the loyalty of a majority of Mary's subjects, and to judge from the breakneck pace of the couriers that passed between the English court and Brussels, where Philip and his father were, the crown was indeed in peril.[7]

Mary was convinced that her sister had to be sent out of the country, perhaps to Spain, where she would be betrothed, should Mary prove childless, to the boy Don Carlos, Philip's son by his first wife. In April the queen "earnestly canvassed" the matter in person, attempting to win the support of the council for her policy and sending off extraordinary messages to Brussels anxiously requesting Philip's permission to act.[8]

The greatest secrecy shrouded these plans, which gathered urgency as the stain of conspiracy spread closer and closer to the princess herself. By June dozens of traitors had been seized and imprisoned, many of them linked to the princess by bonds of service or by family ties. William Howard, lord admiral, Francis Verney, a servitor under suspicion since Elizabeth's Woodstock days, Castiglione, survivor of several prison stays, and, finally, Kat Ashley were all ordered to London in the queen's name.

Mary's guardsmen came to Hatfield to arrest Kat, riding with grim expressions onto the grounds and demanding that Mistress Ashley surrender herself. Elizabeth, no doubt angry that her sanctuary had been violated yet fearful for her beloved governess, made no recorded protest. Yet Kat's guilt was of a sort to drag her mistress down with her. In a coffer at Elizabeth's London residence, Somerset House, Kat had assembled a library of scurrilous pamphlets and libels and other writings against the queen and Philip. For the royal agents to accuse Elizabeth herself of possessing, or at least reading, these treasonable works would have seemed the natural next step, and no one who was at Hatfield on the day Kat was taken into custody could avoid that troubling thought.

The arrest caused "great general vexation," Michiel reported, but it was to be the last blow the queen directed against her sister in this round of their perpetual conflict.

For Mary was slowly losing ground to the enmity and feigned fidelity that surrounded her. Wherever she looked she saw treachery. Many of the important men in the countryside—royal officials, gentry and prominent landholders—had supported the rebellion. Courtiers who had once defended Mary and had sworn to die in her cause now turned against her, and even members of her council were known to have given tacit encouragement to the conspirators. There were assassins among her personal attendants; her chaplain, it was reported, had made an attempt on her life.[9] She avoided appearing in public, and those few who saw her were taken aback by how troubled she looked, and said privately that she had aged ten years.

Her anger still smoldered, to be sure, especially against her sister, but here Philip stayed her hand. Mary's bitter desire for revenge must not be allowed to jeopardize Philip's own suave cultivation of Mary's heir, the next queen of England. For Mary was barren, that was tacitly understood; Elizabeth would in time succeed her. It was only a question of when, and how. When Elizabeth began her reign, Philip would need her good will— and the good will of all those who would resent any harsh treatment of her now by the queen and her husband.

So instead of being committed to strait imprisonment Elizabeth received a gracious message from the queen (shaped, we may presume, by Philip), "consoling and comforting" her on the shock of having her servants arrested and offering, as a palliative to her dejection, a ring worth four hundred ducats.[10]

As the most oblique of rebukes Elizabeth's household was reorganized, with new servants assigned who were unshakably loyal to Mary. Yet lest Elizabeth take this amiss she was assured that, "provided she continue to live becomingly," she would retain Mary's "good will and disposition." Of course, she would have to accept a new governess, a "widow gentlewoman" whom Mary trusted completely, and, as guardian of her wayward establishment, the "rich and grave" Sir Thomas Pope. The princess agreed though Pope himself, like Bedingfield before him, "did his utmost to decline." (Pope's guardianship was as brief as it was uneventful; the fanciful pageantry long associated with his care for Elizabeth is based on forgeries traceable to the eighteenth-century antiquary Thomas Warton.)[11]

What Elizabeth needed, all were agreed, was not a guardian but an iron-fisted husband. It went without saying that Mary was barren; Elizabeth and her husband would sooner or later rule England—unless, as some feared, Philip invaded the country with an army and annexed it permanently to the Hapsburg empire. But though he may have held this in reserve as a contingency plan, his preferred policy was to find a bridegroom for Elizabeth who would also serve as his lieutenant in England.

None of the English candidates was suitable. Courtenay's brief exile ended in tragedy in the fall of this year, 1556, when he caught a fever while hawking and died. Young Lord Maltravers—at one time the most likely, for his virtues and "handsome presence," of the English suitors—was also dead, at only twenty-two, bringing grief not only to his young widow but to his father, for Maltravers was an only son and with his death the line became extinct.[12] The death of the young nobleman must have given Elizabeth pause. Had Mary forced her to marry him, she would now be a widow. She might even have a child.

Then if not an Englishman, a foreigner (or a near-foreigner like Pole, whom Protestants sarcastically urged to "cast aside the abomination of his red [cardinal's] hat," marry Elizabeth and make himself king, since he ruled all anyway).[13] At one time the king of Denmark's son had been suggested, the future Frederick III, at another a Catholic German prince. Much as he might have favored it, Philip could not risk marrying Elizabeth to a Spanish grandee. Being "defiled with English sects," the princess or her servants "might meddle in matters that the Inquisition would take seriously." Then there would be scandal, embarrassment, and possibly even danger, for in the 1550s Protestantism was alive in Spain as it was all over Europe.[14]

By the fall of 1556 the field of eligible men had been narrowed to three. One was Don Carlos, now eleven years old, who could become betrothed to Elizabeth but could not marry her for five or six years, and could hardly be expected to master her even then. Another was Archduke Ferdinand, then twenty-seven. He was a Hapsburg, and the right age, but his suitability was marred by the existence of his common-law wife, his "proud and haughty" temperament, and his envy of Philip and especially of Philip's Flemish possessions.[15] Besides, he was known to have an understanding with the French.

Much the best alternative was Emmanuel Philibert, duke of Savoy, a twenty-seven-year-old paragon who in addition to being a valorous soldier had a "pleasing presence" and fine Italian manners which the English prized. Though he was at present without a dukedom (the French had despoiled Savoy) the duke had royal blood, both Spanish and French, and his family was said to be "of Saxon origin, like the English themselves." Emmanuel Philibert was Philip's first cousin, and loyal to that tie of blood. Beyond this, though, he was a staunch Catholic, and could be counted on to enforce Elizabeth's conformity to the church of Rome. Once they were married, Elizabeth's secret Protestantism would cease to encourage the heretics, for even if she became queen her Catholic husband would prevent her from practicing her faith or changing the official faith of England.[16]

If Elizabeth were to marry, Savoy was Mary's preferred choice for her. Yet Elizabeth herself was extremely reluctant to marry, and when in late

November of 1556 the two sisters met face to face to discuss the issue the meeting ended in a stalemate.[17] But Elizabeth's trip to court resulted in one other meeting: at long last the princess came face to face with Cardinal Pole. They spoke together in Pole's chamber, and no witness took down their words or noted them afterward. Yet some things about their encounter may be imagined—the cardinal's weary kindliness, the sharp exchange of wits, the unspoken acknowledgment that, in Pole, Elizabeth was addressing the queen's alter ego and, in Elizabeth, Pole was addressing England's next ruler.

Whether or not Pole urged Elizabeth to marry—which, given his conviction of women's frailties, he undoubtedly thought best—Mary herself must have been more than a little ambivalent. Philip had commanded her to persuade her sister to take a husband, but Mary herself dreaded it, for to negotiate a marriage contract with a foreign prince or nobleman would mean recognizing Elizabeth as heir to her throne, and as the trueborn daughter of Henry VIII. So Elizabeth's obstinacy was almost welcome to Mary; it allowed her to procrastinate, to put her sister out of her mind for a time, to indulge her own dwindling hopes.

These hopes lived again when Philip returned to England in March of 1557. He came not out of loneliness for his wife but on a practical errand. The imperial forces were at war; he needed men and, especially, money to finance an assault against the Franco-Flemish border. Mary agreed, as the price of her husband's visit, to demand these from her unwilling councilors, and after three months of arguments and admonitions—Mary was not above threatening her advisers with death and confiscation of their property —they gave in. England was at war.

But Mary found, to her chagrin, that Philip had come to demand more than this. He had not given up on Elizabeth's marriage, and now asked Mary's trusted confessor Fresneda to use every possible persuasion on the queen to induce her consent. Fresneda complied. Religion, piety, the security of the kingdom all pointed to the need for Mary's presumed successor to marry, he argued. What if Elizabeth, feeling abused, were to choose a husband for herself, and what if the man she chose "convulsed the whole kingdom into confusion?" She was unpredictable, capricious; she might take it into her head to marry any time. Before the worst happened, a match must be made for her.

The Spaniard was "very dear" to Mary, and she heard him out, yet she remained completely and adamantly opposed to everything he said. Her extreme distaste for Elizabeth's succession rights was hardening into an obsession. She repeated with vehemence the argument she had been making since the start of her reign: Elizabeth was not her sister, Henry VIII was not Elizabeth's father, Mary could not possibly allow Elizabeth to be shown any favor whatsoever, "as she was born of an infamous woman, who had so greatly outraged" Katherine of Aragon and Mary herself.[18]

The confessor, undaunted, persevered so "assiduously and adroitly" that he broke Mary down. She consented, her conscience and honor losing ground to her desire to please Philip and to preserve a Catholic England. A document was drawn up, most likely during Philip's stay in England, which envisioned Elizabeth's future as princess of England and duchess of Savoy. When she produced her first child, the agreement set forth, the duke was to hand over to Philip his castles of Nice and Villefranche as security; if that child actually became king or queen—or if, with Elizabeth dying childless, the duke himself should succeed—then the entire county of Nice and the port and town of Villefranche would become permanently annexed to Philip's possessions. All contingencies were spelled out, with Philip the chief beneficiary in each instance. Mary's name was never mentioned, but the omission was eloquent. No one expected her to live much longer.[19]

Then two days after giving her consent, Mary changed her mind. She would not permit any marriage after all. Elizabeth had no rightful claim, and was completely unworthy besides. Fresneda had to swallow his rage. Cardinal Pole was accused, perhaps rightly, of forcing Mary's reversal. In any case the matter was left in abeyance, and was lost for a time amid the urgencies of war and the brief "warmed-over honeymoon" of the queen and her consort—a honeymoon considerably dampened, so gossips said, by the presence at court of Philip's current mistress.

Early in the new year 1558 Mary's subjects were stunned by the news that Calais, England's last possession on the continent and a vital center of the English wool trade, had been attacked and taken by a French army, and was now the possession of Henry II. Mary was blamed. In her four and a half years as queen she had brought them under a foreign yoke by marrying a Spaniard, humiliated them by her false pregnancy, impoverished them with taxes, and scourged them with merciless burnings and persecution. Now she had lost Calais, and still she demanded that more English soldiers and English coins be sent abroad to aid her ungrateful husband.

"I never saw England weaker in strength, men, money and riches," wrote a scholarly observer early in that dark year. Englishmen "went to the wars hanging down their looks. They came from thence as men dismayed and forlorn. They went about their matters as men amazed, that wist not where to begin or end." And why not, he asked, for his country was in the sorriest of states. "Here was nothing but fining, beheading, hanging, quartering, and burning; taxing, levying, pulling down of bulwarks at home, and beggaring and losing our strongholds abroad."[20] The queen appeared to be moribund, her successor powerless. All the country's vitality had been drained off. "A few priests, men in white rochets, ruled all."

Mary was secretly consoled amid the general gloom, for once again she had been deluded by her physical state and imagined herself pregnant. (She was in fact entering the terminal stage of ovarian cancer.) But her elation was short-lived, and by May, when ten months had passed since Philip's departure and any further hope for a child would be as shameful as it would be futile, she had lost her illusions. Now she concentrated on preserving her shattered authority, grumbling when visiting ambassadors went to call on Elizabeth at Hatfield without obtaining her royal permission first and taking offense at any apparent slight to her primacy.

The personnel of the court, caught between their desire not to alienate the queen and their hope of ingratiating themselves with the woman who would soon replace her, resorted to clandestine visits or elaborate ruses, or contacted Elizabeth through intermediaries.

Elizabeth avoided her sister's wrath by remaining out of sight as much of the time as possible, though when her presence was required at court Mary's enmity toward her burned through her outward politeness. "She dissembles her hatred and anger as much as she can," Michiel wrote of Mary's treatment of her sister, "and endeavors when they are together in public to receive her with every sort of graciousness and honor, nor does she ever converse with her about any but agreeable subjects."[21] Yet her "scorn and ill will" were unmistakable, and whenever she saw Elizabeth the old affronts and humiliations of Mary's childhood rose before her eyes and made her hate the princess all the more. To Mary, Elizabeth represented not only past injuries but present ones: disloyalty, heresy, unchastity, perhaps even adultery, if what Mary suspected of her flirtation with Philip was true. Worse still, Elizabeth represented youth, survival, the future.

A perceptive visitor to Mary's court writing in 1556 had remarked that almost no one he met who was under thirty-five was a genuine Catholic. With some significant exceptions the Protestants who died in the Marian burnings were of the younger generation as well, and Mary's attempt to reeducate her subjects in Catholic ways, now drawing to a close, had been too brief to leave a strong imprint even on the children. God and his true faith might be on Mary's side, as she saw it, but the times were with her sister. Like Katherine of Aragon before her, Mary was doomed to die bereft of a son, separated from her husband, watching her rival triumph.

Throughout the latter half of 1558 the royal court was eclipsed by the shadow-court at Hatfield. Messengers came and went frequently, carrying secret communications about the succession. Noblemen came to pay their respects to Elizabeth now just as they did to Mary, and no longer cared very much whether in paying court to the princess they risked offending the queen. A large and bright comet was observed in the skies over northern Europe that summer, and the English, in the time-honored belief that comets foretold the death of great personages, nodded their heads and took it as confirmation that the change of reigns was near.

Philip too was calculating that before long he would be a widower, and that, in order to secure his hold on England, he would need to woo Elizabeth. He sent his grave, courtly Spanish envoy Count Feria to her and Feria, though too discreet to commit their conversation to writing, reported cryptically that the princess was "very much pleased," and implied that his mission had been a success.[22]

Clearly the English were in process of transferring their loyalty to Mary's successor, and to all outward appearances the actual transfer of power would proceed smoothly and predictably as well. Parliament met in the first week of November, to assure continuity and provide stability while the new queen found her footing, and Mary, in severe pain and weary of life, at last officially declared Elizabeth to be her successor. Two royal messengers arrived at Hatfield with word that Elizabeth was now heir to the throne "by right and law," and the crowd of well-wishers who gathered at the manor house in anticipation of the joyous news of Mary's death rejoiced noisily at this preliminary announcement and waited for better news to come.

While they waited they speculated on Elizabeth's choice of a husband, for no one doubted that she would want a man at her side once she assumed her royal duties. To be sure, no foreign consort would be welcomed— though Swedish and Danish matches were being discussed, and earlier in the year the Swedish king Gustavus Vasa had sent an envoy to Elizabeth to seek her hand for his son Eric.[23] Among English suitors, the talk centered on the earls of Arundel or Westmorland, or the young duke of Norfolk, highest ranking of Elizabeth's Howard relations.

Feria heard that Elizabeth preferred one of her Scottish kin, which spurred him to urge his master's suit the more strongly. That Elizabeth might be persuaded to marry her brother-in-law Philip, whom she had treated with extravagant flattery and flirtation in view of the whole court, seemed to the courtiers a real danger. As Mary's life ebbed they worried over Philip's "intention to have her for himself," and hoped she would show the good sense to refuse him.

But if the waiting courtiers were anxious about Elizabeth's future consort, the country's military commanders had more pressing concerns. During October and November of 1558 the princess, in person and through her agents, was summoning them—or accepting their offers of aid—to stand behind her as she prepared to assume Mary's crown. In one surviving letter from late October she thanked a nobleman for putting his forces at her disposal, and promised that she would remember his service "whensoever time and power may serve." At the same time she was sending word to others, such as Thomas Markham, commander of the extensive Berwick garrison, to bring their troops southward "to serve for the maintenance of her royal state, title and dignity." Markham not only came and swore his allegiance, but brought signed undertakings from other trusted northern captains who swore to back her claim with their lives and the lives of their soldiers—ten thousand men in all.[24]

For if Elizabeth had no apparent rival for the throne, still there were those in the realm who had a stake in prolonging Marian government—and in particular, the Marian church. Cardinal Pole, long-suffering symbol of the Catholic aristocracy and in these latter days almost a co-ruler with Mary, had given no indication that he would make way for Elizabeth without a struggle. Though ill and somewhat wayward in mind, he still held tenaciously to his power. He had only recently burned "one of her chief and well beloved servants," and she was said to be extremely angry with him.[25] To counterbalance Pole's opposition Elizabeth sought the favor of Nicholas Heath, archbishop of York. Though he knew, as everyone did, that as queen Elizabeth would restore Protestantism in some form, the archbishop readily promised his allegiance to her; unlike Pole, for whom religion was primary, Heath felt most keenly his loyalty to the descendants of Henry VIII.

Beyond Pole, and many other stalwart Catholics, there was danger from the Scots and from the French, from Pope Paul IV, and from Philip, who if Elizabeth refused his offer of marriage might in desperation send an invading army to England. To forestall this grim possibility Elizabeth received Feria with marked courtesy when he came to her in the country on November 10, and handled him with the skill of a practiced diplomat.

First she gave him supper, with her confidante Lady Clinton joining them, then afterward she talked with him informally, attended only by three women whose discretion, she assured him, would be absolute as they could speak no Spanish.

Elizabeth began by referring graciously to how grateful she was to Philip for his past friendship, friendship which he had promised her would continue and which was based on "the ancient ties between the houses of Burgundy and England." Feria ignored this grandiloquent reference and brought the conversation closer to home.

Elizabeth, he said, should thank Philip for her imminent accession. Mary had certainly not been responsible for it, nor her councilors; it was Philip, acting behind the scenes, who had brought it about.

She corrected him. She owed what she was to the people, not to Philip or the nobility or anyone else. Feria noted down her particular affection for her people—they would soon be hers—and had to admit that by and large the English did take her part. He forbore, though, to debate the question of who should take credit for her preservation, privately convinced that were it not for his master Elizabeth might well not have survived to outlive her sister.

They spoke of a variety of things: of the peace negotiations then taking place on the continent, and the English commissioners' instructions; of the duke of Savoy, whom Elizabeth had declined to marry, she said, because she feared to lose the people's affection, as Mary had, by marrying a foreigner; of money, of which Elizabeth had been deprived during Mary's reign though Mary had been quick enough to squander coins, and jewels too, on Philip's warmaking.

Through it all Feria watched Elizabeth closely, calculating her strengths and weaknesses as a ruler, aware that, though she had not yet been crowned, she was already a queen.

"She is keen-witted and extremely vain," he wrote. "She has been greatly stamped by her father's way of doing things." (If the peace commissioners agreed to a settlement that did not include the restoration of Calais to the English, she swore to Feria, "it would cost them their heads.") As for religion, there was no hope for her, as she had surrounded herself with councilors and female attendants who were all heretics. Now that she had nothing to fear from the dying queen, she was giving full vent to her pent-up anger. "She shows herself highly indignant at all that was done to her during the queen's lifetime," the count wrote, and though he added no particulars it seems likely that her hostility to Mary colored their entire interview.[26]

At Hatfield by mid-November a holiday atmosphere prevailed. The crowds, "constantly increasing with great frequency," that pressed in through the gardens, shivering in the raw air, were cheerfully expectant. The volume of mail and visitors grew inordinately. No business was being done at court, for Pole was as ill as Mary was, and there was no one in charge of affairs. Instead all business came to Hatfield, and burdened as she was with choosing her council and other household officials, and beginning to formulate her policy toward foreign courts, Elizabeth dealt with it as best she could. Around her all the talk was of the festivities that would accompany her accession, and of the robes and other finery each of the lords and ladies would need "to appear with very great pomp at the coronation of the new queen." There were no suitable fabrics to be found in England; all sent to Antwerp for fine cloths in a rainbow of colors, until it was said that the English had bought up every length of silk in the town.[27]

Then came Hope Wednesday, November 16, the day news came that Mary could not last more than a few hours. The hours passed, the onlookers kept their excited vigil. Finally the next morning the long-awaited message came. The queen had died before dawn, falling into sleeplike peace after hearing mass one last time. And Pole, too, was said to be dying.

With what inner relief Elizabeth uttered the Latin words ascribed to her at that moment—"This is the Lord's doing, and it is marvelous in our eyes" —we can only imagine. Nearly thirty years afterward she spoke of how she had wept at Mary's death. No doubt she wept for her piteous, hated sister, but also for herself, for the sheer weight of the burden of rule that loomed before her. And for release from the long, tense nightmare of her past.

"O Lord, almighty and everlasting God," she was to pray in words of her own, on her coronation day, "I give Thee most hearty thanks that Thou hast been so merciful unto me as to spare me to behold this joyful day. And I acknowledge that Thou hast dealt as wonderfully and as mercifully with me as Thou didst with Thy true and faithful servant, Daniel, Thy prophet, whom Thou deliveredst out of the den of the greedy and raging lions."

PART THREE

"La Plus Fine
Femme du Monde"

15

But whereto shall we bend our lays?
Even up to Heaven, again to raise
The Maid which, thence descended,
Hath brought again the golden days
And all the world amended.

Mary died in the early hours of the morning and by noon Elizabeth had been proclaimed queen in Parliament at Westminster and in the City, where Londoners had long since broken into wild rejoicing. This was their long awaited day of deliverance, their moment of release from the endless, bloody night of Mary's persecution. Throughout the old queen's last illness they had been hoarding their secret delight that her end was near; now they let themselves go in an explosion of celebration.

All the bells in London's hundred churches rang in joyous cacophony as people crowded into the narrow streets to cheer and salute Queen Elizabeth. Shops and markets were closed, work abandoned. By sunset London had become a huge open-air banquet hall, lit by crackling bonfires at every street corner and furnished with meat and drink in lavish abundance. Merchants and gentlefolk mingled with common laborers and the ragged poor in toasting the new queen's health far into the night, dancing and singing until their heads swam from exhaustion and wine.

Several days later, hearing that Elizabeth was on her way toward London from Hatfield, they "went many miles out of the city" to greet her, thronging the roadways and shouting and gesturing "with so lively representations of love, joy and hope that it far exceeded her expectation."[1] And the pageantry was only beginning; still to come was the new sovereign's formal entrance into the City, with cannon booming and trumpets blowing, and, some seven weeks hence, the splendor of the coronation.

From their exile in Strasbourg and Geneva the Protestants who had fled Mary's persecution rejoiced that God in his infinite mercy had taken the old queen to himself and spared her sister to reign in her stead. "We that have long and sorrowfully lacked our country," Cecil's father-in-law Anthony Cooke wrote from abroad, "now have good hope to enjoy the sight of her grace and it." "If the Israelites might joy in their Deborah, how much more we English in our Elizabeth!" wrote the duchess of Suffolk, the Puritan Catherine Bertie, who had wandered fretfully through Germany and Poland while her coreligionists were being burned in England. All through Mary's reign Elizabeth had been the Protestants' hope and treasure, and though they had only the most general idea of her personal faith they knew her to be, by lineage and upbringing, within the Protestant camp. Now that she had come to the throne at last she was certain to fulfill their expectations.[2]

She did not, however, begin to fulfill them right away. She continued to hear daily mass, and her household with her, and commanded "that no one was to dare to molest sacred places nor religious persons, nor to alter the present state of the religion." To all outward appearances Mary's dying wish, that her sister would maintain the Catholic faith in England, was being honored. Nor did her subjects, as might have been expected, vent their anger on the churches or the clergy. For the time being it was enough that the burnings ceased and the mood of repression lifted; the queen would surely act to restore the church of King Henry and King Edward in time.

Besides, for the moment more immediate matters clamored for attention. By an oversight Henry VIII's act of Parliament barring Elizabeth from the throne had never been repealed, even though his later statute had restored her to the succession. Lest this hinder her now she was advised to obtain legal advice at once. She had to give thought, too, to the epidemic of lawbreaking that had begun in the vicinity of the capital. The thieves and cutpurses and murderers that lurked in London alleyways and in the shadow of Westminster Abbey had become bolder than ever, in anticipation of the general pardon they knew would be issued on coronation day. To forestall the thievery and assault Elizabeth gave formal warning that the pardon would not apply to crimes committed after her accession, and that no outlaw or burglar would be pardoned at all.

Preparing for the ancient, intricate ritual of the coronation absorbed much of Elizabeth's time. A churchman had to be found who would be willing to preside, and with Cardinal Pole dead (he had survived Mary by only a few hours) and Heath, archbishop of York, wary of the new queen's private beliefs the search was not an easy one. In the end an obscure suffragan of Heath's, Owen Oglethorpe of Carlisle, was agreed on. Then there were the coronation claims to be settled, with the nobles vying for positions of importance during the ceremonies, and the coronation furnishings ordered.

A whole industry sprang up overnight to supply the robes and ornaments and trappings for this most ostentatious of regal occasions: tailors and seamstresses to stitch the costly gowns and embroiderers and haberdashers and feather-makers to trim them, skinners to provide furs and mercers rich velvets and silks. Upholsterers were ordered to cover the queen's new litter in cloth of gold and the coronation chair in the abbey in cloth of silver. Saddlers and bit-makers prepared gorgeous finery for the horses, while cutlers looked after the ceremonial swords and other arms traditionally worn on coronation day. The queen's tailor supervised the outfitting of the entire court, not only the officials and the queen's ladies but the heralds, henchmen, musicians and guardsmen, many hundreds in all, who would attend her as she rode in procession. No one was overlooked, not even the purveyors of food for the palace kitchens or the queen's laundress, who had a new red dress, or the royal fools, who were to be conspicuous in orange velvet with purple tinsel.[3]

Everywhere, as she plunged into the maelstrom of administrative and ceremonial detail, Elizabeth encountered the ghost of the dead queen. There were bills from Nonnius, Mary's deathbed physician; Philip had sent him to her from the Low Countries, but had never paid him. There were letters of petition and recommendation to Mary, and gifts from her subjects and others to be acknowledged—including eight handsome falcons sent from Albert, duke of Prussia, which Elizabeth gladly inherited. There were the debts which, during her last days, Mary had begged her sister to pay, and wages to be distributed among her hundreds of servants. Her guardsmen were particularly costly, their ranks swollen to four hundred (Henry VIII had had only fifty) because she so feared for her life. Elizabeth let at least half of them go.[4]

One ghoulish incident involving the late queen caused much inconvenience. In Mary's last hours vital documents needed by the peace commissioners negotiating with the French over Calais had been brought to her to sign. She was far too ill to read them, so they lay unattended by the bedside until she died. Now they could not be found anywhere, and the negotiations could proceed only haltingly without them. Mary's chief waiting woman Susan Clarencieux was consulted. The documents had been taken by the embalmers, Mistress Clarencieux announced; the long rolls of parchment had been found useful for wrapping the corpse.[5]

The loss was critical, for the peace talks were England's only defense— and a transitory, fragile defense at best—against the looming menace of the French. Fear of the French overrode all else in the first months of the new reign, "the French king bestriding the realm, having one foot in Calais and the other in Scotland," as the clerk of the council put it.[6] Calais, for centuries an English port, now threatened to become the launching point of an invading army. Mary's loss of the town had meant more than a jolt to English sentiments and severe economic disruption to the vital wool trade; with Calais in French hands England lost control of the Narrow Seas, making it easier than before for the French to send arms and men into Scotland.

For Scotland, in recent years, had become a French stronghold. The ruler, Mary Stuart—successor to her father James V and, as a grandniece of Henry VIII, Elizabeth's cousin—had recently left Scotland to marry the heir to the French throne, the dauphin Francis. Her mother, Mary of Lorraine, was regent for her, surrounded by French advisers and supported by French arms. What lay behind this buildup of power to the north was all too clear: Mary Stuart had a vitally strong claim to the English throne and the Catholic French meant to support her militarily against the Protestant Elizabeth, in Catholic eyes a bastard and a heretic.

Thus as the peace talks went on, Elizabeth and her advisers sent couriers northward with urgent orders to fortify the border fortresses, count and evaluate their ordnance and initiate musters of the fighting men—honest musters, not the fraudulent, inflated numberings that captains usually turned in to make their companies look more impressive. And agents were dispatched to Flanders for the munitions and furnishings of war—hackbuts, helmets, corselets, sulfur and saltpeter.

To be sure, England had in Philip an ally to look to—he was King Philip now, king of Spain and ruler of much other territory besides—so that in theory at least the might of Spain and her dominions broadened England's arsenal. Yet the price of Philip's support was his dictatorship, and further costly involvement of English arms in Spanish wars. At worst, England might become the next forum of conflict between Hapsburg and Valois— a circumstance that would surely, and quickly, reduce the house of Tudor to insignificance and ruin. To show just enough gratitude for Philip's brotherly allegiance to keep the French at bay, yet not enough to invite his active interference in English affairs: that was the narrow course the queen and her advisers must navigate. And everything, including the religious settlement at home, depended on the adroitness of their navigation.

The councilors Elizabeth chose restored the personnel, if not the tone, of her brother's government. Most of them were Protestant—Archbishop Heath, a prominent exception, was before long replaced as lord keeper by Nicholas Bacon—and most of the peers among them were from recently ennobled families. (Arundel, a devout Catholic from an ancient lineage, stood out as unique.)

There were eighteen councilors at first; later the number was reduced to twelve. At their head was William Cecil, Elizabeth's former steward who had long since won her complete trust and reliance. Other councilors were said to be very close to the queen—among them John Mason, whom Feria called "her great confidant," and portly Thomas Parry, since childhood a trusted, if not always trustworthy, intimate—but Cecil alone combined extraordinary intelligence and ability with what Noailles called "a sensitive understanding of his mistress." For four decades he was to serve that mistress, and her kingdom, with an indefatigable competence bordering on the superhuman.

An energetic man in his late thirties, Cecil seemed to take every facet of government as his personal responsibility. As royal secretary he was expected to command detailed knowledge of a wide variety of topics, from foreign and military affairs and secret intelligence to the activities of the church, royal household and local government. But this was only a beginning. Cecil desired to know, and to a remarkable extent managed to know, everything of consequence that happened to anyone of importance throughout the length and breadth of England.

And he displayed that knowledge in the innumerable papers and letters and memoranda he produced—scores of thousands of documents testifying, in their bulk alone, to his tireless labors. Cecil combined the detailed conscientiousness of a meticulous clerk with the comprehensive grasp of a "prying steward"—as one nineteenth-century historian called him—overseeing the estate of England. Yet he was much more than this. He had impressive personal breadth, humanist learning, and much experience of government gained in the two previous reigns. He had, in addition, a remarkable ability to avoid those clashes of public duty and religious conscience that wrecked so many careers in the sixteenth century.

While remaining true to his Protestant opinions he had managed to make himself indispensable to both Mary and Pole, especially Pole, even though both were fully aware of Cecil's obligations to Elizabeth. A few days before he died the cardinal remembered his Protestant co-worker and friend and sent him a beautiful silver inkwell as a last token of his affection. But though Cecil thought it his duty to uphold the reigning sovereign, no matter what her faith or policies, he did not for a moment suppress his private opposition to those policies. Throughout the second half of Mary's reign he recorded in his diary the names of those the queen put to death for heresy, and a bitter chronicle it must have been to him.

A portrait of the secretary at the outset of Elizabeth's reign shows a cool, stern dignitary dressed in sober black with only the smallest of decorative ruffs at the neck. Alert, aloof, he is the picture of self-confident officialdom with his high brow, strong chin and discerning eye. Although Cecil had served his apprenticeship among the corrupt and self-advancing councilors of Edward VI, he had none of their rapacity or dishonesty, and his personal life was notably wholesome. From the sturdy, unostentatious house he leased at Wimbledon he could see the spire of old St. Paul's in the City; the surrounding pastures and fields yielded the beef and grain to feed his twenty-five servants and eight family members. But if Cecil was unusually temperate and humane in his private life he was shrewd, devious, even pitiless when it came to public matters, and it was precisely this Janus-like temperament that made the secretary so valuable to his royal mistress.

She needed, after all, a man of compatible personality, for she had no intention of abandoning her authority to her advisers and letting them rule for and through her. She meant to play the commanding role in her government, and to play it with all the refinements of deceit and misrepresentation she had acquired in Mary's reign, when her life depended on her ability to lie convincingly. Elizabeth and Cecil would conjoin in deception, as they would in every other maneuver of governing, and they complemented one another exceedingly well.

From the start Elizabeth overawed those nearest to her, for she seized the reins of power at once, and boldly. She and she alone ruled. She made all decisions, great and small, though she expected her councilors to advise her exhaustively beforehand and blamed them vociferously when any decision proved ill-advised. The council met daily. The queen did not normally attend its sessions, but did keep herself informed of the substance of its debates. Her preferred method of receiving advice, however, was to meet with individual council members in private, one at a time. These penetrating, no doubt grueling meetings allowed her to examine rigorously varying points of view, to sift and weigh information and arguments, and, perhaps most important, to assess the adroitness of each of her advisers and the degree of his commitment to his point of view.

For Elizabeth, like her father Henry VIII, was determined never to allow her councilors to unite against her. Taking advantage of their ambitious self-seeking and of the personal rivalries that inevitably arose to divide them, she used her exquisite political instincts to play off factions against one another, relying on her ability to gain intimate knowledge of each partisan's character and abilities. Her councilors, a seventeenth-century writer claimed, always "acted more by her own princely rules and judgements, than by their own wills and appetites, which she observed to the last." She took each man's measure, calculated his strengths and weaknesses, and then proceeded to play on these to keep him under control even as she took the utmost benefit from his counsel.

Her tactics baffled everyone, including her principal adviser Cecil. Indeed she was so successful in concealing her own political opinions as they took shape in her mind—while manipulating and intuiting those of others—that modern historians are often at a loss to disentangle her authentic ideas and policies from the false scents and smokescreens and political persiflage with which she surrounded them.

But if Elizabeth's political and intellectual skills served her well, though hardly infallibly, in dealing with her councilors she relied on her volatile, imperious temperament and on her inbred capacity for duplicity and deceit to keep them at bay. She was dangerously unpredictable in her moods. She blustered one minute and beguiled the next. Now coaxing and cajoling, now spitting out ringing oaths and insults, she kept her advisers off balance and perpetually astonished them by the range and mutability of her passions. Beyond this, they came to know that, with Elizabeth, nothing was ever what it seemed. Beneath her surface emotions were layer upon calculating layer of secondary reactions, ploys and schemes. She took pleasure in laying traps for her unwary ministers and ensnaring them later with their own words. Even the wittiest of them were sometimes left tongue-tied and flatfooted in her presence, while all of them, however fleetingly, were on occasion dazzled by her youthful, radiant femininity and sexual magnetism.

Elizabeth had more than enough courage, subtlety and aggressiveness to plunge boldly into the tasks of queenship. She had everything, in fact, but experience.

That she was a novice at foreign affairs could not be disguised. She dismayed her councilors and Feria by asserting that her sister's declaration of war against France was not binding on her—an assertion which, when she found it to be groundless, she quietly dropped. She had at first the overdeveloped suspiciousness of the amateur diplomat; when Feria brought her news that Spain and France had agreed to a truce she assumed at once that King Philip was betraying her, and had to have her fears allayed by Cecil.[7]

But if she was not yet surefooted in the intricacies of diplomacy, her aptitude for statecraft was unmistakable, and she more than made up in strength of personality whatever she lacked in experience of rule.

Feria, in England to safeguard Spanish interests and to try to preserve the influence Philip had enjoyed while Mary lived, has left a portrait of the new queen in the first weeks of her reign. She was extroverted, assertive, masterly. "A very strange sort of woman," he wrote of her in exasperation; she was as uninhibited and free in manner as her father had been, utterly lacking in the passivity and propriety he expected from a noblewoman. She spoke to Feria, as she did to the other ambassadors, candidly and in his own tongue; she complained of her poverty, shone with unabashed pleasure when he presented her with a costly ring ("she is very fond of having things given to her," he observed), and showed herself inordinately fond of disputation. On the whole Feria despaired of her. It was bad enough that she was a woman, but she was worse than that, "a young lass, sharp, but without prudence." In one respect alone she was an improvement over Mary: Elizabeth was likely to bear children once she married. But in every other way she "compared unfavorably" with her sister, from the Spanish point of view.[8]

Yet even Feria had to admit that Elizabeth seemed to him "incomparably more feared" than Mary had been, and that she "gave her orders and had her way absolutely as her father did." Absolutely, that was the key. Elizabeth clearly expected to be obeyed, and was. Her sense of command extended into the privy bedchamber, where she "made a speech to the women who were in her service," ordering them "never to speak to her on business affairs." The royal bedchamber, in the past a locus of much petitioning for offices and favors, became a political wilderness.

Elizabeth did well to keep her wits about her in these early weeks, for the court was in the utmost confusion. Most of Mary's officials and servants had been turned out, and their jobs were left undone or, when finally filled, were given to eager young replacements with more energy than experience. "The kingdom is entirely in the hands of young folks," Feria wrote, "heretics and traitors." The older generation and the staunch Catholics looked on in horror but kept their peace, at least in public; in private they called their new queen "flighty," and applied to her ancient cryptic prophecies predicting that her reign would be short, and that King Philip would soon return to rule again.[9]

Feria found the chaos that surrounded all court business disconcerting in the extreme. When he went to the presence chamber to speak to the queen he found it "crammed with people," all of whom were thrusting gifts at her or otherwise imploring her attention so that she was quite "carried away" by the excitement. If the Spaniard expected to find a peaceful haven in the council chamber he was disappointed. There too all was noise and interruption, with messengers and petitioners crowding in at the doorway and doing their best to listen at the keyhole or peek through cracks in the walls. "Things are in such a hurly-burly and confusion," Feria wrote, at his wits' end, "that fathers do not know their own children."

Elizabeth seemed to rise above the temporary disruptions, and indeed to revel in the chaos, perhaps because it reassured her that all was new and formless, and that she could set her own stamp on her court. One thing she went out of her way to make clear. Whoever had displeased or discomfited her sister, she meant to exalt. Elizabeth was "as much set against her sister as she was previous to her death," and saw to it that everyone realized it. Riding through the streets of the capital she caught sight of William Parr, marquess of Northampton and Protestant opponent of the late queen, watching out of a window along the street. She reined in her horse at once and shouted out a hearty greeting to him, asking after his health (he was convalescing) "in the most cordial way in the world." Parr deserved no special treatment, save that he had been a "great traitor" to Mary, Feria wrote sourly. "He who was most prominent in this way is now best thought of."

The intensity of this climate of revenge is clear from a story the Spaniard told concerning one of the physicians attending Mary in her final days. He was "a young fellow, a harebrained busybody" scorned by his colleagues, and Feria had reason to suspect that he had administered "something noxious" to Mary to hasten her death. He wanted to have the young physician arrested, but hesitated. "I am afraid," he explained, "that if anything is said to the queen about it she would be more likely to reward than to punish him."[10]

But if the courtiers and councilors were taken aback by the flamboyance of their ebullient young sovereign, they reminded themselves that her personal ascendency was bound to be short-lived. For she would surely marry, and soon. On the continent it was taken as a matter of course that Elizabeth would simply step into her dead sister's shoes, presiding over Mary's kingdom, continuing, with a few changes, to be governed by Mary's advisers and marrying Mary's husband. The courteous protection Philip had offered to Mary would now be offered to Elizabeth—indeed it would be ungentlemanly of him not to offer it—and the unbecoming burden of rule would be lifted from Elizabeth's slender shoulders. "It would be better for herself and her kingdom," Philip wrote to his sister-in-law, "if she would take a consort who might relieve her of those labors which are only fit for men."[11] Even Cecil, who was in a better position than anyone to vouch for Elizabeth's mental capacity, was overheard to scold an envoy who had been discussing an important ambassadorial dispatch with the queen. He should never have brought up with her a "matter of such weight," the secretary said, "being too much for a woman's knowledge."[12]

By far the most articulate exponent of the universal abhorrence of women rulers was the Scot John Knox, who in his seething anti-feminist *First Blast of the Trumpet Against the Monstrous Regiment of Women* cursed female rulership as unnatural and repugnant. Though the treatise was directed against Mary Tudor, the Scots queen Mary Stuart and her mother, the regent Mary of Lorraine, and not against Elizabeth personally, she took highly personal offense at it and refused to admit Knox into her realm—a notable break with her current policy of rewarding everyone who had worked to undermine her sister. Knox, who badly needed Elizabeth's support for the cause of Protestant rebellion in Scotland, was caught in his own trap.

He wrote to Cecil, attempting to exonerate himself in a way that would mollify Elizabeth. In his letter he made what must, to him, have seemed an enormous concession. Elizabeth, he said, was an exception to the unalterable principle of female unfitness—a miraculous exception, placed on her throne by God himself to serve his own unsearchable ends. And as long as she admitted that her authority represented an "extraordinary dispensation" from God, and was not grounded in human law or, heaven forbid, in any claim to equality with men ("which both nature and God's law doth deny to all women"), then he, Knox, would be more willing than anyone to "maintain her lawful authority."[13]

Such questions of principle aside, there were good and practical reasons for Elizabeth's household staff, its lower echelons in particular, to look forward expectantly to her marriage. Her consort would have to be supplied with a household of his own, once he came to England, and that would mean hundreds of new jobs; eventually each of their children too would require its own officials, and grooms and other servants, in an endless cycle of burgeoning employment.

The celebrations that accompanied Elizabeth's first Christmas as queen were edged with the special excitement of matchmaking. Since Mary's death the tone of the court had been subdued, its pleasures private, but in mid-December "they began to dance a little before supper," and with the holidays the merriment increased. The queen was said to have her eye on Francis Talbot, son of the earl of Shrewsbury, as well as on Arundel, who was recently returned from his duties as peace commissioner in France. The latter was every inch a suitor, strutting about the presence chamber in new silks and furs and "carrying his thoughts very high." He had borrowed heavily from an Italian merchant in London, telling the man that he would repay once he was married to the queen, and was scattering the money among Elizabeth's most confidential servants—her waiting women shared some two thousand pounds—in hopes that they would speak well of him to her.

Snow was falling lightly over London on the morning of January 14, 1559, the eve of the coronation. The weather had been bad for days, with heavy rain and snow turning to slush and then to deep mud that choked the streets and spattered against the houses and shopfronts as horses passed by. Since before dawn servants had been at work filling in the worst of the puddles and trenches and covering the roadway with gravel and sand, so that when the queen's procession passed it would not bog down in the mire. Through the morning hours the courtiers assembled at the Tower, taking their assigned places in the line of march, all of them "so sparkling with jewels and gold collars that they cleared the air," though the snow continued to fall.

By two o'clock the City was congested with impatient crowds, kept back from the streets by wooden barricades and by liveried whifflers and garders of the city companies. For an hour and more they had watched an interminable parade of harbingers, gentlemen ushers, squires and civic dignitaries, churchmen, judges, knights and peers. The spectacle was splendid—there were a thousand horses, one eyewitness wrote, all as bravely trapped as their glittering riders—but it was only of momentary interest: the people wanted to see the queen.

Then she came, and it was as if the clouds lifted and the sun came out. A great shout went up as her litter rose into view in the distance, gleaming in its gold brocade, and escorted by a host of red-coated footmen whose uniforms, studded in "massive gilt silver," bore the royal arms and the intertwined letters *ER*, for Elizabetha Regina. "Prayers, wishes, welcomings, cries, tender words" greeted the queen, resplendent in "very rich cloth of gold," as stiff and heavy as armor, and she, "by holding up her hands, and merry countenance to such as stood far off, and most tender and gentle language to those that stood nigh to her grace," responded in kind.

"God save your grace!" they cried out.

"God save you all!" she shouted back in a strong, ringing voice. "I thank you with all my heart!"

She seemed to hear every word called out by every well-wisher; she spoke not so much to the crowd as to each individual within it. She had the gift, as her father had in his time, of making everyone within the sound of her voice believe she was speaking to him or her alone.

It was a moment of pure joy, of passionate affection between the queen and her subjects. In that moment, a watching pamphleteer wrote, "there was nothing but gladness, nothing but prayer, nothing but comfort."[14]

So it went throughout the procession route. At each stopping point along the way there was a pageant or a brief concert or a recitation, and Elizabeth, knowing that all eyes would be on her and not on the performers, responded so theatrically—albeit sincerely—that she became an integral part of the show. At Fenchurch, where a child greeted her by speaking a long poem, she reacted with rapturous smiles to every verse of the sentimental doggerel. There was not only "a perpetual attentiveness in her face," but "a marvellous change in look, as the child's words touched either her person or the people's tongues or hearts." Her "rejoicing visage" told all; she was engraving every word on her mind. The queen's heartfelt pantomime was no less a performance than the child's recitation, and when both ended the onlookers burst into cheers and applause.

Elizabeth, concerned throughout to grasp the meaning of every pageant, sent men ahead to find out the theme and import of each display and to quiet the crowd so that she could hear the music and poetic oratory clearly. She commented on the profundity and appropriateness of the presentations, which represented her genealogical descent, the virtues of good governance, the triumph of Time, which had at length brought the realm out of the darkness and idolatry of Mary's reign into the light of divine truth. During this pageant of Time that favorite symbol of Protestants, the English Bible, was "delivered to her grace down by a silken lace" from out of the stage, and she, to the delight of the crowd, clasped it in her arms and kissed it, and cried out that "she would oftentimes read that book," before moving on.

To both the queen and her subjects the pageant of Time had more than a touch of irony about it, for five years earlier, when Queen Mary had ridden through the streets of the capital on her coronation procession, one of the pageants had illustrated her favorite motto, "Truth, the Daughter of Time"—a motto made even more familiar to her people through her coins and devices. Mary's truth had been the falsehood (to Protestants) of Catholicism; Elizabeth must have taken great satisfaction in seeing Mary's motto turned on its head.

At the upper end of Cheapside the city recorder presented the queen with a purse of coins, and she thanked him and the Londoners with a hearty speech.

"I thank my lord mayor, his brethren, and you all," she began. "And whereas your request is that I should continue your good lady and queen, be ye ensured, that I will be as good unto you as ever queen was to her people." The listeners drank in her words, impressed not only by her eloquence but by "hearing so princelike a voice, which could not but have set the enemy on fire." "No will in me can lack," she cried, "neither do I trust shall there lack any power. And persuade yourselves, that for the safety and quietness of you all, I will not spare, if need be, to spend my blood. God thank you all."

The speech drew tumultuous cheers, and as the queen's litter made its way along the remainder of the route onlookers forgot that they were seeing a twenty-five-year-old girl, slight and somewhat delicate, her long red hair flowing unbound and maidenly below the circlet of a princess. In their eyes she became that princely being, a woman ruler.

The final pageant portrayed Elizabeth as Deborah, "judge and restorer of the house of Israel," represented as a "seemly and meet personage, richly apparelled in Parliament robes, with a scepter in her hand, as a queen, crowned with an open crown." It was a worthy riposte to the dour fulminations of Knox, and an omen for the future. Elizabeth was moved. "Be ye well assured," she told the crowd when the pageant oratory had ended, "I will stand your good queen," and whatever else she may have said was drowned out by the "crying and shouting of the people" as she passed on through Temple Bar toward Westminster.

From first to last the procession had been a personal triumph, and not only for Elizabeth but, in a sense, for her pitied mother, restored to honor in the genealogical pageant and portrayed with scepter and diadem, surmounted by her title. And for her tremendous father, who loomed so large in popular memory as the new reign began.

"Remember old King Henry the Eighth!" a voice called from the crowd as Elizabeth's litter rested at Cheapside, and it was noted that she broke into a broad smile. Her father, she knew well, would have laughed with pleasure had he lived to see Anne Boleyn's child, the child of his fondest hopes and deepest disappointment, come into her own at last.

16

Now Besse bethinke thee,
what thou hast to doe.
Thy lover will come presently,
and hardly will he woo:

I will teach my Gentleman,
a tricke that he may know,
I am too craftie and too wise,
to be ore-reached so.

In April of 1559, three months after Elizabeth's coronation, Robert Dudley came suddenly, and alarmingly, into prominence. The queen's tall, athletic master of the horse—by common agreement "an extremely handsome young man," perhaps the handsomest man at court—had been in evidence, though without any particular notoriety, since the start of the reign. He had cut a brave figure in the coronation procession, riding directly behind the queen's litter in solitary magnificence and leading her riderless horse, and it was to be expected that his attractive person would be lent to adorn the tilts and masques and pageants that were the staple of court entertainment. But no one could have predicted at the outset of the reign that Elizabeth would take Lord Robert for her lover.

"During the last few days Lord Robert has come so much into favor that he does whatever he likes with affairs," Feria wrote disapprovingly. "And it is even said that her majesty visits him in his chamber day and night."[1]

Feria's claim, though imprecise, was damning enough, but before long the tales told about the dalliance of the queen and her horse master were so explicit and conclusive that no foreign envoy dared repeat them. "Many persons say things which I should not dare to write," the Mantuan Il Schifanoya told his Venetian employers. De Quadra, who replaced Feria as Spanish ambassador in May, recorded that he heard "some extraordinary things about this intimacy," things he would have found impossible to believe if it weren't for the fact that nearly the entire privy council "made no secret" of the shocking truth.[2]

The love affair between Elizabeth and Dudley was common knowledge, and because everyone knew about it, there was little or no need to write about it. And there was a powerful inducement to silence besides: it would have been extremely dangerous to commit details of the queen's indiscretions to writing. As a result we are left with an abundance of circumlocutions and broad references whose general import is unmistakable, yet on the vital, central issue—whether or not the virgin queen lost her virginity in 1559 (if indeed she had not lost it to Thomas Seymour years earlier)—the records are silent.

To look to Elizabeth's own words for a hint at the truth is frustrating and inconclusive, for in addition to being habitually untruthful the queen took a perverse delight in outraging people. She was much inclined to speak, if not exactly without thinking, then without always thinking very far, and she showed little hesitation when it came to gratifying her everpresent desire to tease, befuddle and generally confound the grave personages who surrounded her.

Thus it would be foolish to put much faith either in her protestations of innocence and chastity or in her coy "confession" to De Quadra in 1561 that she was "no angel" and that she had some affection for Dudley. Had she denied her affection for him her actions would have belied her words, for it was no small part of the scandal that she fondled Dudley like a lover in public.

Then too she may have taken him as her lover out of sheer exultant rebelliousness. For in the first year of her reign—and beyond—Elizabeth was stridently, aggressively self-willed. "Like a peasant on whom a barony has been conferred," an imperial envoy wrote, "she, since she came to the throne is puffed up with pride, and imagines that she is without peer."[3] She had never been educated for her role as queen, and if she had an overabundance of charisma she was woefully lacking in self-restraint. To thwart her own will for the good of her realm was a lesson no one had ever taught her; on the contrary, having been thwarted most of her life, she was now more determined than ever to break free and follow her own desires absolutely. She was, reportedly, "so stubborn and headstrong that she acts regardless of her own welfare and that of the kingdom."[4]

No more explosive arena for self-assertion offered itself than marriage and sex, the time-honored ground of conflict between young and old, parent and child. Kat Ashley and Thomas Parry had stood in lieu of parents to Elizabeth since childhood, and it was no coincidence that her behavior with Dudley was the cause of severe tension between them now.

Parry was said to be grieved and distressed that Elizabeth should act as she did, and this, plus his excessive girth, helped to put him in his grave early in 1561. Kat Ashley, who as mother of the maids presided over the royal bedchamber and no doubt bore the brunt of a good deal of accusatory gossip, made a desperate, and highly affecting, plea for her mistress to come to her senses and see reason.

She began by falling at Elizabeth's feet in abject silence. What was it? the queen asked her, unleashing by her question a long and carefully rehearsed chain of entreaties.

In God's name, Kat begged, Elizabeth ought to marry and put a stop to all the terrible things that were being said about her. The way she treated Dudley led everyone to believe that they were as good as married—or rather as sinful as adulterers, since the horse master was married already. The talk was expanding, and as it spread Elizabeth was making it worse by openly displaying her excessive fondness for Dudley, lowering herself in everyone's eyes and rapidly losing the respect due her as queen.

Could she not see where all this would lead? Kat asked Elizabeth, warming to her subject and perhaps realizing as she went on that she alone could speak as she did, that Elizabeth would tolerate such arguments from no one else. Could she not see that before long her subjects would withdraw their affection, then their allegiance, and that finally there would be warfare between rival claimants to the throne she was no longer worthy to hold? The bloodshed would be on the queen's own head and no one else's; God would call her to account for it, and her erstwhile subjects would curse her name.

It was a calamitous scenario, an unthinkable and ignominious end to a reign that had begun in such joyous celebration. Rather than that all this should happen, Kat concluded, "she would have strangled her majesty in the cradle." Having said that she held her peace.

Elizabeth, who had at the tip of her tongue a well-rehearsed speech of her own in defense of her unmarried state, at first responded with gracious condescension, acknowledging that she knew Kat's words were the "outpourings of a good heart and true fidelity," and that she was, of course, willing to marry if only to set Kat's mind at ease and to console the rest of her subjects. Yet marriage was a weighty matter requiring much reflection, and Mistress Ashley must always keep in mind that up to this time the queen had "had no wish to change her state."

Finding no solace whatever in this response—and Kat knew only too well how skilled Elizabeth was at speaking many words yet saying nothing—she renewed her entreaties.

For the love of God, she implored, Elizabeth must commit herself to one of the many suitors who hung about the court. Let her settle on a worthy, responsible match, one befitting her rank and pleasing to her kingdom, for if she hesitated longer she would be courting divine punishment. God in his wrath might "call her away from this world before her time," Kat warned as sternly as she could—and having no heir of her own body, her legacy would be strife and chaos.

Elizabeth's response to this was not so sure-footed. She began by arguing loftily that God, who had preserved her and made her queen, would continue to provide for her—and for England—as he always had, her life or death being incidental to his inscrutable plan. But having said that, she turned to defending herself against the gossip that there was "something dishonorable" between her and Dudley, and the more she argued on her own behalf the more heated she became. She had given no one cause to accuse her, she insisted; she hoped she never would. Yet—and here self-pity intervened—"in this world she had had so much sorrow and tribulation and so little joy." Her implication was clear: surely she had earned what happiness Dudley brought her. And besides, if she showed him favor, he was deserving of it, for his "honorable nature and dealings." And in any case whatever went on between them went on in the presence of her ladies and maids of honor—an assertion which, whether it was true or not, Kat Ashley would probably have been able to confirm or refute.

Then came her final challenge, and it was just such remarks as this one that lent more than a whiff of truth to the rumors of her unchastity. "If she had ever had the will or had found pleasure in such a dishonorable life," Elizabeth said to Kat, "from which God preserve her, she did not know of anyone who could forbid her."[5]

It was the last word, the ultimate royal pronouncement. And it must have made Kat despair.

The confrontation was overheard by Elizabeth's personal servants and its contents were reported, or more likely sold, to an agent of the Holy Roman Emperor Ferdinand I, who along with the other continental sovereigns had a keen interest in the English queen's intimate life. Other information reached the emperor at the same time. All the bedchamber ladies swore that the queen had "most certainly never been forgetful of her honor," and that they had "never noticed anything." Yet Elizabeth continued to heap honors on her horse master, and to caress him "more markedly than is consistent with her reputation and dignity." She made him a Garter Knight, choosing him over the earl of Bedford, which everyone, especially the earl, found to be a glaring injustice. She gave him several monasteries, a house at Kew, profitable commercial licenses and a princely gift of £12,000 in coins "as an aid toward his expenses."

In the usually parsimonious queen such generosity betokened extravagant love indeed—and extravagant folly. It was no wonder the Spanish ambassador reported that, along with Cecil, Dudley "ruled everything," and that King Philip had best ally himself quickly with the upstart horse master who would surely become king before long.[6]

The queen's shameless attachment to a married man was only the most recent—albeit the most startling—evidence of her unpredictability and unconventionality. Was she simply reckless, thoughtless, "naturally changeable," as Feria believed her to be, or was she, at some deep level of cunning, perfectly in control of everything, including her own extravagant passions? "To say the truth I could not tell your majesty what this woman means to do with herself," Feria wrote to King Philip shortly before he left England, "and those who know her best know no more than I do." Feria's successor De Quadra was equally baffled. "I am not sure about her," he reported, "for I do not understand her."[7]

What was evident by the spring of 1559 was that, for all her inexplicable proceedings, Elizabeth was having marked success in meeting and overcoming the intricate tangle of problems that faced her in her first six months as queen. Most pressing was the issue of religion, a sore spot on the body politic rubbed more raw by the shock and violence of the Marian burnings.

Protestants were a tiny minority in England in 1559, but many in that minority were in London, and when they massed in their hundreds to sing psalms in unison the effect was of one mighty voice, impassioned and indomitable. By the spring of 1559 the marks of Protestant anger against the Marian church were everywhere: church windows smashed, altars overturned and robbed of their ornaments, crucifixes with their faces cut and scratched, statues of the saints torn from their pedestals and burned or broken to bits. The capital was defaced, "as if it had been the sacking of some hostile city," and visitors noted the abundance of anti-Catholic books and ballads for sale, the plays performed in hostels and taverns which mocked the late queen and her husband and Cardinal Pole, the taunting of the clergy as they walked in procession through the streets.[8]

That Elizabeth would placate the fervor of these zealots by restoring the Protestantism of her father and brother was in no doubt, but the situation called for caution. There might be anticlerical mummeries at court—one Epiphany play featured crows in cardinals' habits, asses dressed as bishops and wolves representing abbots—but in Parliament religious legislation had at first to proceed slowly and conservatively, for the shape of the religious settlement was bound up with England's dangerous passage through the shoals of foreign war.

Once Elizabeth took the fatal step of breaking away from Rome, it was feared, the pope would excommunicate her and leave her realm "a prey to all the princes that will enter upon it." England was poor in soldiers, captains and arms, and lacked even the money to buy them, while her fortresses, Philip's chancellor Granvelle said, were scarcely "able to endure the breath of a cannon one day." With the pope's blessing the French and Spanish would pour into the country and dismember it—unless, of course, they could be persuaded that it could be taken by easier and less costly means.

Here Elizabeth showed her inbred mastery of intrigue. By keeping her ambassador in Rome, keeping the mass (with minor alterations) in her chapel and delaying the religious reform in Parliament she forestalled papal excommunication, meanwhile leading both Henry II in France and Philip in Spain to believe that England was theirs for the wooing. Philip wooed in earnest: he was the first and greatest of all Elizabeth's royal suitors, and for several months she allowed him to think that, despite all, she might marry him. At the same time, however, she was treating secretly with an agent of King Henry—who was said to be hiding in Parry's chambers in the palace—and allowing the French to hope that she might break with her dangerous Spanish ally if only King Henry would be reasonable about the return of Calais.

With the French and Spanish thus distracted she continued to muster men and gather war materials, "scraping money together from all sides, paying nothing and giving nothing to her people, and spending very little" so that she could begin to restore her credit with the moneylenders in Antwerp who might finance her warfare. Early in March the recruiters beat their drums in the streets of London and the muster rolls grew longer, while English agents in Flanders ordered gunpowder and bowstaves and corselets and made solemn pledges to pay for them a month or two hence. Berwick Castle was fortified against the French in Scotland, though the expense of the repairs threatened to imperil the treasury's fragile solvency.[9]

In fact Elizabeth had all along been gambling, not on war but on peace, and at the last moment, on Palm Sunday, March 18, word reached her that her negotiators on the continent had arrived at an accommodation to end the hostilities. Calais, unfortunately, was to remain in French hands for at least another eight years; after that, in lieu of returning it to England, the French agreed to pay five hundred thousand crowns as compensation. But there was the hope that the territory might after all be returned, or that before then the amity between the French and Spanish might dissolve once again.

With peace in hand the pace of parliamentary action on the religious settlement quickened, and toward the end of April the Acts of Supremacy and Uniformity were passed. The queen became head of the church in England—though she preferred to use the title "supreme governor"—and King Edward's second Prayer Book of 1552 (with a few modifications) was reintroduced. To attend mass became a crime punishable by imprisonment —life imprisonment if the offender repeated his crime three times. Catholic England was officially dead, though it was to flourish underground for centuries. It was a day of anger and disillusionment for the Spaniards. "We have lost a kingdom," Feria wrote bitterly, "body and soul."[10]

Summer brought a temporary respite from the tensions of statecraft, the first such respite Elizabeth had known as queen. For a week she entertained a delegation of French envoys who came to England to ratify the peace treaties, feasting them so lavishly it was hard to believe she was nearly bankrupt. The magnificent palace of Whitehall became a garden of delights, with hunting parties in the park and sumptuous outdoor banquets. One feast was spread in the palace gardens, the tables laid in an open-air gallery enclosed with hangings of gold and silver brocade and with "wreaths of flowers and leaves of most beautiful designs, which gave a very sweet odor and were marvellous to behold." Elizabeth presided in regal robes of purple velvet, adorned "with so much gold and so many pearls and jewels that it added much to her beauty."[11] The French ladies managed to upstage their hostess; their broad-beamed farthingales, no doubt cut in a fashion not yet seen in England, were so wide that they overflowed the banquet tables, leaving so little room that some of the English had to sit "on the ground on the rushes" to eat. But English robes were of perennial beauty—or so Elizabeth seemed to say when she presented a noble French boy with some of the late King Edward's long unused finery.

June was filled with "musical performances and other entertainments," singing and dancing and, in the evenings, trips on the river in the royal barge. On the twenty-first of June the queen left London to begin her summer journey, or progress, through the countryside, but at first she went no farther than Greenwich, where a vast military spectacle had been arranged.

As the queen looked on, surrounded by the ambassadors and other court notables, some fourteen hundred soldiers marched onto the lawn, "mustering in their arms, all the gunners in shirts of mail." With banners flying and guns and pikes at the ready, they stood to attention while Dudley and others rode up and down reviewing them and dividing them into two armies for a mock battle. At a signal the skirmishing began, to the martial sound of trumpets and drums and flutes. The soldiers rushed on one another as if in earnest, "the guns discharged on one another, the morris pikes encountered together with great alarm; each ran to their weapons again, and then they fell together as fast as they could, in imitation of close fight."[12] Elizabeth showed herself "very merry" at the sight, and let it be known that the muster, and the tilting which followed it, were done "to her great delight and satisfaction."

There were more festivities in the coming days. The queen went to Woolwich to launch a fine new ship for her navy, christened the *Elizabeth*, and returned to Greenwich to watch more military games—among them a "great casting of fire, and shooting of guns, till twelve at night." The recent peace, these exercises proclaimed, had not dimmed England's warlike spirit; let other nations take warning.

Elizabeth played her part in these events with her customary exuberance, showing particular excitement whenever Dudley rode by in the lists or on the parade ground. Yet her vibrancy had a manic quality; more and more it was nervous energy that fueled her as the strain of a heady romantic passion combined with the increasing pressures of disapproving gossip and demeaning advisers to drain her vitality and lower her spirits. Worry over her health, which had never really been strong, increased the longer she delayed in choosing a husband and settling the succession. Her physicians bled her from the foot and arm in June, though from what cause no one recorded. In August she developed a "burning fever" which continued to vex her for several weeks, its onset coinciding closely with Kat Ashley's scolding, imploring plea that she put Dudley aside and take a suitable husband.

Every day, she confided to one foreign envoy, she was pestered with petitions from her subjects "desiring her for her honor's sake and for the welfare of her kingdom" to give up her single life. Everyone had a case to make—Kat Ashley, Parry, Cecil, her councilors. Some favored a foreign match, others an Englishman, still others, and their numbers were growing, anyone but Dudley. Most anguishing of all, there was pressure from Dudley himself, who wanted not only her heart but a share in her rule, and whose ardent wooing set her at odds with herself and made her want to yield to him her hard-won independence.

By mid-August Elizabeth appeared to be "somewhat dejected," and her ladies confided that she had "been quite melancholy in her room of nights and had not slept half an hour." Never very clear-headed in the mornings, she now showed herself "quite pale and weak" on arising, and the thought of facing the array of English and foreign suitors who thronged her presence

chamber and vied for her attention cannot have soothed her sleepless-
ness.[13]

Besides Dudley, there were two principal English wooers. The earl of
Arundel, a fit but unprepossessing man of middle age, was excessively
hurried in his speech and ill-considered in his judgments. He had his
ancient lineage to recommend him, but little else; Elizabeth could, and did,
enjoy his palace of Nonsuch, which her father had leased to him in gratitude for his services, without making him her consort.

The other Englishman was, potentially, a far better match for Elizabeth.
Sir William Pickering was a handsome, urbane pleasure-seeker, a man of
the world who had traveled widely and knew many languages. In sophistication he was more than a match for the queen; he liked women and was
comfortable with them, and was rumored "to have enjoyed the intimacy
of many and great ones." In a court full of timid flatterers and ambitious
schemers Pickering stood out as a man who went his own way and lived
his own life, amiably and somewhat mysteriously. Diplomatic missions kept
him on the continent a great deal, but when he was in London it was noted
that, despite his small fortune, he "lived at times in great state," "like a
prince all alone in a stately house."

It became clear that Pickering intrigued Elizabeth when, on his return
to England in the spring of 1559, she met with him privately for some five
hours, keeping their meeting a secret from Dudley, who was hunting at
Windsor. Dudley sensed the rivalry, and was seen to show less friendliness
toward Pickering than in the past; odds-makers at court, accepting bets on
all the potential suitors then in residence, were posting Pickering at four
to one.[14] But appearances deceived, and in fact Sir William was not a
serious contender. He did, however, emerge from his long discussion with
the queen to make an insightful observation. He knew women well, and
was a good judge of the true intentions that lay behind their coquetry. And
Elizabeth, he felt sure, "meant to die a maid."[15]

Of the foreign suitors, several, such as the French duke de Nemours and
Duke William of Savoy, were not considered worthy of a wager. Others
mounted such elaborate displays of courtship that they could not be dismissed, despite their outlandishness. Prince Eric of Sweden—who became
King Eric XIV in 1560—sent a delegation of his countrymen to the
English court, all of them wearing red robes with badges showing a crimson
velvet heart pierced with an arrow. Their wooing was as clumsy and obvious
as their liveries, though more welcome: they scattered expensive gifts
among the court notables and chief servants, calculating that the sheer
weight of their silver would be sufficient to win the queen's favor. Everyone
was showered with costly bribes, from the maid of honor who carried a

polite greeting to the Swedish ambassador and came away with a trinket worth three hundred crowns to the queen herself, whose "grand present of tapestries and ermine" was meant only to hint at the "many millions" she could expect to receive if she married Prince Eric.

But the suit was hopeless. To English eyes the bearlike Swedes were ridiculously funny and ill-bred, and thick-headed besides. Their appeals were so earnest and their English so poor that they failed to notice when the courtiers made fun of them, and no one joked more mercilessly or laughed harder at the jokes than the queen herself. In the end, though Prince Eric paid Elizabeth the compliment of sending his younger brother as an envoy, with a large and imposing retinue, she turned the offer down —ostensibly because she found the deportment of Swedish royalty appalling. "How should we ever have agreed to such a difference in manners," she remarked in dismay. "For, however much I might accommodate myself, it is greatly to be feared that they would never give up their habits." Even after the dejected northerners returned home she continued to refer to "the barbaric king of Sweden" with fastidious contempt.

Of course, Elizabeth knew full well that the Swedes were not disinterested wooers, and that what lay behind Prince Eric's professions of love— besides his eagerness to add England to his own lands—was a promise of French support and allegiance. For if the queen chose Eric she would refuse the much more tempting offer of a Hapsburg match—something the French, despite their recent rapprochement with the imperialists, had every reason to oppose.

It was the Hapsburg candidate, in fact, who appeared to stand the best chance of winning Elizabeth's hand. He was Archduke Charles, son of the Holy Roman Emperor Ferdinand and reputed to be, at least from the standpoint of England's interests in Europe, "the best match in Christendom" for her. His brother Ferdinand she dismissed for his overweening Catholicism and his illegible handwriting—"the worst she had ever seen" —not to mention his large and stocky German concubine. But young Charles was reported to be, "for a man, beautiful and well-faced," with a small waist and a broad chest and "well-thighed and well-legged" besides. His stoop was not noticeable when he was on horseback, and he had come through an attack of smallpox with remarkably little disfigurement. Never mind, De Quadra told her, that others had presented the archduke as a "young monster." The truth was entirely otherwise. He did not have an enormous head, nor was he really as addicted to hunting, or as "unfit to govern," as rumor held. Best of all, he showed marked leanings toward Protestantism, and if the queen liked his portrait well enough, he might be willing to come to England to woo her in person.

In retrospect it seems clear that Elizabeth never seriously considered marrying Archduke Charles, but throughout most of 1559 she succeeded in giving the appearance of being serious about him, and so in distressing the French. Cecil, Parry, the young duke of Norfolk—not to mention many others on the council—were well disposed toward the Hapsburg marriage, though as time went on their desire for it was fed more and more by their growing apprehension about Dudley.

"Not a man in the realm can suffer the idea of his being king," wrote De Quadra in November, and new rumors of attempts against the lives of Dudley and Elizabeth lent weight to his words. In October stories of a plot to poison the queen and her horse master at a banquet given by Arundel had the queen "much alarmed." A second plot was disclosed a few weeks afterward, and the subject of Dudley's murder was "all common talk and threat" among the courtiers.[16]

Dudley was "very vigilant and suspicious," Elizabeth uneasy, unable to brazen out her danger. Her advisers, normally divided by bitter personal rivalries, now appeared to be uniting in their determination to ensure Dudley's ruin by any means necessary. And the queen, her energies drawn in many directions by the rhythms and necessities of government affairs, now had an added anxiety. One of her chamber staff, a servant named Drury, was, along with his brother, suspected of being part of the plotting. There were assassins, or accomplices of assassins, among her personal servants. How could she, or the man she loved, be safe?

Meanwhile the scandal brewing around the presumed lovers was becoming so ugly and so corrosive that Elizabeth's chances to marry abroad were imperiled. Her good repute was crumbling under the massive weight of accusation. "I have heard great things of a sort that cannot be written about and you will understand what they must be by that," De Quadra reiterated. Elizabeth was a Medea ruled entirely by her lusts, a woman of neither "brains nor conscience," a "passionate ill-advised woman" with "a hundred thousand devils in her body."[17] The slander came from all sides; so many voices were raised in frank, unambiguous accusation, so very few in the queen's defense.

And in the last analysis, as her advisers fully realized, what mattered was not the sin—if sin there was—but the appearance of sin. Never mind the facts: before long Elizabeth would be so cheapened by the presumptions alone that no man would risk staining his own honor by marrying her. It was this obvious, cruel truth that she refused to face—unless, as some hinted darkly, she was so diabolically lecherous that she wanted to destroy all opportunity for marriage, so that she would be free to enjoy not only Dudley but many lovers.

Emperor Ferdinand was becoming protective of his son the archduke. He asked his ambassador in England, Baron von Breuner, to discover as best he could "on what foundation the somewhat discreditable rumors that are being spread from certain quarters touching the honor of the queen, are based." The calumnies could no longer be dismissed as groundless gossip, as they came from "so many sides" and "always had the same tenor." Von Breuner, no doubt terrified that if he confirmed the scandal he would forever discredit himself as a diplomat—for it would mean admitting that for some months he had been working to betroth the archduke to a dishonorable woman—wrote back that the love between Elizabeth and Dudley was no more than an innocent romance. But Emperor Ferdinand was far from being convinced. He allowed the negotiations to proceed, but would not allow his son to visit England. And unless he came to England, Elizabeth declared, she could not possibly even consider marrying him.[18]

By the spring of 1560 the alarm over Dudley approached panic when he himself announced that "if he lived another year he would be in a very different position from now." It was a ringing challenge, a defiant boast that he would soon have Elizabeth entirely in his power.[19] Queen Elizabeth and King Robert: it was only a question of time.

But what would he do about his wife? She lived obscurely in the country, never coming to court and never seeing anyone who did. She was ill, some said, but others denied it. She was despondent—as who in her situation would not be?—and seemed at times to hint at taking her own life. That she felt abandoned by her husband, humiliated by the stories all Europe knew, fearful of the impetuous, attractive queen may be surmised. Did she feel that she was in danger as well?

As Elizabeth and Dudley spent a blissfully companionable summer together, enjoying the long warm afternoons, riding and hunting together in the forests far from the accusing tongues of the court, the common conviction grew adamant. The lovers must be plotting to remove the one obstacle to their happiness. By divorce, or poison, or by the hand of a murderer they meant surely to do away with Dudley's wife.

17

O Besse the knave is growne to proude
take him downe take him downe
Such twiges must needes be bound.

A my Dudley was found dead at the bottom of a flight of stone steps, her neck broken, on the eighth of September, 1560. Robert Dudley was now a widower. He could marry the queen.

On the day of Amy's death Elizabeth went hunting, as she had been doing for some days past, and Dudley was almost certainly with her. Only the day before he had described in a letter how well she felt—the fresh air and exercise invigorated her—and how she had "become a great huntress," following the chase "from morning till night." She was mad for reckless speed, the horse master wrote. Her own geldings, though she "spared not to try them as fast as they can go," were too tame for her; she wanted "strong, good gallopers" from Ireland, hobbies barely broken in and with the wildness of the open country about them.[1]

She was thoroughly enjoying her summer. Only a few weeks earlier she had been joking and flirting with seventy-five-year-old Paulet, marquess of Winchester, when she stayed at his house at Basing. His hospitality was so munificent, she said, that it made her "bemoan him to be so old." If only he were a younger man, she swore, she could "find in her heart to have him to her husband before any man in England." Here in the country there were fewer censorious stares and accusing tongues; even Cecil, who strove to be the voice of reason and conscience, had been absent much of the time in Scotland, and when he returned he found that Dudley was working effectively to undermine his influence with his mistress.

Elizabeth was returning from the hunt, in fact, when she remarked to the Spanish ambassador that "Robert's wife was dead or nearly so," and asked him not to make the knowledge public.

De Quadra was stupefied. There was only one conclusion to be drawn: Dudley, very likely with Elizabeth's complicity, had murdered his wife, either personally or through hired assassins. The circumstances could hardly have been more suspicious. Lady Dudley had been alone in the house when she fell to her death; the servants had conveniently been sent away. Tales of her ill health were an obvious smokescreen, spread by Dudley or his agents to disguise the murder. After all, Cecil had sworn to De Quadra only a few days earlier that Amy Dudley was in truth "quite well, and would take very good care they did not poison her."[2] Evidently she had eluded the poison, and her husband had had to use more violent means to rid himself of her.

And what of Elizabeth's role? Dudley would not risk taking such drastic action without her approval; the matter touched her far too closely. And she hardly seemed distraught at the news. Beyond her announcement to De Quadra, she had told the courtiers of Amy Dudley's death by saying, in Italian, that "she had broken her neck." Nothing more. Elizabeth was frequently offhanded, even high-handed, in her treatment of weighty matters, but this seemed unusually flippant and heartless even for her. Having outraged her entire kingdom during the months of her intimacy with Dudley, she had at last taken the irrevocable, criminal step of condoning murder. This scandal she could never live down.

Shocking as the event was, De Quadra was not entirely unprepared for it. Cecil, beside himself with anxiety over Elizabeth's irresponsibility and in despair about his own position, had only recently spoken to the ambassador with uncharacteristic openness.

Elizabeth, he said, was abandoning the business of government entirely, and turning everything over to her lover—a disastrous course, given his selfish greed and inexperience, not to mention the passionate hatred he inspired from "all the principal people in the kingdom."[3] She meant to marry Dudley in time, Cecil said, and with this catastrophe in view he was thinking very seriously of retiring. His pleas that the queen "act aright, live peacefully and marry" went unheeded; her mind was made up, and the "ruin of the realm" was sure to follow.

Then Cecil told De Quadra a curious thing. Elizabeth, he said, "wished to do as her father did." Certainly she had been following in the old king's footsteps so far, giving rise to gossip, deliberately provoking scandal, indulging her personal desires at the expense of her reputation. All this and more Henry VIII had done when he found himself at the center of a romantic triangle, with an unwanted wife, Katherine of Aragon, and a much desired mistress, Anne Boleyn.

But in a larger sense what King Henry had done was to assert his personal sovereignty in the sexual realm as ruthlessly as he asserted it in the political realm. The women he became entangled with, whether as wives or lovers, emerged much the worse from the encounter, while the king remained unshackled and dominant. By proclaiming her preference for the single life, by refusing the suitors who pursued her, by her seeming indifference to the urgent issue of the succession, and most of all, by her shameless liaison with Dudley, Elizabeth was achieving the same results her father had achieved: sovereign mastery of her sexual life, at the expense of others.

The secretary stopped far short of the ultimate conclusion, that the queen would continue to "do as her father did" to the end of her reign. That she might not marry at all was inconceivable to him; therefore she must intend to marry Dudley. De Quadra, who had watched her closely for over a year and had learned to be wary of both her capacity for deception and her inner incertainties, made a more cautious assessment. "Certainly this business is most shameful and scandalous," he wrote of the Amy Dudley affair, "and withal I am not sure whether she will marry the man at once or even if she will marry at all, as I do not think she has her mind sufficiently fixed."[4]

But this was an exceptionally sophisticated judgment. Most people, in court and out, leaped to the simplest and most sordid conclusion, that the queen had allowed her lust for Dudley and her jealousy of his wife to mislead her into joining her lover in murder.

Even as they put on mourning for Amy Dudley and came to pay their formal respects to her bereaved husband the courtiers cursed him as a murderer and struggled to keep their violent emotions in check. Affronted beyond measure by Dudley's presumptuous crime, insulted by his preeminence with the queen, nonetheless their fear forced them to treat him with outward respect, for they thought it likely he would become king before long. And they were furious with themselves for giving in to their fear, instead of standing up to him and accusing him to his face, or, better, coming up behind him with a sword and running him through.

In the country at large the uproar was immediate and strident. "The cry is that they do not want any more women rulers, and this woman may find herself and her favorite in prison any morning." The guilty death of Amy Dudley confirmed every other scandalous tale that had ever been told about Elizabeth and Dudley, including recent rumors that she had borne his child. People recalled every detail of her questionable past, the accounts of her indiscretions with Thomas Seymour, the stigma she bore as the child of Anne Boleyn, her less than regal upbringing as Henry VIII's bastard daughter—and maybe not his daughter at all, despite her resemblance to him.

Incriminating stories surfaced. The queen had been returning from a banquet at Dudley's London house, one of Arundel's servants said, and had fallen into conversation with the torchbearers who were lighting her way back to the palace. She had talked freely of Dudley, saying that she would make him "the best that ever was of his name." His father had been a duke; to better that rank, Dudley would have to be king.[5]

Before Amy Dudley had been dead ten days Francis Knollys, Elizabeth's second cousin, warned of the "grievous and dangerous suspicion and muttering" throughout the Warwickshire countryside. There must be a formal investigation—an "earnest searching and trying out of the truth," with due punishment to follow if it was merited. Knollys knew well that he was recommending, at the very least, close scrutiny of Dudley's activities, and that they might not bear scrutiny. Yet the alternative to Dudley's incrimination was rebellion, and in view of that he was emboldened "faithfully, reverently and lovingly" to write as he did.[6]

And what of the object of all the suspicion and vituperation? Dudley, presumed villain and absolute master of Elizabeth, was before long sent away from court, to his house at Kew. There he stayed, frustrated, anxious, more than a little bewildered, while she coped with the tumult.

The letter Dudley wrote to Cecil—the man whose security in office he had only recently shaken—betrays little of the arrogance or mastery ascribed to him. He thanked Cecil for a visit he had made, and asked him "what he thought best for him to do." He begged the secretary to voice any suspicions he had, so that Dudley could lay bare what he knew and be better advised how to act. The letter lacked clarity, though it had the half-poetic, half-rhetorical wording and cadence of its highly educated (if not highly intelligent) author. "I am sorry so sudden a chance shalt breed me so great a change," Dudley lamented elegantly. He "sued to be at liberty, out of so great bondage," and found himself "too far, too far from the place he was bound to be"—at court, by the side of his beleaguered lady the queen.

"Methinks I am here all this while, as it were in a dream," he mused, lost in reverie. But he gathered his senses sufficiently to remind Cecil not to forget the "humble sacrifice" he had promised him, and to plead that, though he was out of sight, he might remain strongly in mind—an absolute certainty, given the angry mood of the court.[7]

Elizabeth may have sent Dudley to Kew to protect him. Norfolk, "chief of Lord Robert's enemies," was so incensed by the latest example of Dudley's "presumption" that he was beside himself with rage. As England's only duke he saw himself as defender of the privileges of the nobility against arrogant parvenus of all sorts, and the horse master who aspired to be king —by any means necessary—had now given him intolerable provocation. Norfolk had been overheard to warn that if Dudley "did not abandon his present pretensions" he would not die in his bed. And Cecil, for one, feared that the murderous temper the duke (and many others) displayed would prove to be a danger not only to Dudley, but to the queen.

With Dudley away from court Cecil resumed his former preeminence, still shaking his head over Elizabeth's wrong-headedness but no longer in such despair about his own future role as her chief councilor. The queen's safety was paramount, and he was attending to it, drawing up "Certain Cautions for the Queen's Apparel & Diet" meant to protect her from the wrath and treachery of her alienated courtiers.

More care should be taken, the secretary noted, to preserve the orderly guarding of the privy chamber, with an usher and the prescribed complement of gentlemen and grooms at all times. Too often the back doors of the "chamberers' chambers"—where the queen's gentlewomen were quartered—were left open and unattended, and little notice was taken of the stream of "laundresses, tailors, wardrobers, and such" that came and went through them. Anyone could slip in and attack the queen. Or more fearful still: anyone could introduce into her chambers one of those refined and subtle agents of death that were the hallmark of the age.

Poisons, slow-acting or immediate, ingested by mouth or through the skin; they came in a hundred forms, and had to be guarded against in a hundred ways. From now on, Cecil cautioned, no meat or other food prepared outside the royal kitchens should be allowed into the privy chamber, without "assured knowledge" of its origins. Perfumed gloves or sleeves or other garments were to be kept away from Elizabeth, unless their hazardous odors were "corrected by some other fume." And even the royal underwear—"all manner of things that shall touch any part of her majesty's body bare"—had to be "circumspectly looked to" in future. No unauthorized person was to be allowed near it, lest some harmful substance be hidden in the folds of the linen to menace the queen's person. But all precautions were imperfect, and as an extra safeguard Cecil strongly advised that Elizabeth should take some medicinal preservative "against plague and poison," just in case some evil reached her unawares.[8]

Amy Dudley's funeral was very grand. The queen did not attend it but many of the black-robed courtiers did, whispering to one another that the mourners and attendants and ceremonial accouterments must have cost Dudley two thousand pounds or more. He paid it in order to ease his conscience, they may have added—but (officially at least) only to atone for adultery, not murder. The inquiry Knollys had begged for had been held, and the final pronouncement was that Amy Dudley's death had been accidental.

Of course, no one believed it; not in 1560, and not for centuries afterward. Now, however, the verdict seems plausible. Twentieth-century medical studies have reconstructed the incident to show that Amy Dudley, a victim of breast cancer, probably suffered a spontaneous fracture of the spine just before she plunged down the stairway to her death. Why such a gravely ill woman was left alone that day, why she was out of bed, above all why her husband was not with her are mysteries beyond the reach of medicine, then or now.

On November 20 a rumor swept the court that Dudley had been "married to the queen in the presence of his brother and two ladies of the chamber." It was not true, but it seemed the logical outcome of events, and so it was believed—for a time. Having been convinced for so long that Elizabeth was in love with Dudley, and longed to marry him—for what woman did not long to marry the man she loved?—her subjects expected that, now that he was a widower, and cleared, officially, of wrongdoing in his wife's death, she would not hesitate to take him for her husband.

No letters or other records survive to tell us what Elizabeth was thinking or saying about her beloved during these tense months. A court messenger who saw her at about the time of the marriage rumor noted that she "looked not so heartily and well as she did by a great deal." Surely, he conjectured, "the matter of Lord Robert doth much perplex her."[9]

Perplexity, extreme annoyance, above all doubt must have troubled her. Unless, as hardly seems likely, Elizabeth and Dudley were in fact accomplices in murder, Lady Dudley's death must have come as an unpleasant surprise. With Amy Dudley alive, Elizabeth could let her passions run free, leaving their outcome forever inconclusive. But with Amy dead, she would be forced to declare herself, to make good those displays of affection for Dudley which had, quite possibly, as much defiance in them as lust. She was trapped. Dudley had become, or soon would become, yet another importunate suitor, along with Arundel and the Swedes and the imperialists representing Archduke Charles.

But had he trapped her by design? Did she believe him to be completely innocent of murder when everyone else around her thought otherwise? After all, just as an assassin might strike at Elizabeth herself in a hundred subtle ways, so Dudley could have sent others to act for him. It was even possible that some overzealous servant of Dudley's, eager to carry out what he thought was his master's unspoken will, had pushed Amy Dudley down the stairs. And Dudley, having communicated his desire, was in a way responsible for what happened.

Unanswered questions must have plagued Elizabeth, questions about the extent of Dudley's selfishness and ambition, about his trustworthiness, about the actual degree of harm she might do to the realm by marrying him. Or to herself: in her darkest moments Elizabeth must have forced herself to consider the wisdom of marrying a man who, just possibly, had not scrupled to kill his first wife.

In the end a great deal rested on Dudley's strength of will and character. As the new year 1561 opened he made a great effort to promote his chances by striking a bargain with Philip II. Philip would give his blessing to Dudley's marriage to the queen in return for the future consort's promise to promote Spanish interests and govern England according to Philip's guidelines. Elizabeth appeared to be well disposed toward this, up to a point. She took the necessary steps toward raising Dudley to the peerage —a prerequisite to any marriage between them—though before the patent of nobility could be delivered she slashed at it with a knife and destroyed it. And she asked De Quadra point blank what Philip's reaction might be "if she married one of her servitors," the way several prominent ladies of the court had done.[10]

But she vacillated, refusing on one pretext or another to take decisive steps toward marriage. Dudley, frustrated and perhaps surprised at his inability to control Elizabeth, became "discontented" and sought advice. Talk forcefully to her, Dudley's brother-in-law Henry Sidney told him. Convince her once and for all to "make a stand" against the offended and hostile courtiers and throw herself on the mercy of the king of Spain. Then, secure in King Philip's support, seize the moment and marry her.

Never mind the king of Spain, thundered the bluff soldier Pembroke, unlettered and untutored in the ways of courtly love. Leave her no choice. Tell her she must either marry you or release you to "go to the wars" in her service, making a complete break.[11]

Though Dudley continued to insist that "it was only fear and timidity" that kept Elizabeth from making up her mind to marry him, by March his position appeared to be weakening. He had followed Sidney's advice, but not Pembroke's. ("He is faint-hearted and his favor is founded on vanity," De Quadra observed with relish. "He dares not break with the queen.")

In the battle between royal sovereignty and male authority the latter, to everyone's amazement, was losing. Cecil had been right, at least for the time being. The queen had decided, for now, to keep control of herself and her private affairs in her own hands.

"Lord Robert's recent discontent has ended in her giving him an apartment upstairs adjoining her own," De Quadra reported drily in April, "as it is healthier than that which he had downstairs. He is delighted."

18

Adew, derlyng,
Adew, swettyng,
Adew, all my welfare!
Adew, all thyng
To god perteynyng,
Cryst kepe yow frome all care.

On August 19, 1561, a French ship anchored off Leith in south-eastern Scotland, and a royal passenger stepped into a longboat and came ashore. She was Mary Stuart, Queen of Scotland and the Isles and widowed queen of France; since 1558 she had claimed, at least tacitly, to be queen of England as well.

She was not quite nineteen, with glowing auburn hair and almond-shaped hazel eyes, and her complexion—the sovereign mark of beauty—was as white and unblemished as fine linen. Her portraits reveal less than classic features; eyes set somewhat too close together, nose too large and too long. And her expression has more in it of determination than of sensuality or seductiveness. Yet to contemporaries Mary Stuart was a captivating, ensorceling beauty—"personally the most beautiful in Europe," a Venetian wrote—and to the undeniable charms of her person and manner was added the delight of a "very sweet, very lovely" speaking voice.

She had one startling drawback—at least to vulgar eyes. She was nearly six feet tall, and in an age when men over six feet were giants and a woman of five feet was of average height Mary stood out as a marvel of nature. But the poets who praised her snowy bosom and exquisite hands were too tactful to refer to her lofty stature, and her queenly authority was enhanced rather than weakened by the fact that she towered over a good many of her male relatives and courtiers and looked all but the tallest of them squarely in the eye.

Mary came ashore with some trepidation, for the people of Leith had not prepared an elaborate welcome for her and no doubt most of them stared rudely at this tall, pale woman with the elegant clothes and extensive retinue. France had been home to Mary for most of her life; its sunny skies and green countryside, its farms and prosperous villages were the only world she knew. Scotland, on this August day at least, was enshrouded in thick fog. The country looked barren and treeless, the people ragged. And though there was nominal peace both within the realm and with England, turbulent factions locked in uneasy truce threatened to renew open warfare on any pretext.

Scotland had been a bleeding wound since the start of Elizabeth's reign, with religious and political quarrels converging in the entangled strife of rebellion, civil war and conflict with foreign powers. And England, inevitably, had become deeply and inextricably involved.

The threat of a French invasion of England through Scotland became graver than ever when King Henry II died suddenly in July of 1559. The throne went to the sickly adolescent Francis II, Mary Stuart's husband, but power rested in the hands of Mary's uncles, the cardinal of Lorraine and the duke of Guise. Now both Scotland and France were Guise regencies, with the cardinal and the duke ruling in France and their sister, Mary of Lorraine, mother of Mary Stuart, regent in Scotland. Such a situation invited French aggrandizement as never before, yet strong countercurrents were gaining force in Scotland which were working to undermine the authority of the regent.

Scots Protestants, animated by the fervor of John Knox, rose in righteous opposition to the Catholic church in Scotland and the French-controlled government that supported it. At the same time, the Scots nobles, their power shackled by ever tighter restrictions from the court, merged their political and confessional grievances and joined with the Protestant clerics to form the "Congregation," a body committed to reform of the church and government.

Warfare between the Congregation and the royal forces soon showed that the rebels were at a severe disadvantage, despite clandestine financial support from England, and by December of 1559 Elizabeth had to make a painful decision. Would she intervene openly on the side of the Protestants, and risk bringing in the full might of France in opposition? Or would she stop short of committing her army and treasury on so large a scale, knowing that without her aid Knox and his coreligionists were doomed, and leaving the Guises more firmly entrenched than ever?

Cecil, a veteran of the English wars against the Scots in the 1540s (he fought at the battle of Pinkie) and warm advocate of forceful, undisguised English intervention, was exasperated beyond measure when Elizabeth held back. Her decision was wrong, her view of the situation ruinously ill-advised; he made up his mind to resign. "With a sorrowful heart and watery eyes," he wrote her, he found himself unable to continue in her service as secretary. He would be glad enough to serve her in any other capacity—"though it were in her majesty's kitchen or garden"—but his conscience would not permit him to remain in the council unless the queen agreed to pursue an aggressive policy in the north.

Cecil was essential to Elizabeth's government: she gave way. In February of 1560 she was reportedly seen every day riding abroad on a swift jennet or a great Neapolitan courser, "making a brave show and bearing herself gallantly." She was showing herself off as a superb horsewoman—something the people enjoyed—while at the same time making good on her military intentions. She had ordered an army mustered to go northward under Lord Grey, with Norfolk in supreme command at Berwick.

The campaign proved to be costly and militarily wasteful, but the diplomatic efforts which accompanied it succeeded, thanks to Cecil. His shrewd bargaining, coincident with several pieces of unexpected good fortune—the regent died, and a political conspiracy in France loosened the stranglehold of the Guises—led to a vital and far-reaching agreement. The Treaty of Edinburgh, negotiated at the low point of French influence in Scotland, removed the threat of invasion from the north and, as it proved, insulated England from this time forward against the danger of war on two fronts.

The following year, 1561, brought a dramatic change in Scots fortunes. The Protestant party was in control, and the young queen Mary Stuart, distant in France, was mourning the deaths of her mother and her feeble young husband King Francis. With her once-powerful Guise relatives now out of power, Mary returned to her kingdom of Scotland, sobered by bereavement and variable fortune, prepared to play the difficult role of a Catholic queen ruling aggressively Protestant subjects. To rule effectively Mary would need the help of her royal cousin in England; without that help she could hardly hope to hold on to her throne.

Yet Elizabeth's friendship had a price, as Mary found to her inconvenience when she asked for a safe conduct through England on her way north. If Mary ratified the Treaty of Edinburgh—which she had so far refused to do—then Elizabeth would be glad to guarantee her safe passage through England, and no doubt would give her a royal reception as well. But the treaty contained a clause calling for Mary to renounce her claim to the arms and style of England—a claim she had been making for three years. Amend that clause and she would ratify the treaty, Mary countered. They were at a stalemate: eventually Elizabeth sent the safe conduct without winning what she sought from Mary, but it was too late. By the time it arrived Mary had already set sail for Scotland, remarking melodramatically that if her ship chanced to run aground in England and Elizabeth chose to take her captive, even to execute her, then so be it. She might even be better off dead.

It was just this sort of reckless bravado that made Mary appealing to Elizabeth as a successor. Of course, there were numerous obstacles to such an arrangement: Henry VIII's will, which designated the line of succession excluding the Stuarts, Mary's Catholicism, above all Elizabeth's distaste for any formal succession scheme, which would only promote rebellion by officially designating the next heir to the throne. Elizabeth, remembering vividly what it had meant to be "second person" in the realm, with all the temptations and intrigues that went along with that unenviable position, hesitated to name her successor. Yet there was much that she could do short of a final designation that would indicate her preference and secure Mary's interests—provided Mary was cooperative.

In fact Mary was looking more and more suitable as an heir, given the principal alternative.

Of the seven women named to succeed, after Edward VI, in Henry VIII's will, one (Mary Tudor) had reigned, one (Elizabeth) was reigning, two (Jane Grey and Frances Brandon) had died and three (Catherine Grey, Mary Grey and Margaret Clifford) were still living. Catherine Grey, elder of Jane Grey's two surviving sisters, was looked on as heir presumptive.

Catherine was twenty-three in 1561, a solemn young woman with a long face, rosebud lips and a long, prominent nose like Elizabeth's. There was a definite family resemblance between them, and Catherine, like Elizabeth, had known something of the perils of political intrigue. At fifteen she had been a pawn in Northumberland's scheme to seize power; when her sister Jane married Northumberland's son Guildford Dudley, Catherine married Henry Herbert, Pembroke's son, though the marriage was never consummated and Herbert eventually divorced her. This humiliation was the capstone of a miserable childhood in an unloving family, and by the time Elizabeth became queen Catherine felt ill-used and undeservedly neglected.

Elizabeth hated her, whether for her rivalry in the succession, for her bitterness, or perhaps because Catherine hated her first. In any event Catherine was brought to court but kept in a relatively inferior post. (When Mary was queen Catherine had served in the privy chamber, among the women of highest rank, despite Mary's rumored antipathy to her; now she served among the lower-ranking women of the presence chamber.) Thus when she saw a chance to advance herself and began to receive the respectful treatment she felt she deserved—albeit from a questionable source—Catherine seized her chance.

In the spring of 1559 she had been befriended by Count Feria, before he returned to Spain. Feria had won her trust by listening sympathetically to her complaints. Catherine had told Feria candidly that Elizabeth, should she die childless, did not want her to succeed, which together with her demeaning position among the gentlewomen "dissatisfied and offended" her. Feria had lost no time in informing his master of this unlooked-for opportunity, and contingency plans were made to involve Catherine in Hapsburg designs on the English succession. In the following months English agents abroad reported hearing of plots to kidnap Catherine Grey —who because of her discontent would most likely aid her kidnappers— and to marry her either to Philip's son Don Carlos or some other Hapsburg candidate. Feria had won from her a promise not to marry anyone without his consent, and his successor De Quadra continued to cultivate her good will.[1]

To counteract this potential subversion Elizabeth pretended suddenly to discover her cousin's merits and appeal. She flattered Catherine, paid the greatest attention to her, and took to calling her "her daughter"—"although the feeling between them can hardly be that of mother and child," De Quadra noted wryly. Catherine had once again been placed among the distinguished ladies of the privy chamber, and even this had not seemed to satisfy Elizabeth, who talked freely of adopting her cousin to make her her daughter in fact.

Hypocritical though it was, Elizabeth's extravagant attention seemed to appease Catherine for a time. But in mid-August of 1561, just at the time that Mary Stuart was stepping off the boat at Leith, it was once again discovered that Catherine had been led into dangerous indiscretion.

The sharp eyes of the chamber women detected a telltale swelling at her waist; Catherine was unmistakably pregnant. And, so she claimed, she was married to the child's father: the young earl of Hertford, son of the late Protector Somerset, who was away in France.

Elizabeth, "not well quieted" with this startling proof of treachery, ordered Catherine committed to the Tower and summoned the earl home to imprisonment as well. No doubt she took out her anger on the mother of the maids, Kat Ashley, for her lax supervision of the girl and on the rest of her women for shielding Catherine in her deception and betrayal.

For secret though it had been, the marriage had clearly taken place with the connivance of at least some of the courtiers. Eight months earlier, while Elizabeth herself had been away from court hunting, the couple had exchanged vows, hurriedly, at Hertford House in Westminster. They had not acted on their own; intriguers calculating that Elizabeth would before long marry Dudley had urged them to it. These intriguers had located a priest to perform the ceremony (now nowhere to be found), had witnessed it, and had, as custom and law required, witnessed its consummation as well.

Such treason, such monumental disrespect shook Elizabeth's strained nerves. "She is extremely thin and the color of a corpse," De Quadra reported. Her women told the ambassador that she was in a "dangerous condition," and was becoming dropsical, like her sister Mary. To others, ever mindful of her intimacy with Dudley, her pallor and weakness were easily explained. She "looked like one lately come out of childbed," Lady Willoughby muttered. She was no better than Catherine Grey—indeed she was worse, for Catherine had at least been married.[2]

The scandal surrounding the death of Dudley's wife was a year old, yet from time to time it continued to flare into prominence. Just at this time Arundel and others, bent upon injuring Dudley (who was more in favor than ever), were said to be drawing up copies of the transcript of the inquest into his late wife's death. If De Quadra is to be trusted, their scrutiny was not entirely fruitless. "More is being discovered in that affair" than Dudley wished, the ambassador wrote. Yet what the discoveries were he did not say.[3]

For Elizabeth the course of events had had an unexpected, and unfortunate, sequel. Since she chose not to marry, went one line of reasoning, it must be because she was incapable of bearing children. Her refusal to marry Dudley was seen by some as a conclusive argument for this; beyond it, one had only to remember Mary Tudor's grotesque false pregnancies—not to mention the curse of childlessness that, so people said, had fallen on Elizabeth after her sinful involvement with Thomas Seymour—to realize that Elizabeth was more than likely barren.

To be sure, contradictory rumors flourished. While some were saying the queen was dropsical, others said her swellings were those of approaching motherhood; to some she looked as though she had just risen from childbed, while others swore she could never conceive. Amid the confusion two things seem clear. First, Elizabeth was susceptible to illness, especially in the aftermath of emotional shock. And second, no one among her immediate advisers ever doubted her ability to bear children—or if they doubted it, no record of their doubt remains.

In October of 1562 a crisis brought the problem of the succession into sharp relief. Elizabeth was at Hampton Court and, "feeling unwell," decided to take a hot bath. After her bath she caught a chill and, soon afterward, took to her bed with a high fever.

There had been a minor epidemic of smallpox at court in recent weeks; a number of highborn ladies had been gravely ill, and several, including the countess of Bedford, had died. The survivors remained out of sight, anguished in their convalescence by the deep, angry scars left by the disease, scars that, no matter how assiduously they were treated with creams and herbs and medicinal plasters, refused to heal. Disfigurement was the chief bane of smallpox, when the disease was not fatal. Handsome men became repulsive; beautiful women with clear, glowing complexions were left almost as hideous as lepers, their skin discolored and aged and their features distorted by the pits and chronic sores left behind when the contagion was past.

Evidently the queen had contracted the disease, and it was officially announced at the palace that she had taken to her bed with smallpox. For the next few days, though listless and ill with fever, Elizabeth kept an eye on affairs from her sickbed, leaving to others—chiefly to Dudley—the supervision of the English fighting force that was en route to France.

Just as she had sent an army into Scotland in support of the Protestant rebels there, so Elizabeth had determined to come to the aid of the French Protestants, or Huguenots, in their struggle against the French regent Catherine de' Medici. French political fortunes had shifted once again, and Elizabeth, ever hopeful of regaining Calais, had seen her opportunity. The regent Catherine was weak, and growing weaker as religious warfare became widespread. Huguenot raids and plundering invited murderous Catholic retaliation, and the government seemed powerless to halt the spreading chaos.

By the summer of 1562 warfare and governmental crises combined to make English intervention overwhelmingly attractive to Elizabeth, and when her offers of personal mediation were refused by the regent she ordered her diplomats to negotiate a secret treaty with the rebels. In return for English money and troops, the Huguenots agreed to turn Calais over to the English once it was surrendered, in the course of the war, by the French crown.

With this agreement concluded, three thousand English troops had left Portsmouth and Rye late in September for the French coast, and on October 11, the day after the onset of the queen's illness, three thousand more were to embark. It was a large and costly undertaking, and the councilors were noisily divided in their attitude toward it. Elizabeth's indisposition was inconveniently timed, to say the least; they must have shaken their heads and resigned themselves to several weeks of inconvenience while the disease ran its course.

But it did not take its normal course. The physicians expected the fever to abate on the fourth day, a Wednesday, when the red marks that were the characteristic sign of smallpox would appear and the disease would pass into its second stage. But Wednesday came and went, and the queen's fever only grew higher; there were no red spots, and no sign of the usual transition to the next stage.

Elizabeth lay still and pale in her darkened chamber, her narrow face pinched by pain, her undernourished body thin and bony. At her bedside was Mary Sidney, Dudley's sister, who braved contagion to keep her vigil. There was little enough to be done for smallpox: red cloth at the windows to filter the light and, with luck, prevent scarring; a warm fire; red cloth to swaddle the patient in. The physicians were all but helpless. Either the queen would recover or she would die; her fate was in God's hands.[4]

Since the start of the reign it had been predicted that Elizabeth would die young. She was twenty-nine, and had reigned nearly four years already; it was time for the prophecies and astrological calculations to be fulfilled. Even as she lay in her sickbed at Hampton Court two Catholic conspirators, relatives of the late Cardinal Pole, were being interrogated about their scheme to land troops in Wales and seize the English throne for Mary Stuart. They had not conspired against Elizabeth, the Poles insisted; an astrologer had assured them months before that she would be dead long before their plan went into effect.[5]

No one dared to repeat the predictions about Elizabeth's mortality; everyone thought about them. The courtiers calculated the likeliest heirs to power in the event of her death and hastily aligned themselves accordingly. The devout prayed, the shrewd negotiated. Everyone clamored for the latest news from the council chamber, where the succession was being debated. Everyone, that is, but Robert Dudley, who amassed "a large armed force under his control," some six thousand strong, and waited for events to take their course.

The councilors had been summoned as soon as there was grave concern about Elizabeth's condition. With the country at war and no successor designated, they alone stood for an orderly transition of power should the worst happen. Cecil, in London, learned of the crisis at midnight; he rode upriver to Hampton Court in the early hours of the morning, full of apprehension. Soon the others were assembled, and three long days and nights of argument and advocacy began.

Faced with choosing among the various candidates for the throne the councilors must have struggled to weigh the religion, personality, military strength or weakness of the candidates—not to mention the abstruse legal issues of legitimacy and statutory right. Minor candidates apart, there were two genealogical factions vying for preeminence: the Stuart line, descended from Henry VIII's elder sister Margaret, and the Suffolk line, heirs of Henry's younger sister Mary, who when she married Charles Brandon became duchess of Suffolk.

The Stuart claim appeared at first glance to be the stronger, given Margaret Tudor's seniority in age, but the leading Stuart claimant, the Scots Queen Mary, was not English and had not been born in England. In law she could not inherit property in England, and even if these difficulties were somehow cleared away there would still be the bar of her Catholicism and the incontrovertible fact that the will of Henry VIII had excluded the Stuarts from the throne.

The leading Suffolk claimant, on the other hand, was in the Tower, along with her infant son. Catherine Grey was Protestant, English-born, and demonstrably fertile—no small advantage. She had King Henry's will on her side, and she was nearby, just a few hours downriver from Hampton Court, while Mary Stuart was hundreds of miles away to the north. But Catherine had the disability of her precontract with Pembroke's son, her treasonable marriage, and other obscure legal disadvantages arising from her grandfather Charles Brandon's marital entanglements. And Elizabeth was known not to favor her.

Then there was Henry Hastings, earl of Huntingdon, who belonged neither to the Stuart nor to the Suffolk camp but was a Yorkist, a descendant of Edward III. The Yorkist claim had been effectively moribund for several generations, and Huntingdon was not in himself a strong enough personality to bring it to life. But he had married Catherine Dudley, Robert Dudley's sister, and the troops Dudley was bringing together at the palace, it was said, would be committed to the earl's cause in any succession dispute. De Quadra believed that both Elizabeth and Cecil favored Huntingdon over the female claimants (though there was some evidence to the contrary), in large part because he was a man. But like Mary Stuart, Huntingdon was not named to the succession in Henry VIII's will, and was at a disadvantage, as an ardent, radical Protestant, in religion.[6]

Hour after hour the beleaguered councilors met, hounded by the anxious courtiers, dogged by prolonged tension and lack of sleep, working against a nearing deadline as Elizabeth's remaining strength ebbed. Three points of view emerged. One party favored the most straightforward course of action, to follow King Henry's will and recognize Catherine Grey as queen. Another, including Dudley, Norfolk, the soldierly Pembroke and a number of other pragmatists, favored Huntingdon. A third group cautioned against any hasty choice and urged that the entire succession issue be placed in the hands of the leading jurists in the realm—ostensibly a wise and statesman-like solution, but in fact, so the Protestants believed, a Catholic ploy. The leading jurists were conservatives in religion, and were certain to pronounce in favor of a Catholic. Worse still, their pronouncement would be slow in coming, giving time for military intervention by one of the Catholic powers, France or Spain.

The hours passed, and the wrangling continued. From the queen's apartments word spread that Elizabeth, having lost her power of speech several hours earlier, had slipped into unconsciousness. She had burned with fever for seven days. This was the final crisis. Reluctantly, with as much excitement as apprehension, the court prepared to go into mourning.

Then suddenly there was another bulletin. The queen had regained consciousness, eaten a little jelly, and fallen asleep—to all appearances a normal, healthy sleep—and her fever had broken. By the time she woke again, in the middle of the night, there were red marks on her hands and face, and she had enough appetite to eat a light meal. The next morning, though swollen and covered with blemishes, she had just enough strength to meet with her indecisive councilors.

She called them to her bedside and told them her preferred plan for the succession. Her beloved Dudley was to rule, she said; he could not be king, but he could be Lord Protector, as Edward Seymour had been nearly fifteen years earlier. Dudley should have a noble title and an annuity of twenty thousand pounds. And lest anyone should try to challenge his authority by slandering his honor, she swore solemnly that he had never been her lover.

"Although she loved and had always loved Lord Robert dearly," De Quadra reported her as saying, "as God was her witness, nothing improper had ever passed between them."[7]

Then, taking advantage of her lucidity, Elizabeth made the oral bequests customary at royal deathbeds. Everyone in her household was to receive a grant of money, and she named the staff members one by one and specified the amounts they were to be given. Tamworth, a groom who slept in Dudley's chamber, was to have an income of five hundred pounds a year. And her cousin Hunsdon too was singled out for special recognition and recommended to the council's favor.

None of the councilors thought to argue with these dispositions; Elizabeth was assured that everything, including Dudley's protectorate, would be instituted according to her request.

Clearly she did not expect to live, and it was with as much surprise as relief that the councilors and courtiers learned each day that, though afflicted with severe pain and itching from her blistered skin, the queen was coming through her ordeal, and was not likely to succumb as so many others had. Mary Sidney had come down with smallpox too, but like the queen she was expected to recover.

By October 29 Cecil was reporting that Elizabeth was "out of all peril to come by her disease." She was shut away in her chamber, treating her complexion, and was not expected to appear in public for some time "owing to the disfigurement of her face." Dudley and, less often, Norfolk were the only councilors permitted to confer with her; had the councilors not insisted, it would have been Dudley alone.

The danger was past, for the moment, but the court and, no doubt, the queen had been badly shaken. Even Cecil seemed to have lost his composure. When in conference he spoke "excitedly, confounding and mixing the various points" of his discourse, and he was for a time uncharacteristically preempted in visible leadership, if not in actual stewardship, by Dudley and Norfolk.

It was Dudley more than anyone who had come out ahead. To his informal influence had been added the official sanction of membership in the royal council. He had demonstrated his military resourcefulness, and his raw armed might; anyone who hoped to make a bid for the throne would from now on remember his six thousand men, and reconsider. Most of all, Elizabeth's true regard for him and loyalty to him had come out in her dying declaration. She believed him to be her most capable successor; she had intended to bequeath him her most precious possession, her kingdom. Her feeling for him clearly went far beyond flirtation, far beyond passion (though only the most gullible can have accepted her urgent denial of their intimacy). Wisely or not, she had conferred on Dudley as on no one else her complete, trusting and heartfelt love.

19

Conduct thy learnèd company to Court,
Eliza's Court, Astraea's earthly heaven.

James Melville, Mary Stuart's ambassador and sharp-witted diplomat, arrived at Westminster at the end of September, 1564, and took up lodgings near the court. Melville was twenty-nine, a Scots gentleman who had spent the better part of his life abroad—first as a page at the French court, then later in Italy and the German-speaking lands of the Hapsburg emperor. He was a man of the world, calculated to appeal to the urbane but ill-traveled Elizabeth. Or so Queen Mary hoped.

Relations between the two queens had recently turned sour. For two years and more there had been plans for a face-to-face meeting between them, yet each time an obstacle had arisen and at the last minute the meeting had been called off. Then, in recent months, the issue of Mary's marriage had led to "inward griefs and grudges" which their letters to one another had only made worse. Melville's journey was intended to patch up the quarrel.

Reconciliation was important, for Elizabeth now appeared to prefer Mary to all the other succession candidates and had in mind a brilliant, if involuted and somewhat perverse, plan to make her heir to the throne.

Everything hinged on Mary's marriage—to Dudley. The idea was so startling that the Scots representative who first heard of it, early in 1563, could not bring himself to take it seriously. Yet Elizabeth was indeed serious, acknowledging in a secret dispatch to her own agent in Scotland that the man she had in mind for her cousin to marry was "such as she could hardly think we would agree unto." That Elizabeth should send her lover away to a distant court and marry him to a younger and—by repute at least —a more beautiful woman who coveted her throne seemed sheer self-punishing madness, yet there was a ruthlessly exacting logic behind the plan.

There were very few men whom Mary Stuart could safely marry, from Elizabeth's point of view. If she married one of the leading Catholic princes —Philip II's son Don Carlos, for example, or the ever-available Archduke Charles of Austria—then her claim to the English throne would give her husband the pretext he needed to make war on Elizabeth. A minor foreign match might be less hazardous militarily, yet would offer the disadvantage that in time the Tudor crown would pass to Mary's heirs, who would have almost no English blood at all. And such minor figures often became allied to major powers, a dangerous probability in this case.

With a husband chosen from among the Scots or English nobility, on the other hand, there was the hazard of rebellion—unless the nobleman selected was known to be unswervingly loyal to the English monarch. And who was more loyal than Robert Dudley?

So Elizabeth offered him to Mary, wincing as she did so at the recollection of Mary's derisive remark when she heard of Amy Dudley's death: "The queen of England is going to marry her horsekeeper, who has killed his wife to make room for her."

The sacrifice Elizabeth was making was a measure of her frustration and weariness, for over the last six years she had been hounded and harassed by the overriding urgency of her own marriage. Dire emergencies apart, every governmental issue took second place to this, and as the years passed Parliament, the councilors, the ambassadors and the princes they served, the people at large all grew more and more strident in their single reiterated demand: whom would Elizabeth marry, and when?

Parliament she bullied, or at least outtalked; the councilors, since she had to live among them day after day, were less easy to combat. They were restive and quarrelsome, never exactly out of control yet nearly always out of temper. They were accustomed to dealing with men, to being surrounded by men, ordered by men, giving orders to men. Having a woman at the head of things offended the immemorial propriety of kingly rule; it was an anomaly to be tolerated only if it was to be temporary. And after six years Elizabeth was threatening to make it permanent. Privately they spoke their resentment, publicly they were irritable and impatient, and the level of tension was so high that they sometimes came to blows.

Crotchety Arundel, his dignity wounded by Elizabeth's rejection of his suit, picked a quarrel with Admiral Clinton one day in the presence chamber. They were discussing the appropriate punishment of religious dissenters, with Clinton arguing for severity and Arundel countering that harsh punishment could lead to a counterreaction "unfavorable to the queen's interests." So they argued on, heatedly, until they insulted one another with "rough words" and "fell to fisticuffs and grabbing each other's beards." Large as the presence chamber was, and no doubt crowded with people, Elizabeth could not help but notice the brawling; she ended it by calling the courtiers to her and, pretending she hadn't seen anything, inviting them to "play before her," and so forcing them to make peace. All the same the incident was unseemly, and embarrassing to visitors who saw it as "a great sacrifice of the queen's dignity." It would never have happened in the presence of a king, or even a prince consort.[1]

All the squabbling, the resentment, the silent censure would end once she married—or at least designated a successor. There would be an end to the tiresome suitors, the secret meetings to discuss the succession which, when she heard of them, made her "weep with rage," the tremors of fear that passed through the court whenever she caught cold or suffered with diarrhea or was merely "cumbered with pain in her nose and eyes." Ever since her brush with death two years earlier there had been heightened alarm about her mortality; the prophecies "everybody talked of," together with the vigilant presence of Mary Stuart just over the border, combined to make Elizabeth "much in fear" of falling ill, and put her under even more stress. Then, too, there was always the nightmare possibility that through inadvertence Elizabeth might lose her precarious balance on the highwire of diplomacy and England might be plunged into full-scale war. To save herself and her realm she might then be forced to marry—or unalterably commit herself to marry—in great haste, without time to choose wisely, without time even to see the man to whom she would have to hand over herself and her authority.

To exorcise these bedeviling vexations Elizabeth was willing, at times perhaps eager, to make Mary Stuart a present of Dudley—whom she could not realistically marry—as the price of her peace of mind.

Melville had no sooner settled into his Westminster rooms than he received a visitor from court. Christopher Hatton, a resplendent courtier, arrived bringing a message of welcome from the queen and informing him that she would see him the next morning at eight, when she customarily went for a walk in her privy garden. Then an old friend of Melville's came calling—Nicholas Throckmorton, long in the thick of Scots affairs and a partisan of Mary Stuart. Throckmorton brought Melville up to date on current affairs and counseled him on "how to proceed with the queen." In case Elizabeth became recalcitrant, Throckmorton said, Melville should "use great familiarity with the ambassador of Spain," for that would spur her to be more cooperative.

Nothing could be accomplished without the assent of Cecil and Dudley, Throckmorton warned. Although he himself "had no great kindness" for either of them, he instructed his friend on the best approach to use with them, and with "every courtier in particular," for at Westminster as in Edinburgh personalities counted for as much as issues.

In the morning Hatton reappeared to escort Melville to the palace. With him came a gift from Dudley—a fine horse trapped in a footmantle laced with gold, led by a servant. The horse, he was told, would be at his disposal throughout his stay.

When he arrived Elizabeth was walking briskly up and down an alleyway in the garden, not only to improve her circulation in the chilly morning air but out of anger—or a pretense of anger. She was blunt and brusque with Melville, interrupting him with questions and "tossing words" with him about the injurious language of Queen Mary's last letter.

They spoke French, Melville apologizing that he had been in France for so long that his lowland Scots-English was rusty and Elizabeth, perhaps with some feigned reluctance, conversing with equal fluency. It was her cherished conceit that, whatever language a foreign envoy spoke—and none of them spoke English—she was sure to have trouble with it, as she was more practiced in other tongues. Thus she boasted to one ambassador in 1564 that she "found some difficulty in speaking French, having so long been accustomed to speaking Latin." But to another man she claimed that her Latin was poor, as she "had more practice in the Greek, Italian and French languages."[2] "I understand German quite well," she told an imperial envoy haughtily, "although I do not speak it." Early in her reign, when Count Feria was still at court, Elizabeth had attempted, with a remarkable degree of success, to read documents in Portuguese, though she had to ask for Feria's help.[3] And invariably, whatever foreign language she spoke, she made certain it was highly audible, speaking "in so loud a tone as to be heard by everybody."

Thus she loudly announced to Melville that she had written a "despiteful" letter to Mary and had delayed sending it only because she feared it was not vehement enough. The Scotsman, no doubt prepared, thanks to Throckmorton's counsel, to have Elizabeth try to throw him off balance by just this sort of tactic, was quick with his response. Elizabeth, he said— possibly with faint condescension—though her French was excellent for one who had never been to France, was obviously misled by Mary's

"French court language," which was full of double meanings and tended to be "frank and short." They debated the matter, and finally Elizabeth allowed herself to be won over, tearing up her own angry letter and declaring herself ready to renew the former friendship.

Then she came to the really important issue. Had Mary decided whether or not to marry Dudley? Here Melville did not have to improvise. He had his instructions. Such an important decision, he said, could not be made until there was a formal meeting between representatives of both queens —for Mary, her half-brother the earl of Murray and her secretary Maitland, and for Elizabeth, he supposed, the earl of Bedford, governor of the border castle of Berwick, and Dudley.

Here Elizabeth interrupted. Melville "made but small account" of Dudley, she objected, whereas in fact she was about to make him a very great nobleman, far greater than Bedford, and he, Melville, would witness the ceremony before he left her court. She expanded on Dudley's merits and on what he meant to her, as they continued to stroll up and down beside the clipped hedges in the privy garden.

"She esteemed him as her brother and best friend," Melville wrote later in his *Memoirs*, "whom she would have herself married, had she ever minded to have taken a husband. But being determined to end her life in virginity, she wished that the queen her sister might marry him, as meetest of all other with whom she could find in her heart to declare her second person."

Above all, Elizabeth explained, the marriage would quiet her apprehensions. Once Dudley became prince consort in Scotland, "it would best remove out of her mind all fears and suspicions, to be offended by any usurpation before her death. Being assured that he was so loving and trusty, that he would never permit any such thing to be attempted during her time."[4]

The more he saw of Elizabeth in the following days, the more Melville was convinced of her determination to remain single, despite her surprisingly candid demonstration of her infatuation with Dudley. She might threaten to marry if Mary's "harsh behavior toward her" made it necessary, she said, yet Melville called her bluff.

"I know the truth of that, madam," he told her. "You need not tell it me. Your majesty thinks, if you were married, you would be but queen of England; and now you are both king and queen. I know your spirit cannot endure a commander."

But when in a mood of self-disclosure she took him into her bedchamber and opened up a little cabinet of treasures, among them a miniature of Dudley, she was as coy and secretive as a young girl in love. On the paper wrapping of the tiny portrait Elizabeth had written "My Lord's picture," and when Melville asked to see who her lord was she "appeared loath to let him see it," drawing it away from the candlelight and refusing to unwrap it until his "importunity prevailed." Dudley was in the room at the time, "at the farthest part of the chamber," talking with Cecil; perhaps Elizabeth's coquettishness was directed to him. In any case, she refused to let Melville take the miniature home to Mary, also refusing to send her Scots cousin "a fair ruby, as great as a tennis-ball," that she kept in her little cabinet along with the portraits.

The coyness vanished, the shrewd negotiator reappeared. If Mary would follow Elizabeth's advice and marry Dudley, she said firmly, the portrait, the ruby, and everything else she had would come to her in time. Meanwhile, as a token of the wealth to come, she would send Mary "a fair diamond," which would have to content her.

The ceremony creating Dudley earl of Leicester was the high point of Melville's stay in Westminster. It was done in the vast presence chamber at St. James's, "with great solemnity," the new peer bearing himself with all the gravity of a nobleman born, not made. The title he was to receive had an extraordinary significance, for the earldom of Leicester had traditionally been a royal title, held by a younger son of the reigning sovereign. This distinction, together with the queen's gift of the manor of Kenilworth and of a number of lucrative offices and grants, swept Dudley into the highest rank of the aristocracy; it made him, in fact, a worthy husband for a queen.

Elizabeth sat on her throne, flanked by the nobles in their robes and by the foreign dignitaries then present at court. Dudley appeared clothed in the surcoat and hood of a baron—for he had to be created baron before he could be made earl—and made a threefold obeisance. Escorted by Hunsdon, Clinton and others Dudley came and knelt before the queen, who as his patent was read aloud put on his baronial mantle. Then, "the trumpets sounding before him," Dudley retired to change into the rich robes of estate of an earl, and reentered the chamber in more exalted company.

The earl of Sussex (an outspoken enemy of Dudley's) walked at his right, and the earl of Huntingdon (whom Dudley had supported as successor during Elizabeth's near-fatal illness two years earlier, and who was said to "walk in his shadow") was on his left. Dudley's elder brother Ambrose, an old-fashioned lord who was said to prefer the company of huntsmen to courtiers, walked in the procession carrying his brother's golden sword; Elizabeth had created Ambrose Dudley earl of Warwick earlier in the reign. The Garter King of Arms bore the patent of nobility, and the other officers of arms led the way.

Again Dudley knelt before the throne, stiff and solemn and exceedingly handsome in his velvets, and as Cecil read out the words of the patent creating him earl of Leicester Elizabeth took the sword from Warwick and girded it on around his neck. But the excessive dignity of the moment, and the embarrassing habit she had of caressing Dudley in public, made her mischievous; she "could not refrain from putting her hand in his neck, smilingly tickling him," in view of all the court.[5]

Melville stood near her as she did this—indeed to a large extent the entire spectacle was for his benefit, so that when he returned to Scotland he could impress Mary with Dudley's personal importance and exalted rank —and as Dudley rose, now a peer, she asked Melville "how he liked him."

The reply was bland and diplomatic, and Elizabeth decided to bring up the sensitive issue of Dudley's chief rival for Mary Stuart's hand.

"Yet you like better of yonder long lad," she said, pointing to the tall, blond nineteen-year-old who carried her royal sword of honor. He was Henry Stuart, Lord Darnley, a grandson of Henry VIII's sister Margaret Tudor. Like his cousin Queen Mary he had been excluded from Henry VIII's will despite his royal blood, and his intriguing mother Margaret Douglas, countess of Lennox (herself a claimant to the English throne), had been promoting a match between Darnley and Mary for the past several years.

Elizabeth was not entirely averse to Darnley as a husband for her cousin in Scotland—in fact, Melville believed Darnley was her second choice, after the new earl of Leicester—but his Catholicism, his youth, and above all the ambitions of his parents made her very uneasy about him.[6] Darnley's father Matthew Stuart, earl of Lennox, was just then in Scotland, ostensibly looking after his estates but actually, Elizabeth knew, working to advance his son's cause. And she may have known, or correctly guessed, that Melville had come to London not only to meet with Elizabeth herself but to see the countess and to further Darnley's chances.

Melville must have been taken off guard by Elizabeth's frank question. "No woman of spirit would make choice of such a man," he said presently, "who more resembles a woman than a man." Darnley was in fact notably athletic and lusty, yet beardless and, in Melville's view, "lady-faced." Compared to Leicester he was only a good-looking boy, while the earl was a broad-shouldered, full-bearded man with an imperious eye and a commanding presence. There was no question which Elizabeth preferred; Mary's taste was to differ.

During the nine days he spent at Westminster Melville was "favorably and familiarly used," passing his days and evenings at the palace and habituating himself to the quotidian activity of the huge royal household and to the habits and life of the now candid, now impenetrable personality at its center.

Elizabeth talked with him every day, sometimes two or three times a day, and he always found her full of eager, insistent questions. She wanted to know everything about the books he liked to read, the countries he had seen, the people he had encountered in his wide-ranging travels. Queen Mary had specifically advised Melville to "leave matters of gravity sometimes, and cast in merry purposes," knowing that Elizabeth loved to laugh and also liked her conversation varied. So, knowing how vain she was and how much attention she gave to dress, he described the styles and costume women wore in the various countries.

Here he had nothing new to teach her; Elizabeth already possessed clothes from all over Europe. To prove it she put on a different mode every day from then on, one day French, the next Italian, and so on. Melville was much taken by her in her low-cut Italian gown and abbreviated bonnet, and when in her forthright way she asked him which of the styles most became her he pleased her by answering that he liked the Italian gown on her best. She too liked it, she wrote, because the bonnet covered very little of her "golden colored hair," of which she was very proud. "Her hair was more reddish than yellow," he went on, "curled in appearance naturally." Elizabeth was as competitive as she was vain. "What color of hair was reputed best?" she asked him, her own reddish gold or Queen Mary's auburn waves? And which was fairer, Mary or herself?

The fairness of both queens, Melville pronounced judiciously, "was not their worst fault."

Elizabeth brushed this diplomatic answer aside and insisted on a real response. Which of them was fairest?

Elizabeth was the fairest queen in England, Melville said, and Mary was the fairest queen in Scotland.

The question was a perilous one, if Elizabeth wanted the truth, for her own complexion was pitted with the marks of smallpox—not hideously, but noticeably—and she was a mature thirty-one, to Mary's fresh-faced twenty-two.

Melville inched closer to giving her the compliment she demanded. Both queens were the fairest ladies in their respective lands, he said. Elizabeth's skin was of a more ivory hue, although Mary was "very lovely."

Which of them was taller?

Without hesitation Melville admitted that Queen Mary was taller.

"Then she is too high," was Elizabeth's triumphant response. "I myself," she added, "am neither too high nor too low."

Elizabeth asked next what sort of outdoor pastimes and other accomplishments Mary enjoyed, and the ambassador told her that as he left Scotland Mary had just returned from a hunting expedition in the highlands. As for more sedentary pursuits, when the work of government was not too pressing she read histories, and sometimes played the lute and virginal.

"Does she play them well?" inquired Elizabeth.

"Reasonably well, for a queen," was Melville's somewhat jaundiced reply, which gave Elizabeth just the opportunity she sought to win another point of comparison with her absent rival.

She went about it craftily, contriving to have Melville discover, as though by chance, how gifted she was at the keyboard. That evening after dinner Hunsdon came up to Melville and took him to a gallery in the queen's wing of the palace. There, if they were lucky, Hunsdon said, they could hear Elizabeth playing the virginal; she would not know she was being observed, and so they could count on hearing her play with full feeling and abandon. They listened, and sure enough they could detect, in the next room, the playing of a skilled keyboard performer.

Perhaps to assure himself that it was really the queen playing and not someone else, Melville pushed aside a tapestry covering the doorway of the room where the performer was. It was indeed Elizabeth, and as she had her back to the doorway Melville quietly stepped into the room and stood there for a while listening to her play "excellently well." But as soon as she caught sight of him she stopped and, appearing to be surprised to see him, strode frowning toward him "seeming to strike him with her hand." She never played publicly, she said, but only when alone, "to shun melancholy." Melville apologized, saying that he was so charmed by the sound that he could not help himself, and she forgave him, inwardly pleased to know that he would be forced in candor to report to Queen Mary that Elizabeth was a better musician than she was.

But this incident did not lay the rivalry to rest. Before he left her court Elizabeth insisted that Melville watch her dance, for in this arena as in that of musical performance she felt confident of her superiority.

Most likely reports of Elizabeth's agile dancing had already made their way to Scotland, for the French envoys who had escorted Mary there three years earlier had been entertained at Elizabeth's court on their way home, and had been treated to a memorable scene. One of the banqueting halls at Greenwich was prepared for a feast, the walls covered by a celebrated set of glowing tapestries representing the parable of the five wise and five foolish virgins. After the French guests had enjoyed a sumptuous meal of many courses, Elizabeth's maids of honor entered the room to perform a ballet. The queen had dressed them exactly as the virgins in the tapestries were dressed, and each carried an exquisitely chased silver lamp. In the course of the charming ballet the maids—who were "very pretty, well behaved and very well dressed," a discriminating observer wrote—invited the Frenchmen to dance with them, and even persuaded the queen to join in. All eyes were on Elizabeth as she began to dance, and her measured, rhythmic steps and lovely coloring showed to great effect in the torchlit chamber. She danced, the same observer recalled, "with much grace and right royal majesty, for she possessed then no little beauty and elegance."7

Who danced best, Elizabeth demanded to know after she had given him a demonstration of her skill, Mary or herself?

Mary "danced not so high, and disposedly as she did," he told Elizabeth, and did not venture to say anything further.

Before he left her court Melville tried to persuade Elizabeth, who said again and again how much she wanted to see Mary in person (the portraits they had exchanged being no substitute for a face-to-face encounter), not to wait for a formal royal meeting but to escape with him into Scotland in disguise. Seeing that she enjoyed the fantasy he elaborated further. He would smuggle her across the border, disguised as a page; she could then enter Mary's palace incognito and, after a secret conference, return in the same way as she had come. No one need know that she had so much as left her bedchamber; one trusted waiting woman and a groom of the chamber would have to be let in on the secret, but everyone else would simply be told that the queen was ill, and could not be disturbed in her sickbed.

"Alas! If I might do it thus," Elizabeth said with a sigh when Melville had finished. Was she sincere? He could not tell, but he was certainly leaving her in a more amiable mood toward Mary Stuart than he had found her. Elizabeth had enjoyed her long hours of conversation with the urbane, imperturbable Scotsman; his embassy left her more curious than ever to see her cousin.

Leicester, however, was uneasy. Seizing an opportunity to talk to Melville privately the earl asked him confidentially whether there was any chance that Mary might in fact accept him as a husband. Melville responded coldly, as Mary had instructed him to do, whereupon Leicester— perhaps with relief in his voice—became apologetic and fawningly deferential.

Of course he himself was not so pretentious as to presume that he was of sufficient rank and dignity to be a suitor to a queen; he "did not esteem himself worthy to wipe her shoes." No, the suggestion came from his enemy Cecil, who wanted to send him away. He himself would hardly have been so foolish as to put himself forward as a suitor to Mary, since he would then have been certain to offend both queens, and lose their favor. Surely Melville could see the difficulty of his position, he concluded, and would beg Mary's forgiveness for his apparent presumption. In fact he was guiltless; the entire scheme arose from "the malice of his enemies."

Melville, who had every reason to believe that Elizabeth, not Cecil, was the most enthusiastic proponent of the plan, held his tongue. Either the anxious earl was being duped or, quite possibly, his show of self-protective alarm was itself part of the queen's intricate design, intended to confuse Melville and brake the progress of the suit she had seemed so earnestly to urge. After nine days in Elizabeth's quixotic company he believed her capable of anything.

Melville's leavetaking was as ceremonious as his welcoming had been. Cecil walked with him through the courtyards of Hampton Court to the outer gate, where his traveling party awaited him, and before he mounted his horse the secretary put a valuable gold chain around his neck as a farewell gift. Other gifts Melville had already packed away, chief among them the jewels the countess of Lennox was sending to Queen Mary's officials and the diamond ring she was sending to Mary herself. Melville's negotiations with the countess and her son Lord Darnley had gone well; the countess, he was convinced, was "a very wise and discreet matron," and had "many favorers" in England.

The queen was not there to say goodbye, but she had given Melville a letter at his final audience, expressing her pleasure at his visit and assuring Mary that she had "acquainted him with all her inward griefs and desires."

She had indeed acquainted him to an extraordinary degree with that private self she seldom shared with anyone save Leicester. As he rode northward Melville must have wondered often how he would describe that private self to his mistress in Edinburgh. He would start with externals: Elizabeth's striking looks, her shrewd, agile mind and sharp tongue, her intellectual eagerness and burning thirst to surpass her rival. But for the rest, he was for the moment at a loss. How could he convey the elusive core of the remarkable being who ruled England, whose spirit "could not endure a commander" and whose mercurial temperament embraced so many moods? For this he would have to rely on a few haunting images, describing to Mary how Elizabeth had stalked angrily up and down amid the late-blooming flowers in her privy garden, how she had leaped like an elegant goat in the swift Italian galliard, how she had sat alone at her virginal, her fingers flying over the keys, her concentration intense, determined in her impassioned virtuosity to drive off the inward griefs that assailed her.

20

To laugh, to lie, to flatter, to face:
Four waies in Court to win men grace.

In the 1560s, nearly forty years after Cardinal Wolsey deeded Hampton Court to Henry VIII, the fantastic storybook palace was still the chief monument of the Tudor dynasty. Beneath an endless roofline of asymmetrical turrets and pinnacles and whimsically curlicued chimney stacks were some eighteen hundred habitable rooms—"or at least with doors that lock" —set amid formal gardens where painted dragons and lions and unicorns rose above the fruit trees and banks of flowers. The Thames flowed by, "a little pleasantly rapid," to the south of the palace, fish "playing and in sight" within its clear waters. Visitors to England invariably took home tales of "that stupendous place," Hampton Court, and it was here, in fact, that the pageantry of Queen Elizabeth's court and household could be seen to best advantage.

When the queen was in residence the palace was alive with movement and activity. Skilled workmen repaired rotted paneling and patched plaster; painters renewed the faded colors on the royal emblems and crests which decorated the walls, and gilders re-applied liquid gold where vandals had scratched it off. Servants in blue liveries went from room to room, putting up and taking down tapestries, curtains and bed hangings, carrying trays of food or armfuls of bedding or other "rich implements." An army of grooms brought heavy loads of firewood from the woodyard to stack beside the palace's thousand hearths, where yeomen waited to lay the fires and warm the rooms.

In the long galleries the officers of the household paced up and down with stiff authority in their long robes, their white staves of office in their hands. They scrutinized the walls, the furnishings, the unsavory carpeting of rushes that covered the floors, peering into the guest rooms to make certain each guest had been provided with a well-made bed, a lively fire and a light meal of wine and white bread. At the dining hour the household officers made their way to the chambers of important visitors, to escort them to their places in the great hall. There another cohort of servants and officials saw to the serving and removing of dishes of food and ewers of wine, while out of sight in the cavernous palace kitchens, lit red with the flickering light of open hearths, cooks and scullions "wrought both day and night" to prepare the hearty roast meats and savory sauces and sweet confections that were brought to the banquet table.

The palace courtyards were never empty. Horses clattered through at all hours, bearing the queen's personal messengers—forty of whom were always ready to be dispatched—or the swift riders with the diplomatic post. Noblemen arrived to take up residence for the winter season, bringing their wives and servants and dozens of trunks, their horses and panoplies of arms, even their hounds and hunting gear. Others departed, some under the cloud of royal disfavor, others disappointed in their ambitions and deeply in debt, their stay at court having broken their spirits as it robbed their purses. Tradesmen came through with carts of foodstuffs and coals and building materials, while tailors and clothiers and purveyors of finery and jewels watched nervously as the carters unloaded their trunks and coffers of precious goods.

An Italian awestruck by the expanse and luxury of Hampton Court praised it for being "replete with every convenience," but he was inexact: the palace had every convenience but one, indoor plumbing.

The stench of the great royal establishment must have been at least as awe-inspiring as its architecture, and detectable from nearly as far away. To be sure, Wolsey had gone to enormous expense to provide fresh spring water to the palace, through some three miles of lead pipe, but it was for drinking and cooking and washing only: there was no sewage system. Combined with the overpowering odors from the discarded kitchen garbage and stable sweepings and foul-smelling rushes, full of spilled food and sour wine and animal droppings, the stink of the servants' privies must have made an alarming assault on the senses.

The "close stools" used by gentlefolk (portable wooden toilets which had to be emptied by hand) were no less odoriferous. Even in the queen's privy chamber, a contemporary wrote, where the close stools were disguised "in sugared cases of satin and velvet," the air was often so "sour and noisome" that anyone who entered would be strongly tempted to turn around immediately and leave.[1]

Rather than attempt to eliminate the malodorous atmosphere the queen and her courtiers tried to counteract it. They held aromatic pomanders to their noses when passing through noxious chambers. They perfumed their persons (which they rarely washed), their garments, even their hats and shoes and jewels. They burned juniper wood or sweet-smelling herbs in their rooms, and surrounded themselves, whenever possible, with flowers. Elizabeth, who loved flowers, wore them pinned to her clothes, ordered them strewn on the floor of the royal barge, and had her revels master construct outdoor pavilions whose walls were masses of fragrant blooms. The queen and those who served her walked through the raw stench and rankness of the palace in a perfumed fog, afraid to venture into ordurous environs unshielded against contamination.

Unswept, unscoured, full of slops and slime, Hampton Court after weeks of habitation became uninhabitable, and the queen and all the others moved on. By then the vermin, engorged by the rich diet of discards that fell to them in the great hall and the private apartments, were multiplying so fast that the queen's ratcatchers and mole men could not keep up with them, and beneath their silken doublets the courtiers were bitten head to foot by fleas.

The expense of the huge establishment invariably surpassed the £40,000 allotted to it by Parliament, and the surviving household records make it easy to see why. Despite the existence of regulations setting out, in extensive detail, the daily menus for the queen, her retainers and servants, and prescribing the exact allowances of bread, wine, beer, fuel and light for all persons authorized to come within the court gates, in practice such constraints were disregarded.[2] The queen's meals were twice as large as they were supposed to be (though the excess was enjoyed by her servants and officials; Elizabeth herself was a very light eater), and featured twice as many delicacies. The "fasting days" the budget called for were ignored completely; when they came around the table was heaped as high as ever. Officials whose positions allowed them prescribed meals from the queen's bounty abused this privilege with spectacular greed. They ordered lavishly from the palace kitchens, far exceeding in quantity and quality the limitations imposed on them by the written rules, and they even detoured to their own country houses shipments of food destined for the royal larders.[3]

Economy, where servants and household staff were concerned, depended on uniform meals served to large numbers, but of the hundreds of places

Chalk drawing of Henry VIII in old age, ascribed to Holbein.

Anne Boleyn, painted by an unknown artist.

KATHARINE PARRE

Catherine Parr c. 1545, portrait attributed to W. Scrots.

The Lady Mary after Queen.

Mary Tudor, sketched as a young
girl, perhaps by Holbein.

King Philip II of Spain.

Elizabeth Tudor as a young girl of about fourteen, painted by a Flemish artist.

Thomas Seymour, by an unknown artist.

Coronation portrait of the twenty-five-year-old Elizabeth, painted by an unknown artist c. 1559.

Queen Elizabeth painted by an unknown artist c. 1560, when she was about twenty-seven.

Queen Elizabeth at about age thirty, painted by a Dutch artist.

Robert Dudley, earl of Leicester, in a painting attributed to Steven van der Meulen, c. 1565.

Miniature of Elizabeth by
Nicholas Hilliard.

Francis Walsingham,
Elizabeth's principal
secretary.

ANNO ÆTATIS
SVÆ | 31

The duc d'Alencon, Elizabeth's beloved "Frog," whom she hoped to marry in the 1580s.

Walter Ralegh in 1588, painting attributed to the monogrammist "H."

William Cecil, Elizabeth's principal minister and close associate for nearly forty years.

The earl of Essex, attributed to Marcus Gheeraerts.

Queen Elizabeth, a portrait attributed to Marcus Gheeraerts the Younger.

SERO, SED SERIO

Robert Cecil, Elizabeth's principal minister in the last years of her reign, painted in 1602 and attributed to J. de Critz.

Mary Queen of Scots, painting by an unknown early seventeenth-century artist after a portrait by Nicholas Hilliard of c. 1578.

Head of Elizabeth Tudor, from her tomb in Westminster Abbey.

set daily for the staff and superior servants only a few were occupied. Most people preferred to dine in their apartments, on food of their own choosing; their uneaten share of the common meal was joyfully appropriated by others further down in the hierarchy of office. Economy also demanded that food be available only to certain persons and at certain hours. But the kitchen never closed, and the wine and beer cellars, far from being properly regulated, were also open all night to all comers.

Worst of all, though, was the burgeoning, uncontrolled overpopulation of the court, with the number of private servants—that is, servants of servants—and personal retainers of the great and lesser aristocrats mounting every year without check. And it was bad enough that there were hundreds of these extra, unauthorized servants, all of them elbowing their way into the dining hall for the large midday meal; what was more appalling was that so many of them brought their wives and children along to be fed as well. There were barely enough accommodations for the staff at the best of times. Servants' rooms were tiny, and meant for sleeping only, and everyone slept two to a bed; with whole families sandwiched into space meant for one the squalor (and irritation) must have been unendurable.[4]

No one, whatever his or her rank, was truly comfortable at Hampton Court, but the discomforts had to be balanced against the potential rewards: power, or its illusion; wealth, or its promise; fame, or its counterfeit notoriety. Most of all, there was for ambitious men, ambitious families, the heady, buoyant sensation of constantly being on the threshold of advancement, of having an assigned place in the vast, finely choreographed dance of ascendancy that was court life.

This life had its formal rituals—extraordinary ceremonies such as Leicester's elevation, or the daily solemnities carried out to honor the serving of the queen's meals or the making of her bed, or the formal "good night," following which the courtiers were left to their own amusement and the queen, who slept little, often went to her desk and worked late. On Sundays there was always the small-scale pageantry of Elizabeth's procession to and from the chapel, the long train of her regal gown carried by a countess, her retinue a showy parade of two hundred tall guardsmen in red velvet, the council members, bearing the royal scepters, and a dozen highborn young ladies. As she passed everyone knelt and, by custom, held out to her "letters of supplication from rich and poor" (some written by people in genuine distress, many by that crowd of eager, insatiable petitioners who had been given one taste of royal favor and lived, as Elizabeth fully meant them to, in expectation of more). She accepted them all "with a humble mien," and responded to the display of deference with a full-voiced "Thank you with all my heart," as the trumpeters blew the fanfare signaling dinner.

A spectacular annual ceremony was the giving and receiving of New Year's gifts—an affectionate English custom which at court became calculated and mercenary. In return for carefully weighed goblets and basins and other objects in gold and silver, their worth precisely determined in advance, the queen received from the members of her court an array of fantastic and beautiful gifts. Some people gave her purses of coins, to be sure, but others contributed suits of clothing, jewels, ornaments and other personal gifts. In 1562 the array of presents included an elaborately decorated crossbow, a golden hourglass filled with glass sand, table coverings of needlework and a portable desk, upholstered in velvet embroidered with gold. Cecil gave the queen a royal seal carved in bone and tipped with silver; one of the women of her privy chamber, Lavinia Terling, a portrait of "the queen's person and other personages," enclosed in a finely painted box.

The apothecaries presented Elizabeth with medicines on New Year's Day, and the grocers spices—boxes of ginger and nutmegs and a pound of cinnamon. The chief clerk of the spicery came forward with pomegranates and apples, and boxes of comfits—sugar candies in various flavors. The most fanciful of the edible gifts were the huge structures built of marzipan. One of the yeomen of the chamber wheeled in his "very fair marchpane made like a tower, with men and sundry artillery in it." The master cook presented his with a flourish—a marzipan made like a chessboard, the different squares different flavors. And the surveyor of the works, an architect, surpassed all with his giant sugared construction of St. Paul's Cathedral, its steeples reproduced with loving exactitude in candied paste. The latter gift had a touch of nostalgia about it, for the great steeple—by far the tallest spire in London—had only recently been struck by lightning and the church destroyed by fire, obliterating a venerable link with London's medieval past.

There were incidental pastimes in plenty at Elizabeth's court. Card-playing, gambling, fortune-telling and tennis were among the indoor amusements; when the weather was fine, there was riding and hunting as well. Every well-bred gentleman studied fencing, while ladies took music lessons and did embroidery. Both men and women spent many hours with their tailors and dressmakers and other outfitters. And both perfected their dancing, an art much regarded at Elizabeth's court.

When she was not performing herself, the queen liked to watch her courtiers dance, settling herself on cushions in her presence chamber and beating time as the musicians played. The men she watched with particular pleasure, as they handed their swords to the nearest page and took their places in line. There were prizes for the best dancer, and less immediate rewards as well. Grace on the dance floor was an advantage when it came to preferment to office, and the hours spent learning the fashionable Italian steps and polishing one's leaps and pirouettes paid well in career advancement.

Revelry in the early years of Elizabeth's reign was modest. There were none of the costly spectacles that had drained the treasury of Henry VIII, and whenever possible the queen encouraged and attended large-scale pageantry paid for by others. The London festivities of May-games and midsummer musters she gladly attended, and often, of course, she had plays performed at court. (These might or might not find favor; one group of players that appeared before her in 1559 "acted so disgraceful, that they were commanded to leave off.") Masking as such was limited, at least in the first half of the reign, both because of its expense and, at times, because the great halls of the palaces were not in sufficiently good repair. At Hampton Court one Christmas the revels master struggled manfully against the elements, hampered by gaps in the walls and drafty windows. In desperation, he ordered the toils master to provide him with large tents "to keep away the wind and snow from driving into the hall."[5]

The most lavish occasions at Elizabeth's court were feasts and masques given in outdoor "banqueting houses" especially constructed for these entertainments. Compared to the barnlike indoor halls of the royal palaces, which averaged a hundred feet or more in length, the outdoor banqueting houses were huge pavilions three or four hundred feet in circumference, their thick canvas walls held up by great ship masts forty feet high. In June of 1572, when an important French envoy visited the court, a vast banqueting house was constructed and some five hundred workmen were hired to decorate it with birch boughs and ivy and roses and honeysuckle. The canvas walls were cunningly painted to look like stone, and the ceiling was a phantasmagoria of painted foliage and heavenly bodies and pendant artificial flowers and vegetables—pomegranates, melons, cucumbers, grapes, carrots—"spangled with gold, and most richly hanged." Three hundred "lights of glass" sparkled overhead on the night the banqueting house was inaugurated, and the effect was magnificent. Though built to be temporary, this structure was still in use twelve years later, in 1584, and by then birds had moved into the boughs and overhanging greenery and sang as if in a forest while the feast went on below.[6]

To live moderately and sensibly in so vast a setting as a royal palace, amid outsized backdrops and surrounded by gargantuan excess, must have called for steely self-discipline and extraordinary mental poise. Court life, with its hundred temptations to greed, to gluttony, to ruthless betrayal and hidden vice, pulled its victims in many directions and often left them rudderless.

"Inside their heads is a perpetuum mobile," a visiting foreigner wrote of the English courtiers. Another found them so befuddled and naive in their blind greed that they were "like children, who gladly exchange the precious stone for a single apple."[7]

Edgy, off balance, their nerves in rags, those who lived at court were easily seized by fads and fancies, particularly in dress. Appearance was everything: it was no wonder that they strove to outdo one another, as in the game of preferments and politics, in the cut of their doublets and the modish elegance of their shoes and hats.

It was the men who took the lead. Their trousers, or hose, once short and moderately full, grew to knee-length and bulged like stuffed pockets, while their lace-trimmed, jewel-buttoned doublets too grew longer and more elaborately ornamented. Everything—doublet, hose, coat, cloak, and the dozen accessories no gentleman of fashion went without—had to match or harmonize with everything else, and the scores of yards of golden brocade and crane-colored silk and murrey velvet that went into a complete suit of clothes could far outstrip the wearer's income.

But there was more: bright silk stockings, garters fringed with gold or shining spangles, shoes of soft perfumed leather or velvet, covered with rosettes of ribbons and lace, an ornamented rapier or dagger sheathed in an embroidered velvet scabbard. Velvet hats set off the costume, perhaps with long feathers in their brims which swept out an arc two feet wide. Scented gloves, "sweet as damask roses," dripping tassels and Venice gold, a large and beautiful handkerchief, held in the hand, jeweled rings, a heavy watch, a protective amulet, perhaps a locket enclosing a curl of hair from a favorite lover—all these and more freighted down the well-dressed courtier and must have made him insufferably self-conscious.

His earrings, coiffure and rouged cheeks must have contributed even more to this narcissism. A jewel or pearl at the earlobe enhanced a gentleman's carefully shaped curls, clipped coquettishly short or grown long into a ruff-length page boy. His mustache too was often kept long, and his beard —washed, combed, plaited into braids or bound with bands—was the object of infinite attention. Only yokels let their beards grow in their natural contours; men of fashion chose the shape that made the most of their painted faces. Lean, pinched faces could be made commanding and broad, fat faces narrow, with the help of a clever barber. Satirists joked at the expense of "weasel-beaked" men whose well-meaning barbers left too much hair on their cheeks until as a result the ill-formed gallants "looked like big hens, as grim as geese."

But beards were not only styled—they were also dyed, in a myriad of colors to match a man's coloring and clothes. From Nordic blond to fiery

Irish red to amber or auburn, any hue was possible, along with the startling, but undeniably trend-setting, shades of purple and orange and speckled yellow.

Women departed less spectacularly at first from the conventions of dress that had prevailed in Queen Mary's reign. The time-honored layering of stiffened farthingale, then petticoats, then kirtle, then gown was preserved, but the bodices became more rigidly shaped—the shape supplied by an interior scaffolding of wood or steel—and sleeves became tight and straight, ending in wrist-ruffs. The farthingale, which could stand alone on its whalebone or cane hoops, ballooned out until in its English version it surpassed its French original, which by law could be no more than four feet wide.

In 1564—a year of deliverance for hundreds of overworked laundrymaids and chamber servants—Mistress Dinghen Vanderplasse came to England and taught the English how to make starch. The huge ruffs that were coming into fashion, made of yards and yards of cambric or lawn, were fragile constructions held out from the face by hundreds of sticks of bone or wood, all carefully put in place one after the other by frustrated servants. They could be worn only once; in order to be re-used ruffs had to be laboriously washed and ironed and folded and re-shaped, the tiny wooden stays inserted afresh. With Mistress Vanderplasse's formal instruction in starching and starch-making the laundry and chamber staff were able to save days of tedious work.

Starched, the great ruffs stood out from the face on their own (or over a wire framework); if treated with care, they could be worn several times at least if freshened with a hot "poking stick" inserted between the folds. Of course, they were still vulnerable. The wearer had to keep away from walls and hangings and other people's ruffs; a slight jostling could disarrange his neckwear fatally. And, of course, he had to avoid candles and torches —and wet weather. Great ruffs, in the rain, were said to "strike sail and flutter like dish-clouts."

Preoccupation with dress and personal adornment, far from being an incidental oddity of life at Elizabeth's court, was in the mid-1560s becoming central to that court's affect and mental outlook. The lust for ever costlier fabrics and ever more conspicuous fashions, the willingness, even eagerness, of the courtiers to be squeezed and stuffed and strapped into rigid and confining garments that forced them to move with stiff awkwardness while holding their heads "monstrous steady," the perverse determination with which women pulled their hair into labyrinthine knots which gave them headaches and men sweated and strained before their tailors until they fainted from exhaustion—all these were symptoms of a characteristic malaise of Elizabethan society that was to become more and more pronounced.

"In these days," the historian Camden wrote, "a wondrous excess of apparel had spread itself all over England." The craze for new, exaggerated, garish clothing "grew into such contempt, that men by their new fangled garments, and too gaudy apparel, discovered a certain deformity and arrogancy of mind whilst they jetted up and down in their silks glittering with gold and silver, either embroidered or laced."

Ascham, a close observer of this "deformity and arrogancy of mind" at Elizabeth's court, wrote at length in *The Scholemaster* of the misordered manners that had overtaken the courtiers along with their huge hose and outrageous doublets. They were braggardly, aggressive, unblushingly self-assertive in every situation. Men "unknown to the court" they shoved aside, haughtily facing them down and trying to appear "big, dangerous of look, talk and answer." To their betters they "bore a brave look" and affected warlike oaths and swaggering gestures. They loved to hear themselves speak, Ascham asserted, especially some "brave proverb" or foul vulgarity borrowed from the London underworld. And always, no matter how small their incomes or how costly the fashion, they had to have some "new disguised garment or desperate hat," and they must be the first to have it, before the fad went stale and their pride shriveled with it.[8]

To be sure, Ascham was aging, made cantankerous by chronic fevers and indulging, in part, an old man's contempt for the young. But others less prejudiced by their own circumstances described the same phenomenon; the elderly humanist was merely the most articulate critic of a generally deplored trend. "Innocency is gone, bashfulness is banished," Ascham wrote in his Latinate style, "much presumption in youth, small authority in age, reverence is neglected, duties be confounded, and to be short, disobedience doth overflow the banks of good order, almost in every place, almost in every degree of man." Englishmen had become infected with "Italianate" ways, their insolence extending even into the spiritual realm. They mocked both the pope and the Protestant divines, following no authority save themselves.

And the same grotesque garb and braggardly misbehavior that tainted the "great ones" of the court had begun to infect their social inferiors. In London the "misorder of mean men" was so great that a watch was set at every city gate to seize "misordered persons in apparel." But the effort was futile: not only did the worst of the swaggering courtiers side with their sartorial imitators in the capital but the queen herself, when confronted with extravagantly dressed Londoners in the presence chamber, seemed rather to enjoy than to disapprove of them.

The queen herself: in fact, she was the heart of the problem. For however much she might complain about the money her courtiers wasted on silks and jewels, about disregard for the sumptuary laws and of the acts against outlandish apparel, she herself was the most conspicuous exemplar of splendid excess. Ascham might rage against "Italianate" manners and Parliament deplore the Florentine and Milanese merchants who "licked the fat from English beards," but Elizabeth liked Italians and Italian ways. "I like the manners and customs of the Italians better than those of all the rest of the world," she boasted in 1564, "and I am, as it were, half Italian."[9]

Her wardrobe was a fantasy world of modish extravagance—gowns of elegant black satin and regal purple velvet and silks and brocades in the flattering shades she favored—russet, tawny, peach, marigold, lady blush. Each gown bore a fortune in ornament: aglets or knots or tassels of gold, gold or silver braid, pearls, garnets, even rubies in profusion. When she moved she sparkled as brilliantly as a diamond with refracted light, or threw back the warm gleam of pearls.

Her jeweled necklaces, pendants, rings and bracelets were yet another layer of coruscating richness. She wore proudly all the great gemstones her father had brought into his jewel house when the monasteries surrendered their wealth, and to these she added hundreds of others, until they hung from every inch of her outer garments and blazed from her ears, fingers and hair.

Every kind of fashionable trinket hawked by foreign merchants Elizabeth bought—dozens of pairs of embroidered gloves, cauls and hoods of every design, muffs, earpicks, scissors, jeweled watches made like flowers or reliquaries, brooches, pins, and a great many jeweled fans, their feathers a billowing rainbow of hues, their handles of gold or ivory studded with shining stones.

And just as Elizabeth's continuous display of costly adornment taught her gentlemen and ladies to crave fashion and court ruin, so her colorful, unpredictable and usually indecorous behavior gave them a model of raucous disobedience.

She swore, she shouted, she forgot her manners and swaggered unconscionably before the abashed visitors in the presence chamber. "God's death!" she roared when a luckless councilor or official offended her; she swore, in fact, "by God, by Christ, and by many parts of his glorified body, and by saints, faith, troth, and other forbidden things," and she seemed to like it when those around her swore too—though they swore at her, surely, to their peril.

Of all the maidenly virtues modesty was, perhaps, the least in evidence in Queen Elizabeth. She thumbed her nose and shook her fist at the great powers of her time and, when driven to it, sent her soldiers against them as well. Like the self-vaunting gentlemen Ascham despised, she professed reverence for nothing and looked to herself in everything. She loved the sound of her own voice. "It is her wont," wrote a diplomat much wearied by the queen's torrent of language, "to make long digressions and after much circumlocution to come to the point of which she wishes to speak." "As a rule," wrote another, "she speaks continuously."[10]

Truculent, violent, disagreeable, arrogant, always majestic: such was the queen of Hampton Court. Her loud, authoritative voice echoed fearsomely down the long galleries of the great palace, and the hive of mighty and lowly subjects who served her there, however they plotted and cursed her for the stubborn woman that she was, trembled at the sound.

PART FOUR

"A Very Strange Sort of Woman"

21

The doubt of future foes exiles my present joy,
And Wit me warns to shun such snares as threaten mine
annoy,
For falsehood now doth flow, and subjects' faith doth ebb,
Which would not be if Reason ruled, or Wisdom wove
the web;
But clouds of toys untried do cloak aspiring minds,
Which turn to rain of late repent by course of changed
winds.
The top of hope supposed, the root of ruth will be,
And fruitless all their grafted guiles, as ye shall shortly
see.

On November 14, 1569, three hundred armed horsemen rode to Durham Cathedral and, bursting into the sanctuary, overturned the communion table and broke it in pieces. They snatched up the Protestant service books and English Bible, and burned them in a huge bonfire. As crowds gathered they destroyed or defaced every other symbol of Anglican worship they could find, until the great Norman cathedral stood as it had a generation earlier, a Catholic shrine.

A makeshift altar was erected, and as the soldiers watched, their arquebuses and daggers at hand, high mass was sung. The crowd grew until the vast nave was filled, and the worshipers knelt to be absolved of the Protestant heresy to which they had, against their consciences, acquiesced.

It was a dramatic hour. Many wept, and gave thanks for the restoration of the faith they had never ceased to nourish in secret. But amid their rejoicing they were apprehensive, for what they were doing, however pleasing it might be to God, was treason against the queen.

The Catholic north had been brewing rebellion for many months. Mary Stuart, still Elizabeth's presumed heir, had taken refuge in England from her hostile Scots subjects, and her presence put heart into dissatisfied Catholics, especially when they heard that she was to marry the duke of Norfolk, the leading peer. Rumors and prophecies fed the religious resurgence. The queen's council was said to be divided, her power ebbing. Political unrest was written in the stars. Predictions circulated that the coming year "would witness much trouble and difficulty, and that there was danger of a great change." Those who dared cast the queen's horoscope, and read there uncertainty and peril.

Even without the aid of occult predictions it was evident that trouble was coming. Musters had been held in the summer, and some sixty thousand men had come forward to pledge themselves to arms in the service of their lords, the earls of Westmorland and Northumberland. And in this feudal north country, where the ties between lords and their vassals and tenants had not been diluted by that overriding loyalty to the sovereign that prevailed farther south, the musters created in effect a private army.

The queen had been only too aware of the sharpening of discontent in the north. That craggy, wild land with its barren moors and its rough-hewn, secretive people was foreign to her, but its heritage of rebellion was not. When she was a child of three the Pilgrimage of Grace had erupted in the north country, uniting into one massive rising angry feudatories, countrymen crushed by inflation and ardent Catholics who yearned to restore the old faith. Her father had moved swiftly and vengefully to crush the rising, yet its mystique had seized the folk imagination and its symbols—chiefly the image of the Five Wounds of Christ—remained compelling.

Now, with Mary Stuart in England to rekindle the Catholic cause, Elizabeth became justly alarmed. As in 1536, religious enthusiasm threatened to coalesce with political grievances and local ambitions to engender revolt. Her commander Sussex analyzed the dangerous attachments of her discontented northern subjects. "Some specially respect the duke of Norfolk," he wrote, "some the Scottish queen, and some religion, and some, perhaps, all three."

The forces the queen was able to put into the field should rebellion come were untried and ill-prepared. There were no professional soldiers, only manorial and county levies, and recent musters had revealed their inadequacy. Summoned in haste from their labors in the fields and villages, the disorderly ranks could not discipline themselves or follow commands or handle arms—when arms were available. Many men were listed in the muster rolls as "naked," meaning they had neither armor nor weapons, and if called up suddenly to defend their districts against rebels they could be expected to brandish nothing more menacing than pitchforks. Few in these makeshift bands could be expected to stand their ground courageously in the face of better-armed opponents; many, their commanders candidly advised, were likely to prove disloyal.

Elizabeth had no illusions about her fighting forces. A determined challenge from a strong authority with a tincture of legitimacy could melt them away or turn them against her. If Norfolk married Mary Stuart, Elizabeth confided to Leicester, she herself would be a prisoner in the Tower within four months.

It was a difficult passage, for the choice lay between seizing the initiative, and thus forcing potential traitors to show themselves, and waiting in fear for them to choose their own best moment—which might, of course, never come. Under the circumstances, caution seemed foolhardy. In September of 1569 the queen set her defenses in motion, entrenching herself behind the thick stone walls of Windsor Castle and ordering her militia to arms.

Predictably, the conspirators were flushed out, and in the end were weakened because Elizabeth had chosen the time. Norfolk, who as rumor had it was indeed deeply implicated in plans to determine the succession, capitulated and threw himself on the queen's mercy in October, and the two principal conspirators in the north, the earls of Westmorland and Northumberland, showed such misgivings that they had almost to be shamed into action by their hardier womenfolk and bellicose gentry.

But once the earls at last determined to act revolt was for a time at flood tide. Thus it was that in mid-November, after the conspiracy had lost its most prominent supporter, Westmorland's and Northumberland's soldiers marched from Durham to Darlington to Ripon to Tadcaster and on toward York, following the antique banner of the Five Wounds of Christ.

The assault on Durham Cathedral, with its spectacular destruction of Protestant furnishings and its Bible-burnings, was a high point of the rising. The fervent iconoclasm unleashed a torrent of Catholic piety. Worshipers in town after town came by the hundreds to be absolved from the excommunication they had brought on themselves by conforming to official Protestantism. The priests who absolved them were themselves penitents, for they too had conformed to Elizabeth's church, to their heartfelt regret. The outpouring of pent-up sentiment was if anything more formidable than the political defiance. Masses were sung, prayers raised, sermons expounded with great fervor and devotion; the prodigals had returned to the fold.

To be sure, not all of those who knelt to join in the Catholic celebrations came voluntarily; some were herded in at swordpoint. One of the queen's partisans, an eyewitness, described how the rebels swept into a town, exhorted the people to join them in their cause of freeing the queen from those who had "misused her," and then, when they did not respond with sufficient heartiness, resorted to bribes and threats.[1]

But reports reaching Cecil indicated that between the appeals to piety and to patriotism and the frank promises of reprisals against those who did not take up arms the rebel force was numbered in the thousands, and growing. The Catholic rumormongers who strutted self-importantly up and down the aisles of St. Paul's in London, claiming to have the latest and best information of the situation in the north, boasted of the rebels' strength. Elizabeth and her councilors grew solemn. They did not dare to underestimate the danger, especially as Sussex, president of the royal executive body in the north parts, the Council of the North, was sending disconcerting messages about the trouble he was having raising troops to quell the rising.

Despite his urgent appeals, Sussex wrote on November 18, he had been able to raise no more than four hundred horsemen; the local landholders and communities were jealously holding on to their own men, in self-defense. The ranks of footsoldiers were thin too, and those at the Berwick garrison at least were shamefully feeble. The queen's cousin and commander Lord Hunsdon looked them over, and found many to be elderly veterans or near cripples incapacitated by wounds acquired in earlier conflicts. They were "meeter for an almshouse than to be soldiers," he reported scornfully.

And they were mutinous, or close to it. Sussex's men "found fault with the weather," complaining of the snow and rain and frowning up at the sky to look for signs of storms, at the same time making no secret of their resentment at being drafted for the queen's service. The men of Berwick had to be cautioned sternly not to "utter any misliking of the queen's most royal person or her most gracious proceedings," or to so much as hint at favoring the ideals or designs of the rebels.[2] Meanwhile the rebels, at Ripon, were said to be descending on the town with five thousand foot and twelve hundred horsemen, staunch behind their banners, invoking the aid of the townspeople and the saints.

For ten years and more Catholicism had slumbered in England. But the outward acquiescence to the established church was misleading, not only in the north but throughout the country. Hundreds of thousands, conceivably even a majority of the English, were still Catholics. The public devotions of the northerners in 1569 were carried out regularly by their coreligionists elsewhere in secret. Clerics led their congregations in the Protestant services, then retired to say private masses. The faithful said their prayers and observed the traditional offices in their bedchambers, where they could read Roman devotional books undisturbed.

Some parishioners even took their Catholic primers to church, Protestant preachers complained, "and prayed upon them all the time when the Lessons to be reading and in the time of the Litany." Many of the elderly, who had been brought up in the pre-Reformation church, insisted on saying their rosaries during the communion service, and went on saying them under their breath when the clergy took their beads away.[3]

The government may have had little to fear from grandmothers stubbornly repeating their rosaries but it had much to fear from the Catholic powers of Europe who might be expected to lend English Catholics their aid. The conspirators in the north had already benefited from this aid. A papal agent in London, a nefarious Florentine banker named Ridolfi, had supplied Westmorland and Northumberland with a large sum of money to buy arms and equipment. The French king Charles IX (or rather his mother, Catherine de' Medici, for Charles was a minor) had promised to send five thousand of his soldiers to aid in restoring Mary Stuart—and the Roman faith—in Scotland and, if possible, England as well. And the Spanish, not to be outdone, had assured the earls that they too would send men in the spring of 1570—which had been the conspirators' planned season for their rising—and as proof of their firm intentions had sent an envoy to London who, when the time came, was under orders to abandon his diplomatic pose and command the Spanish troops.[4]

But at the heart of the danger lay Mary Stuart. Demanding, scheming, utterly beguiling, she fretted restlessly at Tutbury Castle under the nervous supervision of Elizabeth's cousin Francis Knollys. She was in effect an English prisoner.

Mary's recent past had been a bloody season of impetuous romances, fearsome passions, and murder. The young, "lady-faced" lad Darnley, whom Mary had married impulsively in 1565, had proven to be a thoroughly contemptible husband, drunken and bestial and insufferably arrogant, and Mary, very unwisely, had turned to another man for companionship. He was David Riccio, a lowborn Italian musician who served Mary as French secretary. Like Leicester at the English court, Riccio had charmed his way to wealth and honors overnight, and in the eyes of the Scots advisers whom he supplanted—not to mention the snarling Darnley —the Italian deserved death, especially as it was widely believed that the child the queen was carrying was his.

One night as the pregnant Mary sat at supper with Riccio and one of her ladies, Darnley and an accomplice burst in and seized Riccio, stabbing him again and again and provoking the gasping, dumbfounded Mary to cry for revenge. The result was another assassination: the house in which Darnley was staying was blown to pieces in a huge explosion, and Darnley himself was discovered dead in a nearby garden. The queen was blamed, and universally despised. She had provided the kingdom with an heir—the infant James Stuart—but her misconduct with Riccio and her barbarous murder of Darnley were intolerable. But there was worse to come.

Darnley's death had been planned by yet another of Mary's admirers— though a far from gentlemanly one—James Hepburn, earl of Bothwell.

Bothwell was young, lecherous, brutal, and married. He wanted Mary, and took her; impatient for power, he then kidnapped her and, after a speedy divorce, married her. Within days of her wedding Mary was reduced to suicidal despair by Bothwell's abuse; not only did he treat her cruelly, he made threats against her infant son, swearing he would prevent him from growing up to avenge his father's death. It was almost a deliverance when the Scots nobles rebelled and took Mary captive, forcing her to renounce her throne in favor of the child James. Her half-brother, the earl of Murray, was made regent.

After nearly a year in captivity, in May of 1568 Mary escaped to England where, to her chagrin, she became a captive again. Mary might be a royal personage who had suffered the gravest indignities, and a young woman in need of protection besides, but in the eyes of the world she was guilty of murder and adultery, and could expect no royal honors until her innocence was proved. Elizabeth lectured her (by letter), housed her, and set in motion an inquiry into her guilt. Meanwhile the English got their first real taste of the notorious queen of Scots.

Mary's keeper, the outspoken and highly moral Francis Knollys, found Mary to be every bit as passionate and intense as the queen of England, but without the latter's restraining wariness of action. Her womanly attraction gave her an undeniable advantage—"she hath withal an alluring grace, a pretty Scottish accent, and a searching wit, clouded with mildness," an Irish visitor wrote—but it was her sheer physical energy and implacable determination to defeat her enemies that made her truly dangerous. Knollys watched apprehensively as she rode out hunting, galloping with breakneck abandon through the fields in pursuit of game, and recalled that not long before she had ridden at the head of her soldiers, dashing to the forefront of the troop and exhorting the saddle-weary men to follow her untiring example. "The thing that most she thirsteth after is victory," he wrote to Cecil in June of 1568, "so that for victory's sake, pain and perils seemeth pleasant unto her."

Unlike Elizabeth, who had learned at an early age to avoid decisiveness and was making an art of judicious irresolution, Mary saw things in black and white and acted boldly. She admired, and imitated, courage and daring. In her confinement she paced and fumed, complaining about the shabby gowns Murray had provided for her in her exile—fit only as "coverings for saddles"—and about her tedious inactivity. She spent the long, dark winter days shut in the castle, doing embroidery hour after hour until it gave her a pain in the side, but in her imagination she was ever active. As she sewed, she schemed, with her supporters in Scotland and with the dissatisfied

English lords who in their exasperation with Elizabeth flirted with treason and finally embraced it.

"I have made great wars in Scotland, and I pray God I make no troubles in other realms also," Mary warned Knollys as her patience with the English wore thin. She "played her highness with thunderings and great countenances," and as the year 1569 advanced she drew a web of conspiracy around her.

Mary's attraction as a focus of rebellion, at least on political grounds, would have been far less had Elizabeth's grip on her council and her government been firm. But in fact Elizabeth faced a severe challenge to her authority.[5] Her advisers, having reluctantly indulged her spinsterly authority for more than ten years, had in 1569 finally decided to override it.

Luck alone, it seemed to these aggressive, masterly men, had brought England through ten years of female rule. Accustomed to complete obedience from women—and accustomed to cursing all those who were less than obedient as obstinate, wilful shrews—they were affronted by their queen's stubborn blindness to the inappropriateness of her dominance over them. Dominion belonged to men, not to women; God had ordained it so. In contravening this self-evident law Elizabeth was acting unnaturally, and adding the risk of divine vengeance to the already great risk posed by her own innate incompetence as a woman.

Knollys burst out in a letter to Cecil, complaining that Elizabeth seemed to desire to be "the ruler or half-ruler" of her realm—instead of the meek and passive figurehead through whom her councilors governed. That he could write such words—and others said similar things—after observing for a decade the day-to-day rulership of his strong-willed, astute, clever sovereign says much about the extent of this deep-seated axiom of male mastery. It was not merely that Elizabeth had failed to prove herself worthy of being sole ruler: as a woman she could never be worthy. And as an unmarried woman she gave profound offense to her advisers, and indeed to all men and to God.

It was the radical inappropriateness of her unmarried state, almost as much as the need for a successor to the Tudor throne, that galled several of her councilors to take on themselves the responsibility of settling the succession issue in their own way. Anointed queen she might be, but Elizabeth was also an erring woman in need of correction. She, and her kingdom, had to be saved from her own folly.

The menacing configuration of the Catholic powers on the continent made prompt action essential. In France, there was renewed danger that the Catholic Guise faction, with its everpresent aspirations to use Mary Stuart to seize Scotland and possibly England, might return to power. Throughout 1569 the country was shaken by civil war, and Cecil and many others believed that the outcome of the struggle would be a strong Catholic resurgence.

At the same time Spain, a sleeping dragon throughout most of the past decade, was stirring to militant life. In 1567, Spain's leading soldier, the duke of Alva, brought ten thousand hardened Spanish infantrymen to the Hapsburg Netherlands, and summoned some twenty-five thousand Germans, Italians and Walloons to back them up. In a few short months the land might of Spain was concentrated in Flanders, garrisoned just across the narrow English Channel from Dover, two days away—or less, with a favorable wind—from London.

An invading army, at least in potential, was camped on England's doorstep. Alva was closer to London than Mary Stuart was, and infinitely better equipped to seize Elizabeth's throne.

This was tolerable, if hardly reassuring, so long as England and her traditional Hapsburg ally remained on amicable terms. But early in 1569 there was a bitter and costly quarrel between them. Five Spanish ships carrying some eighty-five thousand pounds—money loaned to Philip II by Genoese bankers to pay Alva's troops—were driven to seek haven in English ports, and Elizabeth, in need of money herself, confiscated their precious cargo. The Spanish made vehement protests, and retaliated by seizing English ships and goods and declaring an embargo on the Netherlands trade, but in law Elizabeth was within her rights. She assumed the Genoese loan, and countered Alva's embargo by seizing Netherlands ships and goods in England.

It was a checkmate, but only an illusory one, for the nearness of Alva's army made the English counterthreat meaningless. Any thought that Elizabeth's soldiery could turn back the Spanish hordes seemed, to Cecil at least, a vain hope. "This realm is become so feeble by long peace," he wrote, "as it were a fearful thing to imagine, if the enemies were at hand, of what force the resistance would be." And Cecil, good Protestant that he was, had ever before his eyes the prospect of a Catholic crusade against England, prompted not by petty commercial quarrels but by religious zeal. Many English men and women shared his grim vision. People whispered to one another, as the year advanced, that before long Alva and his mail-clad minions would be saying mass in St. Paul's.

Given the hazards England faced, Elizabeth must either marry immediately and conceive a successor—something that, at thirty-five, she could still hope to do, if so inclined—or her advisers must arrange for Mary Stuart's recognition as heir, preferably as Norfolk's wife. (Her marriage to Bothwell would presumably be annulled, or declared invalid.) Elizabeth seemed further than ever from marriage: so it must be Mary, and Norfolk.

The duke of Norfolk seemed destined to play a major role in any intervention the councilors might make in determining the succession. He was England's only duke, the natural spokesman for her nobility, and if his leadership capacity was not equal to the task, his ambitions were.

Norfolk was a great peer who lived in the feudal manner. His Howard ancestors had served all the Tudors, conspicuously—if not always with conspicuous loyalty. He was closely related to three queens: Anne Boleyn, Catherine Howard, and Elizabeth herself, and on his sprawling manorial lands, where several thousand of his tenants occupied some six hundred square miles, he was himself almost a king. Five hundred mounted retainers escorted the duke wherever he went, and from among his own tenants alone it was said he could put a force of nearly two thousand armed men into the field. From this formidable base he was building up his power further, allying himself with other great families through marriage (he had survived three wives) and buying up huge tracts of land to add to his private domain.

Heir to a great name and a great fortune, Norfolk glimpsed, however shakily, an even greater destiny, as consort of the queen of Scots and perhaps, should Mary succeed Elizabeth, as king of England. In 1569 he was only thirty-one, just coming into his maturity; the hour, the political timing of others and the ripeness of his own ambition combined to make Norfolk a focus of conspiracy.

It was Leicester who provided the prompting, and orchestrated the intrigue. Pembroke, Arundel and Sussex stood behind the earl, and the Scots regent Murray too gave his approval to the scheme of marrying Mary Stuart to Norfolk. In a letter to Mary in May, 1569, Leicester offered a tempting bargain. If Mary would agree to wed Norfolk, maintain the reformed religion in Scotland, forgive her political enemies and promise perpetual friendship with England, Leicester and his allies would work to restore her to her Scots throne and recognize her as Elizabeth's official heir. She accepted the terms. Norfolk, now her fiancé, pledged his hand to her with a diamond ring.

In the sequel Norfolk, Leicester and the others bungled their work and showed clearly that, however great their indignation at Elizabeth's perverse autonomy as queen, in fact they were no match for her politically. Leicester, having set the stage, withdrew into the wings and waited there, making excuses for his inaction and hanging back from further decisive steps.

Norfolk, having committed himself too extensively to back out, lost his nerve. Afraid to confess—except, foolishly, to Cecil—and equally afraid to act, he did nothing, and so incriminated himself.

For Elizabeth, sensitive to the dissatisfactions and scheming temperaments of her advisers, knew that conspiracy was under way, though she did not know its precise shape. She gave Norfolk every chance to come forward, and when he failed, and finally in September took refuge on his estates, she gambled on his ultimate cowardice and forced him to capitulate. Leicester had done so several weeks earlier, relying, correctly, on Elizabeth's weakness for him to guarantee her forgiveness. The others—Arundel, Pembroke, Sussex—saw that they were beaten and resumed their disgruntled loyalty to the queen.

But there was much more at stake than pretensions to power by a handful of noblemen. Added to the enticing presence of Mary Stuart and the spur of international Catholic intrigue, Norfolk's alignment with the earls of Westmorland and Northumberland ignited popular insurrection in the north. Dormant forces stirred to life—feudal instincts, religious sentiments centuries old, ancient lusts for revenge. A month after the duke was imprisoned in the Tower, his northern allies went ahead with their defiance, unleashing to rebellion a populace in which the crosscurrents of violence ran turbulent and deep.

"We, Thomas earl of Northumberland and Charles earl of Westmorland the queen's true and faithful subjects, to all the same of the old Catholic religion," the rebel leaders proclaimed loudly from the steps of the Market Cross at Durham, "know ye that we with many other well disposed persons as well of the nobility as others have promised our faith in the furtherance of this our good meaning." The queen was being deceived by "evil disposed persons" bent on destroying the Catholic faith and the ancient nobility, the proclamation announced. "We therefore have gathered ourselves together to resist by force and the rather by the help of God and you good people to see redress of things amiss."

So ran the official statement of the rebels' avowed purpose. The old church and the old social order; these, and the crushing of the queen's "evil disposed" advisers—by whom the earls meant Cecil—were the stated aims of the rising. All was to be undertaken for Elizabeth's sake, not in defiance of her. Simple people harangued by the earls' subordinates were told that in fighting for Westmorland and Northumberland they would be rallying to arms for their queen, and some of them, no doubt, believed this. Others responded with devout reverence to the red crosses the rebel forces wore on their shoulders, and believed them to be crusaders caught up in a holy cause.

There was a near-total merging of armed insurrection with militant religion. The earls went to mass at Durham Cathedral accompanied by a display of force and by the time-honored symbols of the country people's cause borne on banners. A cordon of priests led the procession into the church, carrying the banner with the Five Wounds of Christ. After them came the earls and their ladies, then rank on rank of fighting men in white armor, following the ensigns of the great northern feudal families, and after these a company of footsoldiers armed with bows and arrows, bills and spears. Another tall banner waved over their heads, bearing an image of a plow and the words "God speed the plough." The singing of Catholic hymns and the chanting of the priests mingled with the clank of armor and the clatter of wood on steel as the holy company made its way toward the altar of the huge church to hear mass.

Many of the rank and file among the rebels had no difficulty choosing between loyalty to the queen and their higher loyalty, as Catholics, to the pope.

A serving man who sided with the queen encountered three rebels riding along a country road, their faces swathed in mufflers to protect their identities. Recognizing one of them, a man called Smith, he hailed him and asked him why he was so afraid that he had to disguise himself.

Smith replied that, having intended to support Mary Stuart, he was afraid of capture and imprisonment for attempting to alter the succession. He rode about in secret, he said, and "lodged warily." When Norfolk was taken captive, he explained further, the goal of the conspirators changed. Since then "the setting up of religion, meaning papistry, is our purpose."

"How can that be when you shall be rebels to our queen, and so do against your consciences?" was the serving man's question.

"No, that is not so," came Smith's firm reply, "for the pope has summoned this land once, and if he summon it again, it is lawful to rise against the queen, and do it if she will not; for the pope is head of the church."[6]

Such logic prevailed in the minds of the Catholics of the north country. The queen's officers, impatient with this casuistry, condemned the common rebels as "ignorant, superstitious and altogether blinded with the old popish doctrine," while attacking their leaders as vice-ridden, irreligious hypocrites "pretending to popish holiness" as an excuse for treason.[7]

But the earls, not the queen, drew the greater popular support. Thousands threw in their lot with the rebels, and when the royal commanders appeared in the towns and villages to claim fighting men for the queen's service they came away with far fewer soldiers than they expected. Gentlemen remained loyal to the crown but sent their sons to fight with the rebels.

Villagers hid in the woods to avoid the queen's officers, then came out of hiding later to put on the crusading tunic of the Catholics.

Worse still, the men who did come forward to serve in the queen's army were strongly divided in mind. Their fathers and brothers and friends were on the rebels' side, where, they suspected, good Catholics and northern men belonged. Furthermore, the rebels would be sure to punish disloyal queen's soldiers like themselves by destroying their horses and stealing their cattle. And what if, as looked likely, the rebels won? Surely it would be better to desert to them, the moment their victory began to seem certain. One of Elizabeth's most reliable informants on the state of the north, Sir Ralph Sadler, reported to her that she could not count on the fidelity of any of her fighting men, so profound was their ambivalence. "Though their persons be here with us," Sadler wrote, "their hearts are with them."

Sussex, the lord lieutenant, shook his head over the ill-equipped army he had assembled. He had enough men, he thought, or nearly enough—he could use more horsemen—but the mounted men had no spears, the footsoldiers no corselets or pikes. There were neither arquebuses nor the powder to fire them. Meanwhile reports reached him that the rebel army was gathering in "great strength," their numbers at least as large as the royal bands and their weaponry far superior. He dared not risk a confrontation; he waited nervously for munitions and reinforcements to reach him from Lincolnshire and Leicestershire to the south.

Meanwhile the damp, dark days grew shorter and the winter closed in. The looming escarpments of the Pennines were white with snow, and with each new snowfall the drifts grew higher in the dales and pastures of the rocky uplands. The few roads were all but impassable now, and few or no bridges spanned the swollen rivers and streams that veined the sullen landscape.

Sussex could not easily communicate with the court, or even with his own subordinates. The rebels patrolled the icy highroads, seizing royal messengers and even royal troops on their way northward. At Tadcaster, a band of a hundred and fifty footsoldiers was kidnapped by rebel horsemen and impressed for service in their own ranks.[8]

By early December the inactivity of the queen's forces was lending the rebels an air of invincibility. The gentlemen "stood dutifully by the queen," but the common soldiers were wavering, and "dangerous to trust." When the earls' troops besieged the loyalists at Barnard Castle the rank and file of the royal garrison deserted by the hundreds, in the most spectacular fashion. They "daily leapt over the walls in great number to go to the rebels," and several dozen "broke their necks, legs or arms in the leaping." When some two hundred men deserted, including those that were holding the castle gate against the enemy, the commander, Sir George Bowes, was forced to surrender.

Bowes's faithfulness, in contrast to the faithlessness of his men, was affecting, for the rebels had made him pay dearly for his loyalty to the crown. "I am utterly spoiled of all my goods, my corn and cattle carried away, my houses defaced by pulling away the doors and windows," he wrote. "I have nothing but my horse, armor and weapons, brought out of Barnard Castle—which I more esteem than twenty times as much of other things, because thereby I am enabled to serve my good queen."

Barnard Castle fell in mid-December. By then, however, the rebel forces were actually in retreat, their half-frozen, hungry men "wearied with lagging from place to place," and angry that the pay and spoils promised them had never come. Many simply dropped their arms and corselets and went home; those that remained said "they would rather be hanged than serve the earls any more."

From the start the earls had pinned their hopes on a swift and decisive campaign whose aim was the capture of Mary Stuart at Tutbury. They had marched their men due south from Durham, bypassing York—which they could hardly have taken, as they had no heavy guns—and finally reaching Selby, some fifty miles from Tutbury, on November 24. The next day, however, Mary was escorted another thirty miles farther south, to Coventry, where her guard was increased so that the chances of liberating her were slight.

Cheated of their main object, the rebel leaders had no workable alternative strategy. They had seized the port of Hartlepool, in the hope that Alva might send them troops by sea, but the queen's ships had moved in to block the harbor. Meanwhile the same difficulties that were plaguing Sussex at York harassed the earls: icy roads, miserably cold weather, poor communications. And they had little food for their men, and no money to buy more, or to distribute as pay.

Finally on December 11 the first body of reinforcements and supplies sent from the southern army reached Sussex, and he set out for Durham intending to give battle. The earls, their forces rapidly melting away into the hills, fled northward toward the Scots border. The army of the Five Wounds of Christ was no more. There were only two disloyal earls and some hundreds of their mounted retainers, desperate to get to safety among the lawless population of the borderlands.

Sussex, zealous to prove himself after weeks of inaction, was close on their heels. On December 19 he had them almost within his grasp. They were at Hexham, he at Newcastle, a day away. Weary but eager to seize his prey at last, he sat down at midnight to write to Cecil.

"I shall set forward towards Hexham tomorrow," he reported, "and will remove them or make them pay dearly." Should some part of the earls' force elude him there, he would pursue them to the last man, he swore, "wheresoever they fly, over hills, wastes, or water, until I have either given them the overthrow, or put them out of the world."

22

Fie away, fie away! fie, fie, fie!
No, no, no, no, no, no, no, no, not I!
I'll live a maid till I be forty.

Sussex chased the rebel earls and their horsemen energetically, but in vain. They rode hard for the border and, with the help of the outlaw lords who controlled that lawless region, crossed it on the night of December 20, 1569, disguised as local men.

Hundreds of gentlemen who had joined the rising simply melted into the landscape, hidden away in mountain retreats or in the lofts and barns of country people willing to risk death for the cause of Catholicism and Mary Stuart. On Christmas Day there was good news. The earl of Northumberland was captured by the Scots, who eventually returned him to England. The Scots regent Murray was as alarmed as his Protestant coreligionist Cecil at the presence of the Catholic leaders on his southern border, and feared for the security of his own government, not to mention the everpresent hazard that continental powers might become involved. "This matter no doubt has branches yet unknown," Murray wrote to Cecil in a dark mood, "extending, peradventure, to the furthest marches of both realms." The "malice of foreign adversaries" was not far to seek.

The exasperated Sussex turned to the grisly task of punishing the disloyal north. Little blood had been shed in the brief course of the rebellion, but in its aftermath many hundreds lost their lives. Sussex ordered his provost marshal Sir George Bowes to "make very great example" of the laborers and husbandmen who had made up the majority of the rebel army, and Bowes set to his work with chilling efficiency. He and his men traveled from one village to the next, assembling the luckless population, selecting a suitable number of victims from among the "meanest of the people," then hanging them from a hastily erected gallows. Except in the case of men captured in the fighting field, it was difficult to tell the collaborators from those loyal to the queen; Cecil suggested imprisoning townsmen at random and starving them until, "being pinched with some lack of food," they confessed or named the offenders. But this took time, and the queen, though pleased with the thoroughness of the executions, was impatient to expedite the punishment so that she could disband her costly forces and send them home.

By January there were corpses in every northern village and town. In Durham, where the revolt had begun, eighty men were hanged. The ghastly display had its effect—or so it seemed to the provost marshal. The people, he reported, were "in marvellous fear, so that I trust there shall never such thing happen in these parts again." Those who escaped hanging were forced to pay crushing fines to the queen's governors—a harsh duty in a poor region—and to make that duty even more bitter the English soldiers were ordered to lay waste the cultivated lands of the north. Winter food supplies were destroyed, grain and animals confiscated and storehouses plundered of everything of value. Some among Sussex's captains wondered that the queen's own subjects, however great their disloyalty, should be crippled by such merciless devastation.

But the savage revenge did not bring peace. Just over the Scots border the fugitive English rebels, along with several thousand borderers intent on pillage, massed for an immense counterassault. They swarmed across into England, harrying the countryside as vigorously as the queen's soldiers had done farther south, driving off sheep and cattle, taking prisoners, and treating women and small children with a barbarity that left even hard-bitten military men shaking their heads in sorrow. "It would pity any English heart," one of them wrote, "to see the state of the country."

The real heartbreak of the tragic borderland conflict was that it was endless. There were occasional military victories. Hunsdon engaged and defeated a large rebel force in February, and some five hundred of the rebels were killed or taken prisoner. But the battle was not decisive. The cross-currents of Catholic against Protestant, English against Scot were too inveterate to be eradicated. The border folk, hating and hated, seemed forever poised to continue the ancient bloodbath, and the continual shifts and changes in politics on both sides of the border continued to guarantee them cause.

Elizabeth's reaction to her cousin Hunsdon's brief triumph was a trumpet-call of rejoicing. "I doubt much, my Harry, whether that the victory were given me more joyed me, or that you were by God appointed the instrument of my glory," she said in a handwritten note appended to a formal letter of congratulations. "I assure you that for my country's good the first might suffice, but for my heart's contention the second more pleased me."[1]

The warmth and candor of this note almost mask its egocentricity. Hunsdon was "the instrument of her glory." Her greatness, her invincibility, as much as England's, were at stake on the battlefield. At thirty-six, Elizabeth's truculence and assertiveness had, in her finest moments at least, matured into regality. To her people she was "our most dread sovereign lady," as well as being a beloved and familiar figure.

She possessed a huge illuminated genealogical roll, some thirty yards long, meant to be hung on the wall of a long palace gallery. It depicted England's kings "from the creation to Queen Elizabeth," marching in relentless chronological urgency toward the present reign.[2] The roll made of the jumbled, often historically incoherent past an ordered destiny—Elizabeth's destiny. It served as a counterweight to the forces of disorder and criticism in the kingdom and at court, though it may also have been read as a mockery or a warning to a ruler who had so far failed to designate or give birth to a successor.

To keep those around her in fear of her Elizabeth cultivated—or perhaps simply unleashed—a capricious temper. One hour amiable and approachable, she was peevish and ill-humored the next. Her "terrible fancies" were dreaded, when she "gave no one a gracious answer" and, if even slightly provoked, laid about her with words that cut as cruelly as swords.

Anything could bring on an outburst of royal fury—losing at cards, a slow-witted officer stumbling over his phrases, a hint of defiance in a subordinate. She took action direct and uninhibited, and her words often carried the threat of violence. Finding certain pages in the privy council register offensive to her dignity, she ripped them out. Hearing how the unspeakable Darnley had murdered his wife's beloved secretary almost before her eyes, she remarked that, had she been in Queen Mary's place, she would have taken her husband's dagger and stabbed him with it.

If "God's death" was her favorite oath, beheading was becoming her favorite metaphor. Elizabeth sent a warning to the Scots queen through the Spanish ambassador in 1569 advising her "to bear her condition with less impatience, or she might chance to find some of those on whom she relied shorter by the head." Her councilors too were admonished that she would make them "shorter by the head" if they disobeyed or disregarded her.

Yet even at her most strident and vituperative, Elizabeth was vulnerable, for she was physically frail, and her anger was a menace to her constitution. While flinching from her scolding tongue, the council members and officials she shouted at watched her with concern, anxious for her health. In October of 1569, when she heard that Norfolk, whom she knew to be plotting against her, had defied her summons to court and gone to his estate at Kenninghall, she "became so angry that she fainted, and they ran for vinegar and other remedies to revive her." There were other episodes of mild hysteria, overwrought nerves, spells of illness which, considering their frequency and the queen's delicate physique, gave rise to nearly constant worry.

The only thing worse than an unmarried queen was an unmarried queen in fragile health. Elizabeth suffered from stomach pains, catarrh, pains in the head, and fevers which sometimes held her in their grip for days at a time. Her teeth bothered her, and so did one of her legs; now and again she walked with a limp. Rumors of female disorders persisted. If she refused to marry, people said, it must be for the obvious reason that she could not have children, no matter what she herself or her physicians asserted to the contrary.[3] And most worrisome of all, she was becoming so thin and emaciated that everyone who saw her wondered that so fleshless a body could support so fierce a temperament.

She had always been slight and delicate, with a paper-thin complexion almost transparent in its ivory fineness. But the older she grew the more her cheekbones and neckbones stood out sharply in that fair skin, and her body became gaunt and skeletal. In the spring of 1566 a physician examined her. Beneath the stiff layerings of kirtle, farthingale and petticoats he saw an underweight and enfeebled frame, and detected signs of new illnesses to come. The queen was so thin, he reported, that "her bones may be counted." And she was developing a kidney stone, and becoming consumptive. The doctors who customarily attended her, reluctant to take responsibility for keeping such a poorly creature alive, let it be known that in their opinion her constitution was weak and she was not likely to enjoy a long life.[4]

No one had forgotten Elizabeth's terrifying brush with death in 1562—least of all the queen herself. When some children living near the palace of Westminster developed smallpox, she instantly left the palace out of fear of the disease, and generally avoided any areas where infection had been present. Her grave illness had come on her at Hampton Court, and though she did not avoid the palace entirely, "not wishing it to fall into decay," she was decidedly superstitious about it, and made her stays there as brief as possible.[5]

The urgent consideration of the queen's physical frailty overshadowed the Parliament of 1566, however much her robust and colorful defense of her prerogatives during that session belied her delicacy. This was only the third Parliament of the reign. The principal achievement of the first, summoned in 1559, had been to cooperate with the queen in sweeping away Mary Tudor's Catholicism and in defining crown power over the clergy. The second, summoned in 1563, had been called for the purpose of granting taxation but both houses had had the temerity to petition their sovereign on the subject of the succession and had earned her displeasure as a result.

Now, in 1566, exasperation over the unsettled succession was embolden-ing the members to use what leverage they had to try to force the queen to act. Yet their scope of action was exceedingly narrow, for Parliament, in the mid-sixteenth century, had limited rights and a highly subordinate governmental standing. Parliaments were summoned and dissolved at the queen's sole and absolute discretion; the bills they passed became valid only with her approval. The council, not Parliament, was the locus of power, for the latter met only briefly and irregularly, its proceedings guided and constrained by the royal councilors who sat in its midst.

Elizabeth had so far held Parliament in check by exercising her extensive prerogatives. She vetoed bills, she made certain that the man chosen as speaker of the Commons would be reliably on the side of the crown on any controversial issues, she granted freedom of speech to members only on condition that they remain "neither unmindful nor uncareful of their duties, reverence and obedience to their sovereign." At the first hint of undutiful or irreverent talk, she summoned the speaker and blamed him severely, always having behind her words the implicit threat of withdrawing the right of free speech and making the MPs fear the terrible consequences of any treasonable words they might utter.

Yet though the queen had relatively little to fear from Parliament she did rely on her Lords and Commons to supply her, as their obedience required, with revenue for all her extraordinary expenses, and the members who gathered in the fall of 1566, determined, indeed adamant, about ending the suspense over the succession, had decided to pursue what financial leverage they possessed.

Only a few months earlier they had been frightened yet again when Elizabeth had suffered another illness. She had been "so sore visited with a hot fever," a contemporary wrote, "that no man believed any other but death to be the end of it, all England being thereto in a great perplexity." She had recovered—but for how long? To prevent disaster the queen must provide for such an emergency, by naming either her husband or her successor. So thought the members as they assembled, firm in their purpose to withhold a grant of taxes, if need be, in order to compel the queen to do what had to be done.

The situation was all the more urgent in that, by 1566, all of the three leading candidates for the throne had married—unwisely. Mary Stuart had married Darnley, Catherine Grey had married Edward Seymour, and only the year before, in 1565, the "very short, crookbacked and very ugly" Mary Grey had married the "biggest gentleman in the court," the sergeant-porter Thomas Keyes. It was, as Cecil remarked, "an unhappy chance and monstrous," and added the insult of ridicule to the injury of clandestine marriage.

Elizabeth, furious at the marriage, had thrown her little cousin Mary into one prison and the hulking sergeant-porter into another. (Mary would stay there until she was widowed, then would be released to live out her last years in poverty, still, in law, in line for the throne under the will of Henry VIII.) The queen's anger at her other Grey cousin had not mellowed with time. Catherine, her husband and her two babies lived at the Tower, in surreptitious cohabitation, their cold and forbidding apartments meanly furnished with the few broken chairs and frayed bedclothes Elizabeth provided. When the plague was at its most deadly in London the family was moved for the sake of their health, but their ordinary Tower quarters were far from hygienic. Catherine insisted on keeping her monkeys and dogs with her, and her keeper complained that they tore her gowns into tatters and befouled the floors.[6]

Even before the formal opening of Parliament the members began making trouble, scattering leaflets on the streets intended to rouse public ire against the queen and Cecil. On the first day of the session, they fought among themselves over what strategy to adopt, actually coming to blows. Elizabeth ordered her councilors to speak to the delegates and reassure them of her good intentions, in an effort to defuse their excitement and prevent a confrontation. But the fiery Commons would not be pacified, and in fact they succeeded in persuading the Lords to join them in their campaign to force the vital succession issue.

Hearing this Elizabeth exploded. If there was disloyalty in the House of Lords then the leading peer, Norfolk, must be to blame. She was caustic with the duke, and ended by calling him a traitor. Pembroke blustered in Norfolk's defense. She ought not to treat the duke badly, he told her, "since he and the others were only doing what was fitting for the good of the country, and advising her what was best for her, and if she did not think fit to adopt the advice, it was still their duty to offer it."

Elizabeth told Pembroke he "talked like a swaggering soldier," and silenced him. She turned to Leicester, knowing that he had failed to defend her in the Lords.

If all the world abandoned her, she said to him accusingly, she had thought he, at least, would not. He would gladly die at her feet, Leicester answered limply. Dying at her feet had nothing to do with the matter at hand, she told the earl, and turned sharply to Northampton, who had the misfortune to be present.

Him she disposed of with a well-aimed personal blow. Why mince words with her over her failure to marry when his own marital affairs were an obvious embarrassment? He had a wife living, yet he wanted to marry someone else—which required an act of Parliament to accomplish. Let him look to his own domestic problems, and leave hers to her.[7]

Before any of the buffeted peers could recover themselves she had left them, swearing to herself that she would see them all arrested and confined to their homes. Later she had second thoughts about this extreme measure —after all, she was very fond of all three men, and knew that they were desperately trying to maintain their own credit with their parliamentary colleagues while doing their best to keep her favor. But for some time Leicester, Pembroke and Northampton were forbidden entrance to her privy chamber, and the storm in Parliament went on.

Elizabeth summoned a deputation from both houses and harangued them, leaving no doubt how incensed she was over their presumption in threatening to meddle with the succession. What had she done, she demanded to know, to deserve such trespass against her privilege?

"Was I not born in this realm?" she asked rhetorically. "Is not my kingdom here? Whom have I oppressed? Whom have I enriched to others' harm? What turmoil have I made in this commonwealth that I should be suspected to have no regard to the same?"

She had the succession as much on her mind as they did, she told her audience, but it was a complex matter without an easy solution, since to name an official heir apparent would be to invite conspiracy. She warmed to her subject, and her sentences became diffuse and inelegant. She fell, as usual, to boasting about her own courage and resourcefulness, sounding even more like a "swaggering soldier" than Pembroke had.

"As for my own part, I care not for death; for all men are mortal, and though I be a woman, yet I have as good a courage answerable to my place as ever my father had. I am your anointed queen. I will never be by violence constrained to do anything. I thank God I am endued with such qualities that if I were turned out of the realm in my petticoat, I were able to live in any place in Christendom."

Her bravado was provocative, but not definitive. "Since the queen would not marry," came the parliamentary response, "she ought to be compelled to name her successor." Her refusal to do so could only proceed "from feelings which could only be entertained by weak princes and fainthearted women."

To be called a fainthearted woman was one thing, but a weak prince! That she could not allow. Those she scornfully referred to as the "Protestant gentlemen" in the Commons—those "unbridled persons whose mouth was never snaffled by the rider"—had gone too far. They were "inexperienced schoolboys" handling matters far beyond their competence. They were "devils" intent on bedeviling their sovereign, who deserved better from them. As for the Lords, their collective stupidity hardly needed to be pointed out. The succession, she announced archly, "is an affair of much too great importance to be declared to a knot of harebrains."

In the end, Elizabeth won. She made her usual absolute, and absolutely unconvincing, assurances that she meant to marry, and that was the end of it. She did, however, have to lower the tax burden for that session in order to get her way—and she had to admit that, in practice, she lacked the authority to forbid debate on the succession in the Commons.

The delegates went home, having been bested once again by the tall, spare woman who ruled them—a frail woman whose commanding voice seemed to originate in a reed-thin chest and whose determination was evidently rooted in some power beyond sheer animal vitality. She was amazing, infuriating, intimidating. Her success disturbed them, and not only because it meant prolonging their anxiety over the future security of the realm. She was living proof that, in the phrase of a Venetian ambassador, "statecraft is no business for ladies."

The irony was that, in 1566, Elizabeth had in fact made up her mind to marry the Austrian archduke Charles, and her summoning of Parliament was directly linked to that decision. The diplomatic wooing had been rekindled, with exchanges of envoys and portraits and cautious queries about religion and about the archduke's willingness to come to England to allow Elizabeth to approve him in person. Certainly he seemed personally acceptable; despite old stories about his deformity Elizabeth's envoy Sadler found him to be entirely pleasing in face and physique, a suitable consort in every way. His imperial lineage appealed to Elizabeth's vanity, to that side of her that saw herself as last in a line running "from the creation to Queen Elizabeth." She had once told the French ambassador that, though she loved Leicester, she could not marry him because he had no high name or rank to offer her. "The aspirations towards honor and greatness which are in me," she had said, "cannot suffer him as a companion and a husband." And besides, their relationship had soured.

A really serious and bruising quarrel had arisen between them. Elizabeth had begun to flirt, in her customary heavy-handed and obvious way, with an otherwise inconsequential young chamber gentleman named Thomas Heneage. Leicester was injured; she flirted more industriously than ever. Leicester snubbed and insulted and lashed out at Heneage, who retaliated in kind. The queen stepped in, and pointedly took the younger man's part. Leicester, never a very strong man emotionally, retired to his chambers adjoining Elizabeth's and did not come out for four days.

Abandoned by the queen, the earl was easy prey, and his enemies crowded quickly in. Sussex took to stalking him with a large armed body-guard, so that Leicester had to surround himself with an even larger one to protect himself. There might have been bloodshed had the queen not intervened to prevent it. During the holiday season of 1565 the factions declared themselves sartorially. The followers of Norfolk—and his allies Sussex, Heneage and others—were all conspicuous in yellow laces, while Leicester's men wore blue ones. At a court where no detail of dress went unnoticed, the massing of matched laces was tantamount to a declaration of war.

But a more fateful blow was being prepared. The scandal over Leicester's dead wife Amy Robsart had been allowed to slumber while Elizabeth protected her favorite. But now that she had turned away from him the earl's ugly past was revived. Amy's half-brother knew more than he had so far told about the mysterious death, or so he said. It was murder after all, and he had concealed the fact for Leicester's sake. His testimony could send the earl to the block, and Norfolk, Heneage and the others threatened to reopen the case and charge Leicester formally with murder.

Yet Leicester had a potent weapon of his own, calculated to wound Elizabeth cruelly. He began a flirtation with Lettice Knollys, the dazzling, auburn-haired daughter of Francis and Catherine Knollys, universally praised as "one of the best-looking ladies of the court." Lettice was a stunning beauty, more vivid in her coloring than her second cousin Eliza-beth and with none of the queen's aloof intellectuality to blunt her allure. Her creamy skin was youthful and unlined, her rich, dark-red hair as thick and lustrous as a young girl's. Lettice was everything Elizabeth had once been and was no longer: young, ripe, nubile. And she was Leicester's sweetheart.

The disloyalty cut deep; so too did the loss of the earl's constant, affec-tionate presence. Elizabeth was humiliated, her vanity punctured. They quarreled openly, in front of the whole court. She had the last word. "If you think to rule here I will take a course to see you forthcoming. I will have but one mistress and no master." She won the shouting match, but suffered nonetheless. They wept and made up—after a fashion. Yet the good looks of Heneage and Lettice Knollys continued to be a distraction, and Cecil at least believed that the passionate royal romance had decidedly cooled. He was greatly relieved. Now at last she would marry, he thought, and sensibly. There would be no more talk of Leicester as a husband.

Cecil reflected on Leicester's liabilities as a consort for Elizabeth in 1566, and listed them succinctly. The earl had nothing but himself to offer—no "riches, estimation, or power." He was hounded by scandal. Not only did most people think him a murderer, but they were convinced that he was the queen's lover; to marry him would seem to give final confirmation to that belief. As king consort he would devote his energies to enriching his many allies and dependents, and to giving maximum offense to those who had been his enemies; he was a vindictive man. He was very deeply in debt, and the queen would have to pay his creditors. And finally, Cecil wrote, "He is like to prove unkind, or jealous of the queen's majesty."[8]

In fact Leicester's nerves were frayed, his patience exhausted by the long, stressful years of waiting for Elizabeth to make up her mind to marry him. He confided his exasperation to the French ambassador La Forêt. "The earl has admitted to me," La Forêt reported, "laughing and sighing at the same time, that he knows not what to hope or fear. He is more uncertain than ever whether the queen wishes to marry him or not; she has so many and great princes suitors [sic], that he knows not what to do, or what to think."

Leicester's position was a very difficult one, and Elizabeth, with her endless coquetry and changes of mind and mood, made it much worse. She maddened him with her attentions, her gifts of estates and incomes and offices, her solemn vows to marry him—but not this year. He bore her ill-tempered outbursts. "Her blasts," he commented, "be very sharp at times to those she loves best." He was forever on the point of achieving his ambitions—which were boundless—yet he forever remained the queen's handsome pawn, shorn of pride and will. It was no wonder he felt used, and wanted revenge.

Yet despite the open quarreling between the queen and her erring favorite their intimacy seemed, if anything, more entrenched than ever. Their private hours together had a comfortable, domestic flavor. Norfolk came into Elizabeth's privy chamber unannounced one day, and saw her sitting just at the threshold, with Leicester kneeling beside her, talking quietly to her. She heard him, but her attention was divided; she was also listening "with one ear to a little child, who was singing and playing on the lute to her."

There were scurrilous stories about what else went on during these private hours. Leicester "kissed her majesty when he was not invited thereto," and indulged in "familiarities with the queen which disgraced the crown she wore." He entered her bedchamber early in the morning, it was said, before she was up, and "took upon himself the office of her lady in waiting, by handing to her a garment which ought never to have been seen in the hands of her master of horse." As always, the gossip recorded in ambassadorial dispatches sent abroad from the English court stopped short of saying explicitly that the queen and Leicester were lovers, but they meant to imply it, and the result was to make the English look ridiculous.

Arundel and Norfolk, who bore the oldest titles represented in the privy council, determined to speak frankly to the earl, putting politics and personal enmity aside in the hope that openness might clear the air. Norfolk spoke for both, calling Leicester "to a sharp account" for the unforgivable informality and lack of ceremony he showed in Elizabeth's presence, and for what went on between them behind closed doors. "Neither the English nobility nor her subjects," he told the earl, "would permit the continuance of such proceedings." Norfolk recited a list of specific allegations to support his claims, then backed off from his aristocratic hauteur and spoke man to man. He urged Leicester "to be candid, and say if the queen really wished to marry him." If she did, then he and Arundel would use their influence to persuade the rest of the nobility and the people at large "to sanction their honorable union, and stop all this scandal."

Apparently Leicester told him what he had told the French ambassador earlier: that he "knew not what to do, or what to think." Embarrassed uncertainty had become his customary state, and well as he knew her, Elizabeth was as much an enigma to him as she was to everyone else.

She did make up her mind about one thing. She decided not to marry Archduke Charles. The usefulness of the diplomatic wooing of the Hapsburgs as a counterweight to the French was over, at least for the time being, and besides, the archduke had proven to be difficult about the delicate issue of allowing the queen to approve him in person before agreeing to become his wife. After first saying that he would come to England to be inspected he thought better of it, and declined. Meanwhile the even more important stumbling-block of his Catholicism had raised serious objections among the English. (Leicester, desperate not to lose his chances as a potential royal consort, was trying his best to spread alarm in the council and outside it about the dire consequences of a Catholic king.)

In the end, the negotiations ceased. Leicester breathed more easily, and ceased to be hounded by his political enemies and by Sussex with his armed bodyguard. Indeed Leicester's peril may well have influenced Elizabeth's decision, for she was caught on the horns of a dilemma. If she did not want to marry him, she did not want to destroy him either, and his ruin seemed inevitable once she married someone else and he lost his precarious status as her protected, intimate favorite.

Leicester's affection had been the one fixed point in Elizabeth's highly mutable emotional universe. His devotion to her had always seemed to be as boundless as his ambition, and by the late 1560s she assumed the two had fused together to bond him permanently to her side. His disloyalty with Lettice Knollys unsettled that assumption, but did not dislodge it altogether. However their union might be defined, whatever strains they put upon it, he was hers, reliably and permanently.

She boasted of his slavish, self-sacrificing loyalty. "She is quite certain that he would give his life for hers," the Spanish ambassador wrote after a talk with the queen, "and that if one of them had to die, he would willingly be the one."9

Now in the spring of 1570, in the aftermath of the northern rebellion, Elizabeth took stock of the damage that had been done to her authority, and felt doubly betrayed. It was in a way understandable—though inexcusable—for her disgruntled councilors to plot against her, bitter over her refusal to marry and over their own profound discomfort at being ruled by a woman. It was also understandable, if thoroughly reprehensible, for her northern Catholic subjects to rise against her, led on by their own lords and misled into allying themselves with Mary Stuart. These disloyalties were one thing, but Leicester's was another. She had always relied on him to stay with her to the uttermost. Yet as it proved, he had been the chief conspirator against her.

For twelve years she had used the earl as a decoy, a whipping-boy, a smokescreen to put between herself and marriage. She had abused him, but only because she had assumed he would put up with infinite abuse. Now she saw, with some remorse, that she had gone too far.

23

Time, cruel Time, canst thou subdue that brow
That conquers all but thee, and thee too stays,
As if she were exempt from scythe or bow,
From Love or Years, unsubject to decays?

I n her late thirties Elizabeth engaged a Dutch alchemist to concoct an elixir of perpetual youth. She was still a very handsome woman, as she would be for many years to come, but she had entered the twilight of her youth and already the planes of her fine skin bore the shadow-mask of middle age. The rapidly passing years were transforming her from a commanding yet compelling young woman to an eccentric spinster. In her twenties and early thirties the softness and tenderness of her youthful looks had blunted her acerbity; as she approached forty her strong, spare physical presence reinforced her flinty personality and deepened the impact of her brash, often vulgar tongue. She was getting older, and she hoped to defeat age by alchemy.

The Dutchman, Cornelius Lannoy, was installed at Somerset House, where he worked on the queen's elixir in a secret laboratory and made vaunting promises to the money-hungry nobility that he could turn their base metal into gold. In time, however, when the base metal began to pile up in corners and no gold issued forth from it, the alchemist proved to be a fraud. There was no youth potion either; Lannoy was imprisoned in the Tower, guilty of deceiving the queen.

The incident with the alchemist must have sent ripples of laughter through the privy chamber, for there was much ridiculing of the queen among her waiting women. If the men around Elizabeth found her unduly assertive and offensively magisterial, the women who attended her found her to be hilariously, outlandishly unfeminine.

She was under their scrutiny from the time she rose in the morning—usually bad-tempered—until she got undressed late at night. They knew her habits, her moods, when she was ill and when she had trouble sleeping. Others saw her when she was prepared and presentable; they saw her when she was off guard, and none, except possibly Leicester, knew her better.

And they thought she was ludicrous. Her loud, vehement swearing and soldierly boasting made a strange counterpoint to her elegant dress and coquettish adornments. Flowers in her hair, round oaths on her lips, she stormed through her apartments, slapping and stabbing at her women when they displeased her and demanding to be told how beautiful she was.[1] Only the most wildly extravagant compliments would do. She had to be told that no one dared look at her directly, for her face shone like the sun, or that she was as fair as a heavenly goddess, or she would not be satisfied.

In a less strident woman such vanity would have been pathetic. But in Elizabeth it was the stuff of caricature. For with every whoop of her loud laughter, every stab of her mordant wit, every jerk of her restless, wiry body she undermined her womanly beauty and coarsened herself in others' eyes. Bess of Hardwick, countess of Shrewsbury, confided to Mary Stuart, "doubled over with laughter" as she spoke, how the ladies of the court ridiculed Elizabeth and played tricks on her. When Bess herself and Lady Lennox, Darnley's mother, were together talking to the queen "they didn't dare look at one another for fear of bursting into gales of laughter." And Bess's daughter Mary Talbot was in on the joking, mocking Elizabeth with every curtsy she made while "never ceasing to laugh up her sleeve" at her royal mistress.

Of course, Bess and the others were Catholic partisans of the Queen of Scots, and were naturally predisposed to mock their Protestant sovereign. But there was more than partisan sentiment behind the ridicule, and it was not confined to an insolent few. Mean tricks, broad derision and backbiting gossip followed Elizabeth everywhere. Once she went to her dressing table and found it swept clean. Invisible hands had snatched away her comb, her looking glass, her gold bodkin and the silver-gilt lye pot which held the lye in which she washed her long fair hair. There were whispered conversations among the women, and smothered laughter. They gossiped about her fading looks, her quirks and personal oddities, and about Leicester's new sweetheart Douglas Sheffield. They "played and counterfeited" the queen in her absence, one taking the part of Elizabeth, an absurd mannish maiden, the others her servants and victims.

Not all of the serving women were disloyal. Kat Ashley, who held the post of mistress of the maids until her much-lamented death in 1565, was utterly devoted, as were Blanche Parry and Leicester's sister Mary Sidney, who was "as foul a lady as the smallpox could make her" as a result of her faithful attendance on Elizabeth during her grave illness in 1562. Anne Russell, Bedford's daughter, who had married Ambrose Dudley, was a beloved intimate of the queen, while Elizabeth's cousin Catherine Knollys was equally dear to her. When Lady Knollys fell ill of a fever Elizabeth provided her with every possible remedy, and kept her near at hand, visiting her sickbed frequently and sending messengers every hour to inquire about her condition. In the end she died, and Elizabeth mourned her with such fervency that she cought cold and had to take to her bed herself.

Among the most venomous of the privy chamber stories was that the queen "was not as other women" and that therefore all talk of marriage for her was futile.[2] The issue became pressing in the early 1570s, when renewed marriage negotiations began, this time with the French. Of the three sons of Catherine de' Medici, two were left available. (The eldest son, King Charles IX, was married.) Henry, the middle son—the future Henry III—was the prospective bridegroom, and though he was eighteen years younger than Elizabeth the match seemed at first to be a possibility. The young prince was said to be unusually good-looking, with fine eyes and a charming mouth and a manner as sweet as a girl's. His health could not be vouched for, but he seemed to throw himself into lusty pastimes with a good deal of vigor and energy.

And so he did—but it was the unnatural energy of a manic depressive, and a seasoned voluptuary. Further reports from envoys to the French court disclosed the sordid truth. Prince Henry wore more makeup than Elizabeth herself, who wore a good deal. He smelled overpoweringly of strong perfume, and affected a double row of bejeweled earrings. His liaisons with women were surpassed in their decadence only by his assignations with the long-haired, effeminate "Princes of Sodom" who were his preferred companions.

These unseemly habits would have made the French prince thoroughly unsuitable, even without the religious bigotry that also showed itself and soured the English diplomats irrevocably on the marriage. But to add insult to injury, Prince Henry rejected Elizabeth. "He would not marry her," he announced tactlessly, "for she was not only an old creature, but had a sore leg."

That she had a sore leg, at least, was true. She limped badly throughout the summer of 1570, and had to be carried from place to place in a coach —even to the hunt. An "open ulcer above the ankle" gave her much pain and forced her into weeks of invalidism. The affliction did nothing to enhance her marriageability, which even her own envoys had begun to doubt. ("The more hairy she is before," one of them wrote in 1571, "the more bald she is behind.")

Prince Henry's ungentlemanly reference to Elizabeth's lameness was bad enough, but his unkind allusion to her age wounded her vanity intolerably. She alone could joke about that, as she had been doing ever since she turned thirty, "which she called old." At thirty-four she had referred to her possible marriage with a nineteen-year-old as "a comical farce," "an old woman leading a child to the church doors." People would say she was marrying her son, she remarked gaily when young men were proposed to her, yet though she expected those around her to laugh at this she also expected them to reassure her that it was nonsense, given her youthfulness and beauty.

Conversing with Elizabeth about age was a dangerous pastime. When the queen asked Lady Cobham what she thought of the French Prince Henry as a husband the gentlewoman was rash enough—or malicious enough—to speak her mind. "Those marriages were always the happiest when the parties were the same age, or near about it," she said, "but here there was a great inequality."

"Nonsense!" Elizabeth stormed back. "There are but ten years' difference between us!" The extravagant lie was telling. Ten years' difference might just possibly have been smoothed over, but eighteen was a disturbingly wide gulf, especially when the prospective husband was just across the threshold of manhood and the woman was nearly forty.

Lady Cobham was as brave as she was frank, for the women who angered Elizabeth risked injury. According to Mary Talbot, who told Bess of Hardwick who passed it on to Mary Stuart, several women bore the marks of her wrath. One had a broken finger—though to camouflage the truth Elizabeth made the courtiers believe it was an accident, the result of a blow from a falling candlestick—and another had a scar on her hand where the queen had stabbed her with a knife while she was serving her a meal.[3]

It was a sordid picture, more suited to the stalls of fishwives or the squabbling of prostitutes in the stews than to the queen's privy chamber. The violence, the envy, the climate of backbiting and hidden mockery were yet one more element in Elizabeth's odd, unprecedented role as spinster queen. By the early 1570s, as the French marriage project was abandoned —and with it, all serious hope of children—the limited dimensions of that role were becoming sadly clear.

From the start, it had never really been a fair choice. Either she had to go the way of her tragic half-sister Mary, who by taking a husband had traded what precarious authority she possessed for the privation and humiliation of a loveless royal marriage, ending as a victim of the enmity and feigned fidelity that surrounded her. Or she had to endure the extreme, ultimately dangerous disapproval of the men in government—not to mention the shame of public scorn and the undercurrent of ridicule and ugly gossip at court and elsewhere—by remaining single. The second course had seemed the wiser one, and the one best suited to Elizabeth's temperament and gifts. Yet spinsterhood hobbled and wounded her; she cannot have relished her eccentricities, or the foul reputation that followed her, or the poisonous atmosphere of her bedchamber, even though she relished the very real sovereignty she wielded in their despite.

What strength, what brittleness of spirit were required to counteract the pressures and blows that surrounded her—to parry disloyalty in the council, to negate severe personal criticism, to ward off the pain of Dudley's infidelities—only she knew, and she did not record her inner thoughts. And with it all, she now had to watch her youthful features settle into the frowning, careworn rictus of middle age.

To be sure, Elizabeth had ample resources to offset despondency. Youth could be counterfeited—up to a point—by cosmetics and embroidered silk gowns and flattering jewels. Intellectual pleasures were heightened rather than dimmed with maturity, and the queen continued to read and reread the Greek and Latin texts she had learned to love as a young girl. No doubt Elizabeth was often pleased with herself; her large and small political victories and her frequent strokes of luck must have given her immense private satisfaction.

So too did the everpresent absurdities of court life and the wit and word-play of her clever courtiers. She delighted in jokes and funny stories; they made her laugh as if "she had been tickled." Humorlessness and formality invariably amused her. Catherine de' Medici sent a stiff, correct envoy to the English court who addressed the queen with unbearable solemnity. "Monsieur Pasquier (as I believe) thinks I have no French," Elizabeth wrote to Queen Catherine, "by the passions of laughter into which he throws me by the formal precision with which he speaks and expresses himself."[4] At bottom, it may have been that Elizabeth's sharp sense of the absurd made her own life, with its inevitable accretions of artifice and insubstantiality, easier to bear. In any case, while taking out her frustrations on her hapless waiting maids and reading Seneca to "calm turbulence of mind," she bore her sorrows silently, and kept her self-pity to herself.

She could not, however, keep to herself the legend that was growing up around her, the legend of a woman, unchaste and unmarried, insatiable in her sexual appetites and imperious in gratifying them.

The days were long past when Elizabeth was seen as an infatuated young woman dallying with her handsome suitor Leicester. That image was almost innocent compared to the stories circulating in the 1570s. Now the queen was looked on as a practiced, hardened voluptuary. "Every man had a tale to tell" about her unchastity, and about the vice-ridden court she had gathered around her. At Norwich, in August of 1570, several persons were tried—and some executed—for treasonable slander. "My lord of Leicester had two children by the queen," they insisted, and set out a proclamation "touching the wantonness of the court." A rural parson harangued his congregation with tales of how Elizabeth "desireth nothing but to feed her own lewd fantasy, and to cut off such of her nobility as were not perfumed and court-like to please her delicate eye."[5]

When a parliamentary act limited the succession to the queen and "the natural issue of her majesty's body," the phrase led to endless jokes, for "natural children" were bastards, and though no one had ever actually seen any of Elizabeth's supposed children by Leicester there was very strong suspicion that some existed. The earl, it was said, had influenced the phrasing of the act so that, at least, he could "thrust upon the English some bastard of his own as the queen's natural child."[6]

At the European courts elaborate stories circulated about the bawdy English queen. The Venetian ambassador in Spain told how she had thirteen natural children, one of whom she was planning to marry to Cecil's son. The Spanish ambassador De Spes wrote offensive libels about her. The French called her "the hackney of her own vassals," who rode her at their pleasure; they had used the same phrase about Elizabeth's aunt Mary Boleyn half a century earlier, when she and her younger sister Anne had served as nubile young companions to King Francis I and his nobles.[7] When there was talk of a marriage between Elizabeth and the French Prince Henry one of the French courtiers suggested that a sophisticated sort of arrangement might be made in which the queen would wed the prince, while the queen's lover Leicester could inherit the prince's mistress, Mademoiselle Châteauneuf.

Leicester's own reputation was becoming blacker than ever. While it had long been common tavern gossip that "the Lord Robert did swive the queen," and that he was the murderer of his own wife, it was now being said that he was a lecherous philanderer who had murdered the husband of his mistress Douglas Sheffield. John, Baron Sheffield had died in 1568 leaving his twenty-four-year-old widow to the attentions of the lascivious

Leicester. A story circulated that, before Baron Sheffield's death, the earl had written to his beloved assuring her that he was determined to remove "that obstacle which hindered the full fruition of their contentments." In other words, he intended to murder the baron. He summoned his Italian physician, a man skilled in poisons, the story went on, and ordered him to prepare a lethal draft. Shortly afterward the baron was found dead.[8]

But it was not only Leicester who was widening his circle of conquests. Elizabeth too, it was said, was seducing handsome young men and keeping them under surveillance by her well-paid spies when they were not in amorous attendance on her. Prominent among these favorites was Edward de Vere, earl of Oxford, a boyish, hazel-eyed young courtier whose expression combined poetic languor and aristocratic superciliousness. Oxford excelled at those courtly graces Elizabeth admired. He was athletic and acquitted himself brilliantly in the tiltyard, dashing fearlessly, lance lowered, against any and all comers and retiring the victor despite his youth and slight build. He was an agile and energetic dancer, the ideal partner for the queen, and he had a refined ear for music and was a dexterous performer on the virginals. His poetry was unusually accomplished, and his education had given him a cultivated mind, at home with the antique authors Elizabeth knew so well.

He was an ideal companion for her—except, perhaps, for the seventeen-year age difference that separated them—and she was said to "delight more in his personage and in his dancing and valiantness than any other." Rumormongers speculated about Oxford's talents in the bedchamber, and whispered that he was gambling all, including his marriage, on becoming her preferred lover. He was no longer sleeping with his wife, the gossips said, for fear of losing the preferment he hoped to gain by making love to the queen.[9]

But Oxford, at least, was a willing paramour; Christopher Hatton had been taken by force—or so the poisonous Bess of Hardwick and others said.[10] Elizabeth threw herself at him in public, putting him in such an unendurably awkward position that he had to leave her presence—though he returned often enough in private, and joined Leicester in satisfying her prurient desires. Hatton "had more recourse unto her majesty in her privy chamber than reason would suffer if she were so virtuous and well-inclined as some noiseth her," an irate clergyman shouted in 1571, adding more "vile words" that could not be committed to writing by the mortified informant who reported the sermon to Leicester.[11]

A dark, very good-looking man, "of a comely tallness of body and countenance," Hatton came under suspicion in part because of the suddenness of his rise to favor. He was a lawyer, and an intelligent, capable one. But it was as a dancer, the gossips said, that he earned the queen's attention. She made him captain of her gentlemen pensioners, and kept him near her as a dancing partner and reassuringly lovesick admirer. For whatever tales might be told about them, Hatton was much more uxorious than lecherous; he was hopelessly infatuated, indeed almost intoxicated, with Elizabeth, and she nourished his dedicated fondness by calling him her "Mutton" and, eventually, making him lord chancellor.

Yet whatever the truth, the appearance was that Hatton had joined the ranks of the queen's lovers. Her reputation continued to spiral downward. Henry VIII's daughter she might be to her people, with Henry's personal fire and hearty courage, yet she was Henry's daughter too in bawdiness and wayward passion, and this they could not stomach. She seduced men away from their wives or, as with Hatton and Leicester, kept them from marrying at all (a sore point with Leicester, whose family would die out if he had no son, as his brother Ambrose Dudley was childless). She turned the royal court into a perfumed harem, sending away the dignified nobles of the old school and replacing them with dancing fops and lechers. She was wanton and flirtatious, fondling her favorites in full view of the court and encouraging looseness in others by her unmaidenly behavior. Nearing forty, Elizabeth had left young womanhood behind without entering respectable matronhood as a married woman. She was a disquieting anomaly at best; at worst she was a whore.

The archbishop of Canterbury, Matthew Parker, became so deeply concerned about Elizabeth's reputation and its broad consequences that he wrote to his old friend Cecil "in bitterness of soul" in 1572. A man had been seized at Dover, the archbishop informed Cecil, who "uttered most shameful words" against the queen. Leicester and Hatton, the slanderer said, were "such toward her, as the matter is so horrible, that they [the man's examiners] would not write down the words." The incident prompted Parker to write for several reasons. First, he felt some responsibility toward Elizabeth and her long-dead mother Anne Boleyn. He had been Anne's chaplain during the last two years of her life, years in which she had been abused and ill-treated by her fickle and vindictive husband and subjected to the same sort of slander now directed against her daughter. He remembered vividly how Anne spoke to him about her little girl, and the memory moved him to speak out about the ugly situation he saw brewing.

Second, he spoke as primate of the church—its head, that is, under the defender of the faith and governess of the church, Queen Elizabeth. It was his duty as archbishop to unburden his conscience and to complain, not exactly about immorality—for the accusations against the queen were unproven, and came from others—but about the almost incontrovertible appearance of immorality being built up around her.

To be sure, it was all but impossible to stop the wagging tongues and rolling eyes of Elizabeth's lusty-minded subjects. Inquiries by the leading courtiers, arrests, rigorous and sometimes painful examinations, imprisonment, ultimately the threat of execution: all these remedies were at hand, and were being used, against slanderers. Often they had their tongues or ears cut off as well. But as long as Elizabeth continued her present behavior there was no erasing the impression she made. She damned herself. The woman Elizabeth was defiling the sacred person of the queen, the sacred person of the head of the church. And if she was not very careful, Parker felt, she would so undermine her royal authority that she would be overwhelmed by her enemies.

For the slanderer taken at Dover had not stopped at imputing sexual impurity to the queen. He had gone on to predict civil war, with "as many throats cut here in England, as be reported to be in France," where in this year of 1572 internal conflict reached new heights of slaughter with the St. Bartholomew's Day Massacre. Catholic would rise against Protestant, he predicted. Within a year Elizabeth's government would be uprooted and a Catholic regime installed, and then would begin a religious persecution that would make Queen Mary's burnings of Protestants seem gentle by comparison. Elizabeth would be murdered or executed, her bones "openly burned in Smithfield" along with those of her father.[12]

It was a gruesome picture, made particularly intense by the recent news from France, where the full horrors of religious warfare were beginning to unfold. The warfare there between Catholic and Protestant was unlike any European conflict since the age of the crusades. There were none of the chess-game maneuverings, interminable sieges and genteel chivalric conquests and surrenders of feudal war. This was relentless slaughter, carried out by desperate men and women driven by inner conviction to annihilate, root and branch, all those who opposed them in matters of religious conscience. This was the moral against the immoral, good against evil, virtue against sin. And nothing short of mass butchery would please the vengeful God who commanded the killing.

A realm with an immoral sovereign on its throne in this grimly intolerant climate was a realm in peril, particularly when that realm had no firm allies among the other powers of Europe and relied for its security on its geographic isolation alone. It was with this broader danger in mind that the archbishop recorded his "fearful opinion" about the impact of Elizabeth's worsening repute in the eyes of Christendom. He had heard, he warned

Cecil, that the slanderer had not been imprisoned, but had been turned loose to make mischief again. "Sir, if this be true," he ended his letter, "God be merciful to us." He could only hope that somehow Elizabeth would be rescued in her hour of crisis; having told what he knew, he felt he could do nothing but consign her to divine mercy and protection. "God defend her majesty," he wrote with fervor, "and all her trusty friends."

PART FIVE

"That Guilty Woman
of England"

24

Ring out your bels!
What should yow doe els?
Stricke up your Drums for joy!
The Noblest Queene
that ever was seene
In England doth Raigne this day.

T he twelfth year of the reign of Queen Elizabeth being now happily expired," the historian Camden wrote, "all good men throughout England joyfully triumphed, and with ringing of bells, running at tilt, and festival mirth began to celebrate the seventeenth of November, being the anniversary day of the beginning of her reign." This they did, he added, "in testimony of their affectionate love towards her."

The bells rang out in long and loud peals across the land, in villages and towns, chiming in chorus "in rejoicing of the queen's prosperous reign" until the ringers were exhausted and had to call for bread and drink. The celebration was spontaneous, and was quickly absorbed into the national life, so that by the time the next anniversary of Elizabeth's accession rolled around bonfires and orations and pageantry were added to the ringing, and the entire day was given up to public merrymaking and thanksgiving.

Each community celebrated in its own style. At York all the town officials marched in procession to church, at Liverpool the mayor ordered a huge bonfire to be lit in the market square and smaller ones in the courtyards of private houses. The people of Maidstone shot off a salute and, while all the bells rang noisily, enjoyed a great feast of roast venison in the open air. At Oxford, musicians played and there was a sermon, and in token of the queen's own liberality alms were distributed to prisoners and bread to the poor.[1]

The most elaborate rejoicing was in the capital, where the tilting grounds at Westminster were the scene of gilded pageantry and athletic competition among the younger courtiers. The cycle of the itinerant court was adjusted to highlight these events, with Elizabeth making her triumphant annual return to London from her long summer progress in the countryside in mid-November, then settling in for the winter with the tilting as a display of welcome.

The groundswell of conspicuous thanksgiving was in part a collective sigh of relief. Rebellion had erupted and had been swiftly quelled. The treachery in the council and the discontent in Parliament had tested, and proven, Elizabeth's ultimate authority. The most severe crisis yet faced by the queen and her government had been surmounted, and whatever troubles might lie ahead, they would surely be faced with an extra measure of confidence.

For more than a decade, even the most sanguine of the English had predicted ultimate disaster for a poorly defended realm governed by an unmarried queen. Yet now that the crisis had come it had not shaken the realm, nor had it, as yet, opened the way to foreign invasion. And Elizabeth, who seen in one light was still entirely unsatisfactory in her role as a woman, was taking on the lineaments of a heroine in her role as queen.

The thanksgivings were more than this, however. The church bells—Protestant church bells—were being rung in defiance of the pope. For Elizabeth had at last been excommunicated and—in the eyes of the Catholic world—deposed. From now on her Catholic subjects owed her no allegiance, and in fact, owed it to their consciences to turn their backs on her as a heretic and to rebel against her. In 1571, another conspiracy took shape (mostly in the imaginative mind of the chief conspirator) to replace Elizabeth with Mary Stuart, a Catholic conspiracy invented by the Florentine banker Ridolfi and drawing in the gullible, spineless Norfolk and the imprisoned queen of Scots. Ridolfi's scheme collapsed for want of support in Rome and Madrid and, most crucially, for want of backing from the prepotent Alva in the Netherlands. The proven impotence of yet another Catholic scheme against Elizabeth, climaxed by the execution of Norfolk in June of 1572, lent added force to the Protestant jubilation on Accession Day.

So too did several other events. One was the Massacre of St. Bartholomew, which brought home to many of the English the peril faced by their coreligionists on the continent. Elizabeth and her courtiers went into mourning when they heard the news of the relentless butchery in Paris, and when the French ambassador came to court he found the assembled company in somber black, the queen as disapproving as she was incredulous at the inhumanity of the French Catholics toward the Huguenots. Then too there was Elizabeth's illness in the spring of 1572, which again plunged the kingdom into doubt for her survival and reopened the long-unsettled succession debate.

When she recovered, the recovery seemed, in the light of recent events, to be providential. It was as if God himself had spared his chosen handmaiden to lead his chosen people. In the 1570s what had been an implicit religious ethos was becoming a warmly stated militant credo: dare others what they might, Protestant England was in God's hands.

And a new popular ideology was gathering force: the cult of the queen. To the venerable sanctity of monarchy was now being added the worship of Elizabeth as a Protestant symbol, a symbol of deliverance from evil. She was coming to be seen as a national talisman, a luck-bringing treasure, and her physical frailty and lack of an heir only served to make her all the more precious.

On one of Elizabeth's coins, the double rose noble, was a reminder that she had survived to reach the throne by the slimmest of chances. "This is the Lord's doing," the coin read, in abbreviated Latin, "it is marvelous in our eyes." This was the prayer the young Elizabeth exclaimed on learning that her half-sister was dead and that, after so many hazards, she was finally queen. Yet in the years since 1558 the same providential guidance could be discerned; it marked her whole life. She was blessed, and her people were blessed through her. From now on they would see her through a mist of extraordinary veneration, as a being as miraculous for her heavenly protection as for the sacred anointing she had undergone at her coronation.

The biblical precedents for female rulers were recalled, and Elizabeth was now seen as another like them. To be sure, as Calvin wrote to Cecil, female rulership was "a deviation from the original and proper order of nature," "to be ranked no less than slavery among the punishments consequent upon the fall of man." Yet now and then women appeared "so endowed that the singular good qualities which shone forth in them, made it evident that they were raised up by divine authority." Such a one was the English queen, who had come to the throne "for the better setting forth of his own glory."

It was a startling paradox that Elizabeth's subjects continued to regard their unique ruler from two opposing viewpoints throughout her long reign: on the one hand, they viewed her ill-reputed personal life with extreme distaste, on the other, they cheered her as their luck-bringing champion, as brave as she was, for a woman, unconventional.

Certainly she had a princely courage. In 1572 the courtiers gathered in fearful knots to prognosticate about the catastrophes that were sure to follow the appearance of a "blazing star," or comet, visible in the skies over England. There would be an earthquake, some said; others feared war, or the death of a ruler, or that in some terrifying climatic convulsion their "bodies should be parched and burned up with heat." No good could come from looking at the awful phenomenon, and many tried to persuade Elizabeth to avert her eyes. But "with a courage answerable to the greatness of her state," an observer recorded, "she caused the window to be set open, and cast out this word: *Jacta est alia,* the die is cast.' " Caesar-like, she challenged the heavens—and lo and behold, the year passed with no worse calamity than an unusually cold summer.

Nothing did more to spread and enrich the cult of the queen than her summer progresses. When London became hot and unhealthy the court took to the countryside, in a snakelike procession miles in length with the queen smiling and nodding at its rear. Over the forty-five years of her reign she crossed and recrossed the Midlands, East Anglia, Kent, Sussex and the West Country, visiting hundreds of towns and villages and staying in the royal manors and great noble houses in her path. Thousands of her subjects saw her in the flesh; many of these heard her speak, or watched her wave her hand in their direction and smile winningly. Even those deprived of the sight of her heard about her visit from others; the story spread in ever-widening circles of notoriety until almost nothing else was talked of.

To the dull-eyed, thick-featured country folk the arrival of the queen was an enchantment, touching their leaden lives with the sparkle of faery. When they heard she was coming they scanned the highroad, watching for the first sight of that glittering company that formed her retinue. For hours they saw only a straggling line of overloaded carts and wagons, hundreds and hundreds of them, carrying the indispensable goods and furnishings and miscellaneous baggage of a royal court on holiday. Finally, though, the first of the outriders appeared, clearing the way and making certain there were no dangers or unforeseen impediments and alerting the populace to the imminent arrival of the queen.

She came in a cloud of dust and a shimmer of gold. Sitting regally in her gilded coach, resplendent in silk and brocade, jewels at her throat and in her hair, she appeared "like a goddess such as painters are wont to depict." Her servants and guardsmen and equerries rode immediately ahead of her, her privy councilors behind, followed by another liveried company of tall guardsmen and two dozen maids of honor, "bravely mounted and beautifully attired." It was as if Elizabeth's coronation procession had somehow found its way into rural Kent or Suffolk, bringing all the pageantry of the capital along a country road.

When she passed through a town the citizens gave her as magnificent a welcome as they could afford, and went to great lengths to make a good impression. The main street was swept clean of garbage and sewage, and the pickpockets and prostitutes were locked up or sternly warned to seek other districts for the duration of the royal visit. Idiots were kept discreetly out of sight, and the town gallows dismantled. Laborers were put to work improving the fronts of houses and churches and public buildings; householders cleared their courtyards and put their poultry in cages or behind locked gates. The market cross was painted, the ringers alerted to stand ready, at the royal party's arrival, to ring a lusty peal of bells. Carpenters threw together a platform for the costume plays and presentations and speeches of welcome, while the nervous pupils at the grammar school made heroic efforts to memorize the flowery, singsong poetry their headmaster produced to honor their sovereign's visit. Then, with food and drink prepared and musicians and dignitaries assembled, the queen at last arrived— more or less on schedule—and the fanfares and ringing and sonorous speeches began.

When Elizabeth visited the town of Worcester on progress in 1575 she found the usual provincial welcome.[2] Noisy crowds of excited townspeople surged toward her, drowning out the fanfares and churning the well-swept streets into quagmires. It was raining, but Elizabeth graciously paid no attention to the weather, shouting her thanks to the people who wished her well and showing great interest in the formalities of greeting and gift-giving that protocol demanded. As she stood watching the schoolboys' pageant the storm broke in earnest, but rather than let the "foul and rainy weather" deter her Elizabeth "called for her cloak and hat, and tarried to the end." Her consideration for the performers was noted, and the townspeople loved her for it. She seemed to take in everything: the headmaster's strained couplets, the marvelous tall pear tree that had been uprooted from its bed the night before her arrival and transplanted in the square for her to see and appreciate, the overlong speech of Mr. Bell, the orator, whose peroration was less a paean to the queen than a thinly disguised plea for her to relieve the town's economic woes.

Worcester, Mr. Bell solemnly informed her, had always served England's rulers as a rock-solid bulwark against troubles to the west in Wales, and had been favored by Elizabeth's father "of famous memory" Henry VIII and her brother, "that prince of greatest hope," Edward VI. (Queen Mary Mr. Bell tactfully referred to only as "your highness' dearest sister"; he dared not praise her.)

277

Yet the flourishing craft of weaving which was Worcester's sole industry had recently fallen into severe decline. Where once "in good and fresh memory of man," three hundred and eighty great looms had been kept working, providing employment and prosperity to eight thousand weavers and their families, now the industry had fallen to less than half its former size. Worcester's wealth, he lamented, was "wasted and decayed, the beauty faded, the building ruined, the three hundred and fourscore looms of clothing come to the number of one hundred and three score." Five thousand weavers were out of work, their families impoverished. "There is here," he said, gesturing dramatically to indicate the rain-soaked town around him, "almost nothing left but a ruinous city, or decayed antiquities."

Merchants had done it, the orator went on. Grasping merchants, and restraint of trade by the government, and "the number of pirates on the seas," which reduced exports and inevitably led to idle looms. The queen could alter these evils; the town looked to her to do so. Mr. Bell's eloquence gradually wound to an end.

Elizabeth's stay in Worcester was brief. She was lodged at a town mansion called The White Ladies, where she occupied a rather small and cramped room and her attendants bedded down in uncomfortable heaps on the floor. Somehow grazing was provided for the fifteen hundred horses in the royal caravan, though the town fathers remarked ruefully afterward that Elizabeth left "without paying anything therefor."

Still, when the time came to leave Worcester and move on the queen managed to put the townspeople in a mood to transcend such inconveniences. It was her turn to make a speech, and her words were memorable.

"Misters, I thank you all very heartily for your pains," she began, "and I thank you for the great cheer you made to my men, for they talk greatly of it. And, I pray you, commend me to the whole city, and thank them for their very good will and pains." With every sentence the people cheered loudly and wished her long life and prosperity, so that she felt she had to acknowledge their clamor. "And, I assure you," she concluded, "you all pray so heartily for me, as I fear you will by your prayers make me live too long."

"God save your majesty! God save your majesty!" The outcry was renewed as Elizabeth rode away toward the outskirts of the town, turning back to wave her gloved hand and shout her thanks for their good wishes. "I like as well of them as I have liked of any people in all my progressive time in all my life," she confided later to the bishop of Worcester, and her affection was returned with a fervor verging on adoration. The little room she had slept in at The White Ladies, the cup she drank from there, a jar she had used—all were carefully preserved untouched for centuries and shown to visitors as among the most precious treasures of Worcester. The black pear tree she had admired was from that year on incorporated into the town's coat of arms.

Elizabeth's patient and appreciative response to the formalities at Worcester may have sprung more from political instinct than from excessive enjoyment, for her visit to the town must have been an anticlimax of a very high order. She visited Worcester in August of 1575; during most of July, she had been feted and banqueted and sumptuously lodged at one of the grandest houses in the kingdom, Leicester's palatial mansion of Kenilworth.

So lavish was the three-week royal holiday at Kenilworth that the "verses, proses, poetical inventions and other devices of pleasure" offered her there were published, in a work called "The Princely Pleasures at the Court at Kenilworth," in the following year.[3] Everything that could give the queen delight was provided: fair, sometimes hot summer weather, with only a few days of showers; good hunting in the chase—"vast, wide, large and full of red deer and other stately game"; diverting merrymaking by the local populace, endless spectacles and music and other pastimes in the huge house and grounds. "Things so rich, so rare, and in such abundance" were offered to Elizabeth during her stay that ordinary life seemed suspended. At enormous cost, Leicester made Kenilworth into a fantasy world in which his dearly loved lady and sovereign could revel and recreate and savor the beauties of her countryside.

Kenilworth was an ancient castle. Tradition linked it with the reign of King Arthur, though in fact it began as a Norman fortification. John of Gaunt had enjoyed and beautified it, and Henry V had added a "plaisance," or summerhouse, on the shore of the large artificial lake which stretched away to the west of the castle grounds. Leicester added his own large block of buildings, in the light, high-windowed style Elizabethan noblemen were adopting for their magnificent houses in the 1570s. The effect was stupendous. Robert Laneham, one of Elizabeth's gentleman ushers and a man who owed his preferment to Leicester, described the earl's mansion in the most glowing terms: "every room so spacious, so well belighted, and so high-roofed within, so seemly to sight by due proportion without; by daytime, on every side so glittering by glass, by night, by continual brightness of candle, fire, and torch-light, transparent through the lightsome winds." In the evening the radiance from the great house was spread over the landscape like a shining beacon, and the light had never shone brighter than on the night the queen arrived.

She approached amid an ear-splitting peal of guns and a sky-rending explosion of fireworks. The heavy towers and aged battlements of the outworks loomed up before her in the dusk, and then from somewhere high in the leads six trumpeters blew a regal fanfare. The sound seemed to come from giant players, "much exceeding the common stature of men in this age," holding "huge and monstrous trumpets" to their lips. They were meant to be Arthurian heralds, their pasteboard bodies grotesquely lifelike in the waning light. Other fantastic figures greeted her, including the "Lady of the Lake," riding serenely on a movable island in the moat, and a sibyl "comely clad in a pall of white silk," who prophesied prosperity, health and felicity for the queen.

In the following days the chase echoed with the blasting of huntsmen's horns and the baying of dogs as Elizabeth hunted the hart. She was a skilled and eager huntswoman, delighting in the excitement and activity of bringing a swiftly fleeing deer to "take soil," or plunge desperately into water to save himself. She brought down more than one "goodly deer" during this holiday, but spared at least one; with regal magnanimity she ordered her watermen to cut off the ears of this swimming beast "for a ransom" and then let him go.

In the courtyard, thirteen bears were baited by snarling mastiffs as she looked on from a safe vantage point. The dogs were bred for ferocity and fearlessness, and rushed in yowling packs on the tethered bears. The bears in turn waited to catch the dogs off guard, swatting them away with their huge paws and clawing at their hides in a "great expense of blood and leather." The Elizabethans found the frenzied struggles of the injured bears comical—how "with biting, with clawing, with roaring, tossing and tumbling" they tried to free themselves from the tenacious mastiffs that tore open their flanks and leaped for their throats. To see the great beasts shake their heads violently, their snouts smeared with "blood and slaver," amused Elizabeth and "was a matter of a goodly relief" to all.

One day was set aside for queenly ceremony. Five young men were knighted, including Cecil's son Thomas, and afterward Elizabeth received nine men and women afflicted with the "king's evil," scrofula. These she attempted to heal, drawing on the curative power believed to inhere in her as queen. The ritual was one she carried out often. First she knelt in prayer, then, having purified herself, she "pressed the sores and ulcers" of the sufferers, "boldly and without disgust," confident that many of them would find the ministrations beneficial.

Among the open-air spectacles Elizabeth enjoyed at Kenilworth was a tilting match with a historical theme, the tilters representing the Danish conquerors of medieval England and their English subjects. Two companies of mounted lancers dashed into the courtyard, their horses at a full gallop, and clashed head on, their alder poles snapping into splinters. The combat "grew from a hot skirmish unto a blazing battle," and when the knights were unhorsed they fell to fighting on foot, giving "good bangs on both sides." The Danes threatened to carry the field, but the English finally prevailed, to the cheers of the onlookers, and the defeated foreigners were "beaten down, overcome, and led captive." The queen "laughed well" at the tilting, and gave the performers a generous purse of coins.

One Sunday there was country pageantry in all its oafish charm. It was a rustic bride-ale, with the "lusty lads" of the parish marching in to lead the procession. They were dressed in mismatched finery, hats, caps, doublets and jerkins together, some in boots without spurs, others in spurs without boots, and all with a blue bridelace tied around a sprig of green broom. The bridegroom wore a straw hat, set "steeple-wise" on his head, and harvesting gloves, symbols of his able husbandry; a pen and inkhorn were slung over his back, for he had learned to write a little, and wanted it known. (Later he lost these, and looked "ready to weep" for frustration.)

There was a morris dance, performed "after the ancient manner," and then the bride was led in. She was an unsavory maiden of thirty-five, "ugly, foul and ill-favored," with a muddy complexion and an overpowering stench. Her bridesmaids matched her in "fashion and cleanliness," yet they thought themselves the most radiant damsels to be found anywhere, as they danced before the queen.

Evenings at Kenilworth were devoted to grander and more professional interludes. An Italian contortionist performed remarkable feats of agility, his bones seeming to melt as he twisted and turned himself inside out, springing and somersaulting "with sundry windings, gyrings and circum-flexions." Out of doors, firework displays went on hour after hour, the bursts of sparkling light timed to coincide with "great peals of guns"—no doubt the work of Leicester's brother Ambrose Dudley, earl of Warwick, who was Elizabeth's master of ordnance. The shooting squibs and balls of fire defied nature in that they could not be quenched by water. They fell into the moat and artificial lake, and were submerged, yet before long they shot up out of the water again and seemed to burn even more furiously. To those who had seen battle the display was exhilaratingly warlike, and it pleased the queen very much indeed.

The dining offered to the royal party was fit for the gods—an extravagance all the more impressive in that Elizabeth's own very spare appetite was well known. She ate "smally or nothing," but the three hundred different dishes served at one memorable banquet were set upon and devoured by her household and courtiers. Their gluttony, and the somewhat casual and stretched-out serving of the many courses, meant that the afternoon banquet was still being "wasted and coarsely consumed" at midnight, or near it. A masque, unparalleled "for riches of array, of an incredible cost," had to be canceled because of the late hour.

Next to the hunting and the noisy fireworks displays, it may be that what Elizabeth enjoyed most about Leicester's palatial mansion were the gardens. Brisk walks through the gardens of her palaces were a part of her usual daily routine, and the gardens of Kenilworth, with their long expanses of fine grass and shady fruit trees and stone obelisks, made her feel at home. Care had been taken to choose only the most fragrant flowers and herbs, so that the sweet savors of carnations and stocks and violets and many varieties of roses followed her wherever she went. A massive Italianate fountain, festooned with stone figures of Neptune and Thetis and other classical deities, stood at the center of the garden, its stonework a roiling fantasy of "whales, whirlpools, sturgeons, conchs and whelks."

Besides being ornamental, the fountain was "occupied to very good pastime," as it was equipped with a mechanism to squirt water over bystanders when they least expected it. There was also a huge aviary, "beautified with great diamonds, emeralds, rubies and sapphires," and populated with exotic birds from Europe and Africa, "delightsome in change of tune, and harmony to the ear."

When the time came for Elizabeth to leave her departure drew sighs and doleful poems from a new set of allegorical figures. On her last day of hunting Sylvanus, god of the woods, appeared and urged her "forever to abide in this country," running along beside her horse and promising to double the number of deer in the chase and to make a continual spring in the gardens if only she would consent never to leave. Deepdesire, a messenger from the "council-chamber of heaven," addressed her in verse and, while a consort of musicians played in the background, sang his sad madrigal:

> Come, Muses, come, and help me to lament,
>> Come woods, come waves, come hills, come doleful dales,
> Since life and death are both against me bent,
>> Come gods, come men, beare witnesse of my bales.
>> O heavenly Nimphs, come help my heavy heart;
>> With sighes to see Dame Pleasure thus depart.

The "princely pleasures" were ended, but the progress continued—to Worcester, with its pageantry and speechifying, to Lichfield, where a "grand musical treat" was presented in the cathedral, and to Woodstock, where an elaborate display of linguistic erudition by the poet George Gascoigne—author of the Kenilworth masques and poetry—provided diversion for Elizabeth in Latin, Italian and French. The visit to Woodstock drew forth a peculiar mixture of feelings—dreaded memories of the fear and frustration and killing boredom Elizabeth had known there as a young woman during her sister's reign mingled with a sense of triumph and power. For now she returned to that place of her captivity as a queen regnant, surrounded by pomp and poetic flattery, adored by her excited subjects and in firm command of her life and kingdom.

From Woodstock she made her way southeastward to Reading and then to Windsor, filling the autumn days with hunting and excursions to the country houses of her nobles. The formal progress was now over, and she gave thanks for its smooth course in a prayer of her own composing.

"I render unto thee, O merciful and heavenly Father, most humble and hearty thanks . . . for thy mighty protection and defence over me, in preserving me in this long and dangerous journey." "Continue this thy favorable goodness toward me I beseech thee, that I may still likewise be defended from all adversity, both bodily and ghostly."[4] She prayed for sound faith, for the wisdom to lead her kingdom and the church, for defense against her enemies, that they might never prevail against her.

But it was her realm and her people that concerned her most. "Grant me grace, O Lord, that in the end I may render up and present the same again unto thee, a peaceable, quiet, and well ordered state and kingdom." It had indeed seemed peaceable as she traveled its country roads, smiling with pleasure to see the grain ripening in the fields and the trees heavy with summer fruit. As she prayed she must have had in memory the thousands of waving hands and exuberant faces she had ridden past, the laborers and farmers, country clerics and milkmaids, the schoolchildren and servants and the ragged folk who begged along the highroads. These were the people whose well-being she had preserved for nearly two decades as queen, the people who celebrated her Accession Day as if it were the chief feast of their year. "And to my subjects, O Lord God," Elizabeth prayed fervently, "grant, I beseech ye, faithful and obedient hearts."

25

Eliza is the fairest Quene,
That ever trod upon this greene.
Elizaes eyes are blessed starres,
Inducing peace, subduing warres.
Elizaes hand is christal bright,
Her wordes are balme, her lookes are light.
Elizaes brest is that faire hill,
Where Vertue dwels, and sacred skill,
O blessed bee each day and houre,
Where sweet Eliza builds her bowre.

I t was June, and the queen had decided to go on progress.

From the moment the announcement was made everyone in attendance at court froze into a state of apprehension: Who would be required to go along? Would the weather be oppressive? Would there be enough beds for everyone, and enough space in the wagons for clothes and furnishings? How many personal servants would each courtier and household officer be allowed? And the ultimate question, was there any possible way of being excused from attendance on the queen this time, for the duration of this progress?

For in truth, however glorious a royal journey might be to those who observed it as spectators, to those who actually took part it was a nightmare of discomfort and arduous exertion.

Nothing save war was more disruptive to the orderly well-being of court life than a royal progress.[1] All the fixed certainties of assigned quarters and familiar palaces and predictable ceremonies vanished, giving way to improvised accommodation and strange surroundings and a wearying schedule that could never be known in advance because it varied according to the queen's caprice. Everyone, from grooms to footmen to government officials and their assistants, was kept constantly on the alert, grumbling over personal inconvenience while struggling with the usual tasks of service plus the added demands of frequent packing and unpacking, and of spending long hours on the road.

The ceaseless journeying must have been particularly hard on the elegant courtiers, whose fragile embroidered taffetas and Venetian velvets—not to mention their carefully arranged and dyed hair and beards—must have suffered considerably from the outdoor life. Wardrobe inventories of the period do not mention "progress clothes," so we must assume that they traveled in their customary splendor, their coiffures in windblown disarray and their fine gowns and doublets exposed to the weather. Thick felt traveling cloaks must have given a certain amount of protection, but not enough; the dandified gentlemen and ornately dressed ladies of the court must often have arrived at their destinations with their attire disastrously sun-bleached or mud-spattered or covered in a thick layer of dust.

And once they arrived, they were often subjected to further ignominy. Only the very largest of the country houses the queen visited had accommodations for all of those who traveled with her. Most of the time the majority of her attendants slept in neighboring inns or in tents erected in the open fields, like military men on campaign. For the lucky there were manorial outbuildings crammed with pallet beds, or, for those of the very highest rank, tiny rooms with narrow beds in the great houses themselves. Even these quarters had to be shared; beds were slept in in shifts. To protect the claims of rank, however, propriety as well as household regulations preserved the principle that no nobleman should ever be called upon to share his bed with a commoner.

Coordination of the vast annual migration was in the hands of the lord chamberlain, whose task it was to choose the route that would be followed and see to it that lodging and provisioning would be adequate at every stage of the journey. In completing this enormous task he had the help of the gentlemen ushers of the chamber, who rode out in advance to look over the various proposed lodgings for the queen herself and report on their suitability, and the court harbingers, who did the same thing with the needs of her retinue and provision wagons in mind. The day-to-day mapping of the route was left to the waymaker, who had to determine which roads were most likely to be passable at that season, and safe from brigands, always keeping in mind the necessity of avoiding neighborhoods where plague or smallpox had been reported recently. (It was not unknown for Elizabeth to change her route abruptly on hearing rumors of local contagion; the problem was made especially bothersome as such rumors frequently turned out to be "misinformations.")

The choice of specific routes was no easy matter, for between the time the royal harbingers made their tour and the time the queen and her company arrived an unseasonable rainstorm might turn an inviting lane into a stinking bog. Such mischances had to be foreseen, if possible, and there was much informal communication between the waymaker and the local townspeople, intended to avoid disaster. There were other complicating factors. The court on wheels could travel no farther than ten or twelve miles in a day—less in some areas, where the terrain was difficult—and there had to be some sort of accommodation at the end of each ten- or twelve-mile stretch. Then too each full day of travel had to be broken up with a long pause for dinner at midday and possibly for a light supper, and as the queen and her favorites could not be expected to picnic in the fields this meant locating a capacious inn or wayside manor house, or, in extreme cases, having a temporary structure built for the occasion.

Once an itinerary had been drawn up, the individuals and towns selected to provide hospitality had to be informed, officially, and instructed in detail about their obligations. Sheriffs were told to provide quantities of corn and hay, and justices of the peace received notice that the royal purveyors would expect to find plenty of beef and chickens and fresh fish on hand when they came to buy provisions for the itinerant household. Some wine, the officials were informed, would be brought specially from London, but all of the beer to be drunk by the hundreds of thirsty travelers would have to be brewed on the spot—a sizable challenge to local brewmasters.

A particularly sensitive issue was the brewing of the queen's ale. She liked it light and tart, and was very particular about it. If the ale of the country district was not satisfactory, then a London brewer would have to be found to set up a temporary brewery near the progress site. Sometimes the arrangements went awry, and the royal ale cup failed to please. In 1575, Elizabeth was at Grafton, and Leicester, who was with her, recorded her fury when she arrived hot and thirsty and found the ale provided for her to be undrinkable. "It did put her far out of temper," he wrote, to discover the oversight. Ale had been laid down specially for her, but the "marvellous hot" weather had spoiled it, so that it had turned as thick and sweet as malmsey wine, and no one would touch it. There was a hurried scramble to find better ale; servants were dispatched to London and to neighboring houses with empty bottles, and eventually a fresh supply was brought in. Tempers cooled, and Elizabeth became "perfectly well and merry" once more, ready to take up her travels again and to hazard the cellars of her next lodging.[2]

From a governmental standpoint, there was more than a little recklessness about a royal progress. It was an act of daring, in which the queen flaunted her trust in her people and their love for her by making herself particularly vulnerable to kidnapping or assault, and ignoring the risk. Her councilors suffered agonies of worry, and attempted to dissuade her from making the hazardous journeys, but she refused to listen. But beyond her personal risk there was a broader political one. Though the royal council might move with the queen the seat of government remained in the capital, and during progress season that meant that a reliable and efficient system of communication had to be established between London and the country-side, with scores of messengers ready to ride with news or instructions or documents at a moment's notice. For as long as the long courtly holiday lasted the everyday work of the queen and council—work which often involved weighty deliberations and difficult decisions—had to go on under improvised circumstances allowing little margin for inexactness or thought-ful changes of mind. Urgent business must often have had to be postponed, to the frustration of everyone involved, because the coffers of papers and records needed to carry it through had been sealed and loaded onto carts and sent ahead to the next lodging.

By far the most unwelcome members of the queen's traveling retinue were the court purveyors and their deputies, men authorized to buy food and rent carts and horses for the queen. Purveyance was a time-honored feudal right; since medieval times monarchs had demanded that their subjects sell them goods and provide services at fixed prices, set by the clerk of the market in consultation with a group of local men. The purveyors fanned out through the countryside in their hundreds, commandeering horses and carts and announcing the minimal rates that would be paid for them and the length of time they would be needed. (Only the most naive of the farmers and villagers took these promises at face value; most knew that, once they let their horses and carts go, it would be long months before they were returned, if ever. It was better to bribe the purveyor than to trust him to keep his word.)

Despite the publishing of official prices dishonesty flourished. Poultry and cattle, butter and eggs and fruit were seized and paid for at rates so low they amounted to theft, with the corrupt officials pocketing the differ-ence between the money actually paid out and the amount given them to spend by their superiors. The abuse was scandalous. "Her majesty's poor people are many times molested to their great travail and expenses," a Commons bill regulating purveyance read. Purveyors were notorious for giving "untrue information" about authorized prices, and were no better than "thieves and spoilers."[3] Even when they paid the true price—which was rare—they bought more than was in fact needed by the court and resold the surplus elsewhere at a profit. The system invited fraud and led to deep grievances against the court, if not against the queen herself; in truth she too found the purveyors odious and referred to them as "harpies."

The arrangements complete, the day of departure finally came, and the overloaded carts and wagons began to roll slowly out through the palace courtyard and onto the highroad. Among them rode the officers of the bakehouse and cellar, the men of the stable and woodyard, the cooks and assistant cooks and scullery boys and pantrymen. With the menials en route, the household officers mounted to ride, and with them the yeomen and grooms and ushers who occupied the higher ranks in the huge household population. The procession lengthened, and began to string out and bunch up as the individual carts and riders gathered speed or encountered obstacles. There were minor delays; wagons spilled their loads, horses went lame, riders were overcome by heat or became seasick in the swaying carts. Far to the rear, hours after the parade began, the secretaries and clerks and government officials took to the road, then the guardsmen and the queen's personal servants, and Elizabeth herself, perhaps exhilarated at the prospect of country air and country pastimes, perhaps exasperated already by the hundred petty difficulties of travel.

Within a few miles of London the road began to deteriorate. The wide way grew narrow, and the smooth, even surface gave way to deeply carved ruts between steep and slippery banks. The travelers began to curse the "foul and ragged" path, and to fidget uncomfortably in their hard saddles. There was worse to come: roads so pitted they made the horses stumble and slowed the entire caravan to a crawl, high passes with "dangerous rocks and valleys," lanes full of loose stones, making for "careful and painful riding." The riders went on anyway, "up the hill and down the hill," becoming bored and saddlesore and longing for food and rest.

After dinner the procession re-formed, and the carts and riders resumed the languid pace. There were distractions—the sight of green fields and flowering hedges, gossip and flirtation, welcome drafts of wine passed in leather wineskins from hand to hand. No doubt the travelers sang. But the road, with its bumps and jolts, seemed to lead endlessly on, hour after hour, and when at last the riders halted at their destination they were hardly in a condition to behave as they did at Greenwich or Hampton Court, dining and dancing and frolicking with lighthearted abandon. Yet they attempted to do so, following the queen's tireless example, and were granted only a few hours' uncomfortable sleep before beginning their journeying again.

A week or two of this exhausting pace—broken by longer stays at the larger houses or towns along the route—might have been tolerable, but when it was a matter of months only the hardiest of the courtiers and officials could keep up. "I am old, and come now evil away with the inconveniences of progress," one middle-aged man wrote. "I followed her majesty until my man returned and told me he could get neither fit lodging for me nor room for my horse," he explained; at that point he gave up and went home.

If progress time was hard on those who followed the queen, it was equally hard on those who entertained her. During the 1560s and 1570s dozens of outsize mansions rose on country estates, monuments to self-importance and affluence but witness also to the obligation of nobles and gentry to show lavish hospitality to the queen. Some, like Kenilworth, were royal gifts, ancestral manors or castles requiring only extensive renovation and additions to make them worthy to receive the royal party. But many others were built by their owners from the ground up, entailing truly prodigious labor and expense. Christopher Hatton's new house of Holdenby, a sprawling structure not much smaller than Elizabeth's enormous palace of Hampton Court, put Hatton hopelessly into debt—and to little purpose, for it stood unused, full of furnishings and waiting servants, for ten years without receiving a visit from the queen.

Holdenby's rival for size and sumptuousness was Theobalds, Cecil's magnificent, multi-colored country seat whose palatial dimensions dwarfed those of every other noble house in England. Pink brick and white stone formed the façades, which were broken by high windows and crowned with turrets of blue slate. Fanciful chimneys and domed cupolas adorned the roofline, and there were gilded weathervanes and gleaming painted frescoes to complement the eclectic charm of the overall design. In the remarkable gardens of Theobalds the walks stretched for miles along fragrant avenues lined with blossoms and flowering trees. A narrow waterway ran around the perimeter of the grounds, "large enough for one to have the pleasure of going in a boat, and rowing between the shrubs," and there were fountains and wooden columns and pyramids and a challenging maze. In a summer-house water was piped into lead cisterns so that guests could swim on hot days, while contemplating the noble sight of twelve marble busts of Roman emperors.

The taste for massive houses spawned a diversity of structures, some mock medieval, with towers, turrets and keep, some Italianate and classical, with columns and pilasters and friezes, some recalling the fanciful, fairytale style of the 1520s and 1530s. Mansions that were not also military fortifications were a new thing in England, and if some, such as Audley End, "shone forth like a diadem by the decoration of the cupolas and other ornaments to the pavilions," others were overornamented, crudely proportioned monstrosities.

Even the worst of them, though, had their delights, for if the overall form was flawed there were certain to be interior features carried out by gifted craftsmen whose taste surpassed that of their employers. Plasterers created ribbed ceilings of intricate design and friezes with raised medallions and pendants and hunting scenes. Carvers and joiners built wide wooden staircases that curved grandly upward at a stately angle, and fashioned molded paneling for the walls. Elizabethan fireplaces were a splendor of colored marble and alabaster, their high overmantels decorated with allegorical figures or the queen's arms. At night candlelight shone on polished wood and glowing tapestries; during the day the light poured in through huge windows, lit "like so many suns." In their luxury and originality, the great houses paid tribute to the growing ambition and energy of English society, and to that society's focus on its unique monarch.

Having built his great house, the nobleman moved his family and servants into it and waited, often a very long time, for the queen to come and visit him there. Letters to the lord chamberlain helped, as did gifts to the waymaker and the influence of friends at court. Finally the hoped-for, dreaded moment came. The royal harbingers appeared, to announce that the house was on the progress route and would be used, if found suitable. They were shown through the house, their queries answered deferentially and their requests noted. No, they were assured, there had been no plague among the servants or in the neighboring villages. Their business done, the harbingers remounted and prepared to leave for the next manor house on their list. Before they left they indicated a date for the queen's arrival.

Right away the owner of the house moved himself and his family out; they would stay with neighbors or at an inn for the duration of the royal visit. Workmen were summoned who would make repairs and major alterations so that the house would be fit to receive the queen. Servants were sent to request extra plate and furnishings from friends and neighbors, and to buy up all the available oxen and sheep and chickens in the region before the queen's purveyors took them. Wardrobes had to be refurbished. When Elizabeth visited East Anglia in 1578 the fine cloth was bought up overnight. "All the velvets and silks were taken up that might be laid hands on and bought for money, and soon converted into such garments and suits of robes that show thereof might have beautified the greatest triumph that was in England." To stock the deer in the hunting park, an age-old ritual was enacted. Peasants marched into the forest and began to lure out stags by playing on "flutes and other instruments of music." Then, playing continuously, they led the great antlered beasts into the park, where the huntsmen took note of them and marked their lairs; when the queen arrived they would be driven within range of her crossbow.

Next the host summoned his servants. There were certain to be dozens of them; the larger houses had hundreds. He spoke to them, like a preacher to his flock, informing them of the honor the house was to receive and of the special duties they would be expected to undertake. If he was a good master, he was brief and effective, "putting them in mind what quietness and what diligence they were to use." They were to be clean, orderly, attentive, soundless, invisible. As long as they did their work and avoided provoking the servants of the queen, all would go well.

Yet though he might be poised and masterful with his own staff, the host himself was bound to suffer inner torment. The "great trouble and hindrance" of hospitality weighed heavily on him, the cost, the frustrations, the worry over whether or not the arrangements would prove satisfactory. He worried greatly over the timing of the queen's stay, for it was common knowledge that she often arrived later than announced—indeed she occasionally failed to arrive at all—and that she frequently overstayed her welcome. "I trust your lordship will have in remembrance to provide and help that her majesty's tarrying be not above two nights and a day," the earl of Bedford wrote to Cecil as he waited for Elizabeth at Woburn Abbey, "for so long time do I prepare." For so long, and no longer, the earl might have added; he simply could not find food and fodder and fuel enough for more than his allotted time.

There were more serious aggravations. Elizabeth's courtiers seemed to look on progress season as a time of license, when the everyday rules of conduct could be disregarded and they could feel free to make destructive nuisances of themselves. While staying at a country house they rode roughly through the lawns and gardens, tearing through flower beds and churning up the carefully tended lawns. They stripped the orchards of their fruit and trampled the planted fields until they were "despoiled, wasted and spent," and did not stop there. After they had gone, linens and pewter and even heavy pieces of furniture were found to be missing, and hundreds of pounds' worth of goods had to be replaced.

And there was often malice behind the destructiveness and theft. During progress time in 1574 Leicester led a party of his friends and followers on an unplanned hunting party. They left their designated lodging and rode to Berkeley Castle—giving no warning of their coming—and spent the day slaughtering Lord Berkeley's prize deer. They took twenty-seven deer in all, leaving the infuriated Berkeley to sputter in impotent rage; cheated of other retaliation, he failed to restock the hunting park and let it return to a wild state. Elizabeth was displeased, as Leicester had hoped she would be. Behind it all was the earl's plan to acquire Berkeley Castle for himself by putting its current owner into disfavor.

The issue of political loyalty was uppermost in everyone's mind when

Elizabeth visited Edward Seymour, earl of Hertford, at Elvetham in 1591. Early in the reign he had provoked the queen's anger and suspicion by marrying Catherine Grey, and had spent nine long years in the Tower for his offense. Now he was being given an opportunity to demonstrate the depth of his fidelity to his rightful sovereign, and his trouble and expense were judged to be a measure of his trust.

Seymour hired three hundred workmen "to enlarge his house with new rooms and offices." Elvetham was a medieval manor, far too small to lodge the traveling court, so regiments of carpenters and glaziers and joiners labored night and day to erect new structures, built in record time, to house the visitors. A cluster of temporary buildings sprang up on a hillside, at a little distance from the manor house, within the park. A mock "room of estate" for the nobles, with a withdrawing place for Elizabeth at one end, was made like a forest bower, its walls covered on the outside with boughs and clusters of ripe hazelnuts, and hung on the inside with tapestries, its roof entwined with ivy, its floor covered with rushes and sweet-smelling herbs. There was another building "for her majesty's footmen, and their friends," and another long bower for her guardsmen. A large hall was designated "for knights, ladies, and gentlemen of chief account," and alongside were other spaces for Seymour's own servants and Elizabeth's staff. A labyrinth of specialized quarters for food and supplies ranged around the outside—a pantry equipped with five ovens, "some of them fourteen foot deep," for baking bread and cakes and meat pies, a boiling house, a lodging for the cook, and two cavernous kitchens where succulent meat and game turned slowly over the fire on long spits and waiters stood by to serve all comers.

Beyond these quarters for eating and sleeping were other creations: a "ship isle," a hundred feet long and eighty feet wide, with trees for masts, built in a lake, a "snail mount" made of four tiers of privet hedges spiraling upward, and boats full of musicians, one of them "a pinnace full furnished" with masts, yards, sails, anchor, cables and great guns. The lodging, the banqueting, the music and elaborate masquing that Seymour arranged against the backdrop of the ship isle and the snail mount all pleased Elizabeth very much indeed. The earl had gone to immense trouble and expense; he must be among her most loyal subjects. Her frown of suspicion turned into a dazzling smile of approval—though at the first sign of questionable behavior from Seymour the frown would be certain to return.

Though his loyalty had never been in question Cecil too outdid himself in making extensive arrangements and rearrangements in his great house in order to please the queen. She let it be known that her private chamber there was too small, and at once Cecil gave orders for it to be enlarged. It was decorated in the grotesquely eclectic style which Elizabeth and her contemporaries favored. The ceiling was a celestial clock like the famous one at Hampton Court, with the stars in their zodiacal clusters marching across the heavens by "some concealed ingenious mechanism." A fountain gushed at one end of the room, the water falling from a rocky wall "of all colors, made of real stones," into a dish held by sculpted "savages." The most charming feature of the room was the artificial oak trees which lined the walls, so real in appearance that when the windows were opened, birds flew in and perched on their boughs, singing as loudly as they did in the wild.

The principal discomfort of the royal progress, when all was said and done, was the cost. To be sure, there was much competition for the privilege of entertaining the queen—partly because, in the case of individuals, such an opportunity opened the way for royal patronage and increased wealth. In such cases the expense was an investment which, if all went well, offered a substantial return. But few noblemen were wealthy enough—or felt secure enough in their wealth—to take lightly the outlay required, not to mention the aggravation of unexpected increases in cost that were the bane of all extensive entertainment.

In actuality the charges ranged from perhaps three hundred and fifty pounds to as much as a thousand, for a stay of from four or five days to a week or more. This was the basic expense; added to it were payments for the spectacles, for temporary buildings, for a lavish gift to the queen (an inescapable, and often heavy, expense) and for substantial rewards to officers of her household, for new clothes and liveries, and for such freakish extras as payment for food imported from abroad—as when Lord Buckhurst, waiting for the queen at Wytham, found that his neighbors had used up all the provisions for miles around and had "to send to Flanders to supply him, the others having drawn the country dry." Such were the immediate costs. But the long-term expense was that of staffing and maintaining an enormous mansion which stood empty for most of the year, and of repairing and refurbishing it, year after year, in the hope that eventually Elizabeth might make use of it. This was ruinously expensive, and obviously wasteful.

But it was wasteful only from the narrowest of viewpoints, that of a clerk or comptroller. There was another logic evident in the workings of the royal progress. It had the character of a pilgrimage, or rather of a pilgrimage in reverse, in which the saint herself instead of the worshipful pilgrim moved from shrine to shrine. Seen in this light, the great and small houses along the route and the towns and inns that decked themselves to offer hospitality were like expensive wayside chapels, seldom used yet ever available, their cost inconsequential when weighed against their function.

Cecil once described Hatton's house at Holdenby as "consecrated" to the queen. Present or absent, she was its ruling deity, its sole reason for being. To reckon too closely the use she made of it, or the charges that resulted, would have been sacrilege.

26

Come over the born Bessy,
Come over the born Bessy,
Swete Bessey come over to me;
And I will the take,
And my dere Lady make
Before all other that ever I see.

J ean de Simier, master of the wardrobe to François, duke of Alençon, arrived in England in the first days of 1579. He was a dark, dapper French aristocrat, sleek and smooth-tongued, and as simian as his name; Elizabeth, who had pet names for everyone, called him her "Monkey."

Simier was the duke's "chief darling," and close friend, and his coming was significant. Alençon, who was the younger brother of the king of France, Henry III,* had been proposed once before as a husband for Elizabeth, but the discussions had been allowed to lapse. During 1578 they had been revived, with Alençon and Elizabeth carrying on an increasingly ardent courtship, by letter and through intermediaries. Now their mutual flattery, seduction and bargaining had reached a point where some of the English, at least, were saying that despite the age-old enmity between England and France the time had come to join hands in order to "get the queen married."[1] Simier's coming was the last formality to be observed— the final stage in the ritual wooing—before the expected arrival of the eager bridegroom himself.

The duke could hardly have chosen a more persuasive envoy. In Simier's

---

*François became duke of Anjou on his brother Henry's accession in 1574, but continued to be known, and referred to in official papers, as duke of Alençon.

presence Elizabeth bloomed. He was a master of erotic flattery—"most exquisitely skilled in love-toys, pleasant conceits, and court-dalliances," as the historian Camden wrote—and his whispered messages made her blush and gasp and smile like a girl of twenty—and indeed she looked younger than she ever had in the last fifteen years, the French ambassador Mauvissière noted. She was radiant, spirited, altogether lovely—an enchanted being, utterly transformed by the power of love.

The transformation was so profound, in fact, that it left everyone quite bewildered. Could it be that the little Frenchmen, with his "fine knowledge of the delights of love," had become the queen's lover? Was he introducing her to the refinements of French passion, as a way of tempting her to agree to wed his master? Certainly they were in and out of one another's bedchambers often enough. Elizabeth broke in on him early one morning as he was dressing—just as Thomas Seymour had broken in on her long ago at Chelsea—and insisted that he talk with her "with only his jerkin on." He, in turn, raided her bedchamber and took her nightcap to send to Alençon, who already had a handkerchief belonging to her and several other relics from her person.

The infatuation deepened, fed by candlelit banquets and intimate suppers; there were romantic letters and love tokens from the duke, and the thrilling expectation of a meeting. An extravagant ball was held at court, whose chief entertainment was an imitation tournament, an allegory of the romantic battle of the sexes. Six gentlemen were the challengers at the tilt, six ladies defended. In the end the gentlemen capitulated, and the ladies won the day. In this tournament between the French and English, Elizabeth meant to emerge the victor, and the prize—unthinkable though it seemed to those who had watched her avoid commitment for so long—was to be her fine white hand in marriage.

No one was more dumbfounded by the apparent sincerity of Elizabeth's wooing than Leicester, who knew better than anyone how she looked when she was in love. As the weeks passed he continued to play the highly visible political role required of him—that of principal adviser to the queen and gracious host to Simier and eager promoter of the French marriage—yet in private he spread a story that Simier was using "drinks and unlawful arts" to turn Elizabeth's head, and that these love potions alone were responsible for the otherwise unaccountable change in her. (Had he known anything of Simier's private life he would surely have gossiped about that too, for the Monkey was at the center of a particularly sordid and violent recent scandal. Simier's brother had seduced his wife; the Monkey had had his brother murdered, and the wife, wretched with grief and hatred, had swallowed poison.)

Yet enchanted or not, Elizabeth seemed to have her feet firmly on the ground. She was devoting her abundant energies to the practical matters attending a marriage of state, including that most delicate of them all, her fertility. She was forty-five; could she safely bear a child? Within days of Simier's arrival she had called together her physicians to "decide whether she could hope for progeny," or so the Spanish ambassador Mendoza reported. They "found no difficulty"—a prognosis that may well have been more political than medical, given the queen's history of illness and frailty, not to mention the predictable dangers of middle-age childbirth.[2] Cecil, who saw his dream of marriage for Elizabeth at last coming true, was quick to add his optimistic view to that of the royal doctors. In a carefully thought-out memorandum he reminded Elizabeth that women older and less well-endowed by nature than she was had safely given birth. Why should not she, "a person of most pure complexion, of the largest and goodliest stature of well-shaped women," repeat their example? "In the sight of all men," he concluded loyally and gallantly, "nature cannot amend her shape in any part to make her more likely to conceive and bear children."

As telling a sign of the serious intent of the queen was her postponing of Parliament to allow time for the marriage negotiations to mature. It had been set to convene on January 22; now the date was pushed ahead to March, by which time detailed discussions were well under way. Meanwhile the French king and his mother wrote to give their blessing to the match, with King Henry offering to agree "to any alliance or treaty the queen wished in order to bring it about."[3] While the privy council met hour after hour, Simier pranced and preened, and distributed some twelve thousand ducats in jewels among the leading courtiers to appease any dislike they showed toward him. Elizabeth assured him that once the duke came to England, "the business would be carried through," and as if eager to conclude it quickly, before she changed her mind, she began to talk of having the wedding immediately after Easter.[4]

But could she really go through with it, once she saw him? François d'Alençon was very short, very much younger than she, and very, very ugly. People would be certain to laugh at the two of them together, the tall, thin, middle-aged queen and her dwarfish, puny little husband of twenty-five. His nose was large and bulbous to the point of deformity, and smallpox had left his face a hideous battleground of pits and scars. Francis Walsingham, formerly Elizabeth's ambassador in Paris and now her principal secretary, reported after seeing Alençon some years earlier that the pock-holes were "no great disfigurement," adding clinically that they were thick rather than "deep or great." "They upon the blunt end of his nose," however, were both great and deep, "how much to be disliked may be as it pleaseth God to move the heart of the beholder." It was a tactful if devastating evaluation, and did not quite succeed in disguising the Puritan Walsingham's extreme distaste for both the stunted little duke and the lascivious, decadent French court that had bred him.

A portrait of Alençon painted at age thirty, some six years after his wooing of Elizabeth, reveals an undersized, boyish man with a furtive look in his small eyes. A thin mustache barely brushes a young, weak mouth and chin. There is a hint of guilty sweetness in the face, but neither maturity nor virility; if he was a great lover, Alençon hid it well.

He was indisputably a fighter, though, and a scrappy individualist with a family and political history that had much in common with Elizabeth's own early life. As a boy he had been an unloved youngest son, the runt of the family, and he had grown up a hellion, plotting against his royal brother King Henry (who was their mother's favorite) and intriguing, with an unscrupulous abandon Elizabeth would relish, with Protestants and Catholics alike. Alençon was clearly not a man of principle, but he had sworn a dramatic oath to his followers, "that none of them would ever return while his brother reigned, who treated him with so little dignity." The queen had to admire, sight unseen, such panache from a man who was well under five feet tall.

In fact it was Alençon's audacity and determination to win dignity and, in particular, military glory that had prompted the looming dynastic tie between Tudor and Valois. With a pause in the bloody civil war in France, Alençon had offered to fight with the Dutch Calvinists who were rebelling against Philip II in the Netherlands. The situation there had become extremely volatile. Spanish soldiers had kept a stranglehold on the Low Countries provinces during the first half of the 1570s, but later in the decade the Protestant rebels—aided by English supplies, English volunteers, and large sums of English money—had made headway and achieved a measure of self-government and freedom of religion. Hapsburg power waxed and waned, and each fluctuation offered an opportunity for military adventuring. Leicester, though graying now and pot-bellied, dreamed of renewing in Flanders the exploits of his youth, and boasted that he would soon "lead the greatest army to leave English shores in forty years."[5] Leicester's dreams were thwarted for the present, but Alençon, who had made himself unwelcome in France because of his treachery and troublesome ambition, was free to pursue his, provided he was able to pay for his adventuring himself. With his proposal of marriage to Elizabeth came a request for a loan of three hundred thousand ducats.

From the English point of view, the young duke's enterprise was unsettling. Gratified as she might be by any strengthening of the forces opposing Spanish power, Elizabeth did not want the Netherlands to fall to the French, who had never ceased to scheme to use that region as a base from which to take over Scotland and, through Scotland, to take over England. If Alençon was only making a personal bid for glory in Flanders, then he was probably harmless, at least for the moment. But if he was a stalking horse for his brother, then his Netherlands undertaking was a threat, and she would either have to oppose him or—radical solution though it was— marry him.

Easter came and went, and there was no royal wedding. But a marriage treaty was being drawn up, with the old contract between Philip and Mary Tudor used as a model. The same issues arose now as those which had preoccupied the English negotiators when Mary married Philip: Was the bridegroom to be called king of England? What lands was he to have in England, and what dukedoms, and what was to become of him if, as was expected, his wife died before he did? What was to be done about the bridegroom's Catholicism? Was he to be allowed to practice it, and if so, could his foreign servants practice it too?

The councilors attended to their work, distracted by the increasingly vocal opposition to the marriage by the people and by their own political feuds and self-interested aims. They had been liberally bribed by Simier, and a number were in the pay of the Spaniards as well; beyond this, they had to pay heed to what opinions Elizabeth preferred them to hold, for they relied on her to dispense patronage and continue to confer on them the offices that provided their livelihood. (The Catholics among them she slighted, making them better targets for bribes from abroad.) Sussex, who with Cecil favored the marriage, did so almost as much out of revenge against his old enemy Leicester as from loyalty to the queen's wishes. Walsingham, who had become a very important and very opinionated voice in the council, was torn. As a radical Protestant he abhorred the thought of a Catholic consort for Elizabeth, yet as a vehement advocate of English intervention in the Netherlands against the Satanic forces of Spain he had to welcome Alençon for his military ambitions, and for the weight of the Valois name and throne. Leicester was angry, wounded and plainly jealous of Simier. He was moody toward Elizabeth and played on her emotions by taking to his bed with illness just as she was about to issue a passport to Alençon for his journey to England.

Plainly Elizabeth was waiting for the councilors to advise her to marry, as they had, consistently and cantankerously, for twenty years. She was prepared to overlook Alençon's religion (he could worship in private in his chapel), his demand to be crowned king, his insistence that an English port be given to France and that three thousand French footsoldiers—a small invading army—be allowed to guard it. She did not even express any lasting offense when told that Alençon would change the royal style to "Francis and Elizabeth, King and Queen of England," though at first she did find this reduction in her dignity somewhat hard to accept, and was pointedly rude to Simier in consequence. But her pique was short-lived, and before long her infatuation returned. Suddenly, unaccountably, against all odds Elizabeth was ready to get married, and the last obstacle she expected to encounter was the opposition of her male advisers.

Yet oppose her they did, emerging from wearying discussions that lasted from two in the afternoon till two in the morning without a consensus in favor of the marriage. Most were in fact against it; as a body, all they were willing to do was to summarize the arguments for and against, leaving the ultimate decision to the queen herself. As to the specific terms put forward by the French, the councilors had a definite opinion. They called Simier into the council chamber and told him just how exorbitant they thought his master's demands were. The Frenchman was outraged; he jumped up in a fury and walked out, slamming the door angrily behind him.

The French did not give up, however. Before the week was over they were renewing their efforts to win over the recalcitrant councilors. Alençon sent Leicester two handsome Spanish horses as a gift, and Simier had orders to woo the others with "every possible means," for which he was to have a large sum of money. (The money could not have been more welcome; Simier had spent all he brought with him, and had been reduced to pawning some of his jewels in order to pay for the banquets and gifts he continued to offer the English.)

Elizabeth was far from dissuaded by her advisers' lack of endorsement for her marriage, yet she was noticeably disheartened. Her spirits sank, and for fear of serious consequences several of her favorite ladies were brought to court to keep her company. They were lodged in the palace itself, an unusual if not quite unprecedented practice, and were expected to "entertain" the queen and keep her from depression.

No doubt she was struggling within herself, for though she had everyone convinced of her sincerity in encouraging Alençon's suit it cannot have been easy for her to wait for events to unfold. Her uncooperative councilors frustrated her, as did the drawn-out process of negotiation and the long wait for the sight of her bridegroom's reputedly unlovely face. There was mounting evidence that her subjects were angry over the proposed union with France, and their protests were taking disquieting forms. And even if her choice was politically wise, what would it mean for her personally? Would marriage give her joy and fulfillment, or would it mean humiliating subordination and the loss of what authority she had built up over two decades as queen?

Privately, in her inner chamber surrounded by her women, Elizabeth reiterated her determination to make Alençon her husband. She was by turns heavyhearted, agitated, truculent and infatuated, "burning with impatience" for the arrival of the one suitor who had actually agreed to come to England to be inspected without insisting that a marriage treaty be signed first. "They need not think that it is going to end in this way," she said, responding to the negatives from the council chamber. "I must get married."[6]

But the closer marriage came, the more dangerous it began to seem. Pamphlets warning Elizabeth of the perils of closer ties with the French appeared mysteriously in her bedchamber, placed there by unseen hands, and with them were theological writings predicting that if the queen did not give up her claim to be head of the church, "God would punish her within the year." Messages and warnings were surreptitiously left where she would be sure to find them. On one occasion she was taking her usual morning walk in the garden and found an unsigned letter "thrown into the doorway"; its contents so disturbed her that she hurried at once to Leicester's house, staying there all day and night and canceling at least one of her palace engagements the following day.[7]

In addition to the anonymous warnings there was thunderous disapproval from the preachers who came to court to exhort Elizabeth every Sunday. In sermon after sermon they spoke "very violently" on the evils of marriage to a foreigner and a Catholic, and to nearly everyone's surprise the object of these perorations tolerated the torrent of denunciation. She tolerated it, that is, until one Sunday when the cleric unwisely chose to remind his sovereign of her late half-sister Mary. What untold harm, he said accusingly, had been done when Mary chose the Catholic Spaniard Philip for her husband! What suffering that foreign union had brought to England, with hundreds of martyrs burned at the stake and thousands more forced into exile for the sake of their beliefs. He warmed to his subject, calling up images of fiery destruction and no doubt reawakening in Elizabeth all her old hatred and resentment of her sister. She was furious that he should touch her sore spot, even more furious that he should suggest any comparison between the suave, ambitious young Alençon and the cold-hearted tyrant Philip II.

Crackling with suppressed anger, Elizabeth did not wait for the sermon to end but rose and left the chapel as soon as the ill-advised preacher had completed his survey of the previous reign. He was still speaking when she and her crowd of attendants swept out, and observers turned to one another to remark that such an abrupt royal departure had never been seen before.

Criticism was one thing; attempted assassination another. One day when the queen and Simier were in her barge on the river there was the dull crack of a gun. One of the royal bargemen cried out; he had been hit in both arms, and he slumped down in a spreading pool of blood. He had been sitting only a few feet from Elizabeth, and no one doubted that the shot —fired from a neighboring boat—had been meant to hit her, or possibly the Frenchman.

Amid the panic the queen tore the scarf from around her neck and threw it to the bargeman to use as a bandage. She shouted her reassurance, telling him "to be of good cheer," for she would make certain he was well cared for. There were no further shots, and the barge quickly put ashore.

Apparently no one considered the possibility that the gun might have gone off accidentally (though that is what happened, as it turned out). A similar misadventure had marred the lavish entertainments at Kenilworth four years earlier. Elizabeth had been hunting, when an arrow sped past her, barely missing her, and the huntsmen had seized a man with a crossbow, taking him to be an assassin. Then the incident had been variously interpreted, with the crossbowman denounced by some as a traitor and dismissed by others as a harmless hunter who missed his aim while shooting at a deer.[8] Then there had been room for doubt, but now, with the queen about to undertake the most startling gamble of her reign amid threats and protests and dire warnings of imminent peril, she had to assume the worst.

She did not cut herself off from her subjects during these tense months in the first half of 1579, but she did take fewer risks. A special procession through the capital was scheduled, with the queen riding in state over London Bridge—something she had done only once since her accession. The lord mayor was put in charge of ensuring the safety of the royal party and the smooth running of the official and unofficial welcomes. All was in readiness when, the night before she was to make her triumphal entry, a messenger brought the lord mayor a letter from the queen. He must not let a great crowd gather, she wrote; let the citizens turn out in modest numbers to greet her.

Half an hour later another messenger arrived. Let none of the citizens in the streets be armed when she rode past, Elizabeth commanded. Shortly afterward there was a third message. Elizabeth had decided not to come across London Bridge after all; she would go through the city by water, as usual.[9]

In the end the greatest act of treachery came not from an anonymous assassin but from the most trusted of the queen's intimates, Leicester.

For years the earl had led a disorderly, unsatisfactory private life, full of intrigue and mired in gossip. He was the last of his line—and a good thing too, many said, considering his disgraceful ancestry—and he wanted a son. Not a bastard son, but a legitimate heir, born of a recognized marriage to a woman willing to live down the inevitable disapproval of the queen. He had a number of liaisons (his enemies counted dozens), and a long-lasting mistress, Douglas Sheffield, who bore him two children, but his preferred choice as a wife was Lettice Knollys, the queen's beautiful cousin. They were secretly married sometime after Lettice's husband died in 1576, and two years later, when she was heavily pregnant with Leicester's child, her father Francis Knollys demanded that a more formal private ceremony take place. It was a great risk, for the queen was sure to discover the truth in time, yet Knollys did not trust the notorious womanizer Leicester to have carried through a valid wedding ceremony; he had to see with his own eyes that his daughter was properly married.

Simier found out about the marriage, and told Elizabeth, only weeks before Alençon was due to arrive in England. She was already tense and overwrought with fear and expectation; the discovery of Leicester's treachery shocked, then enraged her. It was like Leicester to act behind her back, his pusillanimity was as contemptible as his deceit. As for Lettice, that traitorous "she-wolf," no words were harsh enough to describe her. Leicester, though, would have reason to fear for his life. She ordered him seized and shut up in an isolated tower in Greenwich park, to await stricter imprisonment in the Tower of London.

Angry and wounded though she was, and eager for revenge, Elizabeth must have glimpsed a kind of perverse symmetry in the courses her life and Leicester's were taking. It was said among the people that they had been born in the same hour, so that their lives were attuned from birth; now, having reached their mid-forties, both had decided to marry. And just as in fact the earl was a year older than the queen, so he had married the previous year; she would follow in her turn. There was a melancholy appropriateness about Leicester's marriage, for however she might lament his loss as a potential husband his union with Lettice Knollys left her completely free to choose elsewhere. However tenuous her enduring romantic tie to him had been, it was now formally severed. She could marry Alençon with nothing weighing on her heart.

On August 17 Alençon arrived. There was no public welcome, for though the fact of his visit was an open secret, it was unofficial, and no one was allowed to speak of it. The secrecy, and the private, clandestine meetings between Elizabeth and her boyish admirer added a strong erotic overtone to their encounter. No one recorded what went on at their first meeting, whether the duke played the ardent, aggressive wooer or let Elizabeth set the tone, her warmth and heartiness breaking through the brittle artificiality of her overadorned, overrouged person. They were prepared to find one another at least tolerable; in fact they took pleasure in each other's company, and ended by becoming infatuated.

"The queen is delighted with Alençon, and he with her," the Spanish ambassador Mendoza reported with chagrin. She was "much taken with his good parts," she found him pleasing in manner and, presumably, acceptable in appearance. In short, "she admired him more than any man." Simier was her Monkey, Alençon became her Frog. He presented her with a brooch commemorating his nickname—a golden frog sitting on a golden flower, with the duke's face painted on the frog's back.

To the men of affairs who were accustomed to keeping themselves informed about events at court the near-total privacy of the wooing couple was maddening. Not even the council members were involved. They "shut their eyes and avoided going to court," while letting it be known that they disapproved of the entire proceeding and were disturbed about it. The very fact that the queen was in sole control of her dealings with Alençon and Simier seemed to indicate the uniquely serious character of these marriage negotiations. "Many people who were wont to smile at it now see that appearances are all in favor of its taking place and believe it," Mendoza wrote.

Elizabeth was enjoying every minute of the intrigue, both for its own sake and because it was distinctly unsettling to her councilors. She used Alençon to tease her courtiers, entertaining them at a ball where the duke was hidden, conspicuously, behind a tapestry. As he looked on from his concealment she danced for him—more vigorously and more often than she usually did—and made secret signals to him that called even more attention to his presence.

The wooing, the game of secrecy and the erotic attentions of the personable young duke energized Elizabeth and drew her further and further along the path toward final commitment. She saw in Alençon the "Defender of Belgian Liberty Against the Tyranny of Spain"—the title the Netherlanders had bestowed on him. He was small but mighty; had he not declared, when warned that the French would never accept him as king if he married Elizabeth, that "he would look upon as his enemy any person who advised him to the contrary"?

She must marry, she had declared. Since she must, let it be this man. There were no more wry smiles, no more self-deprecating remarks. ("What a fine idea for an old woman like me to talk of marriage!" she had said only a few months earlier.) Let the closing stages of the negotiations begin.

Alençon's coming had been private, but his parting with Elizabeth was public, and "very tender." She gave him a handsome jewel, and in return he slipped onto her slender finger a sparkling diamond ring whose worth was estimated at ten thousand crowns. The afterglow of their courtship was vivid. For weeks after the duke's departure Elizabeth talked of his virtues, his "good qualities," even the goodness of her future mother-in-law Catherine de' Medici, whose character and policies she had always before despised.

The frog brooch shone from her bodice, the diamond ring gleamed on her finger. For her part, Elizabeth said, choosing her words with care, "she would not prevent his being her husband."

27

The King of France shall not advance his ships in
   English sand,
Nor shall his brother Francis have the ruling of the land:
We subjects true unto our queen the foreign yoke defy,
Whereto we plight our faithful hearts, our limbs, our lives
   and all,
Thereby to have our honour rise, or take our fatal fall.
Therefore, good Francis, rule at home, resist not our
   desire;
For here is nothing else for thee, but only sword and fire.

Alençon was barely off on his homeward journey—pausing at Dover to write his sweetheart Elizabeth four passionate love letters, and at Boulogne to write three more—when a pamphlet was published which denounced him as a scheming, debauched opportunist.

John Stubbs, a lawyer and country gentleman who spoke for the stern, uncompromising reformers known as Puritans, published *The Discovery of a Gaping Gulf Whereunto England is Like to Be Swallowed by Another French Marriage if the Lord Forbid Not the Bans by Letting Her Majesty See the Sin and Punishment Thereof.* The treatise was as infelicitous as its title, yet its plain-spoken arguments were forceful.

What sort of sordid lovemaking was this, that linked a scurvy young lecher to a gaunt old maid of forty-six? (The pamphlet's appearence coincided unflatteringly with the queen's birthday.) Everyone knows the true purpose of "these younger men that seek their elder matches," Stubbs insisted; they are always deceiving rogues, out to steal the woman's money —or in Elizabeth's case, her kingdom. She herself was a pitiable victim; he hated to see "our dear Queen Elizabeth (I shake to speak of it) led blindfold as a poor lamb to the slaughter."

And slaughter it would surely be, for a woman of her years to submit to the agonies and hazards of childbearing. True physicians would certainly confess, if they were candid, "how exceedingly dangerous they find it by their learning for her majesty to have her first child at these years, yea, how fearful the expectation of death is to mother and child: I fear to say what will be their answer." (Cecil, only a few months earlier, had fully satisfied himself from information provided by the queen's physicians and waiting women that she had "no impediment . . . nor lack of natural functions in those things that properly belong to the procreation of children." Her "aptness to have children" was to him beyond doubt; indeed the physicians predicted another six years of fertility, and added that the process would most likely prove rejuvenating.)

The thought of Elizabeth's fleshly union with the disease-ridden Frenchman was repellent to Stubbs. She who exercised a "princely priesthood in Christ Jesus" ought never to touch a man scabrous with venereal disease, "God's punishment on flesh and bones," a man whose immoral pleasures had brought on him the "inevitable plagues" that follow overripe lusts.

Above all the queen must not be deluded about Alençon's true motive: "to seduce our Eve, that she and we may lose this English Paradise." Just as the hated King Philip had once brought to England a swarm of greedy, slovenly Spaniards when he married Mary Tudor, so Alençon hoped to invade English shores with his train of "needy, spent Frenchmen, the scum of the king's court, which is the scum of all France which is the scum of Europe." They would attach themselves like horseleeches to the prosperous English, until they drew off all their wealth and all their strength, then, with Elizabeth under her husband's command, unable to resist, they would complete the conquest in earnest.

The *Gaping Gulf* was monarchical insult of a high order. Stubbs's condescension toward Elizabeth was as maddening as his language was offensive; he assaulted her sovereignty, her judgment, and her statecraft as well as her nubility—and the latter alone was enough to warrant severe punishment. She ordered all copies of the *Gaping Gulf* to be burned, and ordered Stubbs, his printer and his publisher to be hanged.

In reacting as strongly as she did Elizabeth was responding not merely to one outrageously offensive pamphlet, but to an outspoken and influential group of her subjects. By punishing Stubbs she meant to punish all Puritans, and to rebuke their insolence and self-righteous presumption. They were an affront to her rule, for they answered to no authority but the Bible, as they interpreted it, and they did not hesitate to serve as arbiters of morality to anyone and everyone around them, including the queen.

The church Elizabeth had established at the beginning of her reign was a church built on compromise and concessions, politically workable but spiritually insipid. It was inoffensive to the indifferent, but to men and women of fervid religion it was a stale and bland thing, its rituals a hollow if eloquent exercise, its clergy few and mediocre, its doctrine too remote to nourish warm belief.

Many Catholics never accepted it at all, though most of them conformed outwardly to its usages; many Protestants began early in the reign to form a Puritan "counter-church" within it, dedicated to the moral transformation of the entire society. Earnest Puritan ministers met weekly to devote themselves to Bible study and prayer, and strove to purge every vestige of sin from their lives. Inspired lay parishioners joined these weekly "prophesyings," and became consumed by a holy mission to uncover and correct wrongdoing in themselves and others.

The strength of the Puritan movement lay in its radical, uncompromising view of the human condition. Nothing short of absolute commitment to godliness must be tolerated; there must be no accommodation with Satan. Life was a battleground where good struggled with evil, and only those ironclad with righteousness and profoundly serious of purpose could come through the fray unscathed. "Satan is roaring like a lion, the world is going mad," one Puritan wrote to a likeminded friend in 1578. "Antichrist is resorting to every extreme, that he may with wolf-like ferocity devour the sheep of Christ."

Seen from this grim perspective, ordinary events took on the magnified proportions of omens and portents, signs of things to come. Ominous times called for preternatural vigilance. Therefore there must be, in every parish, men who spied out the sins of the erring and wrote them down for correction at the weekly meeting. "Notorious blasphemy, whoredom, drunkenness, railing against religion, scolds, ribalds and such like"—all must be reported, and the perpetrators admonished. But this was only the beginning. Prayers, attendance at endless, hair-raising sermons, long Sundays filled with heart-searching meditations, Bible study and church services: these were the rudiments of the godly life, to be lived in agonized expectation of the end of the world. Puritan children carried their spiritual burden in their names: Reformation, Tribulation, Dust, Deliverance. Flee-Sin kept company in the nursery with Praise-God and Be-Thankful; the baptismal records of the 1570s and 1580s are a theological lexicon of pious names, with Repent and Eschew Evil and Faint-Not frequent among them.[1]

The more frivolous Elizabethan pastimes drew disapproving Puritan frowns. Players were chased out of town, morris dancers forbidden to dance. Seasonal festivals were outlawed when it was found that the pageantry drew greater crowds than the sermons which competed with them. Everywhere the unregenerate complained of Puritan clergy "too sour in preaching away their pastime," everywhere the lighthearted music of pipe and drum was drowned out by the mighty sound of fervent hymns. The Puritans managed to exert far more influence and attract far more attention than their numbers warranted, perhaps because they felt, and looked, alien and out of place among ordinary, worldly men and women. Their faces were compressed into masks of self-denial and censure; they held themselves rigid, and walked with unswerving purpose. Unadorned, plainly dressed, their clothes were a mortification of the flesh and a warning to the gaudy.

Nowhere were they more conspicuous than at Elizabeth's court, where their dull black gowns stood out from among the flashing, gem-encrusted doublets of the other courtiers. The unruly, shoulder-length hair of the redeemed made a strong contrast to the well-tended coiffures of fashionable men, who "frounced their hair with curling irons" and wore long "love locks" tied with ribbons or silk favors. Exaggeration vied with exaggerated plainness, flamboyance with exaggerated sobriety. And the Puritan emerged the more memorable.

Courtly pastimes came in for particular condemnation. Drinking, gambling, dining on dainty foods and indulging illicit lust all brought forth God's wrath and the preachers'. Dancing the violent, exhausting Elizabethan dances, "with disordinate gestures, and with monstrous thumping of the feet, to pleasant sounds, to wanton songs, to dishonest verses," the Puritans decried as contrary to Scriptural law, while swearing was a dishonor to God and an abomination to the Christian community. The queen, who was unusually gifted at both dancing and swearing, was not spared her measure of censure. Her language was especially reproved.

"Your gracious majesty," a Puritan named Fuller told Elizabeth in a book he left for her to read, "in your anger hath used to swear sometime by that abominable idol the mass, and often and grievously by God, and by Christ." She swore, in fact, by Christ's wounds, his death, his head and other venerated organs, and by all the saints, forgetting entirely about the biblical injunctions against such blasphemy. And her subjects imitated her. "By your majesty's evil example and sufferance," Mr. Fuller wrote reproachfully, "the most part of your subjects and people of every degree, do commonly swear and blaspheme, to God's unspeakable dishonor, without any punishment."

This same tone of personal reproach was taken by Puritans in Parliament, where they formed a strong and formidable opposition group. Their strident voices were raised in long-winded and often keenly perceptive diatribes against the clerical hierarchy of bishops and archbishops—"a thing introduced into the church by Satan"—against the Book of Common Prayer—"an unperfect book, culled and picked out of that popish dung-hill the breviary and mass book"—and in particular against Elizabeth's headship of the church. On this issue, and on Elizabeth's general fallibility, the Puritans became increasingly vehement in the later 1570s. At Easter of 1579 a preacher addressing the lord mayor and magistrates of London railed at the queen so violently that he had to be seized and removed from his pulpit. In Parliament, the Puritan leader Peter Wentworth began a tirade against the queen's ineffectual efforts to reform her church. He went on and on, exceeding the bounds of his subject and attacking Elizabeth with unprecedented impropriety. "Certain it is," he shouted, "that none is without fault, no not our noble queen, since her majesty hath committed great faults, yea dangerous faults to herself." He would have said more, but the Commons members themselves, "out of a reverend regard for her majesty's honor, stopped Mr. Wentworth before he had fully finished."[2]

Wentworth was sent to the Tower, yet he and his coreligionists in Parliament were valuable to Elizabeth's government, for along with their fearless criticism went unfeigned admiration for their Judith, their Deborah, their treasured Gloriana. Elizabeth was a sinful, fallible woman whose political judgment failed her when it came to matters of conscience; she was also the Protestant figurehead of her Protestant realm, the ruler evidently chosen by God to lead her people. With their bluff forthrightness the Puritans were among the loudest in pledging to support their queen with their lives and goods, and in articulating that cult of the queen which grew throughout the 1570s. The eternal struggle between good and evil was in the late sixteenth century embodied in the struggle between England and her Catholic enemies, in the Puritan view; it was their clear duty to stand behind their queen in her hour of danger. There was a tenderness in their fervent protectiveness. "It makes my heart leap for joy to think we have such a jewel," one Commons member said of his sovereign, adding that "it makes my joints to tremble for fear, when I consider the loss of such a jewel."[3]

Much as she valued their patriotism and cherished their affection Elizabeth was wary of the Puritans, for their visionary fanaticism often led them astray. At Cambridge, where the movement had its intellectual stronghold, students disobeyed college rules en masse when they went against Puritan beliefs, and smashed windows and pulled down monuments in an upsurge of iconoclasm. Apoplectic Puritan preachers lost control of themselves, until their shrill invective came close to hysteria. Misguided individual believers were driven to acts of madness. One day, while the service was being performed in Elizabeth's chapel in the palace, there was a frightening interruption. A man ran up to the altar, beside himself with rage and shouting "heretical and shameful words." Before anyone could stop him he had thrown down the cross and candlesticks—the ornaments which to

Puritans represented Catholicism—and crushed them by stomping on them with his boots, cursing and swearing at the top of his lungs as he did so. He was crazed, but not with ordinary madness, and instead of being locked away as a simple madman he was brought before the royal council and questioned. Why had he done this thing? they asked him. He held up a Bible, an English translation of the New Testament. "That book had made him," he said. There was no need to say more.[4]

Vehement, irrational, socially disturbing, the Puritans were as much an abomination to Elizabeth as her swearing was to them. Their way was one of ultimatums and absolutes; hers was one of approximations and evasions. They were clearly "dangerous to kingly rule," and she meant to halt the rapid spread of their influence.

The weekly "prophesyings" must stop. She ordered her archbishop of Canterbury, Edmund Grindal, to command the bishops to end them. But Grindal demurred. The clergy needed revitalizing, he said; why should she want to suppress a movement that was so beneficial to spiritual life? He could not bring himself to do it. She could remove him from his see if she liked, but the prophesyings would go on. And while he was on the subject, Grindal went further. Elizabeth's attempts to govern the affairs of her clergy, he said, were dangerously reminiscent of the pope's attempts to control his priests. "Remember Madam that you are a mortal creature," Grindal warned, "and although ye are a mighty prince, yet remember that he which dwelleth in heaven is mightier." There was a strong Puritan flavor in the archbishop's final admonition. Let Elizabeth take heed that she not repeat the error of the biblical king Joash, who "when he was strengthened, his heart was lifted up to his destruction, and he regarded not the Lord."

The queen ignored her archbishop's righteous growlings and, angrily noting his disobedience, sent out her own command to the bishops that the prophesyings must cease. Grindal was suspended from exercising his jurisdiction, but there was no major scandal, for if she had reacted strongly every time one of her servants showed sympathy with the Puritans she would have had leisure for little else. Not only Grindal but Cecil and Leicester aided them and sided with them on occasion; Knollys and Walsingham were Puritans themselves, and in fact it was the inscrutable, sardonic principal secretary whom she suspected of being behind the publication of Stubbs's *Gaping Gulf.*

Francis Walsingham, who had been principal secretary for the last six years, presented Elizabeth with a unique problem. Of all her councilors, he was least likely to allow anything to dissuade him from speaking his mind, and she valued his candor. Yet when he did voice an opinion she had difficulty deciding whether it was the Puritan ideologue speaking or the cultured, sophisticated diplomat and man of the world. For Walsingham was a paradox, a stern, inflexible follower of the purer religion who was at the same time a well-rounded Renaissance courtier. He looked at life through a narrow apocalyptic lens, yet he was capable of delivering his judgment upon it in facile and cultivated French or Italian or German or Spanish. His superb education—he had studied with John Cheke at Cambridge—had been deepened by two years of travel and study on the continent, and he was as adroit and subtle an ambassador as Elizabeth possessed.

But if she relied on Walsingham to draw on his wide knowledge of foreign courts and tongues in advising her she had always to keep in mind that his views were those of a Marian exile, a grim enemy of what he saw as the Satanic forces of popery. He was at his best in seeking out devious plots at home and abroad, while when it came to the feints and tergiversations and half-truths of Elizabethan statecraft he was somewhat ill at ease, especially when to him the way of godliness seemed overwhelmingly clear.

Walsingham's perception of England's situation left no room for ambiguities. The Catholic powers of Europe, he believed, with overmighty Spain in the vanguard, would soon launch a military assault on Protestant England. They would be certain to involve Mary Stuart—who represented a grave danger to Elizabeth and should have been put to death years ago —and would rely heavily on seditious Catholic subjects within England ' accomplish their purpose. Since Armageddon must come, Walsingham argued, it would be best to go out armed to meet it. England must fight vigorously and wholeheartedly against Spain and the powers of darkness on every holy frontier—in the New World, in France where the Huguenots fought the Catholics, in the Netherlands where Dutch Calvinists struggled to oppose Spanish arms. An alliance with Alençon, heir to the Catholic throne of France, was from this point of view unthinkable; it was tantamount to an alliance with Satan. Elizabeth must not marry him, no matter what the cost to her personal happiness or to the continuity of the Tudor line.

That Walsingham was the most determined opponent of her proposed marriage Elizabeth felt sure. Yet much as she would have liked to discount his views as those of a blind and bigoted fanatic, she could not; she had too much respect for his intelligence and sophistication. To be sure, he had said, "I wish God's glory and next the queen's safety," putting religion before patriotism and personal loyalty, but in this he was typical rather than idiosyncratic. No, she would continue to rely on his prescience, his indefatigable energy—he worked harder, and for longer hours, than almost anyone else in her government—and on his dark vision of reality. But she would not tolerate his behindhand propaganda. If he had been to any degree responsible for the Stubbs pamphlet, then he must be made to feel her displeasure.

Elizabeth had said that Stubbs, his printer and his publisher would be hanged, but when it came to charging them there was a dispute over the illegality of what they had done. Was it really unlawful to raise arguments against a prospective bridegroom before the queen married him? The lawyers had not had to face this issue for a generation, not since Mary Tudor had been forced to provide protection to her hated husband Philip of Spain. Some found Elizabeth's vengefulness against Stubbs intolerable; one judge resigned rather than join in the verdict.

On the appointed day in early November the author and his publisher were brought to face their punishment—the printer was pardoned—on a scaffold built in the marketplace at Westminster. There was a large crowd, and people waited uneasily for the cruel spectacle they were to witness, stamping their feet and hugging their arms to keep warm. The weather was unseasonably cold; it would be a harsh winter. Already there was talk of the unusual frosts and storms, and of what they might foretell. Throughout September there had been extremely heavy rains and floods, stopping up the "crannies, pores and vents" in the ground and impeding the earth's customary "windy exhalations and vapors." A comet had been sighted in October, and this, combined with the climatic aberrations, was clearly a portent. It was not difficult to infer its meaning: it foretold a dark event —the death of a great personage, war or natural calamity, or perhaps an ill-omened marriage between the English queen and the French duke.

Stubbs and his publisher William Page had been sentenced to lose their right hands. Stubbs came forward, baring his wrist and placing his hand on a wooden block. His wit did not fail him. "Pray for me," he was heard to say, "now my calamity is at hand." The hand was "cut off with a cleaver, driven through the wrist by the force of a mallet," and the victim, reeling from the shock of the blow and from the sight of his own gushing blood, pulled off his hat with his sound hand and cried loudly, "God save the queen!" Then he fainted.

"The multitude standing about was deeply silent," wrote an eyewitness, "either out of an horror at this new and unwonted kind of punishment, or else out of commiseration towards the man, as being of an honest and unblameable repute, or else out of hatred of the marriage, which most men presaged would be the overthrow of religion." Or, he might have added, out of disbelief at Elizabeth's bloody spite.

Her behavior was indeed erratic as she struggled with her recalcitrant councilors, now commanding, now cajoling them, weeping with vexation one minute and the next squabbling angrily with whoever opposed her. What the Spanish ambassador Mendoza called "her little witcheries," which often brought her the outcome she desired, failed her utterly. Instead the men of the council played on her fears and anxieties. "Knowing her pusillanimity and fear of any adversity," they tried to alarm her with threats of invasion and treachery. How could she possibly think of marrying a Catholic, Knollys cried, when she had forbidden her Protestant subjects to do so? She glared at him; she had not forgotten his complicity in Leicester's marriage to his daughter, nor did she forget that he was a Puritan like Stubbs. "He might pay dearly for the zeal he was displaying in the cause of religion," she said. This was "a fine way to show his attachment to her, who might desire, like others, to have children."[5]

She exasperated Cecil, and quarreled so bitterly with Hatton that he had to stay out of her sight for a week. Walsingham, who spoke his mind as usual and told her flatly what his objections to the marriage were, she dismissed peremptorily. He was good for nothing, she said, but to be a protector of heretics, and she sent him away. Her moods grew more and more unstable, and for the three months following Alençon's departure in August she was crotchety, imperious and demanding. And when for all her moodiness and insistence she found her councilors as adamant as ever in their refusal to endorse her marriage, she became "extremely sad" and was "so cross and melancholy that it was noticed by everyone who approached her."

As for the beleaguered councilors themselves, it was all they could do to put up with their sovereign. Their ranks had thinned. By 1579 many of the names familiar from the first decade of the reign—Pembroke, Northampton, Arundel, Norfolk—had been struck off, with death or retirement or, in Norfolk's case, execution accounting for the absence. Others were aging, and growing querulous with age. Sussex, whose advice was still valuable, complained of being slighted by Elizabeth; he was treated like an old broom, he said resentfully, useful enough when needed but then thrown outside the door and left to rot.[6] Knollys was becoming prim, and strident on the subject of court morals. He wished aloud for "that realm where virtue is honored and vice is bridled," and had to be humored on moral issues. Hatton, now coming into his own as a suave and skillful reconciler of factions and mediator between opposing points of view, gave place to the efficient secretary Walsingham and to Cecil, who still anchored the council with his moderate opinions.

Cecil was getting on in years. He had his ailments, and wore his doublets "cut and voided in the back" for fear of the stone. For years his government work had kept him in "a continual agitation both of body and mind," and as he got older he took more and more pleasure in such undemanding pastimes as telling stories to his grandchildren around the supper table and "riding privately in his garden upon his little mule." Yet Elizabeth continued to rely on him. He was thoughtful, sober, wise. What he called his "dullness" she prized as balanced judgment, a quality she needed when her thoughts were, as she told him once, "in a labyrinth" and needed unraveling.

Leicester was in a kind of limbo, superficially reconciled to the queen yet not restored to anything like his former place in her regard. She had thought better of her initial reaction to the discovery of his marriage, when in cold anger she had ordered him imprisoned. He had spent a week in involuntary isolation, but it was given out that he had merely been shut away to take medicine, and after the week was over he left court to stay at one of his own houses.

Clearly he had forfeited a measure of that sentimental concern Elizabeth had always felt for him, and he feared to lose his power and perhaps his wealth besides. He wrote to Cecil, lamenting his loss of favor and predicting morosely that having sacrificed his youth and liberty to the queen he was about to give up "all his fortune" besides.[7] He felt wronged, a victim of his enemies' malice and a martyr to his own selfless devotion to his unappreciative sovereign. For twenty years he had "faithfully, carefully, and chargeably" served Elizabeth, and had been honorable in all his acts and intentions, he told Cecil. Yet now she had "grown into a very strange humor, all things considered," and her bitterness knew no bounds. He felt like a faithful dog being whipped by an ungrateful master; all in all, he had little to show for twenty years of service. Leicester's capacity for self-pity, which had always been great, was now at its height, and his counsel was not likely to be of much use to the queen or anyone else in the near future.

After weeks of frustrating and stormy deliberations Elizabeth broke through to action. On November 20 she ordered the marriage articles put into final form, and a few days later Simier, who had stayed on after his master Alençon's departure in order to conclude the diplomatic formalities, left England, taking the articles with him.

The thing was done. If the council members had meant to call Elizabeth's bluff, they found she had all along been sincere. She did not dare face the Commons. Parliament, scheduled to meet in October, was prorogued, and popular opposition continued unabated. Through the bitter winter months, when an "unlooked for great snow" froze the rivers and piled in high drifts along the roads and in the towns, Puritan preachers as usual exhorted their congregations to eschew evil and reject the French marriage. The queen swore she would have them whipped, but forbore. In tender letters to her sweetheart Francis the Constant she confessed to a growing concern about his religion. He was her very dear Frog, and she would rather spend the rest of her life with him than with any other prince in the entire world, she wrote, yet her subjects would have no king who professed the Catholic faith. Unless a way around this obstacle could be found, their infatuation might never come to fruition.

Was it the first sign of a rift? Observers in England and elsewhere watched the queen's behavior closely. One observer had never been convinced that all the lovemaking, all the negotiations had been anything but a ruse. "I have always looked upon the idea of a marriage between the queen and Alençon as a mere invention," King Philip wrote from Madrid to his ambassador Mendoza in England.[8] "I nevertheless believe they will continue to discuss it, and even may become reconciled for the purpose, but I believe that she herself is the person who will refuse."

28

Some gentler passions slide into my minde,
For I am softe, and made of melting snowe;
Or be more cruell, Love, and soe be kynd,
Let me, or flote, or sinke, be high or lowe;
Or let me live with some more sweete content;
Or dye, and soe forget what love ere meant.

In April of 1581, King Philip went to his coronation in Lisbon. He was dressed entirely in black, for he was in deep mourning for his wife, but his doublet was cut of rich brocade and his few ornaments were kingly. He stood solemnly before the altar at the coronation mass, decorous and reverent, as he was invested with the crown of Portugal and with Portuguese lands stretching across the known world from Brazil to the East Indies to the Persian Gulf. Spain had brought him the wealth and treasure of the New World; Portugal brought him added riches, riches enough to conquer what lands and kingdoms he did not already possess.

King Philip had reached the summit of his power. No European sovereign had ever ruled over so much land or commanded so much wealth. Yet beneath the carapace of royalty stood a shrunken figure with a gray beard and sad eyes. "They want to dress me in brocade, much against my will," he wrote later to his daughters, describing the coronation. Finery was alien to him; it went against his deep-seated asceticism. But he had resigned himself dutifully to the expectations of his new Portuguese subjects. "They tell me it is the custom here," he explained.

Philip came to his newfound might in a mood of infinite resignation. Adult life had brought him much more sorrow than joy, and he had only recently lost his most cherished companion, his fourth wife Anne of

Austria. Her tight-lipped self-denial had matched his—"she never leaves her rooms, and her court is like a nunnery," a visitor to the palace had noted —and since her death her bereaved husband had aged noticeably. He had now buried four wives in all, and two heirs to his throne as well. Few of Anne of Austria's many children had survived, and those that had the king treasured with a fiercely paternal concern tinged with fatalism. He clung to all the people he loved, yet stood ready to yield them up should God desire it, for he had learned to look on his private griefs as oblations offered by a humble soul to an inscrutable providence. It was the same with his triumphs. They were not his, but God's, and he accepted them reverently but with a devout indifference.

Contemplation of his worldly dominion brought Philip far less satisfaction than his enemies thought. Others were more quick than he to calculate the benefits of his Portuguese conquest: vast lands in Africa, the New World and the Far East, treasure so incomparably rich it made him wealthier than all the European sovereigns combined, twelve great Portuguese fighting galleons, with the dockyards to service them and the skilled mariners to sail and man them. Already the colossus of the known world, in 1580 Spain was becoming even more gigantic, and those who feared her might counted up her men and arms and warships and tried to imagine what was in the abstracted, austere old king's mind to do with them.

To the pope, to Catholic English exiles in Spain and elsewhere on the continent, the answer was clear. Philip should turn his immense fighting forces against "that guilty woman of England," Elizabeth. He who had conquered Portugal, through his great general Alva, in only a few weeks, he whose fleet had crushed the naval forces of Islam at the battle of Lepanto and was indisputable master of the world's oceans—save for an occasional loss to English pirates—should not hesitate to snuff out England. It was not even a question of calculating the military odds. The suppression of Protestant heresy in England was a holy obligation, part of a larger spiritual war between the forces of the church and the forces of the devil. With all the visionary impracticality of homeward-yearning emigrés the English conspirators dreamed of a grandiose "Enterprise," a voyage of conquest in which Spanish arms would unseat Elizabeth and put Mary Stuart on the throne to restore Catholicism.

But it was not the impractical English exiles alone who urged the Enterprise on Philip; it was the pope himself. Gregory XIII, the fiery, impatient leader of Catholic Christendom was inordinately devoted to the annihilation of the "wicked Jezebel" who ruled England, and as the 1580s opened he had begun to attack her on several fronts. He had sent military expeditions to Ireland, the last of which, landing in the summer of 1579, had succeeded in gaining a foothold in the country and defending it against the English for more than a year. He was sending missionaries into England to revive the Roman faith—and with it the determination to change the government. And he had persuaded himself, with a sophistry common in the later sixteenth century, that to condone the assassination of a ruler who was an enemy to the true faith was to act correctly in the sight of God. Through his secretary of state, the cardinal of Como, Gregory XIII had proclaimed that since Elizabeth was the cause of such injury to the church of Rome and was responsible for the loss of so many Catholic souls, anyone who "sent her out of the world" would not be committing any sin.

Philip was certainly in agreement, in principle, with the cause of destroying Protestant England. He had never approved of Elizabeth, either as a sister-in-law or a prospective wife or a fellow sovereign. He had promised the pope that he would rescue Mary Stuart from her captivity and help her to gain her rightful place as queen of England, and he had made, and honored, in part, a pledge of financial support for an invasion. Self-interest too urged action against Elizabeth, and a desire for revenge. For years she had been opposing him in the Netherlands, financing rebellion there and causing him untold trouble and expense. Her captains harassed his treasure fleets and stole his silver—which she then sent to pay the Dutch rebels— and her vigorous wooing of the heir to the French throne played havoc with the precarious peace between Hapsburg and Valois. And if he wanted revenge, it was now in his grasp, for with the combined fleets of Spain and Portugal at his disposal he could at last confront Elizabeth's small but powerful navy in an invasion launched from his own Portuguese coastal ports.

All this Philip knew, yet as he sat at his plain wooden desk, pen in hand, pondering the state of Christendom and praying for guidance, he often became distracted and slipped into a sort of pious reverie. His servants noted the vacant gaze and bemused expression, and worried over their master's health, for he was frequently melancholy and had difficulty taking pleasure in anything but his children and his great womblike palace.

The Escorial was an outward expression of Philip's wayward inner moods, a dark, cavernous edifice whose core was a monastery. The king's own small and sparely furnished rooms faced down onto an ornate, cathedral-like chapel; lying in his simple bed he could watch the mass being performed and hear the choir intone the ethereal anthems of his court composers. He bought masterworks of medieval art for the palace, and commissioned sumptuous new pieces by gifted craftsmen, but all in the service of faith, not beauty.

The Escorial was as much a gigantic reliquary as it was a Renaissance

319

palace; the king applied the same meticulous care to correspondence with relic merchants as he did to government dispatches, reading every word with squinting slowness and writing comments in the margins with a careful and deliberate hand. He was amassing an unusually complete collection of venerable bones and skulls. He found such objects of devotion consoling; like the countryside around the palace, they helped to "elevate his soul and sustain his pious meditations."

The Protestant English, indeed Protestants everywhere, imagined King Philip far differently than this—not as a nearsighted, bemused old man frowning over his relics, but as a dark conqueror brooding in his secret fortress. What they knew of him was ugly rumor: that he had murdered his son Don Carlos, that he was "more papal than the pope," and murderously bigoted, that his cruel soldiers in the New World had killed millions of Indians, chaining them like dogs and starving them to death or torturing them by searing their skin with hot bacon grease.

They heard, through the reports of spies or ambassadors abroad, how Philip presided in grim majesty over the mass burnings of heretics. In an open square at the center of Valladolid or Madrid a high wooden structure was erected where the king sat on his throne, surrounded by the terrifying inquisitors of the Holy Office. He spoke gravely to the crowd, swearing to defend the pure faith against all who would corrupt it, then gave the signal for the awful spectacle to begin.

The bells of the city's churches began to toll as the mounted escort appeared leading the procession of the condemned. They dragged along in their hundreds, wretched figures broken by miserable confinement and wasted from lack of food, wearing the black tunic of prisoners sentenced to execution. On their heads were high conical caps painted with grimacing devils and leaping red flames—images of hell—and on their wrists and ankles they wore chains, or the wounds and welts where chains had been.

As the king and the vast crowd looked on, a preacher delivered a long and chastening sermon. Afterward, with the spectators on their knees and the executioners heaping wood and straw around the heavy stakes to prepare them for the torches, the grand inquisitor intoned the final rites of absolution and condemnation. Then, stern and remote on his high throne, Philip watched as the victims were tied to the stakes and the fires were lit under them.

The horrors of the Inquisition were graphically described in Protestant propaganda, and the English had no difficulty envisioning the moans and screams of the dying, the acrid, smoke-filled air, the snorting and neighing of the guardsmen's horses and the solemn bells. It was said at Elizabeth's court that such open-air burnings were common in Spain. Early in his reign

Philip reportedly ordered two thousand people apprehended for heresy—
men, women and children—and though a great many of these escaped
death, hundreds had suffered.

The Spanish conquest of Portugal came at a time when Philip's fortunes
were rising elsewhere. The American silver mines that financed Spain's war
machine suddenly boosted their yield. The war in the Netherlands looked
more hopeful than it had for years, and the papal adventuring in Ireland
had shown how vulnerable England was in the north, and had tested her
military resources. The Irish rebellion had attracted substantial Scots support, forcing the government to reinforce the garrison at Berwick and to
muster five thousand fighting men.

If nothing else, the improving leverage of Spain in the European arena
caused increased uncertainty in London, where after two years the outrage
of the queen's French wooing had not died down. Elizabeth had counted
on the chaos in the Netherlands to continue to distract and drain Philip's
energies and treasury, but now a breakthrough seemed possible. And another safeguard had been removed, albeit a shaky and impermanent one.
Civil war had been resumed in France, making it unlikely that the French
would be able to intervene to block Philip's advance, should he decide to
launch the Enterprise of England after all.

Like it or not, the English would have to choose between the menace
of Spain and the distasteful prospect of a French prince as Elizabeth's
husband. As King Philip submitted to his coronation in Lisbon, Elizabeth
unfolded the most lavish and extensive entertainment yet offered to visitors
from abroad. Her guests were envoys of Francis the Constant, still her
long-suffering suitor and devoted slave—or so his letters said—weary of
waiting for his elusive bride-to-be but ever hopeful nonetheless.

There were more than five hundred in the French suite, including many
nobles of the highest rank, and one of Elizabeth's own houses was emptied
to lodge the grandest of them. London and Westminster were crowded
with servants and petty knights and liveried retainers, for in addition to the
hundreds of French servitors all the English peers had been ordered to
come to the capital and to bring their full trains with them. If there was
to be a minor invasion of Frenchmen it was just as well to have a counter-
vailing English force close at hand. Leicester, as conspicuous as ever among
the principal councilors, was amassing kinsmen and servants with frantic
urgency, eager to make the most ostentatious display possible to impress
the French.

A fortune had been spent on a newly built banqueting house at Whitehall. Forty tall, thick ship masts held up the canvas roof, which was painted
and gilded with clouds and stars and gleaming sunbeams. Three hundred

glass lanterns lit the huge open hall, illuminating fantastic ornaments bright with paint and shining with gilt. The entire structure was completed in three weeks, with two of the nearly four hundred workmen breaking their legs in the process, and at a cost not much less than two thousand pounds.

This expense, plus the cost of feeding and lodging the hundreds of guests and distributing some ten thousand pounds' worth of silver plate among the official marriage commissioners, should have severely strained the English treasury. But in fact it was Spanish, not English, silver that was being paid out, Spanish treasure captured by Francis Drake on his way around the world.

Only six months earlier Drake had sailed into Plymouth harbor, his ship leaking badly and riding low in the water, weighed down by her precious cargo. During his three-year voyage he had not only circumnavigated the globe but also shattered the myth of Spanish dominion of the seas. To contemporaries this, and not the unprecedented feat of seamanship and navigation, was Drake's principal achievement. He had sailed freely in waters swept by lofty Spanish galleons and heavy-laden treasure ships. He had cruised the coastal lanes, raiding shipping and stealing from the unprotected colonial ports, walking off with jewels and bars of silver. The treasure ship *Cacafuego* had fallen to him, its hold full of silver in such quantities as to be almost incalculable.

This treasure—the many tons of silver, the pearls and rubies and rare priceless emeralds, the chests of gold and plate—had been stored in the Tower, for though Drake's share in it made him a very wealthy man the profits of the voyage belonged to the shareholders: among others, Hatton, Leicester, Walsingham and the queen.

Elizabeth had backed Drake from the start, and many of her leading courtiers had helped to finance the voyage. John Dee, her astrologer and adviser who by the 1580s had become one of the most eminent mathematicians and scientists in Europe, may have been the moving spirit of the enterprise.[1] Dee's profound knowledge of cosmography and navigation— he was a close friend of the globe-maker Mercator, a teacher of explorers such as Frobisher and later of Humphrey Gilbert—was coupled with a kind of antiquarian imperialism. The fascination he and many other Elizabethans had with King Arthur was closely tied to their exploring venture, for Arthur was looked on as a conqueror whose claims to New World kingdoms Elizabeth inherited. Through Drake, Dee reasoned, England was destined to resurrect the Arthurian empire, and in time to overthrow the empire of Spain.

The Spanish ambassador Mendoza wrote sourly to King Philip that Elizabeth was cheerfully dipping into the stored Spanish treasure to pay for the French entertainments. Everything was being financed "from the bars brought by Drake," he wrote, adding that, as if to emphasize the insult to the Spanish, Elizabeth was going out of her way to show personal favor and approval to the adventurer. He was seen entering her apartments frequently, and envious rivals took note of how she seemed never to go out in public without speaking to him. Drake and the queen walked together often in her private garden, and Mendoza's informants told him that they were plotting to raise a new fleet to harass Spanish shipping.[2]

Of course, the ambassador had officially protested Drake's piracy and demanded the return of the treasure, but nothing came of it. Why should Elizabeth return valuables worth £160,000—which was a sum equal to what Parliament ordinarily granted her, and which represented some nine months' customary crown revenue—when it was so much easier to acquire the income this way than through cajoling Parliament or collecting crown debts? Besides, by keeping King Philip's money, she accomplished two further purposes. She interrupted his expected revenue, inconveniencing and hampering the operations of his government, and what was more important, she did grave harm to his credit. The bankers of Antwerp could no longer be certain that the treasure ships from Peru would reach Seville in safety; the English might seize them. Therefore they would have to raise the interest rates they charged the Spanish crown, to compensate for the added risk, and even then they would be reluctant to make new loans. Damaging Philip's credit meant damaging his ability to wage war, and she was more than willing to face Mendoza's indignation and Philip's frowning anger far away in the Escorial for the sake of forestalling war.

Elizabeth had Mendoza convinced, once the French arrived, that nothing could be less important to her than affairs of state. Leaving the marriage negotiations to her advisers, she concerned herself solely with "whether there were any new devices in the joust, or where a ball was to be held, or what beautiful women were to be at court," and so on. She wanted her ladies and gentlemen to look their handsomest; their finery should compare favorably with that of the tasteful and elegant French. The most practical way to ensure this was to lower the price of luxury cloth, and so she commanded all shopkeepers to sell their velvets and silks and fine metallic weaves at a one-quarter reduction.[3]

The queen's long-smoldering passion for Alençon seemed to leap again into flame with his envoys' coming. She sent her beloved a "wedding ring," and said loudly and fervently that "every hour's delay seemed like a thousand years" until she should have her Frog by her side again. Certainly the little duke was rising in the world's esteem, and no doubt in Elizabeth's. He had been offered, and accepted, sovereignty over the Netherlands by the Protestant rebels, and it looked, for the moment at least, as though he might take on the much larger sovereignty of France. His brother Henry III was said to be "much broken" in health, perhaps near death.

If this was true, the courtship took on a much more serious dimension. If Alençon was soon to become king of France, it was not only essential that his suit to Elizabeth be continued—it was essential that he be kept from looking elsewhere for a bride. As king of France the duke would inherit a Catholic throne, and might think better of taking a Protestant bride. Not long before, his mother Catherine had talked of matching him with a Spanish princess, a nightmare eventuality that must have complicated Elizabeth's attitude toward Alençon and clouded her own emotions.

The French were entertained with fairytale magnificence. There was feasting in the extravagant banqueting house, with Elizabeth presiding in a golden dress ornamented with flashing jewels. There were smaller banquets given by the councilors, more intimate but no less superb in the quality of the food and wines. And there was elaborate jousting in which the young paragons of the court, among them Philip Sidney, rode to their sport in fantastic costumes of glittering engraved armor and metallic lace and stiff feathers of gold and silver. The jousting was an allegory of seduction, in which the chaste Fortress of Beauty, representing the queen herself, was besieged by Desire, or the ardent wooer Alençon. The Fortress was assaulted with mock cannons shooting perfumed water and "sweet powder," and the attackers threw flowers against the walls, but no assault on the queen's purity, however metaphorical, could be allowed to succeed. Desire's siege was turned back, and he was instructed by one of the actors in the pageantry to "content himself with a favorable parley, and wait for grace by loyalty."

There were parleys in plenty, but none completely favorable. By early June a marriage treaty had been drafted, but the English had insisted that it contain a clause making it inoperable until Alençon himself returned to England to sign it.

The French envoys went home, overfed and disgruntled, and Elizabeth sent Walsingham to France to press for a military alliance as an alternative to marriage. She had learned that Henry III was not gravely ill after all; this gave her time to explore a fresh diplomatic initiative. But Walsingham, imposing though he was with his sober talk of the need for France and England to join together to oppose Spain before all opposition became futile, could not move the French king or his mother to commit themselves. They mistrusted Elizabeth, and insisted that she marry Alençon to prove her good faith. She would have to continue her intervention in the

Netherlands no matter what they did, after all; it was in England's interest to go on supporting the rebels' cause, with or without a strong ally.

The recent exchange of envoys had strained relations between the two courts, for King Henry was offended that after sending nearly six hundred of his courtiers to England he got only one, Walsingham, in return. (The secretary sent word to Elizabeth in cipher that the king had been overheard to threaten his life.) What was worse, Alençon had become completely unmanageable and haughty. He had an interview with Walsingham— whom he knew to be a long-standing opponent of Elizabeth's marriage— at La Fère in Picardy, with the dowager queen Catherine present. When Walsingham raised the all-important issue of popular dissatisfaction with the French marriage among the English, the duke nearly exploded. He refused to listen to anyone but Elizabeth herself on the subject of their marriage, and he refused, furthermore, to consider an alliance between Elizabeth and his brother to be in any way a political alternative to it. Had his mother not been there, Walsingham told Elizabeth, the little duke would have become far more vehement. As it was, he said flatly that, if an alliance were to be formed, he would personally break it—unless Elizabeth married him.[4]

Obviously Alençon had to be mollified, and Elizabeth immediately sent off a loving letter in which she expressed her affection "most sweetly" and tried to soothe her admirer's wounded vanity. She also sent him the sum of thirty thousand pounds, "brought out from the Tower, in gold, secretly at night by water," with which to mount a new campaign, and he lost no time in putting the money to use. Levying fresh troops he seized Cambrai from the Spanish, leaving the mighty commander Parma disconcerted and, for the moment, in retreat.

Fresh from this victory Alençon sailed for England, arriving at the end of October, out of money but in buoyant spirits. For three years he had pursued the elusive queen of England, convinced of her passion for him and convinced, too, that in time her passion would overcome her political caution. It could no longer be said that he lacked either maturity or manliness; he had proven himself, he was the conqueror of Cambrai. And he was impatient to put an end to Elizabeth's coyness and to demand that she demonstrate the sincerity of her love by pledging herself to become his wife. After all this time his honor was at stake, and his military future as well, for he relied almost entirely on English gold to finance his warmaking.

Soon after his arrival he wrote confidently to his brother and mother, his letter full of hopes. Elizabeth had come privately to meet him when he disembarked, "in order that he might catch sight of her before he arrived," and this romantic meeting made him more optimistic than ever. They spent the better part of each day together, either alone or out of earshot of the councilors and the queen's women, and in private, Mendoza believed, she "pledged herself to him to his heart's content, and as much as any woman could to a man." To everyone's surprise Leicester was not only affable to the duke but ostentatiously servile, waiting on him as he dined and remarking "that there seemed to be no other way for the queen to secure the tranquillity of England but to marry Alençon."

Walsingham too abandoned his Puritan distaste for the queen's Frog, nodding sagely in agreement with Leicester and complimenting Alençon on his abilities and intelligence. "His only fault," the secretary said archly, in the queen's hearing, "was his ugly face."

"Well, you knave!" she blurted out, "why have you so often spoken ill of him? You veer round like a weathercock!"[5]

After ten days of apparent bliss and high spirits Alençon was unnerved when Elizabeth suggested that he take another thirty thousand pounds and return to Flanders. He balked. He would not leave England—indeed he would not set foot outside his apartments in the palace—until she gave an unequivocal response to his proposal of marriage.

Suddenly on November 22 the response came, and in a far more dramatic form than anyone had expected.

It was midmorning, and Elizabeth and Alençon were walking together down a long gallery in the palace. Leicester and Walsingham were nearby —Cecil was in bed suffering from gout—and were keeping watch, from a distance, on the royal pair. By now they had become a familiar sight, she tall and spare, he short and small, she smiling and joking in her broad French, he returning her witticisms with flowery compliments and gallantry. Their exchanges must have been more pointed than usual that morning, since on the previous day the duke and his followers had seemed quite disenchanted with the vacillating English, and discontented to the point of anger with the queen's failure to make up her mind to the marriage.

The French ambassador came into the gallery and spoke to Elizabeth. He was on the point of writing to King Henry, he said, and needed to hear from Elizabeth herself precisely what her intentions were. Her face brightened. Impulsively she turned to her little companion and cried out, "You may write this to the king: that the duke of Alençon shall be my husband!"

Then, to the astonishment of Leicester and Walsingham, she took off one of her rings and gave it to Alençon, and kissed him on the mouth. The meaning of the ritual was clear to everyone present. It was the ritual of marriage by ring and pledge, the time-honored ceremony of union in medieval Europe going back centuries to a time when men and women married without the presence of a priest, merely by promising themselves to one another.

Delighted and amazed, Alençon took the ring and, pulling off one of his own, handed it to Elizabeth. With this they had fulfilled the prescribed formalities of marriage according to the old custom. They were man and wife.

Quickly the queen summoned all the courtiers in the presence chamber into the gallery and repeated her verbal pledge to the duke "in a loud voice." Their excitement at the announcement must have been very great, not only because of its spontaneity—a rare phenomenon at a soporifically overceremonialized court—but because it was a romantic and even an erotic gesture. Traditionally, couples pledged to one another by promise began to sleep together, even if they planned to repeat their vows later before a priest.

This thought may have been behind Leicester's indignant reaction to the dramatic scene in the gallery. His courtly attentions to the duke, which had been so marked before the exchange of rings took place, ceased abruptly, and when he confronted Elizabeth about what she had done a few days afterward he asked her, rather rudely, "whether she was a maid or a woman." Was she sleeping with the man she had informally made her husband?

No, she was still a maid, she told him, adding that she was likely to remain a maid since the condition under which she had given Alençon her pledge—that King Henry would agree to her new extravagant demands in the marriage bargaining—was not likely to be fulfilled. The question was of course a rhetorical one. Like the queen's impetuous embracing of Alençon, Leicester's outburst was largely for show, though in both cases a strong undertone of heartfelt sentiment went into the display. Nothing that had happened between them in the course of their lifelong infatuation—certainly not Leicester's marriage—had weakened his sharply proprietary affection for Elizabeth, and he was jealous of the strutting young duke.

Hatton, ever the queen's faithful, moonstruck suitor, was inconsolable to think he had lost his love—and to a man who would bring her only ruin. Throughout Alençon's courtship Hatton had continued his own, offering thoughtful advice, eloquently expressed, sending charming letters ("I love yourself. I cannot lack you," he wrote disarmingly), giving gifts of clothes and jewels and purses of coins. He was solicitous of her health, and in plague season sent her a ring which "had the gift of expelling infectious airs." It was to be worn, he explained, "betwixt her sweet breasts, the chaste nest of pure constancy."

It was because he cherished the queen so dearly that he hated to see her take the foolhardy step of making an unpopular marriage. When he saw her pledge herself to Alençon he took the scene so much to heart that he spoke to her "with great boldness and many tears" about it. She could only bring trouble to England, he said, and by going so forcefully against her subjects' wishes she was provoking rebellion—and quite possibly deposition and even death. Perhaps because Hatton was so visibly moved, she listened to what he had to say with uncharacteristic mildness. Or, more likely, she restrained herself from interrupting him because she saw now that the thing he feared would never really happen.

The longer Alençon stayed in England the more obvious it became that marriage to him was neither the political expedient Elizabeth clutched at in moments of fear nor the sentimental epiphany she dreamed of. The end of the year found her no closer to formal alliance with Henry III than before, partly, to be sure, because she had begun to press for such impossible conditions as the return of Calais and a virtual declaration of war against Spain. At the same time she was discovering how ugly and truculent her Frog could become when thwarted—a sobering foretaste of what married life with him might be like.

His veneer of lustful gallantry wore thin, and revealed the money-hungry adventurer beneath. He demanded larger and larger payments, thirty thousand pounds, fifty, a hundred. He demanded war subsidies, guarantees of future sums, finally a huge monthly pension. She owed him this, he said, his tone acid with spite. She had toyed with his affections and given him nothing in return. Everyone was bound to laugh at him, and it was her fault. In public the duke kept up his sugary speeches, as she did her warmth and rapt attention to them, but in private the honeyed words dissolved into bullying and blackmail.

And the hypocrisy of his "burning desire" for her was only too obvious. Even as he swooned, or appeared to swoon, with passion and to yearn inconsolably for "the sweet consummation that he desired more than his life," he was finding abundant consolation in the arms of the London whores, some of whom made off with most of the official papers in his lodgings and sold them to the English diplomats.

And what of the quaint, old-fashioned pledge of marriage? Alençon had taken it as seriously as everyone else—except possibly the bride—and had written to his brother immediately to say that he was wedded to Elizabeth as surely as he, King Henry, was wedded to his wife the queen. How could he have written that? Elizabeth asked Sussex. Surely, knowing her intention as he did, he must have realized that the pledge was conditional on completion of the French alliance.

"No, no, madam, you are mine," Alençon cried out in exasperation as he saw everything the English had led him to expect, including a fortune in English pounds, slipping away. "You are mine, as I can prove by letters and words you have written to me, confirmed by the gift of the ring, of which I have sent intelligence to the king my brother, my mother, and the princes of France."[6] He had witnesses, he had documents, he had everything but the ultimate means to make Elizabeth do what he wanted.

"If I cannot get you for my wife by fair means and affection I must do so by force, for I will not leave this country without you." Whatever he may have meant by that—elopement, kidnapping, or more likely simply blackmail—the threat crushed what remained of the romance.

"I grieve, and dare not show my discontent," Elizabeth wrote, beginning a poem on the occasion of Alençon's departure. "I love, and yet am forced to seem to hate." She was two selves, of two minds, not so much about this surly, insistent little man she had loved but about love itself. Though there was a public pretense that Alençon's stay abroad would be brief, and that he would soon return to England to resume his ever-hopeful vigil at the shrine of his beloved, the truth was evident: he was Elizabeth's last hope for marriage, and he was leaving for good.

With him went her long flirtation with the dream of domesticity, her longing to have what remained of her beauty fully, enduringly appreciated by a lover who was also a husband. Whatever his faults, and she had only begun to uncover them, Alençon had brought out in her the sort of cozy intimacy she had never enjoyed with anyone else except Leicester. She had been able to idle away time with him, shut up happily in a small room hour after hour. She had visited him in bed, carrying little cups of soup to him and possibly feeding him herself. As his wife she might have been able to cheat time, to recover through his youthfulness the lost decades of her spinsterhood.

That Elizabeth was at all times hardheaded about the political dimension of her love affair takes nothing away from the poignancy of her loss as Alençon sailed away out of sight in February of 1582. Not that she really wanted him back, for she had had terrible trouble getting rid of him, but once he was really gone her profound disappointment spent itself in a fury of irritability. She scolded her women rudely, no doubt adding slaps and body blows to the insults she shouted at them. She swore mightily and articulately. She greeted everyone who entered the privy chamber with exceeding ill temper, and had a phenomenal battle with Leicester, accusing him of treason and likening him to his faithless, luckless father and grandfather.

Her wound was very deep, but not fatal. She saw the absurdity as well as the poignancy of her last love, and she saw, too, the way to turn it to her advantage in her subjects' eyes.

Having worried the English for years about her desire for Alençon, she soothed and relieved them with her ultimate decision to send him away. Her rhetoric, as usual, did not fail her.

"O what may they think of me," she had thundered on the eve of Alençon's arrival, "that for any glory of my own would procure the ruin of my land!" Let none think that, like some foolish girl, she had considered even for a moment putting her own personal interests before the well-being of England. No marriage could possibly mean more to her than her people's love. "My mortal foe can no ways wish me a greater loss than England's hate," she announced with solemnity, "neither should death be less welcome unto me than such mishap betide me."[7]

But in her poetry she struck a different tone. "I am and am not; I freeze, and yet am burned," she wrote, "Since from myself, my other self I turned." She was forty-eight, and her life had indeed reached a new turning. At an age when most women were ending their fruitful years, Elizabeth Tudor's greatest challenge was just beginning.

29

With brinish teares, with sobbing sighes,
I, Englande, plunge in paine,
To see and heare such secret sectes
amongst my people raine.

A few months before Alençon left England, three Roman Catholic priests were brought out from their imprisonment in the Tower and taken to Tyburn to be hanged. They were tied to a low wooden sled which sank into the mud under their weight. Horses dragged the sled through the streets to the place of execution, through Cheapside and Holborn and on westward along the Strand. Crowds gathered to watch the holy men pass, their gaunt faces shining and smiling despite the suffering to come. A priest who saw them go by wrote later that, as they neared the scaffold, the condemned men actually broke into laughter. "But they laugh!" the onlookers were heard to say. "They don't care for death!"

The joyous fortitude of the Jesuit Edmund Campion, Father Alexander Bryant and Father Ralph Sherwin came as no surprise to the hundreds who gathered to witness their final agony, for already there was talk of miracles. At Campion's trial, with his condemnation a foregone conclusion, the judge had taken off his glove and found his hand all bloody, though he had felt no wound. Bryant, during his wretched Tower imprisonment, had begun to receive divine revelations. His ecstatic visions had fortified him, it was said, as he lay far below ground in a black and airless pit, his body useless from repeated torture and his spirit tested sorely as he was denied sleep and food. Clearly all three men had withstood pain so intense and so interminable that the life had been all but bled out of their rag-shrouded bodies, yet, miraculously, they lived on.

They lived—so that they might die in this way, their sacrifice a potent instrument of conversion. The Catholics in the huge crowd drew nearer to the scaffold, clutching jars and mugs and other vessels in which to catch a few drops of the blood of these holy martyrs when the dismemberment and disemboweling began. A lucky few would be able to snatch bits of hair or torn flesh or scraps of clothing, but this was dangerous, as rank on rank of armed footmen stood by and mounted guards as well. To show any sympathy for the sufferers, to shout out encouragement to them, or utter prayers, or to try to touch them or their remains was to be tainted with their treason, and so to risk death.

For officially these were traitors, and nothing else. That they were Catholic priests was, if not exactly incidental to their treason, extrinsic to it. Francis Knollys and several other royal servants announced this from the scaffold before the executions began, assuring the crowd in stern language that the spectacle they were about to see had nothing to do with religion; it was to be the just punishment of convicted traitors, enemies to the queen.

Yet to Catholics the radiant faces of the three men, pale and emaciated yet lit with fervor, belied Knollys' words, as did Campion's scaffold speech. "If you esteem my religion treason," he told them, "then am I guilty; as for other treason, I never committed any, God is my judge." His voice was reasonable, his words both cogent and persuasive. Some of those who heard him knew that his interrogation in the Tower had been interrupted several times so that he could take part in public disputations, for he was learned and well-spoken. Then he had been denounced as "an unnatural man to his country, degenerate for an Englishman, an apostate in religion, a fugitive from the realm, unloyal to his prince." Then, as now, he had answered the accusation in the moderate, logical fashion that had made him an outstanding scholar at Oxford and won him the personal patronage of the queen. He had discriminated carefully between his faith and his political conscience, between his priestly work—the conversion of souls—and the darker labors of political subversion, "from which he did gladly restrain and sequester his thoughts." His loyalty to Elizabeth was absolute. He wished her, he told the crowd, "a long quiet reign with all prosperity." It was noted as Campion spoke that he had no fingernails; iron spikes had been driven up under his nails until they were torn off.

Campion, Sherwin and Bryant were not the first priests to be sentenced to death in Elizabeth's reign, but their executions had far-reaching significance. For one thing, they came at a time—early in December of 1581— when it was generally believed that the queen was about to marry the

Catholic Frenchman Alençon, and when in consequence there was heightened ill feeling between the hopeful Catholics and the outraged, outspoken Protestants, especially the Puritans.

More important, they coincided with a sudden resurgence of the Catholic faith in England, as astonishing in its swiftness as in its scope.

In the late 1570s English Catholicism awoke, roused from within in response to the unaccountable rhythms of popular piety and from without by a new generation of fiery young priests schooled for martyrdom in the seminaries of Douai and Rome.

That the immemorial religion of the English should revitalize itself after two generations of dormancy—with brief irruptions of vitality during Mary's reign and in the Northern Rebellion of 1569—was perhaps to be expected. Among the common people Protestantism was still the "new religion," though its newness had in fact worn off in the reign of Henry VIII. A surprisingly large number of elderly priests, some of whom had been quietly, devoutly performing masses without interruption since King Henry's days, kept alive the memory of the old Catholic realm, while the legal profession, the peerage, even to an extent the royal court were all strongholds of the ancient faith. It was impossible for even the most scrupulous Puritans to avoid contacts with Catholics, for they were everywhere—in the law courts, where they occasionally defended the archbishop of Canterbury and the queen, at the social gatherings of the aristocracy, serving as officers in noble and ecclesiastical households, in the House of Lords and, of course, crowding the jails and grinning from the gibbets.[1] Of the sixty peers in 1580, twenty were Catholic. Of the others, Leicester and his brother aided Catholics, Cecil had Catholic relatives (as did Walsingham, who boasted of his peerless Protestant son-in-law Philip Sidney but said little of his Catholic son-in-law the earl of Clanricarde). Given the close-knit Tudor networks of kinship and alliance, confessional enmity was imperfectly sustained. Protestant courtiers gave advance warning of raids and investigations to their Catholic intimates, and the queen herself occasionally lent her protection to her Catholic friends.

There were Catholics everywhere, and in the late 1570s and on into the 1580s their numbers grew rapidly, and their attitude changed from one of tacit complicity in the rituals of established Protestantism to militant refusal to conform. They became recusants—subjects of the queen who would not follow the usages of the queen's church. They stayed away from the service, they did not take communion, they did not listen to the sermons. In secret, they heard mass instead.

They gathered wherever there was a priest to sing mass, in the countryside where several hundred might come together in the open air, in caves or barns or the lofts of houses, in the jails, in the capital where they ran great risks and where many were seized while worshiping and taken to prison. With them were seized the articles of worship that nourished their devotion—"their superstitious stuff," the queen's agents called these objects scornfully, "their abominable relics, their vile books." Shiploads of religious pictures, manuscripts, rosaries and images blessed by the pope were confiscated at English ports, with the bones and garments of the saints among the contraband.

And there were new relics to bolster the faith and confirm the recusancy of believers: the remains of English martyrs whose growth in numbers kept pace with the increasing population of nonconforming Catholics.

A priest was executed in July of 1580, and to the many recusants who came to see him die his suffering was particularly edifying. His conversion, or "reconciliation," to the Catholic church three years earlier had been a triumph for the resurgent faith, for until then he had been a Protestant minister. Following his conversion he had gone to Douai to study, had become a priest, and then had decided to return to England to work among the imprisoned Catholics. In the midst of this spiritual labor he had been seized and interrogated, his captivity made nearly intolerable by filth and hunger and vermin; finally he had been brought to his execution, dying with "invincible constancy and fortitude, greatly to the edification of the Catholics," a coreligionist wrote, "and the surprise of the heretics."

So eager were the devout onlookers to participate in the holy death that they caught up every drop of the dead man's blood, wiping it from the boards on which the body was laid and scooping it out of the earth beneath the scaffold. Every trace of the martyr was spied out and preserved, either by believers impelled by devotion or by opportunists eager for profit. "Two days after his martyrdom," it was noted, "there was not a bit of ground left which had been touched by his blood, it having been taken by the faithful, who also offered large sums of money for his garments."[2]

It was this voracious, all-consuming piety that alarmed the queen and her councilors most, for behind it was an ominous fatalism, a commitment to death as well as to religious truth. Seminarists studying for the priesthood at the Douai college—a vital agency of the Catholic renaissance which by 1580 had sent a hundred priests to England—lived and worked in expectation of martyrdom; the college walls were painted with graphic depictions of torture chambers and grisly torments, beatific faces on rent bodies. Ecstasy through carnage: that, in crude terms, was the watchword of the priestly vanguard, and if to the individual this meant simply self-sacrifice in imitation of the crucified Christ, to the queen and her government it was more reminiscent of the St. Bartholomew's Day Massacre than of the life of Jesus.

To care so little for life, to glory in self-destruction, made the priests and the lay Catholics to whom they ministered natural candidates for extremism, or so royal officials presumed. The pope had exonerated in advance anyone who assassinated Elizabeth, and assassination was already becoming the supreme political weapon of the enemies of Protestantism. Even if this fearsome possibility could be forestalled, an armed rising threatened, more widespread and far more harmful than the Northern Rebellion, with its adherents stiffened by uncompromising leadership and made ruthless by their resolute faith.

Where there was one staunch Catholic in 1559, now there are ten, Cecil confided glumly to a colleague. Their fortitude seemed all but unbreakable —though some did, of course, break, and many died. Pain and delirium drove a few to reveal what they knew of the underground church, and even to offer to serve as spies for the government. But to the treasurer these turncoats were highly exceptional, for his informants told him of fresh conversions in staggeringly large numbers. A single priest could reconcile as many as eighty former Protestants a day to Catholicism, and there were many priests at work. The scale of the religious transformation "almost exceeded belief." It had to be stopped, and immediately.

Urgent and thoroughgoing enforcement of the laws against recusancy reached new heights in the summer of 1580. Royal agents spread ou' through the countryside, raiding houses and buildings suspected to be centers of recusancy, hunting down priests, arresting any Catholics reported to be staying away from the Protestant services and subjecting them to a variety of punishments. At the very least, they were fined—twenty pounds for every month of absence from church, two hundred pounds for a year's absence—and ordered to resume attendance or risk more severe retaliation. "Constant" recusants were interned in castles or other fortified places, their goods forfeit to the government unless they agreed to conform. During August the council stepped up its campaign, sending new orders to every county demanding heightened activity on the part of local officials and notifying all Catholics who had been released from prison on bail to return at once.

"The persecution is now very grave," a contemporary wrote. "New prisons are appointed in every county, as the old ones are full of recusants." Thousands were taken, many of them gentlemen and others of substance; thousands more waited fearfully for their lives to be disrupted, perhaps destroyed, by the sudden appearance of grim-faced officers at their gates.

There were other tactics, counter-evangelism being the most obvious. Sermons of recantation by former Catholics were a frequent occurrence in London, though it is questionable whether any staunch Catholics heeded them. Aylmer, bishop of London, tried to persuade Cecil to finance a plan to send committed, rigorous Puritans into Catholic regions—Lancashire, Staffordshire, Shropshire "and such other like barbarous countries"—to reconvert them, but the idea came to nothing.[3] By the time Campion and his companions arrived in England in the summer of 1580 the jails were full of recusants, and many of those who had so far escaped capture were living hunted lives.

The odyssey of Campion and his Jesuit partner Robert Persons lasted only a year, but during those few months of eventful sojourning much was accomplished. Guided by cohorts of eager young Catholic gentlemen they traveled throughout the country, staying in the houses of recusants and always moving on before they could be discovered by the authorities. They preached, heard confessions, celebrated masses and reconciled men and women to the church, welcomed wherever they went by great numbers of the devout. They became famous, both because the royal agents searched high and low for them and because Campion's written explanation of his mission—"Campion's Brag," as his enemies called it—reached a wide audience.

The journeys of the two Jesuits put new heart into an already revitalized Catholicism. Absolutely confident of the ultimate success of the Jesuit Order, Campion looked forward to the probability of his own execution with joyous humility: "We have made a league," he wrote, "cheerfully to carry the cross you shall lay upon us, and never to despair your recovery, while we have a man left to enjoy your Tyburn, or to be racked with your torments, or consumed with your prisons." Many were caught up in this spirit of hope and of fearlessness; Persons recorded how the believers he encountered showed a "wonderful fortitude of mind and readiness to suffer any travail on account of religion," and heard mass with such "sighs and frequent sobs" that he was moved to tears.

Fear of imminent discovery intensified the mood. At any moment, the Jesuits and their hosts knew, royal agents might burst in and arrest them, led by an informer or a heavily bribed servant. "Sometimes, when we are sitting merrily at table," Persons wrote, "there comes an insistent rapping at the door we associate with the police. We all start up and listen, hearts beating, like deer who hear the hunters halloo." There was no time for flight, only for prayer. "Not a word is spoken, not a sound is heard, till the servant comes in to say what it is. If it is nothing, we laugh—all the more merrily because of our fright."[4]

For Campion the tension ended in capture in June, 1581. (Persons escaped to the continent; he was to remain a moving spirit behind plots against Elizabeth.) After months of questioning and torture he came, with the other two priests, to his execution in December.

Hard rain had turned the earth to deep mud around the scaffold by the time the condemned men were in position and the queen's councilors had harangued the crowd into uneasy silence. The onlookers stood huddled together in the cold and wet, miserable yet watchful, waiting to be caught up in a transcendent drama. Campion addressed them, and Sherwin, and the young visionary Bryant, who "with his naturally innocent and angelic face" moved his hearers by his expression of profound joy.

The three stood in wheeled carts beneath the gallows, and the ropes were put around their necks. It was their last moment of life; they prayed, and the crowd prayed with them. Then the carts were jerked out from under their feet. The weight of their bodies pulled the nooses tight, breaking their necks instantly. But Bryant's noose had been carelessly placed, so that when his cart was pulled away he was left hanging by his chin, in great pain, but still living.

Almost at once the bodies were cut down so that the methodical butchery of disemboweling and dismembering—routine for the corpses of traitors—could begin. But Bryant, resisting the executioners, "made great efforts to rise," and continued to cling to life "in full consciousness" as his abdomen was cut open and its organs disgorged. The spectators pressed closer, awed, horrified, amazed at the young priest's unnatural fortitude. This was the miracle they had come to see, a dying man, his body carried beyond bodily limits, defying death.

"Ere the limbs were severed," an eyewitness wrote, "evidently in the extremity of agony," Bryant "raised his mangled body and stood upright on his feet to the great astonishment of all beholders."[5]

All the eviscerated corpses were beheaded, then cut in four sections and displayed prominently in places where Londoners gathered. The ghoulish spectacle was meant to be a chilling warning against treason, but it was a clear invitation to relic-collecting as well. Part of Campion's quartered body was placed on one of the City gates. Someone cut off a finger, and the incident set off "great efforts" in the royal council to investigate and locate the thief. For these executions were set apart from all previous executions of priests and lay Catholics. Within days of the event stories of the queen's cruelty and bigotry were circulating, and Catholic propagandists in England and elsewhere were making the names of the martyrs widely known.

Pamphlets, libels, broadsheets denouncing Queen Elizabeth and the merciless persecutors who served her appeared in great numbers. One book told of "Mr. Norton the Rackmaster," who was in charge of the dreaded oak frame on which prisoners, tied down at the wrists and ankles, were stretched to the bursting point. Norton was said to have boasted that he racked Bryant until he was "one foot longer than ever God made him," and to have kept the wretched Campion stretched on the frame for the whole of one endless night. (Norton, himself tortured by various "domestic afflictions," was much distressed by his adverse celebrity and wrote in his own defense that he acted "only in pursuance of orders and in conjunction with others."[6])

The ghosts of the dead priests proved to be more pernicious than all their sermons and masses when they were alive. The report of their martyrdom was spread by word of mouth and in print, and this, combined with the attacks on the queen and government, led to more conversions to Catholicism. To counteract the slander official declarations of policy toward recusants were issued, in which Elizabeth's mercy and clemency were stressed along with her habit of pardoning at least some of those condemned to execution. But such statements failed to lessen the impact of the recent deaths, especially at foreign courts. "There be men in the world which drink blood as easily as beasts do water," wrote one European Jesuit of the English councilors. And at their head, he added, was the wicked, bloodthirsty English queen.

The queen, just then, was troubled by a pain in her hip, and this, plus upsetting news of a military reverse for the rebel forces and the English troops supporting them in Flanders, made her unusually bad tempered when the Spanish ambassador Mendoza arrived for an audience.[7] He was led into the privy chamber at Richmond, and found her sitting under her canopy of estate, with two councilors and three ladies in attendance.

It was Elizabeth's custom, when receiving ambassadors, to step down from the raised dais beneath the canopy and, extending her hand to be kissed, to greet them formally in Italian. *"Sia il ben venuto, signor ambasciatore,"* she would say gravely, then return to her place. Now when Mendoza entered, however, she was pointedly rude, disregarding his entrance entirely and taking no notice as he approached her. When she did speak it was not to greet him but to complain of the pain that was annoying her and to add that it had been bothering her for a long time.

Though irritated and fatigued himself, Mendoza took the queen as he found her, sweeping off his hat with a respectful gesture and replying that, though she had delayed granting him an audience for a very long time—unconscionably long, he was thinking—he would gladly have waited longer rather than vex her with business while she was in pain. His words were remarkably gracious, under the circumstances; having been put off day after day, he was abruptly told at noon this day that the queen would see him in two hours. He was ten miles from the palace at the time, but rode there as fast as possible, only to be icily informed by three of the tall gentlemen pensioners and then by the haughty lord chamberlain, once he arrived, that he was very late.

Mendoza stood, hat in hand, waiting for Elizabeth to acknowledge his sentiment with thanks as she usually did. Instead she remained silent, holding her hip.

"How about the letter which you have from his majesty?" she asked at length.

Mendoza gave her a letter from Philip II, which angered her as she read it with its accusations of English belligerence and provocation. With "much hectoring and vociferation," the queen said roundly that, had she genuinely wanted to stir up trouble, it would have taken King Philip's fleets far off their courses to prevent her.

Boastful talk was one thing, action another, Mendoza replied, adding without emphasis that the fleets of Spain were so well prepared that they could triumph over any enemy, no matter how large and powerful. He went on to list the mounting irritations that were exacerbating England's conflict with Spain: the money Elizabeth was giving Alençon to enable him to fight the Spanish in the Low Countries, the English pirates plundering Spanish ships, the vast treasure seized by Drake and never returned. How could she have done more than this, the ambassador asked plainly, without openly declaring war on King Philip?

Without a moment's hesitation Elizabeth snapped back "that she neither knew nor understood anything" about any of these things.

But he himself had been telling her about them for three and a half years, Mendoza insisted. Perhaps "it would be necessary to see whether cannons would not make her hear them better."

If he thought to frighten her, Elizabeth said, stiffening in her seat, she would "put him into a place where he could not say a word." But her voice was low and lacking in its customary note of fierce challenge, and Mendoza found the change noteworthy.

In all probability, Elizabeth was weary. Her painful hip throbbed mercilessly, and as she disliked taking medicine she was most likely doing nothing to alleviate it. She was under a good deal of strain. The situation in the Netherlands nagged at her, forcing her ever closer to the brink of actual war, draining her treasury, playing havoc with her private life. Foreign policy demands clashed with the strongly felt desires of her subjects. The men around her, men made increasingly shrill in their counsel and brittle in their views by age and the tense political climate, delivered themselves of their vehement opinions and disapproved of what use she made of them. Cecil shook his head in dismay at England's dangerous position, Walsingham insisted that Elizabeth must strike the first blow at the Catholic enemy, and immediately. Leicester bemoaned the growing numbers of recusants and the queen's apparent blindness to the threat they posed. "The Lord of his mercy open her eyes!" he wrote to Walsingham, praying that God might do what the royal councilors could not.

Elizabeth and Mendoza exchanged threats, but before long both saw nothing to be gained from continuing this and Elizabeth signaled an end to the personal discussion by asking Mendoza to call in his secretary, she in turn dismissing her ladies and summoning two of her councilors to join the talks.

Elizabeth repeated the ambassador's reference to "bringing in cannons" for the benefit of her advisers, resuming her boastful tone, and told Mendoza once more that he need not try to frighten her. At once he became condescending and gallant. Smiling at her "fury and perturbation," he conceded that monarchs were never afraid of mere private men—and as for Elizabeth, "a lady and so beautiful that even lions would crouch before her," she need fear nothing at all. ("You know how timid and pusillanimous she is," he wrote to Philip II afterward in cipher.)

Her anger was soothed at this, or so Mendoza believed, and the conversation turned from insults and threats to substantive diplomatic matters. But there was no escaping the rancor that colored the meeting, or the unspoken issue—the queen's persecution of her Catholic subjects—that overshadowed it. Before long Mendoza and Elizabeth were quarreling again, with the Spaniard passing on a threat from his master that, unless Drake's treasure was returned, the goods of English merchants in Spain would be seized as compensation.

She would do nothing about Drake, she answered firmly, until Philip had made amends for his role in the attempted invasion of Ireland, and after repeating this twice she took leave of the ambassador "very drily."

Hoping to have the last word Mendoza called out that in future he would communicate with the royal council, raising his voice so that the councilors, hearing him, would think that he had initiated the breach and not the queen. But her voice could carry as well. As he was making his way out of the privy chamber he and everyone else in the room heard Elizabeth say, with a great sigh, "*Volesse a Iddio che ognuno avesse il suo, e fosse in pace.*" "Would to God that each had his own, and was at peace!"

30

Here lieth the worthy warrior
Who never blooded sword;
Here lieth the noble councilor
Who never held his word
Here lieth his excellency
Who ruled all the state.
Here lieth the earl of Leicester
Whom all the world did hate.

I n mid-December of 1585 a fleet of fifty English ships sailed into Flushing harbor, carrying "the flower and chief gallants of England." In command was Leicester, his stout torso and pot belly encased in parade armor and his spirits as high as they had ever been.

Destiny called him—at last. Though he was well into his sixth decade he had been given a command—nay, a sacred mission—that many a younger man might envy. He was to lead the English army in the Netherlands, to make war on the army of Spain.

Many saw an epoch-making confrontation in the offing, a battle, not just between overmighty Spain and truculent little England, not just between Catholic and Protestant, but between the forces of the Roman Antichrist and God's chosen people. Protestant patriotism blazed high. "The freehold of England will be worth but little if this action quail," wrote one of Leicester's valiant captains. "The fire is kindled; whosoever suffers it to go out, it will grow dangerous."[1]

Leicester strode the deck of his flagship self-importantly, now giving orders, now looking out across the water in a pose of farsighted leadership. No one was more aware than he that he had not been near a battlefield for thirty years, and that the summit of his military experience was brief service as ordnance master in Picardy during Mary Tudor's reign. He had no military bearing; his paunchy body, thinning gray beard and tired, lined eyes suggested dissipation and world-weariness rather than stout-hearted combativeness. Yet the queen had chosen him as her commander—not her ambitious new favorite Walter Ralegh, nor Leicester's nephew Sidney, whom she disliked, nor any of the other hotheaded younger men who longed to prove themselves in war and who tried their best to push the reluctant Elizabeth into full-scale conflict with her old enemy King Philip.

She had, in the end, chosen Leicester, but not without grave misgivings and maddening changes of mind. His inexperience, his inability to get along with either subordinates or equals without awakening their violent dislike, his questionable statesmanship were all against him; in his favor were his rank and wealth—though he had to borrow very heavily to finance his expedition—his known intimacy with her and his princely status in the eyes of the Dutch. In his favor too was his somewhat diffuse ambition and mildly befuddled grasp of affairs. Elizabeth feared war in that, as a woman, she would have to yield something of her authority to male commanders; in Leicester she hoped she had a commander who would, partly for want of clear-headed schemes of his own, do as she told him.

With her usual "strange dealings" she had made the preamble to the journey a nightmare for the earl. First he was informed of his appointment, then, having ordered a great deal of armor and supplies and having sent some two hundred letters of summons to his fighting men, he received word that the appointment had been held up. She found she could not spare him after all. She was fearful; an ailment plagued her, and she needed Leicester to comfort her when the attacks came and she lay in her bed fearing that "she should not live." He half expected the change of heart from her. She had always been dependent on him, and had never before been willing to let him go so far away from her for so long. She was not only dependent, she was often malicious, never allowing Leicester to forget that he had wounded her mortally by his deceitful marriage to Lettice Knollys and "ever taking occasion," as he put it, "to withdraw any good from me."[2]

From the time of his original appointment in early September until the very day he sailed, December 8, the queen kept him in uncertainty. She exasperated him to the point of collapse. ("For my part," he wrote to Walsingham when he felt he could take no more of her caprice, "I am weary of life and all.") He felt sure that, whatever force he assembled and however well he equipped it, she would disapprove of it and give the command to someone else. Or her illness might return, or some other minor issue might arise to pique her and cause her to cancel all his carefully made preparations.

On the eve of his departure she gave him one final fright. She withheld the money to pay the six thousand footsoldiers and the thousand mounted men that were to make up his army. In panic, he sent a hurried message to Walsingham. If only she would release the funds, he begged, he would sell her some of his lands at a tremendous loss. The lands were worth sixty thousand pounds; she could have them for thirty, and if she sold the wood on them as well, she could make a profit of forty thousand in all.[3]

The funds were released, and the fleet set sail from Harwich, the queen's proud lieutenant Leicester in the van.

As soon as they caught sight of the English ships the citizens of Flushing signaled a noisy greeting. With every encouragement from Sidney, who had been made military commander of the town, bells were rung and cannons fired in a cacophony of welcome. The earl of Leicester was here at last, the mighty English peer, great Elizabeth's devoted lover—almost a king himself.

Certainly he came with a king's retinue. Over a thousand fighting men made up his personal train, and their huge warhorses and grooms and chests of weaponry weighted down the *Sea Rider*, the *Golden Rose*, the *Swan*, the *Crab-Joint*, the *Golden Hag* and the other English vessels as they anchored in the harbor. Leicester's household was enormous—a hundred yeomen and grooms, six dozen titled lords and gentlemen, scores of menials to wash and clean and serve and carry. His chaplains with their gowns and books and golden candlesticks, his choirboys, his cooks and stable staff and company of actors added another hundred at least to the rolls, and beyond these there were the purely military personnel—paymasters and purveyors, messengers, engineers, armorers and ordnance men, trumpeters, drummers and fife-players to march with the troops. Even so the list was not quite complete. Somehow Leicester had overlooked the office of herald, and had to send home for one—hoping to be supplied with a reliable man who could speak Dutch, Latin and French as well as English.

It was a splendid retinue, and Leicester himself looked splendid walking through the streets of Flushing surrounded by his soldiers and liveried servants, as the townspeople cried out "God save the Queen!" and threw down wreaths of flowers in his path.

Leicester was clearly the savior—more than that, the ruler—they had been waiting for. Elizabeth had refused to accept the sovereignty of the United Provinces—the rebel areas, chiefly Holland and Zeeland, still resisting Spanish domination—when it was offered her five months earlier, but Leicester would accept it, or so Sidney told the Dutch.

The idea of an Anglo-Dutch state had been mooted for a decade, but never before had it seemed so inevitable. The United Netherlands brought into being in 1576 by the Pacification of Ghent had split apart three years later, when the predominantly Catholic southern provinces came to terms with the Spanish governor Parma. The north sought to save itself by appealing to Alençon, then to Henry III, and most recently to Elizabeth, but Parma and his Spanish armies marched virtually without resistance into Brabant and Flanders, seizing Ypres, Bruges and Ghent in 1584 and finally capturing Antwerp in this year of 1585. If Holland and Zeeland were to be spared a similar fate, England would have to rescue them, and this meant virtually annexing them to the English crown.

It would have to be England, not France: France had become little more than a feeble ally of Spain. This more than any other recent shift in continental affairs had pushed England into war. In 1584 Alençon, heir to his brother Henry's throne, had died—plunging Elizabeth, his "widow," as she called herself, into deep mourning and causing her to lay aside business for a time while she wept for him. The Protestant Henry of Navarre was next in line, and to make certain he never made good his claim the Catholic duke of Guise conspired with Philip to exclude him. France, once strong and hostile to Spain, had become weak and submissive to her, and this, plus Parma's series of successful campaigns in the Netherlands, left England directly in the path of Philip's devouring armies.

On the day Leicester reached Flushing news came to the English court that in fact the Spanish were preparing for "some great enterprise against England." Military and naval forces were converging on Lisbon: there were sixty ships in the harbor, twenty of them great warships, or galleons, and over sixty thousand troops were billeted in or near the town.[4] Leicester's modest fleet and minuscule army were toys by comparison. Yet the courage of the English made them admired. Elizabeth, one French courtier remarked, seemed "determined to lose like a man, and not like a woman." Whether Leicester would prove to be as manly remained to be seen.

He came to make war—and found himself compelled to make merry instead. For four months he and his train were escorted from town to town, greeted with fulsome Latin orations and poetry, music and cannonades. They walked under gorgeous triumphal arches, admired pageants in which Leicester was likened to the biblical Joshua, sat down to sumptuous banquets of baked swan and roast pheasant and spitted pork. There were fireworks, water spectacles, plays and a "variety of all sorts of wonderful welcomes." There was wine in great abundance, and the English became abundantly, extravagantly drunk—so drunk that, at a banquet in Amsterdam, they amused themselves by throwing puddings and cakes out the windows and watching them splatter over passers-by in the street below.

In letters to the court in London Leicester tried to put all this frivolity in a serious light. The Dutch towns were valuable to Elizabeth; the lavish hospitality of their devoted citizenry was worth whatever delay it meant in warmaking. "I could be content to lose a limb," he wrote enthusiastically, "could her majesty see these countries and towns as I have done." But there was much that he left out of his letters. He did not tell the queen how flattered he was to be the honored, praised center of attention when for nearly thirty years he had been forced to remain in her shadow. He did not send an accounting of all he had had to spend—out of money designated to pay soldiers and wage war—on expensive gifts to the Dutch towns and feasts for the town officials. Most important, he did not tell Elizabeth that, contrary to her express command, he had accepted the title governor-general, and had taken on, for all practical purposes, the sovereignty she had explicitly ordered him to refuse.

Ignorant as yet of this intolerable disobedience, Elizabeth spent the dark winter days in her privy chamber, within whose richly adorned, perfumed confines she worked and read, interviewed ambassadors and councilors, received visitors and friends and supervised and reprimanded her women.

Smothered in adornment, the chamber was dim and stuffy—there was only one window—and frequently overcrowded. For it was here that the sixteen or so women of the queen's entourage dressed their mistress and served her meals and waited for her orders. They were always present or on call, the four chamberers who slept at the foot of her bed, the half dozen "great ladies," all married, who were her official companions and the six young, unmarried waiting maids or maids of honor whose youth grew more offensive to her with each passing year and whose virtue she guarded as possessively as she did her jewels and treasure.

The great ladies had few formal tasks, which meant that during their long hours of attendance on the queen there was much idle time for gossip and flirtation and malicious spreading of rumors. These were Elizabeth's peers, the women she played cards with and talked with and scolded, the women from whom she expected flattery and pampering. They knew what pleased and what offended her, how she liked looking at handsome young men and hated men with bad breath ("Good God," she burst out after meeting with one malodorous ambassador, "what shall I do if this man stay here, for I smell him an hour after he is gone from me!"). They knew—and dreaded—her dark moods, her infirmities, her womanly secrets.

They saw her, as very few others did, without the elaborate mask of creams and lotions which softened and clarified her pockmarked skin and the oily cosmetics, mixed with egg and spread on in thick swathes of dead white and blazing vermilion, that brightened it. They knew intimately that proud, suspicious, handsome, careworn face, the small, squinting, deepset eyes, the nose growing sharper and more hooked with age, the sagging

345

cheeks and jowls and wrinkled neck. Elizabeth's scent, compounded of her syrupy perfume of musk and rosewater, the sweet oil she used on her hands, and the sharp lemon and vinegar odors of her toiletries, must have hung in the air and clung to her attendants even after they left court or retired to their own beds for the night.

To the young maids of honor the queen was a less familiar and more terrifying figure, a strident, querulous taskmistress who though capable of generosity and even of rough good humor was more treacherous than affable. She expected them all to be well educated and to play the lute and have sweet singing voices. More important, she expected them to be docile and decorous, to form a pleasing backdrop for her own overpainted maidenliness. They dressed to complement her dress, and unless they were very foolish indeed they toned down their youthful good looks so as not to outshine her—at least from a distance.

When walking behind the queen on her way to the royal chapel on Sundays or when waiting on her while she ate her dinner in the privy chamber the maids were at least marginally well behaved, though occasionally they talked back to her in a way that "did breed much choler" in her. But when on their own, especially in the coffer chamber where they all slept, they laughed and shouted and created such uproar that the household officers—who slept in nearby chambers—complained indignantly about the noise.

The maids flirted, were occasionally seduced, occasionally married in secret or became recusants, calling forth the queen's fearsome wrath. They were the object of ribald attention. "The maids of honor desire to have their chamber ceiled, and the partition that is of boards there, to be made higher," reads an instruction to the surveyor of the works at Windsor Castle in 1580, "for that their servants look over."[5] It was bad enough that the maids kept the senior servants awake at night; peeping servants added intolerably to the chaos.

While the great ladies and waiting maids gossiped and fondled their lapdogs and pet squirrels and monkeys, the more humble chamberers took on the laborious tasks that fell to them as practical caretakers of Elizabeth's person, hygiene and wardrobe. With their assistants they attended her while she bathed, cleaned her teeth by rubbing them with tooth soap and then with a linen cloth, and applied her beautifying creams and waters and oils. They dressed her hair, combing and brushing it into mounds of curls, building it outward with swatches of false hair, fastening into its serpentine involutions an array of pearls and rosettes and jewels to match those in her gowns and at her ears. They laced and tied and fastened her into eight layers of clothing—from smock to petticoat to bodice, skirt, kirtle, gowns, and sleeves—and then added to these collars, cuffs, stomachers, a ruff, high-heeled shoes in colored leather or silk, scented gloves, jewelry (a great deal of it, the rings tied to the wrists by a twist of black silk), a ribbon at the waist on which were fastened a pomander, a watch, a fan, perhaps a silken mask.

In middle age Elizabeth abandoned the flattering pastels of her youth for dramatic gowns of black and white. In the mid-1580s, while in mourning for Alençon, she wore only black, though an envoy who saw her at court at Christmastime in 1584 recorded how she brightened her costume for the holiday. She was dressed in black velvet, he wrote, "sumptuously embroidered with silver and pearls. Over her robe she had a silver shawl, that was full of meshes and diaphanous like a piece of gossamer tissue. But this shawl gleamed as though it were bespangled with tinsel." Swathed in this shimmering mantle, sitting under her canopy of cloth of gold, Elizabeth must have resembled a goddess, and her regal air and fragile physique can only have added to the otherworldly effect.

Beyond the chamberers were scores of servants and tradespeople who made their contributions to the vast royal wardrobe: seamstresses, dressmakers, jewelers, wigmakers, milliners who supplied gilded trinkets, ornament-makers who brought glittering spangles and tiny golden or silver aglets to besprinkle a gown, grooms to clean, brush and tend the delicate fabrics between wearings, laundresses for the linen and silk women to provide the stuffs from which new petticoats and kirtles were made. The household rolls recorded one woman whose sole daily work was removing the tiny seed pearls that decorated certain garments and sewing them onto others.

Surrounded by the women who served and attended her—women whose unremitting companionship she could never easily escape—Elizabeth resigned herself, in her fifties, to life as a spinster. With Leicester away in Flanders she was more acutely aware of her unenviable status than ever before. To be sure, she had male companions as well. There were the "handsome old gentlemen" of her council—gouty Cecil, flinty Walsingham, tortured now by kidney stones but still driven to untiring labor by his convictions, silver-haired, lovesick Hatton, who was to become chancellor in 1587. There was young Walter Ralegh, a dark, good-looking intellectual and adventurer whose poetic gifts and brilliantly speculative turn of mind nourished Elizabeth's own ever-hungry intellect even as his infatuation with her soothed her vanity. In Ralegh's eyes she was, if not young, at least womanly and desirable, a mysterious and alluring being to be saluted in delicate rhymes.

But there was no substitute for Leicester, and as the weeks passed and there was no news from Flanders of military activity—only of pageantry and overeating, and requests for money—Elizabeth became more and more uneasy about his campaign, and more and more crotchety and unbearable toward her women.

The mood of the court did nothing to soothe the queen's temper. The palace was a hothouse of frenzy and anxiety. The excitement of war and of mounting danger, the growing conviction among the courtiers that theirs was an age writ large in human destiny, and that they must secure for themselves leading roles in the coming drama, made them desperate. The climate of frenzied desperation fed on itself; every time word came of new belligerence from Spain the tension mounted, with whispers of fear alternating with bullying shouts of defiance.

A new generation of gorgeous, swaggering young men came into their own in these tense years, "sword and buckler men" who burned to engage with England's enemies and to stifle fear in the oblivion of slashing combat. Most of them knew only the glory to be gained in war, not its dust and pain and bloody destruction. As they fitted themselves out with fine horses and gilt swords and richly engraved armor they thought little of the risk they undertook; their arrogance and narcissism eclipsed all else.

With their armor off they paraded in gaudy, grotesquely cut painted doublets, huge, jewel-encrusted sleeves and monstrously wide padded breeches, stuffed with wool or rags or bran until they stood out stiffly from the legs and made walking an art. Friends kissed one another's well-tended hands when they met, enemies squared off and glared at one another through intervening knots of admirers. Detached onlookers, new to court or precariously neutral in its web of internal politics, stood nervously apart, balancing themselves carefully on their high-heeled, diamond-studded silk shoes, sniffing their golden pomanders or elegantly picking their teeth with gilded toothpicks.

All was flash, harsh color, vulgar display, along with the din of intense, insistent voices. The queen, with her blazing gowns and high-colored cheeks, her roaring oaths and free talk of severed heads, seemed at one with the strident young warmongers. She sat in the presence chamber at Whitehall amid "pictures of the wars she had waged," plucking the men by their cloaks and pulling them over to talk with her in private.

A visitor to court watched her one day, and afterward described how she "summoned old and young" to her side, one after another, talking constantly and at the same time watching the acrobatics of a group of dancers. She "chatted and jested most amiably" with all who came before her, and singled out Ralegh to tease. "Pointing with her finger at the face of one Master or Captain Ralegh," the visitor wrote, she "told him that there was smut on it. She also offered to wipe it off with her handkerchief, but he anticipating her removed it himself." The incident evoked whispers. "They say that she now loves him beyond all others," the foreigner recorded, "and this one may easily credit, for but a year ago he could scarcely keep one servant, whereas now owing to her bounty he can afford to keep five hundred."[6]

Neither the queen nor Ralegh seem to have danced that day, but those who did caught the tone of hysteria in their mad leaps and "sprightly fire and motion." Slow dances were gone forever, at least for the young and middle-aged; instead they danced the volta, a violent, whirling two-step punctuated by strenuous high jumps and hectic turnings. The Puritans were outraged at this new example of worldly folly, which called for men to embrace women "lasciviously" while turning and lifting them and which led to the unseemly eroticism of skirts raised as high as the knees. But their protests only fed the mania for dance. New steps, old steps quickened to double time, entirely new and tortuously difficult patterns were invented.

What "new kind of dances, and new devised gestures the people have devised, and daily do devise," only God could say, a contemporary wrote. Dancing schools sprang up, with dancing-masters who "leapt, flung, and took on" wonderfully as their eager students watched. Court gallants tried to keep pace with the professionals, but their fevered efforts—made all the more awkward by their outlandish, restricting costumes—often resulted in injured dignity or worse. Often they leaped high—only to fall down hard on their padded breeches. Some "broke their legs with skipping, leaping, turning and vaulting." A few broke their necks.

It was as if they sought to pour all their restive energies into the galliard and volta, to exorcise the infuriate spirit that possessed them through the mindless exertions of dance.

In everything they courted excess: in flirtation and lust, the "ordinary infection" of the court, in the extravagantly flowery language the queen exchanged with her cultured admirers, a language coruscated with excessive alliteration and topheavy with overwrought metaphors, in the inordinate number of epithets—Lady of the Sea, Phoenix of the World, Peerless Oriana, Astraea, Cynthia, Belphoebe, Gloriana—with which the new generation of poets saluted the aging Elizabeth.

Courtly corruption, never suppressed, now flourished with unprecedented venality. Men came to the royal court, joined its ranks, learned its rules and mastered its unsavory politics for only one reason: to make a fortune. (Women came to marry men with fortunes.) It was understood that money was to be made through sophisticated bureaucratic practices involving bribery and theft. To gain an audience with the queen, the lord chamberlain or any other official the suitor had to present "gifts" of money or valuables; lucrative appointments were acquired through favoritism, and favoritism had to be purchased, usually at a very high price.

But once the courtier found a place, however insignificant, within the governmental hierarchy he could begin to broaden his leverage and sharpen his acquisitive powers. Even the most minor posts offered opportunities for graft and embezzlement and large-scale misappropriation of funds. For if official salaries were small, the perquisites that came with them were profitable. Most profitable of all were monopolies, which put into private hands what under another system would have been state regulation of trade and manufacturing. Armed with the power to regulate, the courtier could also bend the regulations—if paid enough to make it worth his while. Conspicuous examples of profiteering were offered by Leicester, Ralegh and Hatton, all of whom were ostentatiously, lavishly guilty of enriching themselves through bureaucratic theft—with the queen's indulgent help.

No group at court, it might be thought, was in a better position to advance their own and others' fortunes than the queen's waiting women. But in practice their influence was limited. They were "like witches," Ralegh said, "capable of doing great harm, but no good." They could tarnish reputations but not enhance them, and only the latter power could be turned to substantial profit. So unlike other highly placed court officials the great ladies and maids of honor had to be content with such modest profits of office as the queen's cast-off gowns and perfumed shoes, and with what fees they could earn by selling information about Elizabeth's private life and habits to foreign ambassadors and their agents.

Theirs was a frustrating role, made more frustrating by their mistress's unforgiving scrutiny and bad temper. It was no wonder that, when an opportunity for real malice and revenge against the queen presented itself, they took advantage of it, and did great harm indeed.

By early February the news from Flanders—a good deal of which reached Elizabeth through her waiting women—was becoming alarming. Leicester had made himself Absolute Governor of the United States of the Netherlands, a blunder which greatly increased English obligations to the Dutch and which was bound to escalate Spanish belligerence. Worse still, he had failed to send a letter of explanation to Elizabeth, or a personal envoy who could make her understand why he had gone against her orders. (In fact, Leicester had dispatched his servant William Davison to do just that, but foul weather was delaying Davison's crossing.)

But what increased Elizabeth's "extreme choler and dislike" tenfold were the rumors—entirely without foundation—about Lettice Knollys.

Lettice was preparing to join her husband, to cross to Flanders and take her place as wife of the Absolute Governor. Her pride and presumption knew no bounds. She was planning to take with her "such a train of ladies and gentlewomen, and such rich coaches, litters, and side-saddles," that she would seem more a queen than Elizabeth herself, whose own gilded vehicles would seem mean by comparison. Lady Leicester was to be nothing short of a second queen, in effect, with "such a court of ladies as should far pass her majesty's court" in England.[7]

The image of the handsome, auburn-haired Lettice Knollys, ever Elizabeth's despised rival, at the head of a competing court was unbearable. It was no good telling the queen that the rumors were "most false," that Lettice, as surprised as anyone when the story reached her, grew pale and trembled with fear, knowing what Elizabeth's anger could lead to. The malicious rumors had their effect, and they not only caused the queen endless vexation but nearly wrecked Leicester's entire campaign.

All the furies were let loose. Those who thought they had seen the full extent of the terrifying Tudor wrath now saw that they had been mistaken. She shouted her rage, at Leicester's unimaginable arrogance, at his traitorous disobedience, at the unforgivable insolence that had led him, ingrate that he was, to think that he could drag his unmentionable wife across the Channel to play at being queen while he played king. The hand which had created Leicester an earl, which had raised him from dishonor to position and wealth, could "beat him to the dust." Every day she drew up new plans to abort his military mission and order him home; every day Cecil, braving her fury, besought her to "suspend her judgment" until she heard from Leicester directly, or through an envoy.

She drew up a peremptory letter blasting him for his unheard-of effrontery. "We could never have imagined, had we not seen it fall out in experience, that a man raised up by ourself, and extraordinarily favored by us above any other subject of this land, would have in so contemptible a sort broken our commandment, in a cause that so greatly touches us in honor," she wrote imperiously. "So great a wrong," she went on, should not remain "in silence unredressed." Leicester was to obey the bearer of the letter—who would insist on his immediate return—without fail, or he would surely "answer the contrary at his uttermost peril."

But Cecil and his fellow councilors detained the bearer of the letter until after the belated arrival of Leicester's servant Davison, who undertook the unenviable task of placating the deeply injured queen. The incident had stirred up all her old grievances against Leicester, and she recited them one after another in "long and tedious" fashion. Her bitterness overflowed;

clearly it would take more than soothing words from a subordinate to assuage her mood. (Hatton sent word to Leicester that an expensive gift —bought, of course, from the military funds—would help.)

Eventually Davison and the councilors wore her down, and persuaded her, with some difficulty, that the stories about Lady Leicester were nothing more than the inventions of troublemakers. By June all talk of recalling Leicester ended. But by then his campaign was dissolving in enmity and squalor, and the beleaguered earl was wishing he had never left Harwich.

Even before the long honeymoon of feasting and pageantry had ended, he had found himself in conflict with the Dutch, who continued, much to his bewilderment, to oppose and hamper his authority while they looked to him to save them from the armies of Spain. Despite himself he was swept into the vortex of religious and political faction, while constantly called on to make peace between his captains and their fractious counterparts among the local forces. Elizabeth was more angry with him than she had ever been since his rash marriage, yet he was at a loss to know how to satisfy her, for her instructions had warned him "rather to make a defensive than an offensive war," and "not in any sort to hazard a battle without great advantage." Heavily outnumbered as he was by Parma's troops, he could hardly expect to stumble into a situation where "great advantage" would be his; even more discouraging was word from England that the queen was undermining his warlike posture by trying to negotiate peace terms with the enemy. He was condemned to preside over an expensive, ignominious stalemate, and the realization broke his morale.

The one military effort he launched, a daring assault on a fort dominating the town of Zutphen, resulted in a loss that broke his heart. His nephew Sidney died of wounds suffered in the assault, and the elaborate hero's funeral Sidney was later accorded could not disguise the relative insignificance of the English gain.

"Forget not money, money," Leicester wrote to Walsingham, and the plea echoes plaintively throughout his correspondence with the court. Elizabeth promised further funds, but did not keep her promises, especially after she learned that Leicester had flouted her parsimony by increasing his own and his soldiers' rate of pay. But she was far away in London; he was on the scene, and knew that the excess money was needed if the men were to have enough food, not to mention boots and cloaks and arms. He had come to lead stalwart soldiers into battle; instead he was forced to listen while "sick, lame and shrewdly enfeebled" men cried out to him for help. He contributed what he could from his own money, but as he had gone deeply into debt his ready funds were small. He did what he could; meanwhile the summer campaigning season ended, and in the fall the Absolute Governor was quietly summoned back to his sovereign's court.

Leicester made the return journey from Flushing in as disheartened a mood as he had ever known. Glory had been within his grasp, and then had been denied him. He found the courage to face the queen, but his tired eyes were full of self-pity. He had failed her, and whatever her share of that failure, the blame must be his. Unutterably weary, he made a brief appearance at court, then left Elizabeth in a monumental quarrel with her advisers and made his way to Bath to take the waters.

31

But sorrow and plagues for their offences,
Battle and famine, and all pestilences,
As a desolate land, brought it shall be;
What shall be more, none know but He.

E ngland in the 1580s was a land ravaged by profound unease. There was cause for anxiety everywhere: in the war, and rumors of war, that took on substance when Leicester sailed for Flanders; in the shouted exigencies of the Puritan preachers, exhorting men and women to hold firm against the devil; in the alarming rise in the number of witches, so virulent they threatened to "overrun the whole land"; in the severe food shortages that drove people to riot and curse the times, the gouging middlemen, and the queen.

Certainty had vanished. There were only guesses, conjectures, troubled whispers. Elizabeth warned her subjects in a proclamation "not to be moved by murmurers and spreaders of rumors, the dissemination of which is to be punished as the spreading of sedition."[1] Yet the rumors persisted, for this was an age with no consensus of received fact, and without such a consensus to rely on, hearsay was more comforting than fearful ignorance. Prophecy, however grim, was most comforting of all, for it made the future the product of past foresight, a preconceived, and therefore tamed, prospect.

The queen would live only a few years—or a few months—more. The queen would die a violent death. An invasion was imminent. (It would have taken a very poorly informed prophet indeed not to predict this.) A Dreadful Dead Man was coming, who would rise from his grave to overturn the present order and install a new one. These pronouncements were made, sometimes with the aid of a large folio book of "painted pictures of prophecy," to villagers hounded by worry over their failed crops and hungry children.[2] Grim as the prognostications were, they were eagerly received, for they offered a glimpse of something transcendent, something visionary and otherworldly, that lifted the burden of everyday want and brought a sense of awe and wonder.

The credulity of Elizabeth's subjects gave their anxieties very broad scope. They were fearful not only for the future, but that in some occult fashion history might reverse itself, forcing them to contend again with the past. Many associated the Dreadful Dead Man of prophecy with the late king Edward VI, and imagined that he would soon return to them. "Up Edward the Sixth, the time is come," began one prophetic saying, and in response to expectations held by "great multitudes of the simpler sort," he did indeed return—in the form of several impostors. The impostors were seized and locked away, but not before many people had seen and heard them, and they had helped to strengthen the widely held conviction that the boy-king lived on. There was nothing in King Edward's tomb but a lump of lead, an Essex blacksmith said. A soldier returning from the Low Countries swore that Edward was alive and well in Spain, or perhaps it was France. Another man, a "very simple person," told the authorities the same story he told his neighbors. King Edward had not died in 1553; instead a substitute boy had been put to death in his place, while the king himself was taken secretly to Denmark, where he became the reigning monarch.[3]

The unsettled past returned in many forms to haunt the Elizabethans. There were stories of a child born to the childless Mary Tudor, smuggled out of England to be raised to adulthood on the continent, where he awaited the propitious moment to claim his throne. Tales had been told since the start of Elizabeth's reign about the children she had with Leicester; currently, in the 1580s, a boy representing himself as their son was making himself known at Catholic courts abroad. Imagination merged with sacrilege in the disordered mind of an Englishman calling himself "Emmanuel Plantagenet," who was brought before Cecil in 1587. He was the son of Queen Elizabeth by God the Father, the madman told the treasurer haughtily. And greater than the Archangel Gabriel's was his authority in heaven.

The ultimate prophecy was that the end of the world was near. History was clearly in its "last days," people told one another, for the signs and wonders predicted in the biblical Book of Revelation were everywhere apparent. There were comets and eclipses in the skies, and downpours and snowstorms and heavy flooding on the earth. There was even groaning and travail under the earth, for during Easter week of 1580 a mighty earthquake shook southern England, tearing huge gashes in the walls of castles and knocking down chimneys and church towers.[4]

A loud noise like roaring thunder broke over Kent, and then the earth jerked and heaved with a "wondrous violent motion, and shaking of all things." In London stones fell from venerable buildings onto the heads of people rushing into the streets, and the playhouses swayed so violently that playgoers leaped down out of their seats into the pit for safety. New prayers were introduced into the litany for protection from earthquakes, but the disaster was feared less for its own sake than as a portent "terrible in signification of things to come."

Three years later, on an April Sunday in 1583, the same crowds that had fled the great earthquake were watching the heavens, waiting in fascinated terror for "some strange apparition or vision in the air" that would signal the end of the world. Saturn and Jupiter were in conjunction, and the astrologers predicted "either a grievous alteration of empires" or "an utter destruction of this world." Many had made an effort to cleanse their lives in expectation of Christ's Second Coming. A contemporary noted how they "talked very religiously, seeming as though they would become sanctified people," and their faces were very pious as they turned them toward the sky.

But as the day went on and the heavens failed to open, the expressions of innocent piety gave way to cynical smirking and by nightfall the crowds were jeering at the astrologers for their "extreme madness and folly." Yet hope, or dread, lived on. For every scornful voice there was a voice of expiation: the calculations were off by a few years, there were other factors to be considered besides the exact positions of the planets. New calculations produced new expectations. The world would end in 1588. It was "most certain."

But for the queen, time might run out sooner than that. In the 1580s, fears were redoubled that she might be assassinated.

The risk had been there since the early years of the reign, when in response to rumors that an Italian poisoner had infiltrated the royal household Elizabeth dismissed all the Italians currently in her service. Another alarm led her to confiscate every key to every door leading to her privy chamber, and to ensure that "great care" was taken by the officers of her guard. She might take consolation from her archbishop of Canterbury, who assured her that no harm would come to her "so long as Virgo," her birth sign and informal regal symbol, "was in the ascendant," but every time word came of new designs on her life there were fresh fears. Wax replicas of the queen and two of her councilors were found in the house of a Catholic priest, who meant to use them to end her life by magical means. One of her chamber ladies was accused of trying "by witchcraft" to discover Elizabeth's life span; from there it was but a small step to shortening it.

In the 1580s the attacks increased in numbers and in gravity, prompted by a macabre fashion for political assassination on the continent and by the violent and uncertain climate of the age. These were the years of the rack and the torture chamber, of the English spy network which set snares for Catholics and conspirators but terrorized the entire population. Londoners became habituated, though hardly immune, to "general searches" undertaken by justices and agents of the queen, who threw the city into panic by going from house to house and routing out wanted or suspected persons. Any "unknown men"—those without certain employment or reliable friends or connections—were seized and locked in churches while the raid went on to its end. The searches themselves were only part of a broader campaign of fear; Walsingham's men "prepared the people's minds" for the raids weeks in advance, by spreading talk of "great stirs" and dangerous foreigners abroad in the capital.

London life was a pattern of alarms and ghoulish horrors: wild shouting in the streets in the middle of the night, torchlit interrogations, the clump of boots on cobblestones. And, in growing numbers, hangings, and their grisly aftermath, the display of heads and chunks of flesh on London Bridge.

In the fall of 1584 there was a particularly ghastly execution. Eighteen people, "among them two women and two young lads," were hanged at one time, and the butchery was rounded out by a barbarous act of mercy. The victims' friends, wrote a visitor to the capital present at the executions, "went up to the gallows, tugged at their legs and struck them over the breasts in order to hasten their death."[5]

The attempts on the queen's life were in keeping with the mode of disordered violence. A Warwickshire man fell into a "frantic humor" and started off, glassy-eyed, for the court where he meant to shoot the queen. Elizabeth was a "serpent and viper," he shouted to anyone who would hear him. He wanted "to see her head set upon a pole." Catholic animus had shaped his thinking—a priest was sheltered in his household—but what pushed him to undertake his desperate mission is less clear. When captured and tried, he strangled himself in his cell.

Another intended murderer was a member of the House of Commons. William Parry looked to be above suspicion. He was not only an MP but an employee of Walsingham's, and in fact his connection with the intelligence network makes his guilt somewhat problematical. Still, he bragged of his plans to kill the queen, and an accomplice denounced him, telling how the two of them had decided to surprise her as she rode in her coach. They would ride alongside her, one on each side, and shoot at her head; she would be an easy target, either out of doors or in the palace, where Parry as a trusted royal servant could assault her during the course of a private audience.

A story was told later that Parry had actually gained his private audience, and had come to it with a knife hidden in his sleeve. He lost his courage, otherwise there would have been regicide and chaos.

True or not, the story added to the general apprehension, and supported the common people's view of their ruler as an endangered, beleaguered treasure whose safety was a matter for grave concern. They imagined her, overwrought and weeping, walking in her garden and lamenting "that she would fain know why so many people sought her life." She tore her breast, the tale went, and said she was "defenseless and unarmed, a miserable woman," yet she "trusted in the Lord God to have compassion on her."[6]

This was the account a traveler heard in London, the romantic, tender fabrication of a worried citizenry. People had told similar stories about Mary Tudor many years earlier, their chivalrous feeling for a woman in peril taking precedence over their respect for their sovereign's courage.

In the fall of 1583 there were revelations of a Catholic plot for an invasion force to land in Sussex and proceed to the liberation of Mary Stuart. The Spanish ambassador Mendoza was heavily implicated, and was expelled. Just as the danger was coming to light and the conspirators, under torture, were revealing what they knew Elizabeth was riding under guard from Hampton Court to London, with the French ambassador Mauvissière beside her. They were deep in conversation, with Elizabeth talking effusively about the Jesuit plots that threatened her.

"Just at this moment," Mauvissière afterward recalled, "many people, in large companies, met her by the way, and kneeling on the ground, with divers sorts of prayers wished her a thousand blessings, and that the evil-disposed who meant to harm her tonight be discovered, and punished as they deserved."

As always Elizabeth stopped her horse to acknowledge the good wishes, and broke off her talk of the Jesuits. It was clear, she remarked to the Frenchman tartly, "that she was not disliked by all."

The prayers of the people were echoed in Parliament. Just before the Christmas recess in 1584 the queen thanked the Commons for their care and concern, and then Hatton spoke. He had with him a prayer, he said, written by "a godly man." It was a prayer "for the queen's preservation," and he asked if he could read it aloud. He began to read, and as he did so the members fell reverently to their knees and repeated the words after him, as if they had been the words of a psalm or a response from the Book of Common Prayer.

In a more militant vein was a movement to circumvent assassination by undercutting its potential benefits. In the summer of 1584 the royal council had prepared a document called the Bond of Association which pledged its signatories to pursue to the death any person on whose behalf an assassin might act. Since any attempt on Elizabeth's life (save the random assaults of madmen) was bound to be undertaken on behalf of Mary Stuart the Bond of Association was in effect a vast counter-conspiracy against her, and as the number of signatures grew—there were many thousands, from every part of the realm—the depth and strength of popular opposition to Mary became more and more clear.

Of all the dark clouds that overshadowed the decade the menace of Mary Stuart was the most abiding, and the least tractable. Would Elizabeth outlive her, or not? The nine-year difference in their ages, and the hazards to which Elizabeth was subjected, suggested that Mary might one day rule England, even if the plotters she so fervently encouraged never managed to bring off the grandiose schemes they concocted to sweep her onto the throne.

The days were long past when the two queens were rivals for admiration. Vanity, wigs and cosmetics aside, they were old women, their bones and temperaments brittle and their façade of mutual gentility worn thin. Mary, in her forties, looked ten years older; captivity had turned her hair white and left her "poor, languishing, sickly body" stiff and aching. Her letters to Elizabeth were querulous, yet not so full of complaints as to risk anger or irritation in her royal relative. It was essential to Mary—indeed to them both—that a semblance of goodwill be preserved. Indeed Mary was full of proposals. Why not make her co-ruler of Scotland with her son James, now entering young manhood? Elizabeth considered the proposal, sent negotiators to Scotland to look into it, and concluded that it was completely impractical. In addition to the risk to England in releasing Mary from captivity, the Scottish lords refused to have their dishonored, deposed queen back—and her son too was most unfilial in his negative response. But the correspondence continued.

With her letters Mary sent Elizabeth wigs and embroidered cuffs and caps ornamented with her own needlework, a reminder of her tedious and empty hours. The damp and drafts in her apartments, she informed the queen, were putting her in "danger of her death," yet she hoped Elizabeth's own health was good. Meanwhile, in secret, she read the letters of English

Catholics in France and Spain, letters full of plans for raising armies of liberation, and wrote them commanding, impassioned, traitorous replies.

Elizabeth, for her part, sent Mary wigs in return and bolts of satin and taffeta and, to improve her health, sent her own physician as well. Elizabeth signed herself "your good sister and cousin," and affixed her royal seal. In her council chamber, however, she wondered aloud what to do with her untrustworthy relative, and saw only too clearly that she would never be able to free her. "Her head should have been cut off years ago," she once remarked to an Italian visitor.7 As the years went by the queen of Scots' execution seemed imperative, and at last inevitable.

To Elizabeth's advisers and to Parliament, the elimination of Mary Stuart was long, long overdue. She was the "monstrous and huge dragon" that menaced England's security, the lodestar of rebellion and treachery and danger from abroad. Her morals were as low as any woman's could be; she had murdered her husband, she was an adulteress, she had seduced her jailer Shrewsbury (according to Shrewsbury's spiteful wife Bess of Hardwick) and borne his child. She had shown herself to be faithless where Elizabeth and her government were concerned. "It is evident," the fair-minded Cecil concluded, "that the Scottish queen has never entered into any treaty but only of purpose to abuse the queen of England with some treacherous attempt or other." In fact there was more to Mary's story than this, but by the mid-1580s only the broad outlines mattered.

Then in 1586 a trap was set for her, leading her to provide the evidence needed to find her guilty of treason. She approved, in writing, a plan for Elizabeth's assassination, and when in October of 1586 she was tried at Fotheringhay Castle by a group of commissioners appointed by the queen her guilt was confirmed.

As sovereign, as guardian of her people's lives and her nation's safety, Elizabeth had no choice but to order the issuing of the proclamation setting forth Mary's death sentence and to sign the warrant authorizing her execution. But something held her back. The fears that gathered around her people clutched at her as well, adding to the deep personal misgivings she fought as the year came to a close.

It had been a hard year, a year of bitter disappointment and failure. War had taken Leicester from her for many months, and had led to conflict and ill feeling between them. War had been waged, and the cost had been great, yet save for the minor triumph at Zutphen there had been no victory. Now a decision had to be made about the Scots queen.

The political hazards in sending Mary to her death were substantial. First, Scotland, and the succession. With Mary dead, her claim would pass to her son James; what was to prevent him from attracting to himself all the powers that had previously supported his mother's claim, then using their forces to conquer England? True, James had only recently signed the Treaty of Berwick, pledging himself to an alliance with England and accepting an annual pension from Elizabeth. He was her presumed successor, and he might be content to wait for the crown to come to him in the course of nature. But what if he chose to betray the treaty? What better excuse could she give him than to put his mother to death?

Then there was France, where Mary was still recognized as queen. French envoys had come to Elizabeth's court to ask that her life be spared, and with war at hand the English could not afford to drive the French, already submissive to Spain, into King Philip's camp. The creation of a Catholic martyr in Mary Stuart might well have that effect.

And what of Spain, and King Philip? Would the death of the woman he looked on as England's rightful queen abate Philip's determination to crush England in battle? Or would it merely shift the explanation of his warmaking, from conquest on Mary's behalf to a war of vengeance, a war to punish Mary's murderers?

For a time Elizabeth took counsel with Cecil on this most difficult of her decisions, but before long she ceased to ask his views and pondered the matter alone. Parliament had shouted for Mary's death, begging the queen to "take away this most wicked and filthy woman" before it was too late. But however unanimous the views and feelings of her advisers Elizabeth could not bring herself to acquiesce. William Davison, recently made a secretary of state because of the increasing burden of office on Secretary Walsingham, believed that it would take more than intellectual and political logic to persuade the queen to sign the death warrant. She would never take Mary's life, Davison said, unless compelled by "extreme fear."

Among the prophecies being spread abroad in 1586 was one concerning the queen of Scots. Once she came to harm, it was said, there would be horrible results. An army of invasion would sail to England and land at Chester. Queen Elizabeth, abandoned by her quarreling Parliament, would become a fugitive seeking safety in Wales. The people would rebel; a rising of "clubs and clouted shoes" would end in victory for the peasants, and meanwhile the Tudor crown would be lost and won by a series of claimants.[8] It was a long, intricate vision of disaster, encompassing most of Elizabeth's worst fears. And it would all come about the moment Mary Stuart's head was severed from her shoulders.

Alone with her thoughts, was Elizabeth haunted by this dire prediction? Did it deepen her already strong reluctance to send a female relative to her death? ("What will they not now say," she asked a parliamentary delegation, "when it shall be spread that, for the safety of her life, a maiden queen could be content to spill the blood even of her own kinswoman?") As a highly educated woman, and one who had more than a slight interest in the occult, Elizabeth believed in the doctrine of correspondence—the teaching that every created thing was linked to every other by a powerful psychic force. To disturb one element in the carefully balanced whole was to send shock waves through the rest of creation. For Elizabeth to authorize the taking of an anointed queen's life was a sacrilege of sorts, a rending of the web which encompassed all; it might well bring death back on her.

There may have been another theme in Elizabeth's tortured musings, made up of antiquarian curiosity and long-buried memories. A queen had been executed in England, fifty years earlier. Anne Boleyn had stood accused of treason, as Mary Stuart was now; like Mary, Anne had been denounced as a wicked, unrepentant woman, faithless to her husband, an adulteress who had plotted the death of her lord and lawful sovereign. Was there in Anne's daughter a superstitious dread of replicating her father's terrible revenge against Anne? Or did Elizabeth merely note the parallels, nod with interest, and then return to her efforts to calculate the reaction Mary's death was likely to produce at foreign courts?

In January of 1587 fresh alarms swept the country. Rumors sprang from one another, creating unprecedented panic and breeding ever more fantastic news of imagined events.

The Spaniards had landed. They were at Milford, thousands strong, their huge cannon rumbling through the Welsh countryside and their grim legions of cutthroat troops marching ever closer to the capital.

The north was in revolt. It was a rising as stubborn and as ill-disposed toward the queen as the rising of 1569, only this time the Spaniards would aid the rebels and nothing could stop them.

London was in flames. The queen—was she still living, or had she been assassinated, as some said?—had had to flee. In all the confusion, the queen of Scots had escaped. She was on her way to the northern rebels. Spaniards were moving toward the burning capital, their crested helmets silhouetted against the red glow of the night sky. Surely, these were the last days of the world.

The whirl of rumor engulfed the court. The image of a realm in chaos shimmered in the air like a horrifying mirage, unreal yet threatening. Elizabeth fought toward her decision, pressed as much by the wildfire of panic as by the urgent necessity for action on a matter of great import.

"For mine own life," she insisted, "I would not touch her." Yet Mary had to die. There was no escape—unless, as a number of people hinted darkly, Mary's jailers took it upon themselves to carry out the pledge of death they had sworn to in the Bond of Association. Elizabeth asked it of them, but the deed was not done. She cursed them, blasting "the niceness of those precise fellows who in words would do great things but in deed perform nothing."[9]

Then came word of yet another plot against her life—on Mary's behalf. The French ambassador and others made plans to kill Elizabeth, though when their conspiracy came to light they had not yet determined whether to poison her stirrup or her shoe, in the Italian manner; or to kill her "by laying a train of gunpowder where she lieth."[10]

There was no longer any reason to stay Mary's execution in order to placate the French. As for James Stuart, she would have to gamble on his coldheartedness toward his mother and his often asserted, carefully protected succession rights.

At the end of January Elizabeth wrote to James. Mary, she said, is "the serpent that poisons me." If she saved Mary, she would herself be destroyed. The agony of decision had passed. Only one simple, fateful course was open to her.

On February 1, Elizabeth summoned Davison, signed the death warrant, and sent Davison off with it to the bedside of the sick Walsingham. It was a solemn moment, but she added a grim joke. "The grief thereof," she said, referring to the document in his hand, "would go near to kill him outright."

32

When after Christs birth there be expired,
Of hundreds fifteene, yeares eighty eight,
Then comes the time of dangers to be feared,
And all mankind with dolors it shall freight,
For if the world in that yeare doe not fall,
If sea and land then perish ne decay,
Yet Empires all, and Kingdomes alter shall,
And man to ease himselfe shall have no way.

The Most Fortunate Armada rocked at anchor in Lisbon harbor, its white sails with their bright red crosses fluttering in the chill wind. There were well over a hundred ships, half of them towering galleons and galleasses and hulking armed merchantmen that loomed "so high that they resembled great castles." These monstrous vessels were meant to frighten the enemy as much by sheer size as by force of arms or firepower, and as the tiny supply boats darted in and out among them, rising and dipping in the strong chop of the harbor waters, they seemed to stand, stately and majestic, like grandees attended by their scurrying valets.

In command of the vast flotilla on this spring day in 1588 was Don Alonso Perez de Guzman, duke of Medina Sidonia, Lord of San Lucar, and Knight of the Golden Fleece. King Philip had made him Captain General of the Ocean Sea only two months before, and in the interim he had struggled to learn what he could about ships and guns and naval warfare, about which, when appointed, he knew virtually nothing. He watched now as the ships were loaded with chests of muskets and pikes, corselets and morions, cannon balls and powder. Horses and cattle were slung aboard in nets and stowed below decks, along with casks and barrels of salt meat and fish, rice, cheese, and other provisions, wine and water. In accordance with the captain general's orders, more men were being put aboard the ships along with the beasts and provisions, sailors kidnapped from other ships in Lisbon harbor, invalids from the hospitals and criminals from the prisons, even laborers who had never before seen the sea, taken from their fields and put to work for the king aboard the great Armada.

There was a shortage of men. Some months earlier, when word of a vast expedition had first gone out, men had come to Lisbon from all over Spain and Portugal, eager to sail with the fleet. But since then, epidemics had reduced the size of the crews and desertion too had become a problem, and as the time for departure neared it had been necessary to make up the losses by commandeering all the men to be found, no matter how unsuitable.

Medina Sidonia had other worries. The gigantic ships carried too few guns, and there were nothing like enough gunners to man them. Many of the vessels leaked, or responded badly under sail, and there were far too few smaller craft to act as a proper escort for the greatships. Food and water were bound to be a problem, for the purveyors to whom the task of provisioning had been entrusted were notorious for supplying tainted meat and sour wine. In addition, it had not been possible to buy enough seasoned barrel staves to supply the entire fleet; most food, wine and water were stored in casks and water butts made from green wood, which were not watertight and in which perishables spoiled quickly.

For this, Drake was to blame. A year earlier, in the spring of 1587, the daring Englishman had raided the harbor at Cadiz, then supply center for the Armada, and in the course of his raid he had burned tens of thousands of seasoned barrel staves—along with some thirty-seven warships and smaller vessels. To Elizabeth's great satisfaction, he had also seized a merchant ship whose cargo of spices, silks and jewels was worth many fortunes. But in the long run, the lumber was the greater loss to the Spaniards, for though the ships could be replaced, the lumber could not.

A strong, almost wintry wind set the colorful pennants and flags flying. Each ship was "furnished and beautified with trumpets, streamers, banners, warlike ensigns, and other such like ornaments," gilded and painted, and as they fluttered from the masts and spars they lent the vast flotilla an air of joyous celebration. But the duke was far from joyous. He found the tasks of command irksome, and the men under him—haughty, jealous commanders who quarreled with one another and looked askance at any admiral set over them—hard to rule. Moreover, he was more fatalistic than sanguine about the Armada's chances for success. The astrologers and prophets were predicting disaster for this year, and given the unsatisfactory state of his ships and crews, they were likely to be right. Certainly the weather was no help. "Unsettled winds" bedeviled navigation, and unseasonable storms sent huge waves crashing against the coast with heavy rain and blasting gales. It promised to be the stormiest summer in years, and the captain general imagined with dread what perils awaited his ships in the dangerous waters of the North Atlantic.

The king too was fatalistic, but with the granite certainty of one absolutely convinced that God is on his side. To King Philip, the Armada was a crusading navy, its mission a holy war. For years he had been urged to turn the might of his soldiers and his ships against England; now, at last, he had made up his mind to do so. By what saurian involutions of thought he had reached this determination no one could say, for with advancing age his abstractedness and self-absorption had increased to the point of opacity. But sometime in the mid-1580s his predestined path had become clear to him. He came to realize that all the wealth and power he had amassed in his long reign, all the gold and silver from the New World, all the lands he had seized and plundered had been brought together for a single purpose: to destroy the heretical rule of Queen Elizabeth.

With an alacrity that startled his ministers—who were accustomed to infinitely protracted decisions from the king, clouded by infinitely detailed objections—Philip ordered the preparation of an enormous fleet. It would sail for the Netherlands, where Parma would be waiting with his soldiery to commence the conquest of England. The Armada would not be itself a fleet of conquest, it would aid in the military invasion. Together, the towering warships and the fighting men in their tens of thousands would overcome England's formidable navy and much less formidable land defenses.

Just where and how the two halves of the Spanish attack force would join together was unclear. In particular, it was left vague how a fleet requiring a deep-water port was to rendezvous with a land army in a region whose one deep-water port was in enemy hands. But these and other tactical considerations were not allowed to deter the expeditious assembling of ships and men and supplies that culminated in the splendid panorama spread before Medina Sidonia's gaze in Lisbon harbor in the spring of 1588. In record time, the most formidable, the most extensive, the most intimidating naval force that ever put to sea had been assembled. Soon it would set sail, and Philip, as the English told one another excitedly, would attempt to "devour all Christendom with invasion."

The English would have been surprised to learn with what alarm their own defensive preparations were viewed by the Spanish sailors manning the Armada. "The enemy now make but little reckoning of us," said Lord Howard of Effingham—half-brother of the traitor Norfolk, and now appointed admiral of the English fleet—"and know that we are but like bears tied to stakes, and they may come like dogs to offend us."[1] In fact, among the intelligence reports reaching the English court from Lisbon were one or two declaring the "great fear" felt throughout the Spanish fleet that England was more than adequately prepared to encounter their ships and men.[2] Drake was especially terrifying. The Spaniards called him "El Draque," the dragon, and found his powers of navigation and extraordinary luck in combat too remarkable to be explained by human abilities alone. He was a sorcerer, they said, who sailed and waged war by means of magic.

Yet taken overall, the reports were much more disheartening than encouraging. Wildly inflated estimates of the Armada's size and strength reached the council chamber: there were over two hundred ships, carrying thirty-six thousand men; there were three hundred ships, half of them giant ships of war; there were four or five hundred ships, ready to debouch onto English soil the largest land army ever assembled.[3] And it was surely assembling, the spies in Dunkirk wrote. There were thirty-seven warships in the harbor, ready to ferry Parma's men to their rendezvous with the hulking escort fleet. Horses were being brought to Dunkirk in great numbers, and all the abbeys in the region were pressed into service grinding wheat to bake biscuits for the soldiers.

So vain was King Philip of his monster fleet that he publicized its specifications. Detailed lists of the ships, their guns and their crews were available in Rome and Paris and Amsterdam in the spring of 1588, and though the numbers on these lists were inflated they were more reliable— though no more comforting to the English—than the dispatches of spies. Printers in Amsterdam, ever eager to incriminate the Spaniards, augmented the official itemization by listing the scourges and whips and instruments of torture the great ships carried in their holds. By the time these lurid documents reached England they were fleshed out by stories of how, once the invasion force landed, all adult English men and women would be tortured and killed, leaving their orphaned infants to be suckled by an army of seven thousand Spanish wet nurses—to be carried, along with the scourges and whips, in the Armada's capacious holds.[4]

Throughout the stormy spring and early summer the English defense was mounted. The lords lieutenant of the counties were ordered to muster bands of footsoldiers and the nobles and gentry received messages from the queen commanding them "to attend upon her with such a convenient number of lances and light horse as might stand with their ability." In the interest of security, watches were to be set in all towns by night and all suspicious persons detained. The hunt for priests and for the recusants who concealed them was intensified, for no one could predict what English Catholics might do once their Spanish coreligionists came ashore in force. All along the coasts, villagers were told to prepare beacons, to be lit as warning fires when the Armada hove into sight. Nothing of possible use to the invaders was to be left unguarded; even cattle grazing near the sea were driven inland, to prevent them from falling into Spanish hands.

An ingenious if somewhat makeshift barrier was erected to block the passage of any enemy ships up the Thames. Huge, heavy chains and ships' cables were locked together and stretched across the river from Gravesend to Tilbury, held in place by a cordon of small boats anchored in the river and by a hundred and twenty tall ships' masts laid end to end.[5]

But the main line of defense was the navy, and in addition to Admiral Howard's main fleet there were two smaller squadrons, one at Plymouth under Drake, who was named vice admiral, and another light squadron to patrol the Channel, headquartered at Dover. A full complement of sailors was mustered ("There is here the gallantest company of captains, soldiers and mariners that I think ever was seen in England," the ebullient admiral remarked), and even the Thames watermen were called to serve. Carpenters and shipwrights had labored to fit the ships until, in Howard's words, "there was never a one of them that knows what a leak means," though this had often meant working by torchlight at night as well as during the day, and persisting despite the "extreme gales of wind" that lashed at the harbors.

By June the fleet was ready, the ships dancing out the recurrent storms "as lustily as the gallantest dancers at the court." Ashore the trained bands were beginning to converge on Tilbury, designated as the headquarters of the land forces. If any resisted serving the queen in that perilous hour, no record of their resistance remains—though there was some concern on the part of the country people that taxes levied to support the soldiers might become a permanent burden. For many the approaching confrontation with the Spaniards must have come as a great relief. To meet at last the enemy they had dreaded for so many years can only have filled them with a sort of millenarian exhilaration. Whether they prevailed or were defeated, the outcome would at least be clear, the long uncertainty ended. "It was a pleasant sight," a contemporary wrote, "to behold the soldiers as they marched toward Tilbury, their cheerful countenances, courageous words and gestures, dancing and leaping wheresoever they came."

As the English marched toward Tilbury and their expected rendezvous with the enemy, the ships of the Most Fortunate Armada were foundering in a howling storm off Cape Finisterre.

Since leaving Lisbon in early May, the fleet had been overtaken by a series of disasters. First contrary gales had kept them windbound off the Portuguese coast, with some ships unable to hold their own against the headwinds and drifting off far to the south. Then, once the fleet finally began its northward progress—traveling with exasperating slowness because of the leaden pace of the supply ships and the fitful, unpredictable winds—the men began to fall sick from drinking foul water and eating rotten food. The green barrel staves were taking their toll. Cask after cask of provisions was opened and found to be stinking and crawling with worms; only the rice was unspoiled. Then, just as the captain general was about to halt the expedition, a sudden tempest had arisen, scattering the vessels and seriously damaging some of them, and forcing a general run for port.

After so many delays and catastrophes it was hard to see the beneficent hand of God guiding the Armada's destiny. June, so Medina Sidonia had been led to understand, was the best sailing month of the year, when calm seas and fair winds prevailed even in the roughest waters. Yet June had been even more stormy than May. If God could not seem to provide a safe passage even in the most halcyon season of the year, then perhaps it was a sign that he meant the fleet to fail in its mission.

Yet such a suggestion hardly seemed credible. How could God be displeased with an undertaking which in every particular bore the stamp of a holy crusade? The ships had been christened with the names of the saints: *San Francesco, San Lorenzo, San Luis* and *San Martin.* Holy images and crusading crosses had been painted on every waving ensign and pennant. The flagship's principal banner, blessed with elaborate ceremony in Lisbon cathedral just before the fleet's departure, carried on its face the crucified Christ and on its back the Virgin, her eyes upraised in supplication. *"Exsurge, Domine,"* read the scroll beneath, *"et judica causam tuam!"* "Arise, O Lord, and vindicate thy cause!"

None of the usual vulgarities incident to expeditions of sailing men were allowed to defile this sanctified campaign. Before leaving the harbor the ships had been swept clear of prostitutes, and the men had purged themselves of their sins and communicated in the cathedral. Nearly two hundred monks and friars sailed with the fleet to perform daily masses and lead the crews in prayer. At sunrise and sunset the ships' boys gathered at the mainmasts to sing religious hymns, and the sailors were dissuaded from indulging in "profane oaths dishonoring the names of our Lord, our Lady and the saints." The watchwords for each of the days of the week—for Monday, Holy Ghost, for Tuesday, Most Holy Trinity, for Wednesday, Saint James, for Thursday, the Angels, and so on—were a pious reminder of the Armada's transcendent purpose. "From highest to lowest," King Philip's instructions to the men read, "you are to understand that the object of our expedition is to regain countries to the church now oppressed by enemies of the true faith. I therefore beseech you to remember your calling, so that God will be with us in what we do."

"God will be with us"—so Medina Sidonia had believed, especially after a most holy man, a friar, had expressed to him his most profound certainty that Spain would be the victor in the coming contest. His officers too, men of long experience in battle, seemed serenely content to anticipate a victorious outcome, though they were candid in admitting that the English would have the advantage of them in ordnance and maneuverability. "We fight in God's cause," one of them explained. "We are sailing against the English in the confident hope of a miracle."

Yet as he sat in his flagship in the harbor of Corunna, surrounded by his storm-battered ships, the captain general lost heart. The expedition might be in God's hands, but the immediate responsibility was his own, and he could not in conscience proceed with it. Even an inexperienced sailor such as he was could see that the galleys, formidable though they might be in Mediterranean waters, were holding up badly as oceangoing ships. The bulky merchantmen listed badly and lagged far behind the more responsive vessels. The storm had underscored the fleet's vulnerability, but even without it there would have been reason enough to reconsider the entire venture.

"To undertake so great a task with forces equal to those of the enemy would be inadvisable," Medina Sidonia wrote in a sobering letter to King Philip, "but to do so with an inferior force, as ours is now, with our men lacking in experience, would be still more unwise." "I am bound to confess that I see very few, or hardly any, of those on the Armada with any knowledge of or ability to perform the duties entrusted to them." He particularized the difficulties one after another, hoping that his sovereign, with his logical mind and reverence for detail, would find the disadvantages overwhelming. "I have tested and watched this point very carefully, and your majesty may believe me when I assure you that we are very weak," he concluded. "The opportunity might be taken, and the difficulties avoided, by making some honorable terms with the enemy."

Philip found the duke's letter disconcerting, especially as Parma, in the Netherlands, took the same overall view. (Parma's army had fallen from thirty thousand to seventeen, which made him doubt whether an invasion of England could be attempted without leaving too few men behind as garrison troops.) But it did not disconcert him for long. Human limitations, however severe, could not be allowed to impede a divinely appointed mission. At the Escorial, the masses and prayers in the huge, ornate royal chapel went on day and night; in the towns and villages of Spain statues of the Virgin and the saints were carried in procession through the streets to ask God's blessing on his Invincible Armada. The captain general must have faith that all would be well, that the troubles he faced would be surmounted. King Philip ordered him to proceed.

Obediently Medina Sidonia complied, and on July 12, with his fleet re-victualed and repaired, he gave the command to weigh anchor.

A week later, on the afternoon of July 19, an English captain sighted the Spanish fleet while his bark was cruising the mouth of the Channel. He came into Plymouth to report. By evening the beacon fires were burning along all the headlands, their thick columns of smoke and red glow visible far inland and out across the Channel to Dunkirk. Within hours the chain of warning lights had spread far to the north and west, until by morning it had reached the Scots border. The Spanish were upon them. The great battle was at hand.

Three days after word reached the capital that the Armada was within striking distance of the English coast, the queen appointed Leicester to be commander of the Camp Royal at Tilbury. The appointment warmed the heart of the sick old earl, who ever since his return from the Netherlands campaign had suffered nearly as much from Elizabeth's coldness and angry neglect as he did from the illness that was slowly killing him. His old age was proving to be harsher and bleaker than he could have imagined. His marriage had grown cold and was in any case disfigured by bereavement. (His son by Lettice had died in infancy—of epilepsy, so Leicester's enemies said, as a punishment from God for the father's immorality.) A sensational book, *Leicester's Commonwealth*, revived in lurid detail every scandal ever spread about him, accusing him of seducing most of Elizabeth's women (sometimes "keeping a mother and two or three daughters at the same time"), of being "plunged, overwhelmed and defamed in all vice," of murdering those who stood in the way of his advancement and generally of making himself the most hated man in England, which he very probably was. The years of lechery and criminality had left him "broken within and without," the anonymous author said, and in 1588 the phrase was not far wrong.

The hatred he aroused, and his wealth and apparent power at court, made the earl a target for assassination. Several of the plots against the queen included killing Leicester as well, and during 1587 a conspiracy had come to light that envisioned his murder by one of a grisly variety of means. Either he was to be killed when his house at Wanstead was burned, or he was to be poisoned, possibly by a lethal liquid slipped into his perfume.[6]

Early in 1588 Leicester wrote to Elizabeth "beseeching her to behold his wretched and depressed estate, and restore him to some degree of her former grace and favor." Her belated reply had been the appointment as commander of Tilbury, and even though he realized that the command was a restricted and somewhat honorific one, he accepted it gladly. The title was grander than the post itself: Lord Steward Her Majesty's Lieutenant Against Foreign Invasion.

Elizabeth sent Leicester off to Tilbury with words of "great comfort," spurring him to squeeze the maximum of activity out of his aging frame and inflating his self-importance to new heights. "Nothing must be neglected to oppose this mighty enemy now knocking at our gates," he wrote to the council, dashing off the letter in great haste while en route from Gravesend to Chelmsford to supervise the raising of troops. "There is no looking back now to any oversight past." Present oversights offended him, however. There were too few officers appointed to serve under him, an implied insult to his rank. And he was jealous of Hunsdon, appointed to command the special forces raised to protect the queen; he asked the council to word Hunsdon's commission "so as not to interfere with his own authority."[7] He tangled with the arrogant earl of Oxford, who refused the command Leicester offered him and made such a disdainful nuisance of himself that the earl was "glad to be rid of him" after he stalked off in anger.

In his first expansive days as lord steward Leicester encouraged Elizabeth to visit the camp in person to "comfort these thousands" as she had comforted him. Fortunately for him, her coming was delayed for some days; in the interim he was able to turn the chaos of unprovisioned troops, half-erected fortifications and rain-soddened equipment into something like an orderly camp.

The military crisis with Spain pulled Elizabeth out of an ugly contretemps with her advisers. All the hidden strain in her personal life had broken to the surface with the execution of Mary Stuart, and in the aftermath of that infinitely distasteful event she had lost not only her self-control but, for a time, her governmental sense. The chief scapegoat, William Davison, was sent to the Tower while the queen sought to have him hanged without a trial. (Finding this impossible, she had him tried, condemned to an indeterminate imprisonment and heavily fined.) The councilors feared for their lives.

It seemed for a time as if the brash, bullying woman with her loud talk of severed heads was about to order executions in earnest. She inquired of the justices "whether her prerogatives were not absolute" and succeeded in calling up, in the minds of her senior advisers, the specter of her terrifying father Henry VIII. With advancing years both the old king and his father, Henry VII, had now and then lapsed into a twilit sanity in which they stumbled about, red-faced and speechless with anger, or attacked their companions with lunging violence. The older Henry had withdrawn into secretive paranoia, the younger into raging tyranny.

There was more than a hint of this affliction in Elizabeth Tudor, but unlike her father and grandfather she had never until now allowed her personal eccentricities to damage her discrimination as queen. In the three or four months after her royal cousin's death she came very close to losing her judgment, and allowing her feelings of resentment to lead her into direct conflict with the men through whom she ruled. In the end she did not provoke a governmental conflict; instead her revenge took the form of excluding from court those she meant to punish, then, after a period of painful exile, allowing them to return but exposing them to savage and bitter abuse. Cecil, whom she at first wanted to imprison in the Tower along with Davison, was exiled, then vilified in this way; though old and ill he was made to suffer through the queen's tirades, being called "traitor, false dissembler, and wicked wretch" in tones far sharper than the words themselves. Walsingham stood up better to such ill treatment than Cecil, though he too was ailing and the stormy scenes must have worn down his nerves. The queen addressed him with icy disdain to his face and spoke viciously about him behind his back; he confessed to behavior toward her that was "nothing gracious."

The military emergency that began to loom in the spring of 1588 relieved this atmosphere of sordid tensions and turned the queen's enmity in a more appropriate direction. Not that she welcomed the Spanish assault: in fact she shut her eyes to its inevitability until the last possible moment, doling out funds to pay troops and victual her navy with a tightfistedness remarkable even for her ("King Harry, her majesty's father, never made a lesser proportion of supply than six weeks," complained Admiral Howard when he found out he was to be allotted only a month's provisions at a time) and continuing to negotiate with Parma until mid-June, many weeks after the Armada had left Lisbon harbor. But once she accepted its inescapability the danger began to lift her spirits; she rose to meet its challenge, in a flamboyant gesture of self-display that left an indelible mark on English memory.

On August 8 she sailed on the ebb tide to Tilbury in her royal barge, surrounded by a small flotilla of other rivercraft carrying her trumpeters, her tall gentlemen pensioners and the yeomen of her guard. A flourish of trumpets and drum rolls announced her arrival, and as she disembarked a great shout went up from the men.

She rode through their ranks on a huge white warhorse, armed like a queen out of antique mythology in a silver cuirass and silver truncheon. Her gown was white velvet, and there were plumes in her hair like those that waved from the helmets of the mounted soldiers.

Every man the queen passed fell to his knees and called on God to preserve her, until the extravagant reverence became as embarrassing as it was repetitious. She sent a messenger to precede her and to beg the men to forbear. Yet the shouts of blessing could not be restrained, and the soldiers appointed to stand guard outside her lodging that night toasted one another with cries of "Lord preserve the queen!" until the early hours of the morning.

It had been more than two weeks now since the first sighting of the Spanish fleet, and very little news had reached the Camp Royal about the fate of the two navies. Word came that Drake had seized a galleass, and captured the fleet's "admiral or vice admiral" along with it. One of the greatships had sunk. Two Spanish carracks had been taken by the ships of Flushing and Zeeland. So far, it seemed, English losses had been small. The arrival of the queen greatly encouraged the men, but they knew well in what peril they lay. There were perhaps ten thousand in the neighborhood of the camp, all told—a respectable, but hardly an invincible force. They could not stand long against the Spaniards if they landed; they could not even protect London, for the huge boom of ships' masts and chains that had been built across the mouth of the river had collapsed, leaving open to invaders the pathway to the heart of the country, the court and government.

The following day, August 9, Elizabeth again rode through the camp, this time with a retinue of heralds and sergeants, guardsmen and musicians. Leicester and Lord Grey, marshal of the camp, rode before her, richly dressed "in princely garments of great price, bearing their hats and feathers in their hands." Eight footmen escorted her warhorse, her ladies riding behind her and a troop of guardsmen bringing up the rear.

This time the queen did more than acknowledge the shouts of the men by energetic nods and waves and brief words of thanks. She made a speech, at once rousing and moving, her words carefully chosen to appeal to their patriotism and to their lifelong affection for her.[8]

"My loving people," she began, "we have been persuaded by some that are careful for our safety, to take heed how we commit ourselves to armed multitudes, for fear of treachery. But I assure you, I do not desire to live to distrust my faithful and loving people. Let tyrants fear. I have so behaved myself that, under God, I have placed my chiefest strength and safeguard in the loyal hearts and good will of my subjects; and therefore I am come amongst you as you see, at this time, not for my recreation and disport, but being resolved, in the midst and heat of the battle, to live or die amongst you all, and to lay down for my God and for my kingdom and for my people, my honor and my blood, even in the dust."

She spoke simply, her words interrupted often by cheers. Only the men nearest to her could make them out; to most of those at the camp she was a tiny, gesticulating figure in white, her cuirass gleaming dully and her orange wig bobbing enthusiastically up and down with each shout of approval.

"I know I have the body of a weak and feeble woman," she was saying, "but I have the heart and stomach of a king, and of a king of England too, and think foul scorn that Parma or Spain, or any prince of Europe should dare to invade the borders of my realm; to which, rather than any dishonor shall grow by me, I myself will take up arms, I myself will be your general, judge, and rewarder of every one of your virtues in the field."

Thunderous noise greeted this appeal of the thin, aging woman to lead her troops into battle, and with a final promise to pay the unpaid, meanly fed men—a promise she was to break—Elizabeth ended her speech.

Had this been stage drama rather than plain reality battle would immediately have been joined, or word would have come of a decisive clash between the fleets, decisively ended. But in truth the sequel was anticlimactic.

There had been fighting in the Channel, as it turned out, some of it fierce and prolonged. But according to the messages reaching Tilbury, it had been inconclusive, and had ended in confusion in the first days of August.

The Armada had sailed majestically up the coast, a massive crescent of seagoing castles. Forbidden by King Philip's orders to land, the fleet had anchored off Calais to wait for Parma's men, fending off the English ships as best they could but suffering a good deal of damage from the furious pounding of the latter's awesome guns. Admiral Howard had been wrong: it was not the English but the Spanish ships which were like bears tied to stakes, lumbering and clumsy for all their strength, with the smaller but more deadly English mastiffs tearing at them from all sides.

Medina Sidonia sent message after message pleading with Parma to embark with his army, yet there was no sight of them; in fact the Spanish forces were blocked in by the Dutch. Alternately blinded by thick smoke from the English cannonades and by the driving rain and heaving seas that washed over their bows and broke their bowsprits and foremasts, the Armada captains raged against their commander, against Parma, and against their own ill fortune. On the night of July 28, the English sent blazing fireships into the midst of the enemy vessels; they scattered, and several foundered. Pounded on the following day by the English off Gravelines, and then by yet another in the series of gales that made winter of this freak summer, the Invincible Armada sailed northward, pursued by the English until, short of powder and provisions, they had to give up the chase off Scotland.

A wreckage of spars and sails, ropes and bodies floated in the Channel, witness to much destruction, but the English captains felt cheated of victory and speculated anxiously about the Armada's imminent return. Surely the fleet would not sail home to Spain without making another attempt to complete its task; it must have taken shelter somewhere—perhaps Denmark—to refit, and would be back soon. In the meantime Parma must be belatedly preparing his invasion, and would cross in his own ships with the next favorable tides in a matter of days.

And the English seamen, who had served bravely despite widespread illness from rough seas and sour beer, and had gone on uncomplaining when the fresh water ran out and they were forced to drink their own urine, had now begun to die of typhus by the hundreds. Shipboard mortality left some vessels with too few men to weigh their anchors. "They sicken one day and die the next," wrote the admiral. "It is a most pitiful sight to see the men die in the streets of Margate."[9]

In all the Catholic cities of Europe the bells were rung for a great Spanish victory. The Newfoundland fishing fleet, on its way to Dieppe, had witnessed a monumental naval battle with the English losing many of their ships. Other reports told how Drake had been captured, and gave assurance that Parma must already be in London. From Paris to Venice to Rome the fantastic news traveled, with the few contrary reports dismissed as unreliable. It was to have been a year of disaster, and disaster had indeed fallen on the English, as all good Catholics had known it should. In the Escorial the royal chapel resounded with masses of thanksgiving; in Seville and Madrid rejoicing crowds gathered around bonfires to celebrate the defeat of the wicked heretic Elizabeth and the capture of the devilish dragon Francis Drake.

But the revelry, like the misgivings of the English captains, was premature. The Armada, many of her ships listing badly and others damaged beyond repair, was battling vainly to return home, and losing ground with every mile. Another storm caught them nearing the Orkneys, and by the time the fleet was opposite the Galway coast more and more of the great-ships were wallowing low in the water and sinking out of sight. New tempests drove many of the remnants onto the Irish coasts, where survivors were executed by English soldiers or by the Irish in their pay. Of the overmighty fleet assembled in Lisbon in the spring, only half the ships made it back to their home waters.

Not for many weeks was it known in England that a great victory had been won, the great power of Spain checked for a season. Parma and his army did not come, nor did the Armada reappear. Instead, there were stories of dead horses and mules washing ashore—to save water and excess weight the Spanish had thrown all their animals overboard—and of wrecked galleons driven onto rocky shores or broken up by giant waves. Gradually it became clear that the boasting on the continent was nothing more than wishful thinking. The Armada had been shattered, a victim of the English guns, the treacherous weather, and its own inherent weakness.

"She came, she saw, she fled," read derisive Protestant broadsheets celebrating the miraculous defeat of the unconquerable Armada. In retrospect her proportions seemed impossibly vast, her menace unprecedented. She had come, Ralegh wrote, with "so great and terrible an ostentation" that no other fleet could ever match it; the ships were so huge, Camden recorded with Vergilian pomposity, that the winds were tired of carrying them, and the ocean groaned under their weight. A mistimed, mishandled venture was seen as a providential debacle, an epic chapter in the canon of Protestant history.

But the depositions of the few Spanish survivors who were not at first killed restored the disaster to human scale. They told stories of slow starvation on the crippled ships, of drownings, of wounded men crying for food and water, of scurvy and maddening despair. By the power of the saints a few, a very few, had come through their hour of martyrdom alive.

Late in October, nearly three months after the battle in the Channel and its tragic aftermath, Geoffrey Fenton, secretary for Ireland, went walking on the coast of Sligo. The secretary had been an official of the queen's government for many years, and had seen much slaughter and bloodshed in the Irish wars. Yet nothing in his experience matched the spectacle that awaited him on that raw autumn day. In a walk of less than five miles, he wrote to Cecil afterward, he counted more than eleven hundred Spanish corpses on the beach, washed up, bloated and decaying, by the incoming tide.

PART SIX

"A Lady
Whom Time Had Surprised"

33

I weepe for ioy to see the world decay,
Yet see Eliza flourishing like May.

I t was a brisk December afternoon when André Hurault, Sieur De Maisse, disembarked from the royal barge at the privy stairs of Whitehall Palace and greeted the gentlemen who waited to receive him there. He came as ambassador of Henry IV of France—the former Henry of Navarre —and he had been entrusted with the unenviable task of sounding out Queen Elizabeth on the subject of the war with Spain.

The year was 1597, nine years after the Spanish had surprised themselves and all Europe by failing to conquer England with the Invincible Armada. But far from ending the war the Armada debacle had, paradoxically, toughened Spain so that a decade later her navy was stronger than ever, far stronger than it had been when Medina Sidonia left Lisbon harbor with his doomed flotilla. The rejoicing in England in 1588 had soon turned to apprehension, for Spain not only rebuilt her warships but moved her land forces into Picardy and Brittany in an aggressive attempt to acquire a French port from which to invade England.

Recently King Philip had been active in Ireland as well, sending supplies and gold to support the rebel leader Tyrone and ordering soundings taken along the coast to locate a deep-water landing site. Even as De Maisse mounted the river stairs behind his escort and made his way along the covered walkway leading to the lower rooms of the palace, the court was alive with talk of the latest news from Ireland. The English governor had just died—some said of poison—and Tyrone and his Spanish allies had begun to burn dozens of villages and slaughter all who opposed them.

The ambassador was led into the presence chamber, where he was requested to seat himself on a cushion. The queen, he was told, would see him presently.

In contrast to the dark, low passage into the palace from the river side, which De Maisse had found "passing melancholy," and "with no appearance for a royal house," the presence chamber was all garish color and coruscation. Tapestries flowed in bright blues and reds and burnished golds on the walls, whose surfaces, where they were not covered by the rich hangings, were painted and gilded. There were thick Persian and Indian carpets draped over every table and cupboard, as well as soft rugs on the floors. Oddities of all sorts—ostrich eggs, coconut cups, earthenware art objects and miniatures in crystal and mother of pearl—were mounted in silver and displayed about the room, while outsize ornaments in the shape of frogs, salamanders, golden flowers and giant walnuts gleamed with semiprecious stones.

But the dozens of courtiers who stood about the chamber, brilliant in their overstuffed, overembroidered finery, outshone by far all other ornaments in the room. With their orange and purple beards and their flashing earrings, their jeweled swords and daggers and bright doublets in fashionable shades of "Lusty Gallant," "Drake's Color" and "Dead Spaniard," their sheer gaudiness inspired awe.

But remarkable as they were, the splendors of the presence chamber were not what the Frenchman had come to see. They were nothing more than a backdrop for the principal treasure of the court, and of England—the rare, peerless and altogether extraordinary sixty-four-year-old queen.

In the forty years since her coronation Elizabeth Tudor had never ceased to be the object of intense speculation and scandal, but in the last decade her fame had transcended itself. She had become the stuff of legend.

She had outlived most of her contemporaries. Few in Europe could remember a time when she was not England's monarch. She had outlived nearly all of those who, at her own court, had shaken their heads over her sickliness and fragile woman's body, and muttered that her reign could not be a long one. Among her councilors and intimates, Hatton was dead, and godly Walsingham, blind Blanche Parry, and her beloved Leicester. His brief lieutenancy at Tilbury had been his last; he had died, virtually alone and certainly unmourned, save by the queen, a few days after that command ended. Only Cecil, a portable invalid carried from room to room in an upholstered chair, was left to carry on.

Elizabeth seemed immemorial—and unique. For forty years she had governed alone, without a husband (though certainly not without lovers, it was said), showing, at least in retrospect, an amazing capacity for stubbornness as well as for rule. Her unmarried state—which in fact she had several times been on the point of cheerfully abandoning—had become in her old age the centerpiece of her legend. By an irony of history, this woman of exceptional passions would be known as the Virgin Queen.

Her gorgeous palaces had become half-museums, half-mausoleums where aristocratic tourists paid to see the great queen's perfumed virginal made all of glass, her bed with its gilded beasts and multi-colored ostrich plumes spangled with gold, her brown velvet throne "studded with very large diamonds, rubies, sapphires and the like that glitter among other precious stones and pearls as the sun among the stars." They were shown her "bathing rooms" at Windsor, their walls and ceilings all mirrors, and the breathtaking throne room at Hampton Court, called the Paradise Chamber for its incomparable richness in gold and silver and gems. A very few of these tourists received brief audiences with the queen herself, but none of them wrote down their impressions of her with anything like the penetrating scrutiny of De Maisse.

As he waited on his cushion in the presence chamber the ambassador must have had in mind all that he had been told about the old queen's habits and personality.[1] For his own part he was already favorably impressed, for she had paid him the honor of giving him apartments "wherein Drake had formerly lodged," pleasing him very much. His informants, however, described her as an aging termagant, "a haughty woman, falling easily into rebuke," inclined to think herself far wiser than her councilors and mocking them contemptuously and holding them up to ridicule. Diplomats found her exceedingly difficult to confront, it was said, because she only listened to them as long as what they said was agreeable; as soon as they raised a disagreeable subject she interrupted them with a harangue of her own, often managing to misinterpret their point of view in the process. Usually she misrepresented the entire conversation to the council afterward, so De Maisse was advised to write out his message and arguments and present the written document to her advisers. Worst of all, he learned, Elizabeth was particularly inclined to show her noisy bad temper whenever she heard the name of France or of Henry IV.

After a while the Frenchman was led along a dark passage into the privy chamber, the inner sanctum of the queen, and there, "seated in a low chair, by herself," he found Elizabeth.

Her appearance was startling. She wore, not the customary English gown and kirtle, but a gauzy dressing gown of cloth of silver, unfastened in front so that "one could see the whole of her bosom." Her high-piled red wig was stuck full of gold and silver spangles, and was made still higher by a crowning garland of silver cloth. Two long, fat curls hung down almost to her shoulders, ending at the high jeweled collar of her gown.

She rose and came forward to embrace him, and De Maisse noted that, although her body was still youthful and her movements graceful, her face was long and thin and "very aged." As she greeted him, and began to apologize for not having received him sooner, he found it hard to understand her. She was missing a great many teeth, especially on the right side of her face; those she retained were "very yellow and unequal," and unbecoming in the extreme.

Straining to catch her words through her lisp, he managed to grasp her meaning. She had been ill, she said, looking at him kindly, with a swelling in her right cheek—indeed she could not remember ever having been so ill before. Then glancing down at her robe, she began to excuse her informal dress. "What will these gentlemen say to see me so attired?" she said, looking over at her councilors who were grouped together at the far end of the room and scolding them. "I am much disturbed that they should see me in this state."

De Maisse was a diplomat seasoned in years and experience, yet he found this bizarre mixture of bawdiness and coquetry disconcerting, especially as the queen punctuated her talk by continually grabbing the open front of her gown and flapping it back and forth as if she were too hot, "so that all her belly could be seen." Though her neck was wrinkled, he noted, the skin below was "exceeding white and delicate" all the way down to her navel; the display, though grotesque, made its intended impression.

The ambassador proceeded to the subject matter of his mission, the issue of peacemaking, and found to his relief that the queen neither interrupted him nor flew into a rage at the mention of France. Yet he found her difficult to talk to all the same, for she was never still. At first she sat in her chair, twisting and untwisting the fringe of her gown, then she got up and began to pace around the room—remarking that this was a habit of hers which often tired out ambassadors—and all the time she fairly trembled with nervous energy, showing marked impatience and agitatedly opening and shutting her gown. The fire was too hot, she complained, it was hurting her eyes. She called for her servants to put it out, and the Frenchman paused in his discourse while buckets of water were poured on the sizzling logs.

Elizabeth's overabundant vitality amazed him. He had prepared himself to confront a very old woman, crotchety perhaps, but frail. Instead he found himself faced with a fidgety, restless being whose animal spirits appeared to be waxing rather than ebbing. There was an air of the macabre about Elizabeth; she was like a lively, clacking skeleton whose energetic jerkiness belied her wrinkled cheeks and bare gums. She had in fact lived through her grand climacteric, the dreaded age of sixty-three which few of her contemporaries reached and fewer passed. In that "fatal" year she had for a time seemed to be near death; prolonged insomnia and fevered swellings of her chest and head had prompted her advisers to prepare for a change of reigns, fortifying the court with arms and ordnance and taking steps to guard the treasury at Westminster. But she had recovered quickly enough, and there had been no repetition of the crisis. Even the leg ulcer that had made her limp as a much younger woman seemed no longer to affect her, nor were her hearing or her vision impaired. She had in recent months been troubled by a "desperate ache" in her right thumb, which was as annoying as it was painful since it prevented her from writing. But she hid it, and vehemently denied that it could be gout ("the gout it *cannot* be nor *dare* not be"), and by denying it, she seemed at least for the moment to have cured it.[2]

Under the circumstances, De Maisse made his audience a brief one. He rose to go, and Elizabeth, walking with him to the door, reiterated her coy chagrin "that all the gentlemen he had brought should see her in that condition," and called for them to say their goodbyes. Then, embracing them all "with great charm and smiling countenance," she let them go.

While talking with the queen De Maisse had recognized individuals among the councilors in the room: Cecil, "very old and white," Admiral Howard, much at the heart of affairs and highly honored since his Armada victory, and Cecil's son Robert, who had become principal secretary the year before and who was generally accounted to be "the greatest councilor in England," with whom Elizabeth spent hours in "private and secret conference."

Young Cecil, in 1597 just entering his mid-thirties, was as startling in his appearance in one way as the queen was startling in hers. Elizabeth called him "Pygmy"—a name she knew he detested—but he was not only short, he was hunchbacked, and according to De Maisse, "had small grace and appearance." In an age that believed a crooked soul went with a crooked spine, Robert Cecil was at a severe disadvantage, and his self-consciousness about his appearance did nothing to improve it. He was an urbane and clever man, at home in the witty world of the theater and loving the excitements of gambling and high society. Precocious as a politician and man of affairs, he had sat in Parliament at the age of eighteen and had risen rapidly in Elizabeth's government. Robert Cecil was a worthy successor to Walsingham, to his own father and, reaching back through the century, to

Cromwell and ultimately to Wolsey among the great Tudor drudges who bore the title of royal secretary. All had shared, beyond intellectual force and keen judgment, a capacity for long hours of exceedingly detailed labor; young Cecil was cast in their mold. A man who saw him at court wrote how he hurried his slight, oddly shaped body through the presence chamber on his way to meet with the queen, walking "like a blind man, his hands full of papers and head full of matter."

One figure had been conspicuously missing from the privy chamber: the most flamboyant, the most popular, and many said the most able man at court, the earl of Essex.

Leicester's stepson clearly had greatness of a kind in him. He was built along heroic lines. Tall, broad-shouldered, with the bluff, slightly awkward movements of an athlete and soldier, Essex had the clear, wide forehead, soulful eyes and sensitive expression of a poet. His long face was ruddy in color and grew more so when he talked heatedly of the subject that obsessed him: warfare, and in particular, his own military exploits. "He is entirely given over to arms and the war," wrote De Maisse when he finally met and talked with Essex, "courageous and ambitious, and a man of great designs, hoping to attain glory by arms, and to win renown more and more."[3] The Frenchman also detected his principal flaw. "He is a man of judgment," he wrote, "but one who believes no counsel save his own; when once he has undertaken a thing it is impossible to get it out of his head."

Yet De Maisse would have agreed that, by the mid-1590s, Essex's judgment (coupled with Leicester's patronage and his own marked physical prowess) had brought him a long way. After the death of his penniless, debt-ridden father, Lettice Knollys' first husband Walter Devereux, nine-year-old Essex had been brought up in Cecil's household, along with the hunchbacked boy Robert. By age seventeen he was being advanced at court by his stepfather Leicester, and brought attention to himself by insulting Ralegh and striking him. "What comfort can I have to give myself over to the service of a mistress that is in awe of such a man?" he declared dramatically, running away and hoping to join the fighting in the Netherlands.

He did fight there, and later in France, with considerable distinction, acquiring a reputation not only for brave and audacious soldiery but for old-fashioned chivalry as well. Duels and challenges to single combat suited his temperament perfectly, while drawing attention to his fighting ability and making him popular. But he did not entirely neglect civil for military affairs, and managed to convince Elizabeth of his statesmanship so that she appointed him a member of the council in 1593.

The queen found Essex as exasperating and delightful as a man as he had been as a boy. She called him her "Wild Horse," and felt toward him not only a strong tie of blood—they were cousins, as Elizabeth and Lettice were —but an even stronger one of sentiment. Essex was, after all, the stepson of her lifelong love, and even before Leicester's death she was installing Essex in his court apartments.[4] She put up with his hotheadedness and disobedience, his dueling and violence, though she did complain loudly "that someone or other should take him down and treat [*sic*] him better manners." He was an intelligent, exuberant, extremely handsome man, good company and a brilliant escort for her, and he knew how to please and flatter her. He sat up late partnering her at cards; he sat at her side for the first performance of *A Comedy of Errors;* he wore her favor in the tiltyard and organized athletic entertainments for her pleasure. She was in her sixties, he in his thirties, yet there was nothing grandmotherly in her affection for him. His marriage to Sidney's widow infuriated her—though her fury abated in record time for a secret marriage, two weeks—and she rushed at "the fair Mistress Bridges," one of her waiting maids, with "words and blows of anger" when she learned that the girl was flirting seriously with Essex.

Essex was clearly the rising star at court, yet his absence from the privy chamber on the day of De Maisse's audience was not only conspicuous but eloquent. He felt wronged, and he was showing his feelings, as he customarily did, by staying away from the queen and the council table.

"The court is ordinarily full of discontent and factions," De Maisse commented in his written observations, "and the queen is well pleased to maintain it so." In 1597 the factions were very clearly defined: the Cecils, with Admiral Howard, were on one side, opposing Essex, some of the younger men in government and the young military men who admired Essex's swashbuckling style and who had come to maturity during a decade and more of war. Between the elder Cecil and Essex there was respect and a kind of courtly mutuality ("they render strange charities to one another," De Maisse wrote), but greed corroded their relations; Essex was waiting impatiently for Cecil to die so that he could take over the latter's lucrative post as keeper of the wardrobe.

For their part, the two Cecils and their adherents eagerly pushed the bellicose Essex into hazardous military ventures—he hardly needed their encouragement—and then waited smugly for him to kill himself or, equally to their advantage, to damage himself financially and politically. "If he comes back victorious they take occasion thereby to make him suspected by the queen, and if nothing is accomplished then to ruin him." In time, they sensed, Essex would overreach himself and bring about his own destruction.

If he did, it would very likely be because he was blind to the immense personal capacities of the queen. Their relations fell into the time-honored mold of disdainful lady and flattering, admiring courtier. "Most fair, most dear, and most excellent Sovereign," he addressed her in his letters. "While your Majesty gives me leave to say I love you, my fortune is as my affection, unmatchable. If ever you deny me that liberty, you may end my life, but never shake my constancy." But Essex thought little of the abilities of women, and saw no reason to exempt the queen from his belittling censure. The English court, he told De Maisse confidentially, "labored under two things, delay and inconstancy, which proceeded chiefly from the sex of the queen."[5]

These ungallant sentiments were shared by a great many of the men at Elizabeth's court in her last years. "Ah, silly woman! now she shall not curb me, she shall not rule me!" blurted out one of the blunt soldiers who resented a woman's authority. "God's wounds! This is to serve a base, bastard, pissing kitchen woman; if I had served any prince in Christendom, I had not been so dealt withal." The offender was tried for his slanderous remarks—among them, that Elizabeth had "pissed herself with fear" at the time of the Armada—yet it was not possible to bring charges against every man who looked forward to the day when the kingdom would again pass into male hands. However the common people might cheer for the old queen whenever they caught a glimpse of her, the aristocracy and political elite were more than ready for her presumed successor James VI of Scotland to assume power. Her government, the French ambassador noted, "was little pleasing to the great men and the nobles, and if by chance she should die, it is certain that the English would never again submit to the rule of a woman."[6]

Over the next several weeks De Maisse saw Elizabeth a number of times, and with each audience he came to appreciate her more. Her eccentricities of dress and manner continued to disconcert him. Constantly in motion, she talked constantly as well, digressing into long, musing anecdotes or memories so that the ambassador had often to bring her back to the business at hand. She repeated herself, she indulged her musing memory, yet De Maisse was astute enough not to confuse this deliberate, self-flattering self-indulgence with senility.

He had often to humor her vanity. She was forever calling herself foolish and old, "saying she was sorry to see him there, and that, after having seen so many wise men and great princes, he should at length come to see a poor woman and a foolish." This called forth, as it was meant to, overstated reassurances about her "blessings, virtues and perfections," her prudent sovereignty and wise judgment.

Her concern for her appearance was clearly obsessive. "When anyone speaks of her beauty she says that she was never beautiful," De Maisse wrote, "although she had that reputation thirty years ago. Nevertheless she speaks of her beauty as often as she can." Concern for her looks caused Elizabeth to cancel an appointment with the ambassador one day. She had made herself ready, and had already sent her coaches to fetch him and his entourage to the palace, when she thought better of it and called it off. "Taking a look into her mirror," she said that she looked too ill to be presentable, and "was unwilling for anyone to see her in that state."

When presentable she was breathtakingly garbed, either in robes of her favorite silvery white or in elegant black and white. At one meeting she "wore innumerable jewels on her person, not only on her head, but also within her collar, about her arms and on her hands, with a very great quantity of pearls, round her neck and on her bracelets. She had two bands, one on each arm, which were worth a great price."[7]

Yet striking as her appearance was, it was nearly eclipsed by the force of her personality, and by her remarkable sway of mind. Her arrogance about her talent for rulership was absolute. Having been "intended for affairs of state, even from her cradle," she governed with a degree of astuteness none of her present councilors could match. ("They were young," she said, "and had no experience in affairs of state.") She impressed De Maisse as a "very great princess who knows everything," yet her manner was endearingly candid and on occasion playful. De Maisse introduced to her a secretary who was a member of his legation. She "made good cheer to him" as he knelt before her, saying that she remembered having seen several of his letters. "She began to take him by the hair," De Maisse wrote, "and made him rise and pretended to give him a box on the ears."

The more he saw of her the more the Frenchman was astonished by Elizabeth's liveliness. One afternoon she remarked "that she was on the edge of the grave and ought to bethink herself of death," but then abruptly contradicted herself. "I think not to die so soon, Master Ambassador," she said, "and am not so old as they think." And indeed as De Maisse watched her leave the room at the conclusion of his audience, "retiring half dancing to her chamber," he could well believe it.

The true test of the old queen's acuity, of course, was her ability to come to terms with affairs of state. Here he found her to be not only shrewd, calculating and utterly statesmanlike, but minutely informed about recent events and conditions in many parts of Europe. She had spies everywhere, she confided, and especially in the port cities of Spain. She paid them well, but expected complete loyalty and diligence from them. "If they failed to send true advertisement of all that was being done," she remarked simply, "she caused them to be hanged." De Maisse had occasion to see for himself how the queen insisted on being the first to be informed. A courier arrived at Whitehall bringing letters from France. When he made the mistake of giving the ambassador his letters before delivering Elizabeth's, she made her extreme displeasure known and "caused him to be reprimanded for it."

The business on which he had come to England was urgent, yet De Maisse found himself staying on, week after week, without being able to conclude it. Elizabeth beguiled him by her digressions—which he knew full well were meant to delay the negotiations as well as being "her natural way." They talked of the classics ("she knows all the ancient histories, and one can say nothing to her on which she will not make some apt comment"), of her pleasure in dancing and music (she had some sixty musicians, she said, watching her maids dance and "following the cadence with her head, hand and foot"), of how she still liked to play the virginals and how, in her youth, she had "known six languages better than her own."

"A great virtue in a princess," the Frenchman commented at this.

"It is no marvel to teach a woman to talk," the queen shot back wryly. "It were far harder to teach her to hold her tongue."

They talked of religion, with Elizabeth firmly denying as "malice and lying" all the stories then current about her in Rome. It was not true, she insisted with vehemence, that she had ordered a house burned to the ground knowing that over a hundred Catholic women were taking refuge there; in fact there had been only "one or two" women. It was also an absolute falsehood that she had ordered Catholics to be wrapped in bearskins and baited by dogs; the Roman spies sent to London to touch the bears and see for themselves could confirm this. No matter what scandalmongers said, she had never allowed any Catholic to be harmed who was not a traitor, and no one could condemn her for ordering traitors to be punished. Her conscience was "clear and transparent as crystal," she said, sounding very much like her father when pressed on a sensitive topic. And echoing a famous saying of her sister's, she added "that she wished they could see the inside of her heart in a picture and that it was at Rome, so that all could see it as it was."

Christmas came and went, with its elaborate feasting and music and merriment. No doubt the queen danced with Essex—after displays of pique on both sides, they made up their quarrel—and there was entertainment by companies of actors, among them the lord chamberlain's company with its actor and playwright Will Shakespeare.

In the third week of the new year De Maisse pressed for definitive word to take back to King Henry. What did Elizabeth mean to do about the war with Spain, and, more specifically, about the English troops she had in France?

The subject galled her. "They were but thieves and ought to hang," she said, becoming so angry that the ambassador was alarmed. Seeming to forget his presence she ranted on about the worthless soldiers, lisping through her bad teeth and muttering so that he could not make out her words. She had already sent for them to return home, she told him when she became calmer. But they both knew that the larger issue of peacemaking hung over them, unaddressed and unsettling. King Henry was desperate to make peace with Philip II, yet Elizabeth, peace-loving though she was, had to urge him to continue the war—even if it had to be, as in the past, at her expense. She had no choice. Only months before a vast fleet of Spanish ships had sailed against England, and though bad weather had forced it back to its home port there were reports of a fresh fleet being prepared.

She called De Maisse to come closer, and talked to him in a low voice so that none of her advisers could hear. She gave him a private message to take to King Henry. She said to tell him that she was an old woman, and capable of nothing on her own; her nobles were unstable, and changeable in their moods and opinions, and her ordinary subjects, no matter how loudly they might swear their love for her, were nonetheless fickle and inconstant.

She had to fear everything, Elizabeth went on—hostile Parliaments, a depleted treasury, a bitter and war-weary populace that had already sent twenty thousand men to die in the wars abroad. At this she quoted an appropriate Latin tag, and looked "greatly sorrowful."

No one knew King Philip better than she did. In fact she had talked of him often to De Maisse, telling the ambassador again and again how over the years he had sent fifteen assassins to England to kill her. Yet her spies now told her that Philip was little more than a walking corpse, being kept alive "by force" by his physicians and by his daughter who nursed and fed him.

If only King Henry would wait. Only a few months more, at the most, and the old enemy would be dead.

The message would not please his master, De Maisse knew, nor would it stop him from making peace with Spain. King Henry would desert Queen Elizabeth, and there would be a diplomatic rupture. He cannot have enjoyed taking his leave of the great queen with this knowledge weighing on his mind, but her graciousness lightened the parting. She talked briefly of personal things, saying how pleased she was to have befriended De Maisse and complimenting him on his diplomatic finesse.

391

She embraced him twice, and then embraced the gentlemen who attended him, charming them all as she had on the first audience.

Then she turned to Admiral Howard, who had come up to join the group, and commanded him to give De Maisse a good swift ship for his homeward voyage. Her last words were a dark jest. Watch out, she warned with a laugh, that the Spaniards don't take you prisoner.

34

Fly from her, Age; sleep, Time,
before her throne;
Our strongest wall falls down,
when she is gone.

T he government had run perilously short of money by 1600, and
Elizabeth, calculating the value of the heirlooms in her Jewel House, was
forced to lay sentiment aside and pawn her family treasures.

Many of them had been her father's. There was his gold admiral's
whistle, which he had once worn when he strode the deck of his flagship
the *Great Harry*, wearing a sailor's uniform of cloth of gold. There were
his thick gold bracelets—far too large for his daughter's reed-thin wrists—
enameled with his motto, *Dieu et mon droit*. There was his great seal, and
the gold chains he had worn for the annual feasts of the Garter Knights,
and even two pairs of spectacles, "garnished with gold," which he had worn
when he read his books and perused his documents. These and other
precious things—jeweled crucifixes, objects in Venice gold, an enormous
sapphire (had it belonged to Anne Boleyn?) "in the shape of a heart, with
a hole in it"—brought nearly ten thousand pounds from the merchants who
bid on them, while the "coarse rubbish" that remained was sent to the mint
to be melted down into gold and silver coins.

There was simply not enough income to cover the painfully high expenses of war. "The receipts are so short of the issue," wrote Robert Cecil,
"that my hair stands upright to think of it." It was not only that the costs
of government were greatly swollen by bills for weaponry and military

provisions, and by the unending demands for soldiers' pay, it was also that severe inflation had caused the actual value of crown revenues to shrink. Parliamentary subsidies were large but inadequate, and when Elizabeth tried to collect on the promissory notes she held from the French and Dutch she had little success. There was nothing for it but to sell crown lands, raise loans and, finally, auction off the heirlooms in the Jewel House.

If the queen was in want the men of the court who looked to her for their livings were fighting to the death for the crumbs from her table. The great fortunes of the 1570s and 1580s were long gone, and the richest courtiers of that era had died greatly in debt to the crown. Hatton left unpaid an immense sum he had borrowed from Elizabeth, and Leicester, however sincerely grieved by his bereaved sovereign, was hardly in his grave before she forced his widow to sell off the contents of his magnificent houses and turn over the proceeds to the royal treasury. Walsingham found at the end that the godly did not invariably prosper; he died so overwhelmed by debt that his coffin had to be hidden away from his creditors, and buried at night.

The "grasping days" of the 1590s clutched at the elegantly ruffed throats of the courtiers and turned their customary greed and acquisitiveness to clawing theft. With trade withered by the war, monopolies were the only route to solvency, and the men in power battled one another for the right to control the sale of soap and leather and wine and starch. That the sale of monopolies led to disastrous inflation for the people at large and to court corruption on a massive scale did not make the system any less appealing to those caught up in it, for if they blamed anything or anyone for the twilight madness of the late Elizabethan economy, they blamed the queen.

It was the old queen's "nearness" with her money, people whispered to one another, that was at the bottom of all the trouble. That, and her damnable spite, which led her to keep men waiting months, even years longer than necessary for appointments or licenses and made her set faction against vicious faction merely for her own amusement. What in a younger ruler they might have admired as political skill they condemned in Elizabeth as an old woman's malice—and to an extent they were right. To the young men at her court she was thrice alien: as sovereign, as female, and as a relic of an earlier, irrecoverably different age and generation. By 1600 they had become "very generally weary of an old woman's government," and were overheard to make "turbulent speeches" calling for a change of reigns.

And in truth, however admirably regal she might seem when appearing in public on Accession Day or the Queen's Birthday, with the fresh young waiting maids around her and the sumptuously attired gentlemen of her guard in her train, Elizabeth was rapidly aging and lapsed at times into slatternly disarray or senile fury.

Usually garish with jeweled coiffure and layers of finery, she sometimes forgot adornment and went "quite disfavored, and unattired." She lost interest in food entirely, even in the sugared sweets she was normally greedy for, and ate only plain bread and soup. No doubt her swollen gums and black teeth gave her much pain, and made chewing a torment.

But it was her black moods that frightened her servants and made the councilors shake their heads and remark that she could not live long. "She walks much in her privy chamber," wrote John Harington, one of the elderly queen's favorites, "and stamps with her feet at ill news, and thrusts her rusty sword at times into the arras in great rage."[1] She always kept a sword beside her now, Harington wrote, for the "evil plots and designs" against her life had become so commonplace that she never felt safe.

The Spanish assassins she had kept such close count of, sent by King Philip, came no more after 1598 when the old king died. But there were others, prompted by revenge or political impatience or lunacy. A desperate military captain with a few sworn companions burst into her private apartments as she sat dining with her ladies; at the last instant, when he was at the threshold of the room where she was sitting, he was captured. In the presence chamber a burly madman, a sailor by profession, drew his dagger and would have plunged it into Elizabeth's heart had the guards not rushed to stop him.

It was no wonder that the frowning queen stamped her feet in rage and lay about her with her rusty sword, for she was closing out her reign as she had begun it, in imminent peril from enemies at home and abroad. France had, as she feared, made peace with Spain in 1598, leaving England completely isolated. Under Essex's supervision, the country was being organized for semi-permanent war, with the county levies brought under the coordinated direction of military superintendents and with new military districts designated. There was talk of compulsory military training for all men aged eighteen to fifty, and there was talk, too, of how much better off the country would be with a bold, vigorous young man to rule it.

He was at hand, that bold young man, and his ill-timed, ill considered bid for power brought to a head all the war weariness and growing popular grievances that blighted the last years of the reign.

Essex, the queen's brilliant, exasperating "Wild Horse," had by the late 1590s outgrown his court offices and was impatient for a new challenge. His breakneck ambition had reached the bursting point, and he felt that his aristocratic, chivalrous spirit was being enervated by the besmirching vulgarities of court politics. His respected enemy, old Cecil, died in 1598 and Essex had no taste for direct combat with Robert Cecil or his allies.

Essex had the rudiments of true nobility: high-heartedness, eloquence, purity of aim and raw courage. Honor, especially his own personal honor, meant a great deal to him and it was an instinct beyond simple arrogance that made him want to keep himself pure from the corrupting influence of ignoble men.

"All the world shall witness," he wrote of his ambitions, "that it is not the breath of me, which is but wind, or the love of the multitude, which burns as tinder, that I hunt after, but either to be valued by her above them that are of no value, or to forget the world and to be forgotten by it."

To be valued by Elizabeth was one thing, to be ruled by her was, for Essex, quite another. The eccentric old queen and the blazing young swordsman confronted one another again and again in a one-sided battle of wills. She invariably won, but he saw each loss as only a temporary setback, and steeled himself for the next encounter. When she struck him at the council table and "bade him get him gone and be hanged," his pride was cut to the quick, and forgetting where he was and whom he threatened, he put his hand to his sword to avenge the insult. He did not strike—others checked him—but with the full force of his outraged manhood he swore that he would never take such treatment from anyone, not even Henry VIII, and left the chamber in a rage.

It was undoubtedly best for all concerned that Essex was allowed early in 1599 to leave court to take on the most galling of England's immediate troubles: the rebellion in Ireland. In the latest and most grave of a series of rebellions Hugh O'Neill, earl of Tyrone, had with Spanish aid so weakened England's hold on Ireland that the situation called for an urgent and heavy counterstroke.

Ireland was a purgatory for common soldiers and commanders alike, a militantly uncivilized region where for many generations the English had tracked the long-haired, treacherous Irish through a quagmire of malarial bogs. Essex set out in the spring of 1599 with an army of reconquest seventeen thousand strong, yet his chance for glory was blighted by the impossible conditions he found once he arrived, as well as by his own mercurial moods and wayward judgment. Six months after he left England he was on his way back, his army reduced to a quarter of its strength and his own fighting fervor quenched by dysentery.

Elizabeth took one look at Essex's muddy face and exhausted body— with typical brashness he had not stopped to think or to wash before rushing into her privy chamber at Nonsuch—and saw that he had become too weak and too unstable to be of further use to her. "An ungovernable beast," she remarked cryptically, "must be stopped of his provender." Essex was tried for misconduct, denied his court offices, and, worst of all, denied the income from his monopolies. More than this the queen dared not do, however, for the hero had grown dangerously popular, and his admirers dangerously numerous and angry.

It was not only that London was full of swaggering swordsmen who toasted Essex and sang ballads about his exploits in the taverns; he had become the cherished idol of the impoverished, embattled populace at large. For the 1590s were a "famine decade," when four successive years of disastrously poor harvests brought the anxious, overtaxed people to the edge of starvation. The number of "poor folks who died for want in the streets" was rising rapidly, and throughout the north and west the years of scarcity led to bread riots and to impassioned outbursts of violence against the royal government. Elizabeth's reign was coming to a close, not with the prosperity and contentment she might have hoped for two decades earlier, but amid groans of hunger and the rancorous shouts of protesters forced, as they said, to feed their children on "dogs, cats and nettle roots." Such people cried for a savior, and with very little provocation they might have been persuaded to follow Essex into rebellion.

When put to the test, however, in February of 1601, their loyalty remained with the queen. Essex, consumed by ambition and maddened by frustration, plotted to seize the court and the Tower, and then to raise the Londoners in rebellion. Elizabeth, forearmed, saw to it that her court was well defended, forcing the earl either to submit or to appeal directly to the people.

He made a hotheaded dash through the London streets, shouting "For the queen! For the queen! A plot is laid for my life!" But though he caused great excitement with his mad alarm, and with the several hundred swordsmen who thundered at his heels, his dash for glory was deadborn. The royal officials were in the streets too, proclaiming Essex a traitor and ordering barricades raised to prevent his passage. Lacking allies on the council, deprived of the income he might have used to finance a civil war, Essex had only his soldierly rabble and the common folk to rely on. These might have been enough, had the rising been carefully timed, but without planning or preparation it could not succeed, and Essex was soon captured and executed.

It was to prove the last crisis of the reign. Disaffection continued, and "turbulent spirits" went on vilifying the queen and wishing her dead, but no new Essex arose to rally them and besides, the next ruler was already hovering over the court like a disembodied spirit waiting to take form.

In Edinburgh, King James VI was "giving it out very constantly but in secret and indirectly that her majesty was sick and in peril." He was Elizabeth's undoubted successor, though no official statement proclaimed him so; his son Prince Henry was referred to as "Prince of Wales" in anticipation of his father's succession. James now played the role that had been Elizabeth's when her sister was queen. There was discreet correspondence between one of his servants and one of Cecil's about the procedure to be followed when the queen died, how the news would be carried north and the new reign proclaimed, with armed men and ordnance brought in to secure the court against any possible disturbance. Courtiers began to send letters and gifts to the Scots king, flattering him and asking to be remembered "when he came into his kingdom." That they should desert the setting for the rising sun was only natural, yet Elizabeth found her subjects' behavior disconcerting and often muttered, *"Mortua sed non sepulta"*—dead but not yet buried—under her breath.

If she showed no remorse over Essex's death it did leave her heavyhearted with regret. She wept for him, and for old Cecil, whose death "often drew tears from her goodly cheeks," as no doubt she wept for the several generations of intimate servants and friends she had outlived. Suddenly, unaccountably, she would burst into tears at the realization of her own mortality, weeping less, perhaps, for the inevitability of death than for the certainty that when it came she would have to face it alone. Essex had been the last of her close companions. Now that he was gone she had no one to confide in, and the thought saddened her.

"A queen's declining," wrote Essex's secretary Sir Henry Wotton, "is commonly even of itself the more umbratious and apprehensive," than that of a king, and in truth all sunsets are misty. Much as Elizabeth fought to keep melancholy at bay there was much to depress her. She had achieved a reputation for greatness, if not for goodness, yet for all her capacity she would bequeath to her successor a distempered and overburdened realm, cankered by an unsound economic system, huge debts, acrimonious religious differences, brutal persecution of Catholics and widespread poverty and misery.

The affection her presence invariably called forth from her excitable subjects still heartened her, yet she knew it to be an insubstantial thing. She was under no illusions about their volatile passions, and she knew that when the time came they would cheer as lustily for King James as they now cheered for her.

The months following Essex's failed rising in 1601 were among Elizabeth's worst. She appeared weakened, physically and emotionally, and contrary to her usual habits she "walked out but little" and "meditated much alone."[2]

She still enjoyed the occasional hospitality of her nobles, however, and Robert Sidney, younger brother of Philip Sidney, described a visit she made to his house in the fall of the year.

It was a progress-time spectacle in miniature. Six drummers and six trumpeters sounded a greeting at her arrival, and the lord and lady of the house stood waiting in their finest garb, he in "goodly stuff of the bravest cut and fashion," she in a purple kirtle fringed with gold. The son of the house made a welcoming speech, to which the queen replied graciously, and then the musicians in the gallery began to play and the women danced for her, making her smile with pleasure. There were refreshments—the queen ate two helpings of sugary cake and drank a cordial from a gold cup—and then the company went outdoors to watch an athletic youth perform "gallant feats" on horseback, mounting and dismounting with agile leaps and charging with a lance.

It was a happy afternoon for Elizabeth, who had herself dressed in a rich velvet gown for the occasion and sat contentedly on an improvised throne while the festivities went on around her. It pleased her that the women dancers stepped out of their order and came up one by one to curtsy to her before resuming their places again, and if she did not join them in the dancing she did feel energetic enough to tour the house. She was "much wearied in walking about" from room to room, and though the effort tired her and she had to call for a staff to lean on when going up stairs, she announced that she wanted to come back another day.

She shone in full glory a few weeks later when in the crowded council chamber at Whitehall she made her last and most heartwarming speech to the Commons, closing out an embittered parliamentary session in which she had lost ground politically. She thanked the members for their loyalty and love, and spoke a little of her troubles ("To be a king and wear a crown is a thing more glorious to them that see it, than it is pleasant to them that bear it"). She assured them of her continued commitment to their welfare. "There will never queen sit in my seat," she told them, "with more zeal to my country, care for my subjects, and that will sooner with willingness venture her life for your good and safety, than myself. For it is my desire to live nor reign no longer than my life and reign shall be for your good."

As always, she moved them by her straightforward eloquence—though she spoke indistinctly now, and her voice was the high, shrill voice of old age—and even more by her presence. There she was, a withered spinster nearing seventy, boasting that God had given her "a heart that yet never feared any foreign or home enemy"; it was enough to make the most recalcitrant of her political opponents want to lay down his life for her. The boast she made had immediacy to it, for there was a Spanish occupation force in Ireland five thousand strong. It was not inconceivable that the queen might yet have to heft her rusty sword and brandish it against the enemy.

But if her heart was still stout the old queen's legs were weak, and growing weaker. At the opening of Parliament, walking in procession in all her heavy robes, she suddenly became unsteady on her feet and would have fallen "if some gentlemen had not suddenly cast themselves under that side that tottered, and supported her."[3] After she had ridden on horseback for a mile or two her legs would become numb, forcing her to dismount and to call her footmen over to massage them; their "earnest rubbing" eventually restored her circulation so that she could go on.[4]

"Lord bless her, lord keep her, lord lengthen her days," the balladmongers sang, and to this Elizabeth added a fervent amen. She was in no hurry to die, and the days as they passed were all too short. The unending work of government went far to fill them. Cecil was always at hand with his stacks of papers, and there was much to read if she was to maintain her reputation as "a great princess who knows everything." Her active intellect strove on, always returning to the classics she had first studied with Ascham so many years before.

She read and reread, translated and retranslated, finding in the Greek and Latin writers much that was enduring, if not eternal. Seneca suited her forthright, fatalistic philosophical stance. "It is best to suffer that thou canst not mend," read her translation of one of his letters. "In this rotten bower our life we must lead." "It is no delighting thing to live, for so thou enterest into a long journey, where sometimes thou must needs slip and then up again, and so sometimes thou fallest, often times art wearied, and driven to cry out."

Such heavyhanded sentiments suited Elizabeth's mind and temperament. She distrusted subtlety—though no one of her generation was more capable of appreciating it—and turned to Seneca's morose truisms with a sense of relief. For the exquisite complexities of contemporary theology she had no patience whatever, though she read the works of Augustine and Jerome with "great pleasure." Religious disputes seemed to her as fruitless as they were murderous. "If there were two princes in Christendom who had goodwill and courage it would be easy to reconcile the differences in religion," she told De Maisse, "for there was only one Jesus Christ and one faith, and all the rest that they disputed about but trifles."[5]

Though as an old woman Elizabeth presided over a cultural flowering as brilliant as any in European history it would be a distortion to imagine that she had more than a minor role in it. As queen she patronized poets and playwrights both actively and passively; she protected them when they were threatened by repressive forces and she was proud to read and attend their plays. But they belonged to the coming generation, not to hers; their effulgent virility was at odds with the reassuring verities she sought in the texts of her youth. Shakespeare besought her to rail against fortune; Seneca taught her to accept it, and to soldier cheerfully on. "An evil soldier is he who with sighs follows his captain. Wherefore let us take our charge not like the grudging sluggard, but as the joyful man, nor let us leave this course of fair workmanship, in which all our sufferance is well engraven."[6]

In her long last years Elizabeth slogged on with the determination of a footsore man-at-arms, rousing herself time and again from dark thoughts and casting off physical frailties with a revitalizing burst of vigor. A visitor to Hampton Court caught a revealing glimpse of her in a small chamber, alone save for one attendant, "dancing the Spanish Panic to whistle and tabor." Not realizing that she was being observed, the old queen was tossing her head and stamping her feet with crazy abandon, beating out a measure in defiance of time and death.

35

Weepe, little isle, and for thy Mistris death
Swim in a double sea of brackish waters:
Weepe little world, weepe for great Elizabeth;
Daughter of warre, for Mars himself begate her,
Mother of peace, for she bore the latter.
She was and is, what can there more be said,
In earth the first, in heaven the second Maid.

I t seemed as if the old queen would go on forever. Day after day she roused herself and set off on long, vigorous walks in her gardens and hunting parks, tiring out with her brisk pace the attendants who marched unwillingly at her heels. She took "great walks out of the park, and round the park," striding as energetically "as though she were eighteen years old," and if it happened to be raining or windy, or if there were frost on the ground, so much the better. Her advisers watched her in wry disbelief, her tall, wiry figure bent against the wind, her voluminous skirts whipping around her, knowing they could not dissuade her from her resolute exercise no matter what they said.

Her physicians said, simply, that if old age did not soon kill her, all this exertion would. Yet the physicians came and went—Elizabeth buried five or six of them in her last years—while she went strenuously on, taking a perverse pleasure in the way her arduous regimen disconcerted everyone around her.

With the weather "passing foul," the court was moving from Hampton Court to London. A September storm was blowing, with drenching rain bouncing off the canvas-covered wagons and the roadways a mire of potholes. The queen insisted on making the journey to London on horseback, as she usually did.

"It is not meet for one of your majesty's years to ride in such a storm," young Hunsdon told her gravely. (His father, Elizabeth's cousin and lord chamberlain, had died in 1596.) He did not add, though another courtier did in a private letter, that she was "scarce able to sit upright" at the time.

Elizabeth glared angrily at her relative. "My years!" she called out. "Maids, to your horses quickly!" Before anyone could stop her the queen mounted and rode off, and did not stop until she had reached the capital. Hunsdon was in disgrace for two days.

It was part stunt, part pure contrariness. Elizabeth had always enjoyed doing what people told her she could not do, and now that she was elderly it pleased her to surpass in physical vigor men and women half her age. But it was partly the result, too, of a strong instinct for self-preservation. She had always had her own ideas about medicine (she avoided it) and doctors (she distrusted them). The physicians advised rest and conservation of strength, yet she knew she had always thrived on combativeness and churning activity, and if her feats of endurance sometimes left her panting and prostrate, they seemed to energize her as well.

There was, in addition, a grim political purpose behind her relentless exertions. She knew well that King James—along with all the other monarchs of Europe, and all her enemies abroad—received word of her every faltering step, her every bout of pain or indisposition. Every hint of weakness made the vultures swoop lower. (In Scotland, it was said there was "no talk but England, England, of which they think to make havoc, and every man to be a gentleman with the spoil of the English."[1]) There had to be news of another sort to contradict the accounts of feebleness, so Elizabeth set about making herself look conspicuously strong.

So she walked, and rode, and hunted as often as she could, and danced with foreign envoys "to show that she is not so old as some would have her."[2] She drove out in her jewel-encrusted coach, the manes and tails of the horses dyed as orange as her own false hair, and waved and called out to the people she passed with vigorous graciousness. To impress visitors from abroad she paraded in her privy gardens, elegantly dressed and with a fashionable mask covering her face, then lowered her mask and her neckline to reveal her much-faded handsomeness and snow-white skin. ("Even in old age," wrote a German nobleman who saw her in 1602, "she did not look ugly, when seen from a distance.") She never failed to appear when her public expected her to, at the weddings of her courtiers, at the tilts and other celebrations marking her Accession Day, on feast days and other formal occasions. For her to miss the "preaching, singing, shooting, ringing and running" of the Accession Day celebrations would have been seen as a sad foreshadowing of imminent death, and even though her last

Accession Day in 1602 was marred by suspicion of an assassination attempt, she changed her route to avoid the danger and made her appearance as scheduled.

That November 17 was, in fact, the brightest in recent years. The harvest had been bountiful, Lord Mountjoy, Essex's successor as commander in Ireland, had beaten the invading Spaniards and checked Tyrone, and the plague, which had been virulent in the summer months, had receded. Londoners ran to see the queen, endured a dull sermon at Paul's Cross, and applauded the host of young men who ran recklessly against one another in the tiltyard. The queen was "very merry" when a fool appeared riding a horse no bigger than a dog, and as always she took keen pleasure in the bear-baiting. A swindler caused a commotion by selling a great many tickets for a play to be staged that day, then disappearing with the money. When the theatergoers arrived to find no play in progress, they took their revenge by tearing the tapestries from the walls and breaking the chairs and generally "making great spoil." But somehow the vandalism was absorbed in the mayhem of merrymaking, and the day ended joyously.

To an extent the queen's effort to appear forceful and vigorous succeeded. "Her majesty is very well," reported one court-watcher, "and exceedingly disposed to hunting, for every second or third day she is on horseback, and continues the sport long." Another praised her "health and disposition of body," and said he "had not seen her every way better disposed these many years." Yet among those close to her there were always informers ready to tell how, in truth, an hour's riding so enervated Elizabeth that she had to stay in bed for two days afterward, or how often pain in her arm or weakness in her legs made it impossible for her to try to ride at all. She had to take naps during the day to keep up her strength, and even so she was often exhausted, for the sheer effort of appearing to be vigorous was taking as high a toll as the exercise itself.

In the midst of the Christmas celebrations at the end of the year, Harington found the queen in a "pitiable state." She was sadly in decline, yet she was dying by inches, in an attenuated misery that was as much mental as physical. She continued to govern, he noted, despite failing eyesight and increasing absentmindedness; she shouted hoarsely at her servants for forgetting things, when in fact it was she who had forgotten, and she sometimes sent for her officers, then reacted with fury to see that they had arrived, as she thought, unbidden.[3]

Cecil and the others managed her as best they could. In their letters they cautioned one another against letting her read dispatches containing bad news at night, when it might worsen her insomnia and so make her impossible the next day, and on occasion they misrepresented the true state of affairs in small ways in order to quieten her anxieties. Cecil kept up the gallant tradition in his dealings with her, complimenting her, flattering her vanity. The parchment she wrote on, he declared, was the sweeter for the touch of her hand; he praised "the life of her eyes and color of her lips," the one ruby, the other crystalline topaz.[4] Yet his admiration for her statesmanship was sincere, and as her reign drew to its close he gave some thought to the "memory to be left to all ages" of her papers. Among the records of her rule, he wrote, were to be found the remains of "more piety, learning and dolceness [sweetness] than ever prince did leave behind him." It must have saddened him, as it did Harington, to see her bent over her letters and warrants, squinting vainly in the firelight to make out their words, and then to watch her scribble her name at the bottom, her once fine handwriting now crabbed and spidery.

Early in 1603 Elizabeth caught cold, and on January 21 the court moved to Richmond, as rain poured down, for the duration of the unusually severe winter. The dark skies and harsh storms worsened the queen's cold to bronchitis and, along with the death of her kinswoman the countess of Nottingham, lowered her spirits alarmingly.

"The queen loved the countess well," wrote a foreign envoy who had come to join the deathwatch, "and hath much lamented her death, remaining ever since in a deep melancholy that she must die herself."[5]

She had entered her seventieth year, and her body was protesting its burden in a dozen ways. Her head ached, her bones ached, the rheum in her arm made it painfully tender, she had a cough and suffered from a "continual cold in her legs." Food and drink had lost their savor for her completely, and she could no longer escape from her miseries in sleep, for she was wakeful and fretful at all hours of the day and night. She had always enjoyed coming to Richmond, calling it "a warm winter box for her old age," but now, as she fretted out the long night watches in sleepless anxiety, she took no comfort from her surroundings.

Worst of all her ailments was the heavyheartedness that had become nearly inescapable. She sat on the floor, embroidered cushions under her, staring at one spot for hours at a time, her motionlessness relieved only by noisy sighs and bouts of crying.

Her usefulness had ended, and she no longer had the will to rouse herself from the listless sadness that immobilized her. From time to time she "raged exceedingly" at ministers who demanded money and at her nemesis Tyrone, who had managed to turn defeat to his advantage and to force the angry, humiliated queen to pardon him. But for the most part her "notable decay of judgment and memory" prevented her from attending to the tasks of rule.

"She cannot abide discourses of government and state," it was said, "but delighteth to hear old Canterbury tales, to which she is very attentive."[6] She would see Cecil, but was unpredictable about receiving anyone else; "impatient and testy," she often sent others away.

It injured her greatly that, now that her death was close at hand, her servants and officials grew lax in obeying her and paid as little attention to her as if she were dead already. She was "very much neglected," wrote the bishop of Carlisle, "which was an occasion of her melancholy." To many, especially her "long-worn, threadbare, poor old servants," she was of interest chiefly for the possessions she would leave behind when the end finally came. What would become of her jewels, the rich furnishings of her apartments, her hundreds of gowns and perfumed gloves and swansdown fans? Would the new king bestow these treasures on Elizabeth's long-suffering, long underpaid servants, or would he take them for his wife? (Surely not, the gossip went; James and his queen were on distant terms at best, and it was rumored that he would have had her imprisoned if his councilors had not dissuaded him.)

"All are in a dump at court," an observer wrote. "Some fear present danger, others doubt she will not continue past the month of May, but generally all are of opinion that she cannot overpass another winter." The courtiers were nearly as fretful as the elderly queen, kept indoors by bad weather and forced into anxious inactivity by the deadlock in political affairs. Business and careers came to a standstill at Richmond, while as the long weeks passed the palace began to reek more and more strongly of unwashed bodies and unwashed floors.

In the first days of March the queen's symptoms became more severe, and made her so "full of chagrin and weary of life" that she refused to swallow the hated medicines her physicians urged on her and sank into a coma-like lassitude. She would not struggle to live, but she would not go to bed and die either. She sat on her cushions, aware yet fatally indifferent to her surroundings, not speaking, not eating, not changing her clothes. A swelling in her throat broke open, choking her with fluid and leaving her prostrate "like a dead person," but the doctors "found means to dry it up well," and the crisis passed.

It was a long, slow, wearying death, without drama or color—a death out of keeping with Elizabeth's flamboyant life. Glassy-eyed and emaciated, she lingered on amid her cushions, her body malodorous from disease, her finger in her mouth like an idiot or a dazed child. Finally, on the twenty-first of March, she did not resist the suggestion that she take off her soiled clothes and get into bed.

It may have been word of this significant event that caused fears of a "commotion" among the nervous men and women of the court. With the queen in her deathbed it was time to take refuge against whatever trouble was coming. The council had fortified the palace and, in London, had begun to amass wheat in the storehouses to ensure against bread riots. The military danger, if it should come, would be from the north, where King James was said to have fourteen thousand mounted men ready to put into the field. London's defenses were strengthened by a wide ditch dug around its northern perimeter and on eastward to Westminster, though the city's best defense, it seemed, might be its worst affliction. Plague had broken out in both the city and suburbs, and was spreading so rapidly, and so early in the year, that the contagion promised to be far worse than any in memory.

They put the queen to bed in her high wooden bed with its ornate beasts and gilded plumes, covering her with embroidered sheets and laying her bony head on a silken pillow. She was greatly wasted from lack of food, but apart from a little broth, ate nothing, and continued her dulled vigil by turning on her side and ceasing to speak or to look at anyone. Alone despite the others in the room, her last thoughts shrouded in enigmatic silence, the great queen sank toward death.

There was a murmur of voices in the room as meditations and prayers were read; outside it, and in the realm at large, preachers had been instructed to pray for Elizabeth, "that she might be strengthened in weakness, her grief assuaged, her mind purified, and her health restored."[7] At the name of Jesus and when Archbishop Whitgift, who was with her, spoke of heaven she seemed to brighten fleetingly with hope, and hugged his hand. Within hours of going to bed she found she could not speak, and had to indicate by lifting her hand and eyes to heaven that she had full faith in her salvation "by Christ's merits and mercy only."

It was her last gesture. Late in the evening of March 23 she went to sleep, and her favorite chaplain, Dr. Parry, watched over her. In the corridor outside the bedchamber the chief servants and dignitaries paced back and forth, waiting for word to reach them. A horse stood in the outer courtyard, saddled and ready for its rider, who would set off northward as soon as the announcement was made to carry the news of the queen's death to King James. There was "great weeping and lamentation among the lords and ladies" when several hours later Dr. Parry, perceiving that the end had come and beginning earnestly to pray for the queen's soul, indicated that she was dead.

The word was passed, the rider mounted, and then the sound of galloping hoofbeats echoed through the rainy night.

Notes

Burghley Papers	*A Collection of State Papers Relating to Affairs in the Reigns of King Henry VIII, King Edward VI, Queen Mary, and Queen Elizabeth . . . left by William Cecil Lord Burghley, and now remaining at Hatfield House,* ed. Samuel Haynes and William Murdin. 2 vols. London: William Bowyer, 1740–59.
EHR	*English Historical Review*
L.P.	*Letters and Papers, Foreign and Domestic, of the Reign of Henry VIII,* ed. J.S. Brewer, R.H. Brodie and James Gairdner. 21 vols. London: Her Majesty's Stationery Office, 1862–1910.
Relations politiques	Kervyn de Lettenhove, Joseph M.B.C. and L. Gilliodts van Severen, eds., *Relations politiques des Pays-Bas et de l'Angleterre, sous le règne de Philippe II.* 11 vols. Brussels: P. Hayez, 1882–1900.
Salisbury MSS.	*Calendar of the Manuscripts of the Most Hon. the Marquis of Salisbury . . . preserved at Hatfield House, Hertfordshire.* 23 vols. in 19. London: Her Majesty's Stationery Office, 1883–1973.
Sp. Cal.	*Calendar of Letters, Despatches, and State Papers, relating to the Negotiations between England and Spain, preserved in the Archives at Vienna, Simancas, Besançon and Brussels,* ed. Pascual de Gayangos, G.A. Bergenroth, Martin A.S. Hume, Royall Tyler, and Garrett Mattingly. 13 vols. London: His and Her Majesty's Stationery Office, 1862–1954.
Sp. Cal. Elizabethan	*Calendar of Letters and State Papers relating to English Affairs, preserved principally in the Archives of Simancas,* ed. Martin A.S. Hume. 4 vols. London: Her Majesty's Stationery Office, 1892–1899.

State Papers, Domestic   *Calendar of State Papers, Domestic Series, of the Reigns of Edward VI, Mary, Elizabeth and James I, preserved in the State Paper Department of Her Majesty's Public Record Office*, ed. Robert Lemon and Mary A. E. Green. 12 vols. London: Longman, etc., 1856–1872.

State Papers, Foreign, Elizabeth   *Calendar of State Papers, Foreign Series, of the Reign of Elizabeth, preserved in the State Paper Department of Her Majesty's Public Record Office*, ed. Joseph Stevenson et al., 23 vols. in 26. London: Longman, etc., 1863–1950.

Ven. Cal.   *Calendar of State Papers and Manuscripts, relating to English Affairs, existing in the Archives and Collections of Venice, and in Other Libraries of Northern Italy*, ed. Rawdon Brown et al., 38 vols. in 40. London: Longman, etc., 1864–1947.

References to *L.P.*, *Sp. Cal.* and similar collections are to page numbers, not document numbers.

PART ONE

The Improbable Child

CHAPTER 1

1. *L.P.* V, 592.
2. *L.P.* VI, 412, 420.
3. *Ibid.*, 450.
4. *Sp. Cal.* IV:ii:ii, 923.
5. *Ibid.*, 788.

CHAPTER 2

1. *L.P.* VI, 684.
2. *Ibid.* VII, 360.
3. *Ibid.* VI, 658.
4. *Ibid.*, 604, 618.
5. *Ibid.*, 610.
6. *Ibid.*, 629.
7. *L.P.* VII, 424–5.
8. *Ibid.* VIII, 172–3.
9. *Ibid.* IX, 189.
10. *Ibid.* VII, 191.
11. *Ibid.* VIII, 297.
12. *Ibid.*, 204.
13. *Sp. Cal.* V:ii, 39.
14. *L.P.* X, 361–2, 359–60.

CHAPTER 3

1. *L.P.* VIII, 157.
2. *Ibid.* X, 356.
3. *Ibid.*, 380.
4. *Ibid.*, 381.
5. *Ibid.*, 433.
6. *Ibid.*, 380.
7. *Ibid.*, 466.
8. *Ven. Cal.* VI:iii, 1538.
9. *L.P.* X, 104, 339.
10. *Ibid.*, 135.

11. *Ibid.* XI, 346.
12. *Ibid.* X, 377.
13. *Ibid.* XI, 17.
14. *Ibid.* X, 357.
15. *Ibid.*, 333.
16. *Ibid.*, 380, 378. Modern historians concur in finding Anne's guilt an imponderable issue, though one not lightly to be dismissed.
17. *Ibid.* X, 401.
18. *Ibid.*, 371, 382.
19. *Ibid.* XI, 90; Agnes Strickland, *Lives of the Queens of England*, 6 vols. (London, 1873), III, 5–7.
20. *L.P.* XI, 130, 104.
21. *Ibid.*, 202.

CHAPTER 4

1. *L.P.* XIV:i, 507, 515.
2. Strickland, III, 32, citing MSS. Lansd. 1236 f. 35.
3. *L.P.* XIV:ii, 257.
4. Lu Emily Pearson, *Elizabethans at Home* (Palo Alto, 1957), pp. 187–8.
5. *L.P.* VI, 629.
6. *Ibid.* VIII, 101.
7. Cited in Pearson, pp. 183, 186, 190.
8. Roger Ascham, *The Scholemaster*, in *English Works*, ed. William Aldis Wright (Cambridge, 1904), p. 210.
9. Cited in Pearson, pp. 208–9, 191.
10. *Ibid.*, 191, 189.
11. *L.P.* XIV:i, 5; *L.P.* XV, 1.
12. John Nichols, *The Progresses and Public Processions of Queen Elizabeth*, new ed., 3 vols. (London, 1823; reprint New York, 1969), I, x note.
13. M. St. Clare Byrne, *Elizabethan Life in Town and Country* (London, 1954), pp. 208–9; Pearson, p. 182.
14. Ascham, *Scholemaster*, p. 200.
15. *L.P.* XV, 391.
16. *Ibid.*, 636.
17. *Ibid.* XVII, 66.
18. *Ibid.* XVII, 66; *L.P.* XV, 519.

CHAPTER 5

1. *L.P.* XIV:i, 53.
2. *Ibid.* XVIII:ii, 283.
3. *Ibid.*, 115.
4. Frank A. Mumby, *The Girlhood of Queen Elizabeth: A Narrative in Contemporary Letters* (London, 1909), pp. 22–3. There seems to be no evidence to support the often repeated presumption that this period of separation was the result of some misbehavior on Elizabeth's part.
5. *The Whole Works of Roger Ascham*, ed. J. A. Giles, 3 vols. (London, 1864–5; reprint New York, 1965), I:i, 108. For Ascham's life see Lawrence V. Ryan, *Roger Ascham* (Palo Alto and London, 1963).
6. J. E. Neale, *Queen Elizabeth I* (London, 1934; reprint 1952), pp. 23–4; Strickland, III, 225–6.
7. Nichols, *Progresses*, I, x note.
8. Nicholas Udall, preface to *Paraphrases of St. John's Gospel*, cited in G. Ballard, *Memoirs of Several Ladies of Great Britain* (London, 1752), p. 127.
9. Anthony Martienssen, *Queen Katherine Parr* (New York and London, 1973), p. 227.

411

PART TWO

God's Virgin

CHAPTER 6

1. *Burghley Papers*, I, 100.
2. *Ibid.*, 98.
3. *Ibid.*, 70.
4. W. K. Jordan, *Edward VI* (London, 1968–70), II, 18.
5. *Sp. Cal.* IX, 46–7.
6. Jordan, II, 422.
7. The Good Duke is reassessed in M. L. Bush, *The Government Policy of Protector Somerset* (London, 1975).
8. Ascham, *Whole Works*, I:i, lvi–lvii.
9. For what follows see *Burghley Papers*, I, 99–100.
10. *Burghley Papers*, I, 99.
11. *Ibid.*, 99–100.
12. Martienssen, p. 24, citing Vives, *De Institutione Foeminae Christianae*.
13. *Ibid.*, 24–5.
14. *Burghley Papers*, I, 96.

CHAPTER 7

1. *Burghley Papers*, I, 96. "As I remember," Thomas Parry deposed later, "this was the cause why she was sent from the queen; or else that her grace parted from the queen. I do not perfectly remember whether of both she [Ashley] said, she went of herself, or was sent away."
2. *Ibid.*, 101.
3. Ascham, *Scholemaster*, p. 261.
4. *Apologia . . . pro caena Dominica*, cited in Ryan, p. 96.
5. Ascham, *Whole Works*, I:i, lii–liii.
6. Mumby, pp. 69–72.
7. *Ibid.*, 35–6.
8. *Ibid.*, 37.
9. *Burghley Papers*, I, 103–4.
10. Cited in Martienssen, p. 239.
11. *Burghley Papers*, I, 82.
12. *Ibid.*
13. *Ibid.*, 105.
14. *Sp. Cal.* IX, 346–7. Their vehement disavowal of such backing after Seymour's apprehension suggests their involvement, as does the fact that the French king was closely informed of the admiral's activities. The messenger who brought him news of Seymour's arrest "broke one of his ribs in haste."
15. *Burghley Papers*, I, 80.
16. *L.P.* XXI:ii, 320–2.
17. *Burghley Papers*, I, 96.
18. *Ibid.*
19. *Ibid.*, 100.
20. *Ibid.*, 102.
21. *Ibid.*, 101.
22. *Sp. Cal.* IX, 340. Paget's remark may be the source of the apocryphal comment attributed by the fanciful historian Leti to Elizabeth on Seymour's death: "This day died a man of much wit and very little judgment."

CHAPTER 8

1. *Burghley Papers*, I, 70.
2. *Ibid.*, 70–71.
3. *Ibid.*, 72.
4. This story had a very long life. A version of it was still being told on the continent in 1601.
5. Henry Clifford, *The Life of Jane Dormer, Duchess of Feria* (London, 1887), p. 86.

6. *Burghley Papers*, I, 89–90.
7. *Ibid.*, 94–5.
8. *Ibid.*, 89, 102.
9. *Ibid.*, 106–7.
10. *Ibid.*, 108.
11. Mumby, pp. 55–9.
12. John Aylmer, *A Harbor for True and Faithful Subjects*, cited in Strickland, III, 38–9.
13. *Sp. Cal.* IX, 489.
14. *Ibid.*, X, 6–7.
15. *Salisbury MSS*, I, 60.
16. Jordan, II, 20.

CHAPTER 9

1. *Sp. Cal.* X, 186.
2. *Ibid.*, 209.
3. *The Chronicle and Political Papers [of Edward VI]*, ed. W.K. Jordan (London, 1966), p. 71.
4. Viscount Strangford, ed., *Household Expenses of the Princess Elizabeth during her Residence at Hatfield October 1, 1551 to September 30, 1552*. In *The Camden Miscellany*, Vol. II. Camden Society, Old series, LV (London, 1853).
5. Ascham, *Whole Works*, I:i, 175–6; Ryan, p. 112.
6. *Sp. Cal.* X, xxvii, and 114–15.
7. *Ibid.*, 215–16.
8. Jordan, II, 87, 102.
9. Frederick Chamberlin, *The Private Character of Henry VIII* (New York, 1931), pp. 243–4; Jordan, II, 133–4.
10. Jordan, II, 494, 497.
11. *Sp. Cal.* XI, 54–5.

CHAPTER 10

1. *Sp. Cal.* XI, 228.
2. John G. Nichols, ed., *Literary Remains of Edward VI* (London, 1857; reprint New York, 1963), I, cxl.
3. Years later Cecil told his clerk John Clapham that Elizabeth had been in love with Courtenay, and that he was in fact the only man she had ever wanted to marry. John Clapham, *Elizabeth of England; certain observations concerning the life and reign of Queen Elizabeth*, ed. Evelyn and Conyers Read (Philadelphia, 1951), p. 68.
4. *Sp. Cal.* XI, 252–3.
5. John G. Nichols, ed., *The Chronicle of Queen Jane, and of Two Years of Queen Mary . . .* Camden Society, Old series, XLVIII (London, 1850), 69.
6. *Sp. Cal.* XII, 55ff.
7. *The Acts and Monuments of John Foxe*, ed. George Townsend and A.R. Cattley, 8 vols. (London, 1837–41), VI, 414.
8. Patrick Fraser Tytler, *England Under the Reigns of Edward VI and Mary*, 2 vols. (London, 1838), II, 310–11; Mumby, 107–8; Chamberlin, *Private Character of Henry VIII*, 45–8.

CHAPTER 11

1. Neale, *Elizabeth I and Her Parliaments* (London, 1953–1957), I, 148.
2. Tytler, II, 320, 337–8.
3. *Ibid.*, 340–1; *Holinshed's Chronicles of England, Scotland and Ireland*, 6 vols. (London, 1807–8), IV, 56.
4. Tytler, II, 342.
5. Foxe, *Acts and Monuments*, VIII, 607ff.
6. *Ibid.*, VIII, 609.

CHAPTER 12

1. "State Papers Relating to the Custody of the Princess Elizabeth at Woodstock in 1554," ed. Rev. C. R. Manning, in *Norfolk Archaeology*, IV (Norwich, 1855), 176.

2. Tytler, II, 371–2.
3. *Ibid.*, II, 343–4; *Ambassades de messieurs de Noailles en Angleterre*, 5 vols. (Leyden, 1763), III, 95–103.
4. Tytler, II, 366–7.
5. *Ibid.*, II, 415, 396, 367, 405.
6. *Ibid.*, II, 398–9.
7. "State Papers . . . Woodstock," p. 206.
8. Ian Dunlop, *Palaces and Progresses of Elizabeth I* (London, 1962), pp. 16–17.
9. *Ibid.*, 13ff.
10. Nichols, *Progresses*, I, 9–10 note.
11. *Ibid.*, I, 9–10.
12. *Ibid.*, I, 10–11.
13. "State Papers . . . Woodstock," p. 142.
14. *Ibid.*, 176–7.
15. *Ibid.*, 169, 172–3.
16. *Ibid.*, 170, 166, 169.
17. *Ibid.*, 175–6, 179, 182–3.
18. *Ibid.*, 192–3.
19. *Ibid.*, 224–5.

CHAPTER 13

1. *Sp. Cal.* XIII, 135.
2. *Ibid.*, 169; *Ven. Cal.* VI:i, 60–61.
3. *Sp. Cal.* XIII, 145.
4. *Ven. Cal.* VI:ii, 1059.
5. *Ibid.*, 1058–9.
6. *Ibid.*, 1059.
7. *Ibid.*
8. *Ibid.*
9. Carolly Erickson, *Bloody Mary* (New York, 1978), p. 420.
10. *Ven. Cal.* VI:i, 57.
11. Erickson, *Bloody Mary*, p. 413, and sources cited there.

CHAPTER 14

1. *Ven. Cal.* VI:ii, 1059.
2. Peter J. French, *John Dee: The World of an Elizabethan Magus* (London, 1972), pp. 34–5. It is unclear just how Dee came to make the astrological calculations that endangered him.
3. Ascham, *Whole Works*, I:ii, 443–8.
4. *Ibid.*
5. Frederick Chamberlin, *The Private Character of Queen Elizabeth* (New York, 1922), p. 22.
6. Ascham, *Whole Works*, I:ii, 447.
7. *Ven. Cal.* VI:i, 417–18.
8. *Ibid.*
9. Erickson, *Bloody Mary*, pp. 436–7.
10. *Ven. Cal.* VI:i, 479–80.
11. *Ibid.* VI:ii, 484; on the Pope forgeries see Herbert E. D. Blakiston, "Thomas Warton and Machyn's Diary," *EHR* (April 1896), 282–300.
12. *Ven. Cal.* VI:i, 559.
13. *Sp. Cal.* XIII, 238.
14. *Ibid.*, 90.
15. *Ven. Cal.* VI:ii, 1079 and note, 1081 note.
16. *Ibid.*, 1080.
17. *Ibid.* French agents in England were reporting that her jaundice and shortness of breath were likely to be fatal.
18. *Ven. Cal.* VI:iii, 1538.
19. *Sp. Cal.* XIII, 293.
20. Cited in J. E. Neale, "The Accession of Queen Elizabeth I," *History Today*, III, No. 5 (May 1953), 295.

21. *Ven. Cal.* VI:ii, 1058.
22. *Sp. Cal.* XIII, xvi.
23. *Ibid.*, 379.
24. Neale, "Accession," pp. 295–6.
25. *Ven. Cal.* VI:iii, 1563.
26. *Relations politiques*, I, 280–1. On this document see Conyers Read, *Mr. Secretary Cecil and Queen Elizabeth* (New York, 1961), p. 479 notes 2–3.
27. *Ven. Cal.* VI:iii, 1549.

PART THREE

"La Plus Fine Femme du Monde"

CHAPTER 15

1. John Hayward, *Annals of the First Four Years of the Reign of Queen Elizabeth*, ed. John Bruce. Camden Society, Old series, VII (London, 1840), 6.
2. *State Papers, Foreign, Elizabeth*, I, 21, 28, 101.
3. Neville Williams, "The Coronation of Queen Elizabeth I," *Quarterly Review*, CCXCI, No. 597 (July 1953), 398–401.
4. *State Papers, Foreign, Elizabeth*, I, 7. In 1585 or so the number of Elizabeth's personal guard was reported to be about two hundred.
5. *Ibid.*, I, 6.
6. Read, *Mr. Secretary Cecil*, p. 124.
7. *Sp. Cal. Elizabethan*, I, 12, 10.
8. *Ibid.*, I, 12, 10, 8, 7.
9. *Ibid.*, I, 7, 17–18.
10. *Ibid.*, I, 13.
11. *Salisbury MSS*, I, 158.
12. R. B. Wernham, *Before the Armada: The Emergence of the English Nation, 1485–1588* (New York, 1966), p. 237.
13. *State Papers, Foreign, Elizabeth*, I, 209. In his letter Knox ruefully admitted that his "First Blast had blown from him all his friends in England."
14. Nichols, *Progresses*, I, 38. This account of Elizabeth's coronation is drawn primarily from the most reliable contemporary English account, printed in Nichols, I, 38ff and from *Ven. Cal.* VII, 12ff.

CHAPTER 16

1. *Sp. Cal. Elizabethan*, I, 57–8.
2. *Ven. Cal.* VII, 105; *Sp. Cal. Elizabethan*, I, 112.
3. Victor von Klarwill, ed., *Queen Elizabeth and Some Foreigners* (New York, 1928), p. 157.
4. *Ibid.*
5. *Ibid.*, 113–15.
6. *Sp. Cal. Elizabethan*, I, 68, 57–8.
7. *Ibid.*, I, 57, 75.
8. *Ven. Cal.* VII, 27, 80–1, 84; Philip Hughes, *The Reformation in England*, 3 vols. (New York, 1951–4), III, 28–9 and notes.
9. *State Papers, Foreign, Elizabeth*, I, 152–3.
10. *Sp. Cal. Elizabethan*, I, 51.
11. *Ven. Cal.* VII, 91.
12. Nichols, *Progresses*, I, 69–73.
13. Klarwill, pp. 120–1.
14. *Sp. Cal. Elizabethan*, I, 67.
15. *Ibid.*, I, 74.
16. *Ibid.*, I, 95ff, 107.
17. *Ibid.*, I, 119, 110, 101–2. *Burghley Papers*, I, 212.
18. Klarwill, pp. 98, 99, 157.
19. *Sp. Cal. Elizabethan*, I, 141.

CHAPTER 17

1. Read, *Mr. Secretary Cecil*, p. 199.
2. *Sp. Cal. Elizabethan*, I, 175.
3. *Ibid.*, I, 175, 113.
4. *Ibid.*, I, 175.
5. *Burghley Papers*, I, 364.
6. *Ibid.*, 362. One wonders whether any significance ought to be attached to the fact that, within days of writing his letter, Francis Knollys received a large gift of lands from the queen. *State Papers, Domestic*, I, 159.
7. *Burghley Papers*, I, 361–2.
8. *Ibid.*, I, 368. Cecil's minute is undated, but is placed among the documents from fall 1560.
9. Read, *Mr. Secretary Cecil*, p. 202.
10. *Sp. Cal. Elizabethan*, I, 181–2. Frances Brandon, daughter of Henry VIII's sister Mary Tudor and Charles Brandon, had married her steward. Brandon's fourth wife, Catherine, had in her widowhood married a gentleman of her household. Both women were duchesses, and Frances Brandon was in line for the throne.
11. *Ibid.*, 188–9.

CHAPTER 18

1. *Sp. Cal. Elizabethan*, I, 45; Thomas Wright, ed., *Queen Elizabeth and Her Times*, 2 vols. (London, 1838), I, 7–8. The envoys representing the archduke Charles at Elizabeth's court, while pressing for the queen's own consent to marry their candidate, kept Catherine Grey in the background as an alternative should the royal marriage project fail.
2. *Sp. Cal. Elizabethan*, I, 214; Chamberlin, *Private Character of Queen Elizabeth*, pp. 50–51.
3. *Sp. Cal. Elizabethan*, I, 213. On Amy Robsart's death see Ian Aird, "The Death of Amy Robsart," *EHR*, LXXI, No. 278 (January 1956), 69–79 and Elizabeth D'Oyley, "The Death of Amye Robsart," *History Today*, VI, No. 4 (April 1956), 252–60.
4. F. E. Halliday, "Queen Elizabeth I and Doctor Burcot," *History Today*, V, No. 8 (August 1955), 542–4 draws from the seventeenth-century memoirs of Richard Carew an account of Queen Elizabeth's encounter with one Dr. Burcot, a German mining engineer and medical wonder-worker. According to this account, it was Dr. Burcot who cured the queen of smallpox in 1562. But Halliday's inexact chronology mars the plausibility of his argument somewhat, and there are major discrepancies between the course of the queen's illness as described in the later account and the dispatches written by Ambassador De Quadra at the time. Burcot may indeed have treated Elizabeth, but Carew's story cannot be taken as an accurate narrative of that treatment.
   In this reconstruction of the events—whose chronology is somewhat muddled in De Quadra's dispatches—I have relied on *Sp. Cal. Elizabethan*, I, 262ff and in particular the more complete transcriptions in *Relations politiques*, III, 162ff.
5. Chamberlin, *Private Character of Queen Elizabeth*, p. 51.
6. On all the candidates for the throne see Mortimer Levine, *The Early Elizabethan Succession Question, 1558–1568* (Palo Alto, 1966).
7. *Sp. Cal. Elizabethan*, I, 263.

CHAPTER 19

1. *Sp. Cal. Elizabethan*, I, 126.
2. Klarwill, pp. 194, 59.
3. *Ibid.*, 194; *Sp. Cal. Elizabethan*, I, 49.
4. *Memoirs of Sir James Melville*, ed. A. Francis Stewart (New York, 1930), p. 91. Melville's stay at Elizabeth's court in 1564 is well documented in these memoirs, pp. 88ff.
5. Melville, *Memoirs*, p. 92. A formal description of Dudley's elevation is in Nichols, *Progresses*, I, 190–1.
6. *Ibid.*, 82.
7. Cited in Strickland, III, 154.

CHAPTER 20

1. Cited in A. L. Rowse, *The Elizabethan Renaissance, Part 1: The Life of the Society* (London, 1971), p. 134.
2. Allegra Woodworth, "Purveyance for the Royal Household in the Reign of Queen Elizabeth," *Transactions of the American Philosophical Society*, New series, XXXV, Pt. 1 (1945), 3–89.
3. *Ibid.*, 12.
4. *Ibid.*, 13.
5. Dunlop, p. 100.
6. E. K. Chambers, *The Elizabethan Stage*, 4 vols. (Oxford, 1923), I, 15–16 and note.
7. Klarwill, pp. 160, 58.
8. Ascham, *Scholemaster*, p. 207.
9. Klarwill, p. 195.
10. *Ibid.*, 145, 337.

PART FOUR
"A Very Strange Sort of Woman"

CHAPTER 21

1. Wright, I, 331–8. This account of the rebellion comes from Wright, I, 331ff and notes, and Hughes, III, 269–70 and *passim*.
2. *State Papers, Foreign, Elizabeth*, IX, 159, 147; Hughes, III, 269–70.
3. Hughes, III, 247.
4. Wright, I, 331.
5. On Elizabeth's government in the 1560s see Wallace MacCaffrey, *The Shaping of the Elizabethan Regime* (Princeton, 1968).
6. *State Papers, Domestic*, VII, 100.
7. *Ibid.*, VII, 139, 104.
8. *Ibid.*, VII, 114.

CHAPTER 22

1. Hunsdon, Da Silva wrote in 1567, was "not thought much of as a soldier." *Sp. Cal. Elizabethan*, I, 676.
2. *Salisbury MSS*, I, 50.
3. Historians aver that, despite the gossip over Elizabeth's inability to bear children, she was perfectly healthy and able to reproduce. Conyers Read, *Lord Burghley and Queen Elizabeth* (New York, 1960), pp. 210–11; Neale, *Elizabeth I*, pp. 220, 239–40, 244–5; Wernham, p. 259. However, contemporary opinion varied, and rumors were predictably inconsistent. "If my spies do not lie," Feria wrote in 1559, "which I believe they do not, for a certain reason which they have recently given me I understand she will not bear children." In 1561, De Quadra recorded that "the common opinion, confirmed by certain physicians, is that this woman is unhealthy, and it is believed certain that she will not have children, although there is no lack of people who say she has already had some." *Sp. Cal. Elizabethan*, I, 63, 180.
4. Chamberlin, *Private Character of Queen Elizabeth*, pp. 56–7. In February of 1567 the Spanish ambassador Da Silva wrote with tantalizing inexactness that Elizabeth was "apparently well, only she treats her stomach badly." *Sp. Cal. Elizabethan*, I, 615.
5. *Sp. Cal. Elizabethan*, I, 679.
6. Wright, I, 140–1.
7. *Sp. Cal. Elizabethan*, I, 591–2.
8. *Burghley Papers*, I, 444.
9. *Sp. Cal. Elizabethan*, I, 599.

CHAPTER 23

1. The dark side of life in the queen's privy chamber is abundantly illustrated in a letter attributed to Mary Stuart, in *Lettres, Instructions et Mémoires de Marie Stuart, Reine d'Ecosse*, ed. Alexandre Labanoff, 7 vols. (London, 1844), VI, 50–57.

2. *Lettres . . . de Marie Stuart*, VI, 51. It is worth noting a later reference in the same letter to Elizabeth's "having recently ceased menstruating"—a fragment of evidence about her reproductive health. The letter is variously dated 1584 or 1586, though much of its contents are retrospective.

3. *Ibid.*, 54.

4. *The Letters of Queen Elizabeth*, ed. G.B. Harrison (London, 1935, reprinted New York, 1968), p. 52.

5. Nicholas Harris Nicolas, *Memoirs of the Life and Times of Sir Christopher Hatton* (London, 1847), pp. 13–14.

6. Cited in Hughes, III, 261 note.

7. Strickland, III, 207; Nichols, *Progresses*, II, 619 note 1.

8. Conyers Read, "A Letter from Robert, Earl of Leicester, to a Lady," *Huntington Library Bulletin*, No. 9 (April 1936), 17.

9. *Lettres . . . de Marie Stuart*, VI, 52–3.

10. *Ibid.*, 52.

11. Nicolas, *Hatton*, pp. 13–14.

12. Wright, I, 440–1.

CHAPTER 24

1. Roy Strong, "The Popular Celebration of the Accession Day of Queen Elizabeth I," *Journal of the Warburg and Courtauld Institutes*, XXI, Nos. 1–2 (January–June 1958), 91 and *passim*; J. E. Neale, "November 17," in *Essays in Elizabethan History* (London, 1958), 9–20.

2. Nichols, *Progresses*, I, 533–52.

3. *Ibid.*, 485–523. Robert Laneham's account of Elizabeth's sojourn at Kenilworth is in Nichols, I, 426–84.

4. *Ibid.*, I, 601.

CHAPTER 25

1. Much material on the progresses of the Elizabethan court is in Nichols, *Progresses*, Vols. I–III, Chambers, *Elizabethan Stage*, Vol. I, Allegra Woodworth, "Purveyance," Dunlop, *Palaces and Progresses*, and John Buxton, *Elizabethan Taste* (London, 1963).

2. Nichols, *Progresses*, I, 526.

3. Woodworth, "Purveyance," p. 25.

CHAPTER 26

1. *Sp. Cal. Elizabethan*, II, 631.

2. *Ibid.*, II, 627.

3. *Ibid.*, II, 636.

4. On the Anglo–French negotiations, and the issue of Elizabeth's marriageability, see Wallace T. MacCaffrey, "The Anjou Match and the Making of Elizabethan Foreign Policy," in *The English Commonwealth, 1547–1640*, ed. Peter Clark *et al.* (Leicester, 1979).

5. MacCaffrey, "Anjou Match," p. 60.

6. *Sp. Cal. Elizabethan*, II, 675.

7. *Ibid.*, II, 638, 641, 581.

8. *Ibid.*, II, 498.

9. *Ibid.*, II, 641.

CHAPTER 27

1. Nicholas Tyacke, "Popular Puritan Mentality in Late Elizabethan England," in *The English Commonwealth*, ed. Peter Clark *et al.*, p. 78.

2. Hughes, III, 178–9.

3. J. E. Neale, "The Elizabethan Age," in *Essays in Elizabethan History* (London, 1958), p. 26.

4. *Sp. Cal. Elizabethan*, I, 682.

5. *Ibid.*, II, 704.

6. Michael Barraclough Pulman, *The Elizabethan Privy Council in the Fifteen-Seventies* (Berkeley, 1971), p. 48.

7. Wright, II, 103–5.
8. *Sp. Cal. Elizabethan*, II, 664 and note.

PART FIVE
"That Guilty Woman of England"

CHAPTER 28

1. French, *John Dee*, p. 189.
2. *Sp. Cal. Elizabethan*, III, 91, 80.
3. *Ibid.*, III, 93.
4. *Ibid.*, III, 158–9.
5. *Ibid.*, III, 206.
6. *Ibid.*, III, 243.
7. Wright, II, 151.

CHAPTER 29

1. Adrian Morey, *The Catholic Subjects of Elizabeth I* (London, 1978), pp. 133–5 and *passim*.
2. *Sp. Cal. Elizabethan*, III, 153.
3. Carol Z. Wiener, "The Beleaguered Isle: A Study of Elizabethan and Early Jacobean Anti-Catholicism," *Past and Present*, LI (May 1971), 48.
4. Hughes, III, 311.
5. St. George Kieran Hyland, *A Century of Persecution under Tudor and Stuart Sovereigns from Contemporary Records* (London, 1920), p. 292. This account of the executions of December, 1581 is taken from Hyland, pp. 288ff, and *Sp. Cal. Elizabethan*, III, 231–2.
6. *State Papers, Domestic*, II, 48.
7. *Sp. Cal. Elizabethan*, III, 186–90.

CHAPTER 30

1. On Leicester's expedition see Roy Strong and J. A. Van Dorsten, *Leicester's Triumph* (Leiden and London, 1964) and Charles Henry Wilson, *Queen Elizabeth and the Revolt of the Netherlands* (Berkeley and Los Angeles, 1970).
2. *State Papers, Domestic*, II, 265.
3. *Correspondence of Robert Dudley*, Camden Society, Old series, XXVII (London, 1844), 21.
4. *State Papers, Domestic*, II, 291.
5. *Ibid.*, I, 648.
6. Klarwill, pp. 338–9.
7. *Correspondence of Robert Dudley*, p. 112.

CHAPTER 31

1. John Hungerford Pollen, *The English Catholics in the Reign of Queen Elizabeth* (London, 1920), p. 340.
2. Keith Thomas, *Religion and the Decline of Magic: Studies in Popular Belief in Sixteenth and Seventeenth Century England* (London, 1971), p. 422; *State Papers, Domestic*, II, 38.
3. Thomas, pp. 419–21.
4. Alan Haynes, "The English Earthquake of 1580," *History Today*, XXIX (August 1979), 542–4.
5. Klarwill, p. 340.
6. *Ibid.*
7. *Sp. Cal. Elizabethan*, II, 581.
8. Thomas, p. 407.
9. Read, *Burghley*, pp. 367–8.
10. *State Papers, Domestic*, II, 380.

CHAPTER 32

1. *State Papers, Domestic*, II, 461.
2. *Ibid.*, II, 480, 497.
3. *Ibid.*, II, 468, 470, 483.
4. Martin A. S. Hume, *Philip II of Spain* (London, 1897, reprinted New York, 1969), p. 267.
5. *State Papers, Domestic*, II, 507; Miller Christy, "Queen Elizabeth's Visit to Tilbury in 1588," *EHR*, XXXIV (January 1919), 46.
6. *State Papers, Domestic*, II, 391.
7. *Ibid.*, II, 515.
8. On the authenticity of Elizabeth's Tilbury speech, see Neale, *Essays in Elizabethan History*, pp. 104–6.
9. *State Papers, Domestic*, II, 534, 536, 527, 529.

PART SIX

"A Lady Whom Time Had Surprised"

CHAPTER 33

1. *A Journal of All That Was Accomplished by Monsieur de Maisse* . . . , trans. and ed. G. B. Harrison and R. A. Jones (Bloomsbury, 1931).
2. Chamberlin, *Private Character of Elizabeth*, p. 70.
3. De Maisse, *Journal*, p. 7.
4. Alan Kendall, *Robert Dudley, Earl of Leicester* (London, 1980), p. 231.
5. De Maisse, *Journal*, p. 115.
6. *Ibid.*, pp. 11–12.
7. *Ibid.*, p. 83.

CHAPTER 34

1. John Harington, *Nugae Antiquae*, ed. Rev. Henry Harington (London, 1804, reprinted New York, 1966), I, 318.
2. *Ibid.*, I, 312–16.
3. Chamberlin, *Private Character of Queen Elizabeth*, p. 73.
4. *State Papers, Domestic*, V, 252.
5. De Maisse, *Journal*, p. 58.
6. Elizabeth's translation of Seneca is in *Nugae Antiquae*, I, 109–14.

CHAPTER 35

1. *State Papers, Domestic*, VI, 42.
2. *Ibid.*, V, 543.
3. *Nugae Antiquae*, I, 320ff.
4. *State Papers, Domestic*, VI, 260.
5. *Ibid.*, VI, 298–301.
6. *Ibid.*
7. *Ibid.*, VI, 303. Neale sorts legend from authentic incident concerning Elizabeth's last days in "The Sayings of Queen Elizabeth," *History*, New series, X, No. 39 (October 1925), 212–33.

Select Bibliography

ORIGINAL SOURCES

Ascham, Roger. *The Scholemaster.* In *English Works,* ed. William Aldis Wright. Cambridge, England: Cambridge University Press, 1904.
——. *Toxophilus.* In *English Works,* ed. William Aldis Wright. Cambridge, England: Cambridge University Press, 1904.
——. *The Whole Works of Roger Ascham,* ed. J. A. Giles. 3 vols. in 4. London: John Russell Smith, 1864–65, reprinted New York: AMS Press, 1965.
Bullen, A. H., ed. *Lyrics from the Song-books of the Elizabethan Age.* London: Lawrence and Bullen, 1897.
Bülow, Gottfried von and Walter Powell, eds. "Diary of the Journey of Philip Julius, duke of Stettin-Pomerania, through England in the Year 1602." *Transactions of the Royal Historical Society,* Second series, VI (1892), 1–67.
Calendar of Letters and State Papers, relating to English Affairs, preserved principally in the Archives of Simancas, ed. Martin A. S. Hume. 4 vols. London: H. M. Stationery Office, 1892–99.
Calendar of Letters, Despatches, and State Papers, relating to the Negotiations between England and Spain, preserved in the Archives at Vienna, Simancas, Besançon and Brussels, ed. G. A. Bergenroth *et alii.* 13 vols. in 17. London: Longman, etc., 1862–1954.
Calendar of State Papers and Manuscripts, relating to English Affairs, existing in the Archives and Collections of Venice, and in Other Libraries of Northern Italy, ed. Rawdon Brown *et alii.* 38 vols. in 40. London: Longman, etc., 1864–1947.
Calendar of State Papers, Domestic Series, of the Reigns of Edward VI, Mary, Elizabeth and James I, preserved in the State Paper Department of Her Majesty's Public Record Office, ed. Robert Lemon and Mary A. E. Green. 12 vols. London: Longman, etc., 1856–72.
Calendar of State Papers, Foreign Series, of the Reign of Edward VI, 1547–1553, preserved in the State Paper Department of Her Majesty's Public Record Office, ed. William B. Turnbull. London: Longman, Green, Longman and Roberts, 1861.

Calendar of State Papers, Foreign Series, of the Reign of Elizabeth, preserved in the State Paper Department of Her Majesty's Public Record Office, ed. Joseph Stevenson *et alii.* 23 vols. in 26. London: Longman, etc., 1863–1950.

Calendar of State Papers, Foreign Series, of the Reign of Mary, 1553–1558, preserved in the State Paper Department of Her Majesty's Public Record Office, ed. William B: Turnbull. London: Longman, Green, Longman, and Roberts, 1861.

Calendar of the Manuscripts of the Most Hon. the Marquis of Salisbury . . . preserved at Hatfield House, Hertfordshire. 23 vols. in 19. London: Her Majesty's Stationery Office, 1883–1973.

Camden, William. *The History of the Most Renowned and Victorious Princess Elizabeth, Late Queen of England.* 4th ed. London: R. Bentley, 1688, reprinted New York: AMS Press, 1970.

———. *Remains Concerning Britain.* London: John Russell Smith, 1870, reprinted Yorkshire, England: EP Publishing, 1974.

Clifford, Henry. *The Life of Jane Dormer, Duchess of Feria,* transcribed by E. E. Estcourt and ed. Joseph Stevenson. London: Burns and Oates, 1887.

A Collection of State Papers Relating to Affairs in the Reigns of King Henry VIII, King Edward VI, Queen Mary, and Queen Elizabeth . . . left by William Cecil Lord Burghley, and now remaining at Hatfield House, ed. Samuel Haynes and William Murdin. 2 vols. London: William Bowyer, 1740–59.

Dee, John. *The Private Diary of Dr. John Dee,* ed. James Orchard Halliwell. Camden Society, Old series, XIX. London: J. B. Nichols and Son, 1842.

Doughtie, Edward, ed. *Lyrics from English Airs, 1596–1622.* Cambridge, Mass.: Harvard University Press, 1970.

Edward VI. *The Chronicle and Political Papers,* ed. W. K. Jordan. London: Allen and Unwin, 1966.

———. *Literary Remains of King Edward the Sixth,* ed. J. G. Nichols. 2 vols. London: J. B. Nichols and Son, 1857.

Elizabeth I. *The Letters of Queen Elizabeth I,* ed. G. B. Harrison. London: Cassell, 1935, reprinted New York: Funk and Wagnalls, 1968.

Fénélon, Bertrand de Salignac, seigneur de La Mothe. *Correspondance Diplomatique de Bertrand de Salignac de La Mothe Fénélon,* ed. Alexandre Teulet. 7 vols. Paris and London: no publisher, 1838–40.

Forbes, Thomas Rogers. *Chronicle from Aldgate: Life and Death in Shakespeare's London.* New Haven and London: Yale University Press, 1971.

Foxe, John. *The Acts and Monuments of John Foxe,* ed. George Townsend and S. R. Cattley. 8 vols. London: R. B. Seeley and W. Burnside, 1837–41.

Frescoln, Katharine P. "A Letter from Thomas Randolph to the Earl of Leicester." *Huntington Library Quarterly,* XXXVII, No. 1 (November 1973), 83–88.

Hayward, John. *Annals of the First Four Years of the Reign of Queen Elizabeth,* ed. John Bruce. Camden Society, Old series, VII. London: J. B. Nichols and Son, 1840.

Hinton, Edward M. *Ireland through Tudor Eyes.* Philadelphia: University of Pennsylvania Press and London: Oxford University Press, 1935, reprinted Philadelphia: R. West, 1977.

Holinshed, Raphael. *Holinshed's Chronicles of England, Scotland and Ireland.* 6 vols. London: J. Johnson, 1807–08.

Kervyn de Lettenhove, Joseph M. B. C. and L. Gilliodts van Severen, eds. *Relations politiques des Pays-Bas et de l'Angleterre, sous le règne de Philippe II.* 11 vols. Brussels: F. Hayez, 1882–1900.

Klarwill, Victor von, ed. *Queen Elizabeth and Some Foreigners.* New York: Brentano's, 1928.

Leicester, Robert Dudley, earl of. *Correspondence of Robert Dudley, earl of Leycester, during his Government of the Low Countries, in the Years 1585 and 1586.* Camden Society, Old series, XXVII. London: J. B. Nichols and Son, 1844.

[*Leicester's Commonwealth*]. *The Copy of a Letter Written by a Master of Arts of Cambridge to his Friend in London, concerning some talk passed of late between two worshipful and grave men about the present state, and some proceedings of the Earl of Leicester and his friends in England.* Printed in Bacon, Francis. *Collotype Facsimile and Type Transcript of an Elizabethan Manuscript.* London, New York and Bombay: Longmans, Green and Co., 1904.

Maisse, André Hurault, sieur de. *A Journal of All That Was Accomplished by Monsieur de Maisse Ambassador in England from King Henri IV to Queen Elizabeth Anno Domini 1597*, trans. and ed. G. B. Harrison and R. A. Jones. Bloomsbury, England: Nonesuch Press, 1931.

Manning, C. R., ed. "State Papers Relating to the Custody of the Princess Elizabeth at Woodstock, in 1554: Being Letters between Queen Mary and her Privy Council, and Sir Henry Bedingfield." *Norfolk Archaeology: or Miscellaneous Tracts relating to the Antiquities of the County of Norfolk*, IV (1855), 133–231.

Mary Stuart. *Lettres, Instructions et Mémoires de Marie Stuart, Reine d'Ecosse*, ed. Alexandre Labanoff. 7 vols. London: C. Dolman, 1844.

Melville, James. *Memoirs of Sir James Melville*, ed. A. Francis Stewart. New York: E. P. Dutton, 1930.

Moryson, Fynes. *Shakespeare's Europe: A Survey of the Condition of Europe at the end of the 16th Century, being unpublished chapters of Fynes Moryson's Itinerary (1617)*. 2nd ed. London: Sherratt and Hughes, 1903, reissued New York: Benjamin Blom, 1967.

Mumby, Frank A. *The Girlhood of Queen Elizabeth: A Narrative in Contemporary Letters.* London: Constable and Co., 1909.

Nichols, John. *The Progresses and Public Processions of Queen Elizabeth.* new ed. 3 vols. London: John Nichols and Son, 1823, reprinted New York: AMS Press, 1969.

Nichols, John Gough, ed. *The Chronicle of Queen Jane, and of Two Years of Queen Mary, and especially of the Rebellion of Sir Thomas Wyat.* Camden Society, Old series, XLVIII. London: Printed for the Camden Society, 1850.

Nicolas, Nicholas Harris. *Memoirs of the Life and Times of Sir Christopher Hatton.* London: R. Bentley, 1847.

Nugae Antiquae: Being a Miscellaneous Collection of Original Papers in Prose and Verse, written in the Reigns of Henry VIII, Queen Mary, Elizabeth, King James, etc., ed. Rev. Henry Harington. 3 vols. London: J. Dodsley, 1779.

Osburn, James M., ed. *The Quenes Maiesties Passage through the Citie of London to Westminster the Day before her Coronacion.* Elizabethan Club Series, Vol. I. New Haven, Conn.: Yale University Press, 1960.

Read, Conyers. "A Letter from Robert, Earl of Leicester, to a Lady." *Huntington Library Bulletin*, IX (April 1936), 15–26.

Rye, William Brenchley. *England as Seen by Foreigners in the Days of Elizabeth and James the First.* London: John Russell Smith, 1865.

Strangford, Viscount, ed. "Household Expenses of the Princess Elizabeth during her Residence at Hatfield October 1, 1551, to September 30, 1552." In *The Camden Miscellany*, Vol. II. Camden Society, Old series, LV. London: J. B. Nichols and Son, 1853.

Tytler, Patrick Fraser. *England under the Reigns of Edward VI and Mary.* 2 vols. London: Richard Bentley, 1839.

Wedel, Lupold von. "Journey through England and Scotland made by Lupold von Wedel in the Years 1584 and 1585," trans. Gottfried von Bülow. *Transactions of the Royal Historical Society*, Second series, IX (1895), 223–270.

Wright, Thomas, ed. *Queen Elizabeth and Her Times.* 2 vols. London: Henry Colburn, 1838.

SECONDARY AUTHORITIES

Aird, Ian. "The Death of Amy Robsart." *English Historical Review*, LXXI, No. 278 (January 1956), 69–79.

Appleby, Andrew B. *Famine in Tudor and Stuart England.* Palo Alto, Calif.: Stanford University Press, 1978.

Ball, Bryan W. *A Great Expectation: Eschatological Thought in English Protestantism to 1660.* Leiden: E. J. Brill, 1975.

Beckingsale, B. W. *Elizabeth I.* London: B. T. Batsford, 1963.

Beier, A. L. "Social Problems in Elizabethan London." *Journal of Interdisciplinary History*, IX, No. 2 (Autumn 1978), 203–21.

———. "Vagrants and the Social Order in Elizabethan London." *Past and Present*, LXIV (August 1974), 3–29.

Bergeron, David M. "Elizabeth's Coronation Entry (1559): New Manuscript Evidence." *English Literary Renaissance*, VIII, No. 1 (Winter 1978), 3–8.

Bindoff, Stanley T. "A Kingdom at Stake, 1553." *History Today*, III, No. 9 (September 1953), 642–48.

———. *Tudor England*. The Pelican History of England, Vol. V. Baltimore: Penguin Books, 1950.

Black, John B. *The Reign of Elizabeth, 1558–1603*. 2nd ed. Oxford History of England, Vol. VIII. Oxford: Clarendon Press, 1959.

Bradley, Ian. "The English Sunday." *History Today*, XXII, No. 5 (May 1972), 355–63.

Braudel, Fernand. *Capitalism and Material Life, 1400–1800*, trans. Miriam Kochan. New York, Evanston, San Francisco and London: Harper and Row, 1973.

———. *The Mediterranean and the Mediterranean World in the Age of Philip II*, trans. Siân Reynolds. 2 vols. New York, Hagerstown, San Francisco and London: Harper and Row, 1972.

Bush, M. L. *The Government Policy of Protector Somerset*. London: Edward Arnold, 1975.

Byrne, M. St. Clare. *Elizabethan Life in Town and Country*. 7th ed. London: Methuen, 1954.

Chamberlin, Frederick. *The Private Character of Queen Elizabeth*. New York: Dodd Mead and Co., 1922.

Chambers, E. K. *The Elizabethan Stage*. 4 vols. Oxford: Clarendon Press, 1923.

Christy, Miller. "Queen Elizabeth's Visit to Tilbury in 1588." *English Historical Review*, XXXIV (January 1919), 43–61.

Clark, Peter, Alan G. R. Smith and Nicholas Tyacke, eds. *The English Commonwealth, 1547–1640: Essays in Politics and Society presented to Joel Hurstfield*. Leicester: Leicester University Press, 1979.

Cook, Olive. *The English Country House: An Art and a Way of Life*. London: Thames and Hudson, 1974.

Council, Norman. "O Dea Certe: The Allegory of the Fortress of Perfect Beauty." *Huntington Library Quarterly*, XXXIX, No. 4 (August 1976), 329–42.

Craig, Hardin. *The Enchanted Glass: The Elizabethan Mind in Literature*. Oxford: Blackwell, 1960.

Creighton, Mandell. *Queen Elizabeth*. new ed. London, New York, etc.: Longmans, Green and Co., 1899, reprinted New York: Thomas Y. Crowell, 1966.

Croft, Pauline. "Englishmen and the Spanish Inquisition, 1588–1625." *English Historical Review*, LXXXVII, No. 343 (April 1972), 249–68.

Davies, R. Trevor. *The Golden Century of Spain, 1501–1621*. London and Basingstoke: Macmillan, 1937.

Davis, Eliza Jeffries. "The Transformation of London." In *Tudor Studies presented by the Board of Students in History in the University of London to Albert Frederick Pollard*, ed. R. W. Seton-Watson. London: Longmans, Green and Co., 1924.

Dent, Anthony. "Shakespeare's Horse-borne England." *History Today*, XXIII, No. 7 (July 1973), 455–61.

D'Oyley, Elizabeth. "The Death of Amye Robsart." *History Today*, VI, No. 4 (April 1956), 252–60.

Dunlop, Ian. *Palaces and Progresses of Elizabeth I*. London: Jonathan Cape, 1962.

Durant, David N. *Arabella Stuart: A Rival to the Queen*. London: Weidenfeld and Nicolson, 1978.

———. "A London Visit, 1591." *History Today*, XXIV, No. 7 (July 1974), 497–503.

Elliot, J. H. *The Old World and the New, 1492–1650*. Cambridge, England: Cambridge University Press, 1970.

Elton, G. R. *England under the Tudors*. 2nd ed. A History of England, Vol. IV. London: Methuen, 1974.

———. *Modern Historians on British History 1485–1945: A Critical Bibliography, 1945–1969*. London: Methuen, 1970.

———. *Studies in Tudor and Stuart Politics and Government: Papers and Reviews, 1946–1972*. Vol. I: *Tudor Politics/Tudor Government*. Vol. II: *Parliament/Political Thought*. 2 vols. Cambridge, England: Cambridge University Press, 1974.

Emmison, F. G. *Elizabethan Life: Disorder*. Chelmsford, England: Essex County Council, 1970.

Erickson, Carolly. *Bloody Mary*. Garden City, N. Y.: Doubleday, 1978.

——. *Great Harry.* New York: Summit Books, 1980.

Ewen, C. L'Estrange, ed. *Witch Hunting and Witch Trials.* London: Kegan Paul, Trench, Trubner and Co., 1929, reprinted New York: Barnes and Noble, 1971.

Firth, Katharine R. *The Apocalyptic Tradition in Reformation Britain, 1530–1645.* Oxford and New York: Oxford University Press, 1979.

Fraser, Antonia. *Mary Queen of Scots.* New York: Dell, 1971.

French, Peter J. *John Dee: The World of an Elizabethan Magus.* London: Routledge and Kegan Paul, 1972.

Froude, James Anthony. *History of England, from the Fall of Wolsey to the Death of Elizabeth.* 4 vols. New York: Charles Scribner's Sons, 1881.

Fuzier, Jean. "London and Country Cries: Elizabethan Life in Song and Music." *Cahiers Elisabéthains,* VIII (October 1975), 31–63.

Gilbert, Creighton. "When Did a Man in the Renaissance Grow Old?" *Studies in the Renaissance,* XIV (1967), 7–32.

Gilkes, R. K. *The Tudor Parliament.* The London History Series, Vol. V. London: University of London Press, 1969.

Glanville, Philippa. "Nonsuch: A Lost Tudor Palace." *London Archaeologist,* I, No. 5 (Winter 1969), 111–13.

Granville-Barker, Harley and G. B. Harrison, eds. *A Companion to Shakespeare Studies.* Cambridge, England: Cambridge University Press, 1934.

Haller, William. *Foxe's Book of Martyrs and the Elect Nation.* London: Jonathan Cape, 1963.

Halliday, F. E. "Queen Elizabeth I and Dr. Burcot." *History Today,* V, No. 8 (August 1955), 542–44.

Harbage, Alfred. *Shakespeare's Audience.* New York: Columbia University Press, 1941.

Hardin, Richard F. *Michael Drayton and the Passing of Elizabethan England.* Lawrence, Manhattan and Wichita: University Press of Kansas, 1973.

Hartley, Dorothy. *Lost Country Life.* New York: Pantheon Books, 1979.

Haugaard, William P. *Elizabeth and the English Reformation: The Struggle for a Stable Settlement of Religion.* Cambridge, England: Cambridge University Press, 1968.

Haynes, Alan. "The Cadiz Expedition, 1596." *History Today,* XXIII, No. 3 (March 1973), 161–69.

——. "The English Earthquake of 1580." *History Today,* XXIX (August 1979), 542–44.

——. "Supplying the Elizabethan Court." *History Today,* XXVIII (November 1978), 729–37.

Hitchcock, J. "A Confession of the Family of Love, 1580." *Bulletin of the Institute of Historical Research,* XLIII, No. 107 (May 1970), 85–86.

Hogrefe, Pearl. *Women of Action in Tudor England: Nine Biographical Sketches.* Ames, Iowa: Iowa State University Press, 1977.

Hughes, Philip. *The Reformation in England.* 3 vols. New York: Macmillan, 1951–54.

Hume, Martin A. S. *Philip II of Spain.* London and New York: Macmillan, 1897, reprinted New York: Haskell House, 1969.

Hurstfield, Joel. *Elizabeth I and the Unity of England.* New York: Macmillan, 1960.

——. *The Elizabethan Nation.* New York and London: Harper and Row, 1967.

——. and Alan G. R. Smith, eds. *Elizabethan People: State and Society.* New York: St. Martin's Press, 1972.

——. *Freedom, Corruption, and Government in Elizabethan England.* London: Jonathan Cape, 1973.

——. *The Illusion of Power in Tudor Politics.* London: Athlone Press, 1979.

——. "Queen and State: The Emergence of an Elizabethan Myth." In *Britain and the Netherlands,* ed. J. S. Bromley and E. H. Kossmann. The Hague: Martinus Nijhoff, 1975.

Hyland, St. George Kieran. *A Century of Persecution under Tudor and Stuart Sovereigns from Contemporary Records.* London: Kegan Paul, Trench, Trubner and Co. and New York: E. P. Dutton, 1920.

Ingram, William. "The Closing of the Theaters in 1597: A Dissenting View." *Modern Philology,* LXIX, No. 2 (November 1971), 105–15.

Jenkins, Elizabeth. *Elizabeth the Great.* New York: G. P. Putnam's Sons, 1967.

Johnson, Paul. *Elizabeth I: A Biography*. New York, Chicago and San Francisco: Holt, Rinehart and Winston, 1974.

Jordan, W. K. *Edward VI*. Vol. I: *The Young King: The Protectorship of the Duke of Somerset*. Vol. II: *The Threshold of Power: The Dominance of the Duke of Northumberland*. 2 vols. London: Allen and Unwin, 1968–70.

Kendall, Alan. *Robert Dudley, Earl of Leicester*. London: Cassell, 1980.

Knowles, David. "The Eltonian Revolution in Early Tudor History." *Historical Journal*, XVII, No. 4 (December 1974), 867–72.

Lacey, Robert. *Robert, Earl of Essex: An Elizabethan Icarus*. London: Weidenfeld and Nicolson, 1971.

Levine, Mortimer. *The Early Elizabethan Succession Question, 1558–1568*. Palo Alto, Calif.: Stanford University Press, 1966.

Loomie, Albert J. "The Armadas and the Catholics of England." *Catholic Historical Review*, LIX, No. 3 (October 1973), 385–403.

MacCaffrey, Wallace T. "The Anjou Match and the Making of Elizabethan Foreign Policy." In *The English Commonwealth, 1547–1640: Essays in Politics and Society presented to Joel Hurstfield*, ed. Peter Clark, Alan G. R. Smith and Nicholas Tyacke. Leicester: Leicester University Press, 1979.

——. *The Shaping of the Elizabethan Regime*. Princeton: Princeton University Press, 1968.

Machin, R. "The Great Rebuilding: A Reassessment." *Past and Present*, LXXVII (November 1977), 33–56.

Mackie, J. D. *The Earlier Tudors, 1485–1558*. The Oxford History of England, Vol. VII. Oxford: Clarendon Press, 1952.

Maltby, William S. *The Black Legend in England: The Development of Anti-Spanish Sentiment, 1558–1660*. Durham, N. C.: Duke University Press, 1971.

Martienssen, Anthony. *Queen Katherine Parr*. New York: McGraw-Hill and London: Secker and Warburg, 1973.

Mattingly, Garrett. *The Armada*. Boston: Houghton Mifflin, 1962.

Morey, Adrian. *The Catholic Subjects of Elizabeth I*. London, Boston and Sydney: George Allen and Unwin, 1978.

Morris, Christopher. *The Tudors*. New York: John Wiley and Sons, 1967.

Moss, D. E. "Roger Ascham." *History Today*, XXVII, No. 10 (October 1977), 651–57.

Moss, Jean D. "Additional Light on the Family of Love." *Bulletin of the Institute of Historical Research*, XLVII, No. 115 (May 1974), 103–05.

Neale, J. E. "The Accession of Queen Elizabeth I." *History Today*, III, No. 5 (May 1953), 293–300.

——. *The Age of Catherine de' Medici*. London: Jonathan Cape, 1943.

——. "The Elizabethan Political Scene." *Proceedings of the British Academy*, XXXIV (1948), 97–117.

——. *Essays in Elizabethan History*. London: Jonathan Cape, 1958.

——. *Queen Elizabeth I*. London: Jonathan Cape, 1934, reprinted 1952.

——. "The Sayings of Queen Elizabeth." *History*, New series, X, No. 39 (October 1925), 212–33.

——. "Sir Nicholas Throckmorton's Advice to Queen Elizabeth on her Accession to the Throne." *English Historical Review*, LXV, No. 254 (January 1950), 91–98.

Nuttall, Geoffrey F. "The English Martyrs, 1535–1680: A Statistical Review." *Journal of Ecclesiastical History*, XXII, No. 3 (July 1971), 191–97.

O'Malley, C. D. "Tudor Medicine and Biology." *Huntington Library Quarterly*, XXXII, No. 1 (November 1968), 1–27.

Outhwaite, R. B. "Royal Borrowing in the Reign of Elizabeth I: The Aftermath of Antwerp." *English Historical Review*, LXXXVI, No. 339 (April 1971), 251–63.

Owen, A. E. B. "Sir John Wolley's Letter-book as Latin Secretary to Elizabeth I." *Archives*, XI, No. 49 (Spring 1973), 16–18.

Parker, Geoffrey. "Mutiny and Discontent in the Spanish Army of Flanders 1572–1607." *Past and Present*, LVIII (February 1973), 38–52.

Pearson, Lu Emily. *Elizabethans at Home*. Palo Alto, Calif.: Stanford University Press, 1957.

Pike, Luke Owen. *A History of Crime in England*. 2 vols. London: Smith, Elder and Co., 1873–76.

The Plague Reconsidered: A New Look at its Origins and Effects in 16th and 17th Century England. Matlock, England: Local Population Studies, 1977.

Pollen, John Hungerford. *The English Catholics in the Reign of Queen Elizabeth*. London: Longmans, Green and Co., 1920.

Pollitt, Ronald. "John Hawkins' Troublesome Voyages: Merchants, Bureaucrats, and the Origins of the Slave Trade." *Journal of British Studies*, XII, No. 2 (May 1973), 26–40.

Prescott, H. F. M. *Mary Tudor*. New York: Macmillan, 1954.

Pulman, Michael Barraclough. *The Elizabethan Privy Council in the Fifteen-Seventies*. Berkeley: University of California Press, 1971.

Read, Conyers. *Lord Burghley and Queen Elizabeth*. New York: Alfred A. Knopf, 1960.

──────. *Mr. Secretary Cecil and Queen Elizabeth*. New York: Alfred A. Knopf, 1961.

──────. *The Tudors: Personalities and Practical Politics in Sixteenth Century England*. New York: Holt, Rinehart and Winston, 1936.

Reid, R. R. "The Rebellion of the Earls, 1569." *Transactions of the Royal Historical Society*, Second series, XX (1906), 171–203.

Ross, Josephine. *Suitors of the Queen: The Men in the Life of Elizabeth I of England*. New York: Coward, McCann and Geoghegan, 1975.

Rowse, A. L. "The Coronation of Queen Elizabeth I." *History Today*, III, No. 4 (May 1953), 301–10.

──────. *The Elizabethan Renaissance. Part I: The Life of the Society. Part II: The Cultural Achievement*. 2 vols. London: Macmillan, 1971–72.

──────. *The England of Elizabeth: The Structure of Society*. London: Macmillan, 1950.

──────. *Portraits and Views: Literary and Historical*. London: Macmillan, 1979.

──────. *Simon Forman: Sex and Society in Shakespeare's Age*. London: Weidenfeld and Nicolson, 1974.

Ruff, Lillian M. and D. Arnold Wilson. "The Madrigal, the Lute Song and Elizabethan Politics." *Past and Present*, XLIV (August 1969), 3–51.

Ryan, Lawrence V. *Roger Ascham*. Palo Alto, Calif.: Stanford University Press and London: Oxford University Press, 1963.

Salgādo, Gāmini. *The Elizabethan Underworld*. London: Dent and Totowa, N. J.: Rowman and Littlefield, 1977.

Schnucker, Robert V. "Elizabethan Birth Control and Puritan Attitudes." *Journal of Interdisciplinary History*, V, No. 4 (Spring 1975), 655–67.

Shakespeare's England: An Account of the Life and Manners of his Age. 2 vols. London: Oxford University Press, 1916.

Smith, Alan G. R. *The Government of Elizabethan England*. London: Edward Arnold, 1967.

Smith, Lacey Baldwin. *Elizabeth Tudor: Portrait of a Queen*. Boston and Toronto: Little, Brown, 1975.

Stopes, C. C. *Shakespeare's Environment*. London: G. Bell and Sons, 1914.

Strickland, Agnes. *Lives of the Queens of England*. 8 vols. London: Henry Colburn, 1851.

Strong, Roy and Julia Trevelyan Oman. *Elizabeth R*. London: Secker and Warburg, 1971.

Strong, Roy and J. A. Van Dorsten. *Leicester's Triumph*. Leiden: University Press and London: Oxford University Press, 1964.

Strong, Roy. "The Popular Celebration of the Accession Day of Queen Elizabeth I." *Journal of the Warburg and Courtauld Institutes*, XXI, Nos. 1–2 (January–June 1958), 86–103.

Thomas, Keith. *Religion and the Decline of Magic: Studies in Popular Beliefs in Sixteenth and Seventeenth Century England*. London: Weidenfeld and Nicolson, 1971.

Tillyard, E. M. W. *The Elizabethan World Picture*. London: Chatto and Windus, 1943.

Trimble, William Raleigh. *The Catholic Laity in Elizabethan England 1558–1603*. Cambridge, Mass.: Harvard University Press, 1964.

Tyacke, Nicholas. "Popular Puritan Mentality in Late Elizabethan England." In *The English Commonwealth, 1547–1640: Essays in Politics and Society presented to Joel Hurstfield*, ed. Peter Clark, Alan G. R. Smith and Nicholas Tyacke. Leicester: Leicester University Press, 1979.

Vines, Alice G. *Neither Fire Nor Steel: Sir Christopher Hatton*. Chicago: Nelson-Hall, 1978.

Walcott, Robert. *The Tudor-Stuart Period of English History (1485–1714): A Review of Changing Interpretations*. Service Center for Teachers of History, Vol. LVIII. New York: Macmillan, 1964.

Wallace, Willard M. *Sir Walter Raleigh*. Princeton, N. J.: Princeton University Press, 1959.

Wernham, R. B. *Before the Armada: The Emergence of the English Nation, 1485–1588*. New York: Harcourt, Brace and World, 1966.

———. *The Making of Elizabethan Foreign Policy, 1558–1603*. Berkeley: University of California Press, 1980.

Wiener, Carol Z. "The Beleaguered Isle: A Study of Elizabethan and Early Jacobean Anti-Catholicism." *Past and Present*, LI (May 1971), 27–62.

Wiesener, Louis. *La Jeunesse d'Elisabeth d'Angleterre 1533–1558*. Paris: Librairie Hachette, 1878.

Williams, Glanmor. *The General and Common Sort of People, 1540–1640*. Exeter, England: University of Exeter, 1977.

Williams, Neville. *All the Queen's Men: Elizabeth I and her Courtiers*. New York: Macmillan, 1972.

———. "The Coronation of Queen Elizabeth I." *Quarterly Review*, CCXCI, No. 597 (July 1953), 397–410.

———. *Elizabeth the First: Queen of England*. New York: E. P. Dutton and Co., 1968.

———. *The Life and Times of Elizabeth I*. Garden City, N. Y.: Doubleday, 1972.

Williams, Penry. *The Tudor Regime*. Oxford: Clarendon Press, 1979.

Wilson, Charles Henry. *Queen Elizabeth and the Revolt of the Netherlands*. Berkeley and Los Angeles: University of California Press, 1970.

Wilson, E. K. *England's Eliza*. Cambridge, Mass.: Harvard University Press, 1939.

Wilson, F. P. *The Plague in Shakespeare's London*. Oxford: Clarendon Press, 1927.

Woodworth, Allegra. "Purveyance for the Royal Household in the Reign of Queen Elizabeth." *Transactions of the American Philosophical Society*, New series, XXXV, Pt. 1 (1945), 3–89.

Yates, Frances A. *Astraea: The Imperial Theme in the Sixteenth Century*. London and Boston: Routledge and Kegan Paul, 1975.

———. "Elizabethan Chivalry: The Romance of the Accession Day Tilts." *Journal of the Warburg and Courtauld Institutes*, XX (1957), 4–25.

Zagorin, Perez. "English History, 1558–1640: A Bibliographical Survey." In *Changing Views on British History: Essays on Historical Writing since 1939*, ed. Elizabeth C. Furber. Cambridge, Mass.: Harvard University Press, 1966.

Index

About the Author

A Ph.D. in medieval history from Columbia University led Carolly Erickson to six years as a college professor, then to a career as a full-time writer. Since 1968 she has written extensively for both scholarly and popular audiences. *The First Elizabeth,* her sixth book, follows two other biographies of the Tudor dynasty: *Bloody Mary,* a life of Mary Tudor, and *Great Harry* on Henry VIII, both of which have achieved both exceptional critical acclaim and a wide popular readership. Ms. Erickson lives in Berkeley, California, with her teenage son Hal.